Allen Howard. Godbey

Great Disasters and Horrors in the World's History

Allen Howard. Godbey

Great Disasters and Horrors in the World's History

ISBN/EAN: 9783743325180

Manufactured in Europe, USA, Canada, Australia, Japa

Cover: Foto ©ninafisch / pixelio.de

Manufactured and distributed by brebook publishing software (www.brebook.com)

Allen Howard. Godbey

Great Disasters and Horrors in the World's History

GREAT DISASTERS

AND

HORRORS IN THE WORLD'S HISTORY.

A GRAPHIC ACCOUNT OF THE NOTABLE CALAMITIES
WHICH HAVE BEFALLEN MANKIND

IN ALL AGES, BOTH UPON LAND AND SEA.

EMBRACING

THE LOUISVILLE TORNADO, FLOODS IN THE SOUTH, CHARLESTON EARTHQUAKE, JOHNSTOWN FLOOD, STORM ON THE COAST OF SAMOA, NOTED SHIPWRECKS, GREAT FLOODS IN CHINA, HOLLAND AND JAPAN, AND OTHER NOTABLE DISASTERS CAUSED BY STORM, FLOOD AND VOLCANIC ACTION,

AND OF THE LAWS OF THE

NATURAL PHENOMENA THAT PRODUCE THEM.

COMPRISING

THRILLING TALES OF HEROISM, GREAT DESTRUCTION OF TOWNS, CITIES, HOMES AND LIVES, HEART-RENDING SCENES OF AGONY, DREADFUL SUFFERINGS, MIRACULOUS ESCAPES, DARING ADVENTURES, ETC., ETC.,

TOGETHER WITH

NOBLE RESPONSES OF AID.

TO WHICH IS ADDED

AN ACCOUNT OF METHODS OF PREDICTION.

By A. H. GODBEY, A.M.,

Author of "Stanley in Africa," "Light in Darkness," "Missions and Missionary Heroes," etc.

SUPERBLY ILLUSTRATED WITH 150 ENGRAVINGS.

PUBLISHED BY

THE EXCELSIOR PUBLISHING CO.,

ST. LOUIS, MO.

PREFACE.

WHATEVER be the ideas of the public upon a glance at the title page of this work, it is not intended to pander to the morbid desire for the sensational or horrible, characteristic of weak minds. This volume is not a literary morgue.

Mankind is constantly astonished by reports of mishaps and disasters of manifold character, when there is seldom room for astonishment. A large proportion of the calamities reported from day to day are directly due to the haste, greed, and heedlessness of man himself, and need no comment.

But there is a large class of disasters, due solely to meteorological or geological conditions, which surpass all others in magnitude and appalling destruction. In such cases men insist on prating about "mysterious visitations," as though these occurrences were subject to the dominion of no law. To an examination of such is this book devoted.

When in school, the writer was often struck by the persistence with which even the most diligent students would call upon the teachers of physics and chemistry to suspend the recitation and devote the time to illustrative experiments. Physical Geography was constantly pronounced "very dry," because of the scarcity of opportunities for illustration.

The writer has endeavored to present in a form acceptable to the popular palate the general principles of the storm and earthquake so far as they are understood: and numerous narratives of great disturbances have been inserted that a clearer conception of the magnitude of these agencies and their relative importance may be attained by the reader.

Much care has been spent in "steering between Scylla and Charybdis." While it has been designed to avoid merely scientific data, there has been the equally delicate task of avoiding prolix narration and mere sensational tales. It is hoped that the result will be useful and interesting.

If the book shall lead the reader to higher views of the reign of inexorable law in nature, and to a profounder reverence for the Author of Law and his works, the labor of its compilation will not have been spent in vain.

A. H. GODBEY.

TABLE OF CONTENTS.

CHAPTER I.
MYTHS OF THE WINDS.
Old Greek fancies—Their modern traces—Man seeking mysteries—Personifications—The "air-mothers"... 17

CHAPTER II.
CONSTANT WINDS.
Comparative climate—Expansive force of heat—Illustrations—The trade-winds—Effect of the earth's rotation—Return currents and calms... 26

CHAPTER III.
PERIODIC WINDS.
Modified trade winds—The monsoons—Local winds—Sea and land breezes—The simoom: its terrible effects—The khamsin, and similar winds—Moisture in the air: its effects—Rain and hail—Clouds: their varieties—Mountain winds... 34

CHAPTER IV.
TORNADOES AND CYCLONES.
Unheeded law—Peculiarities of storms—Cyclonic storms—Theoretical Illustrations—A "cyclone hot-bed"—Traveling of a cyclone—Its curves in accordance with law—Features of the cyclone's path—Great cyclone of August, 1888—The planetary equinox theory—Objections to it—Safe predictions—Sun-spots—Mysterious providences... 48

CHAPTER V.
THE LOUISVILLE TORNADO.
Perspective of news—Amusing conceits—Distress at the door—The tornado—Warning of the Signal Service—The storm strikes Louisville—Its course—Wreck of Falls City Hall—Rescuing the victims—Fire breaks out—Personal narratives—At the Union Depot............ 65

CHAPTER VI.

INCIDENTS OF THE TORNADO.

The poor to be remembered—Peddlers, publicans and sinners—The freaks of "Providence"—Deaths in the storm remarkably few—Wonderful escapes—Equine antics of confined air—Strange pranks of the wind—The storm at Parkland—At Jeffersonville—The mammoth worshiper—Generosity and independence 87

CHAPTER VII.

MORE TORNADOES.

The tornado in East Kansas—In Southeast Missouri—Great damage in Illinois—Waterspout at Matamoros—Many distinct whirlwinds—Effect of forest and prairie fires—Tornado of Charleston, 1761—Tornadoes at Natchez 1840 and 1842—The Marshfield storm, 1880—Remarkably small loss of life in tornadoes—Tornadoes in foreign lands 114

CHAPTER VIII.

TROPICAL CYCLONES.

Cyclones at our eastern borders—The Nova Scotia cyclone—St. Thomas cyclone and earthquake, 1867—Cyclone of 1876—Barbadoes storm, 1830—Great storm of 1780—Terrible cyclones and storm waves of India—Typhoons in the China seas 142

CHAPTER IX.

PERILS OF THE SEA.

Songs of the sea—The ocean always admired—Its treasures and dangers—Man's greed a source of disaster—Criminal disregard of life—Terrible fatalities in leaky ships—The Arctic seas—The ship Karluk. 159

CHAPTER X.

LIFE-SAVING MASTERS.

Great storm of 1776—Embarrassed and unpreparedness—Diabolical wreckers—Hoodlums—Desperate struggles without a life-boat illustrated by dangers—The life-boat invented—Its usefulness—Lighthouses and sea-bells 179

CHAPTER XI.
GREAT SAMOAN HURRICANE.

Germany and Samoa—Naboth's vineyard—War breaks out—The assembled navy—Situation of the harbor—The hurricane—Fears of the natives—Vessels dragging anchors—Sudden wreck of the *Eber*—Magnanimous natives—The *Adler* overturned—Struggle of the *Nipsic*—Fouled by the *Olga*, and run ashore—Crew rescued by the natives—The *Vandalia* helpless—Bold feat of the *Calliope* cheered—*Vandalia* stranded—Many Drowned—At the last gasp—The *Trenton* drifts upon them—Defiance of the storm—The flag triumphant... 195

CHAPTER XII.
ELECTRIC STORMS.

Byron's fire—Myths of the lightning—Causes of thunder storms—Strange freaks of the lightning—Numerous fatalities—Some curious cases—A lightning stroke a Divine favor—Thunder—Peculiar incidents—Lightning little to be feared—Foolish precautions—A "dysentery conductor" wanted—St. Elmo's fire—Electric halos—Their part in history—The aurora—Popular myths—Aurora described...... 220

CHAPTER XIII.
RAIN, HAIL AND SNOW.

Clouds and cloud shapes—The storm changes national destinies—Cloud halos—Specter of the Brocken—The "beautiful rain"—Amount of rainfall—Snow—Its ravages—Remarkable showers of hail—Prodigies 246

CHAPTER XIV.
FLOODS IN THE SOUTH.

Rivers a universal problem—Character of the Mississippi—Failure of the levee system—The building of levees—Three great sections—Damage of overflows—Fighting for the levee—Storm on the river—Scene at a crevasse—The flood in the rural districts—In the city—Closing a crevasse—Refugees on the levee—Crooked streams... 261

CHAPTER XV.
THE FLOOD OF 1890.

Floods of other years—Warning of the Signal Service—The water rising—At Greenville, Mississippi—The fight for the Morganza line—The waters win—Other crevasses—Extent of the damage—Objections to levees—Levees *versus* outlets—Terrible floods in China—A proposed outlet—Reflection on present policy.................................. 296

CHAPTER XVI.

THE JOHNSTOWN FLOOD.

The dam system of India—American "cheap goods and haste"—The Little Conemaugh Valley—Heavy rains—Johnstown flooded—The artificial lake—A poor dam—No uneasiness—How the water would move—The dam breaks—Terrible rush of the flood—An engine chased—A warning whistle—Locomotives hurled about like toys—Flying for life—Escapes and losses. 324

CHAPTER XVII.

INCIDENTS AT JOHNSTOWN.

Suddenness of the flood—It divides—A chaotic scene—Fire breaks out—Faith of the perishing—Narratives: the Hulbert House; Rev. D. M. Miller's story; Mr. Calliver's escape; Dr. Beale and family—Morning: the stricken multitude; Mr. Rose's narrative; Talmage's letter; the grief of the survivors 343

CHAPTER XVIII.

RELIEF MEASURES.

The people in want—Johnstown after the flood—Human ghouls—Relic hunters—Temporary government—A dictatorship—Hospitals and morgues—Prompt response of the public—Aid from various cities—Losses by the flood.................. 365

CHAPTER XIX.

FAMINE AND PESTILENCE.

Signs and omens—Natural causes—Bengal famine of 1866—Relief Measures—Results—Pestilence and contagion—Black death—Its frequent ravages—Fright—A romance of Florence.................. 354

CHAPTER XX.

THE VOLCANO.

Erroneous views—Myths—Active principle in volcanoes—Atmospheric pressure—Rain at eruptions—Lava, pumice, ashes and tufa—Different phases of action—Stromboli, the "lighthouse"—Lava bubbles—Thrilling adventure—Low!—Theory of a molten earth—Objections to it—The earth cools slowly—Subsidence and chemical action—Distribution of volcanoes—Their work and forms. 364

TABLE OF CONTENTS. ix

CHAPTER XXI.

GREAT ERUPTIONS OF VESUVIUS.

Pompeii long buried—Excavations begun—A hermetically sealed city—Scenes in the town—Pliny's story—Hundreds stifled—Finding the bodies—Subsequent eruptions—Notable convulsion of 1538—The eruption of 1531, 1737 and 1793—Recent observations.................. 421

CHAPTER XXII.

OTHER GREAT ERUPTIONS.

Destruction of Sodom—Arguments—The pitch lake of Trinidad—Ætna: eruption of 1669—Thousands perish—Catania destroyed—Other outbreaks—Iceland; Mt. Hecla—Tremendous eruption of Skaptar Jokul—One-fifth of the people perish—Millions of cubic yards of lava—Disturbances in the sea—Jorullo: a mountain made in a night—Fearful outburst of Sumbawa—Twenty-six people out of twelve thousand escape—Explosions heard nine hundred miles—Other Malaysian volcanoes—Geysers—Terrible eruption of Coseguina—Heard one thousand miles—Eruptions in South America—Force required to send out lava—In the Sandwich Islands—Krakatoa: the greatest eruption in history—A chorus of volcanoes—Awful destruction—Perceived around the world—Unparalleled sea wave... 440

CHAPTER XXIII.

EARTHQUAKES.

Myths of the earthquake—Ancient theories—Modern research—Earthquakes and volcanic agency—Speed of a shock—The atmospheric theory—Earthquakes at particular seasons—The "planetary influence" theory—Character of motions... 481

CHAPTER XXIV.

EUROPEAN EARTHQUAKES.

Legends of the flood—Sparta Destroyed—Bura and Helice engulfed—Numerous convulsions in Asia Minor—Antioch repeatedly destroyed—North Africa suffers—Calabrian earthquake of 1693—A tremendous convulsion in 1783—Immense chasms—People swallowed up—Great landslides—Terrible catastrophe at Scylla—Ruffians amid the wreck—The great Lisbon earthquake—Its vast extent—Awful destruction—Earthquake at Chio—In Switzerland—In Ischia—Distressing scenes in the ruins—Disastrous shocks in Spain................... 406

CHAPTER XXV.

EARTHQUAKES IN THE UNITED STATES AND ENGLAND.

All nature uneasy—The terrifying character of an earthquake—Signs and wonders—" El Gran Ruido," of Guanajuato—Frequency of earthquakes—Earthquake in New England, 1638—A second in 1663—Shock of 1727—Great convulsions of 1755—Damage and great alarm at Boston — " The end of the world!" — Great disturbance in the Mississippi Valley, 1811—Strange feats—The Charleston earthquake Numerous English earthquakes—Comparatively small loss of life... 535

CHAPTER XXVI.

EARTHQUAKES IN TROPICAL AMERICA.

Shocks in Asia: lack of reliable information—The Andes region—Great earthquake of Riobamba—Humboldt's description—Numerous shocks in Venezuela—Catastrophe of Caracas—Effect on the survivors—Frequent convulsions at San Salvador—Total destruction in 1854—Ruffians on the scene—Sudden disaster of Mendoza—Touching incidents—Faithful dogs—Shocks in Peru and gigantic sea wave—Numerous great shocks—The end of all things—The last man......... 563

CHAPTER XXVII.

PREDICTION AND PREVENTION.

Futile efforts to control the future—Law neglected for superstition—Pretentious prophets — Humbugs—Laws of weather changes—Actions of animals—Methods for producing rain suggested—Earthquake indicators—A force beyond control—Possibilities............... 589

CHAPTER XXVIII.

THE REIGN OF LAW.

Knowledge only from experience—Partial mastery by faith—Natural law the ruling force—Good and bad results of faith in the Supernatural—Sin punished—Ignorance punished—Examples—Man slow to learn—Eternal wisdom and goodness—Progress, past, present and future 600

LIST OF ILLUSTRATIONS.

	PAGE.
Cave of the Winds	18
The Simoom	40
Forms of Clouds	45
Path of Cyclones	54
Rotation of Storms	56
Water-spouts at Sea	60
Where the Storm entered Louisville	68
Baxter Park, Louisville	71
Falls City Hall	75
At Work in the Wreck	78
Main Street, between Eleventh and Twelfth, Louisville	82
Union Depot, Louisville	85
Eighth and Main, Louisville	90
Corner Main and Clinton, Louisville	94
Looking East from Tenth and Main, Louisville	96
Corner Jefferson and Twelfth, Louisville	99
On Ninth Street, Louisville	102
Ruined Tobacco Warehouses	104
View of Jeffersonville	108
Wall and Front Streets, Jeffersonville	109
Wreck at Jeffersonville	110
Tenth and Main, Louisville	112
Looking West from Tenth and Main, Louisville	115
View of the Residence District, Louisville	118
Ruined Dwellings	121
Path of Tornado, Olney, Ill	124
Scene at Olney, Ill	126
Whirlwind from Burnt Prairie	127
Tornado followed by Rain Storm	129
Instantaneous View of Tornado	130

LIST OF ILLUSTRATIONS.

	PAGE.
Tornado at Monville	132
Water-spout at Sea	135
Minnesota Tornado	137
Sand-spouts in the Desert	139
Cyclone, Fire and Earthquake, St. Thomas	145
"Drowning with its Terrible Roar"	147
Hurricane in the Tropics	151
Coast of India Submerged by a Storm	156
"He Sinks into Thy Depths"	160
Cast Ashore	163
Wreck of the *Minotaur*	167
Wrecked on a Rock	171
Castaways on a Raft	173
Sinking of the *London*	177
Storm on the Shoals, 1703	180
On a Lee Shore	184
Hovellers Relieving a Vessel	187
The Life-boat	190
The Life-boat at Work	193
Bow of the *Eber* Cast Ashore	201
The *Adler* on the Reef	204
Samoans Rescuing American Sailors	207
The *Calliope* Putting to Sea	210
Bow of the Sunken *Vandalia*	214
After the Storm	218
The Lyse Fiord	221
Ideal Subterranean Storm	225
Harvesters Killed by Lightning	232
Land of the Aurora	243
Field of Waterloo	249
Specter of the Brocken	252
Tropical Flood	264
Making Mats for Levee Fronts	266
Struggle to Hold the Levee	269
A Mountain Torrent	271
"No Time for Prayin'!"	273
Funeral During the Flood	275
Breaking of the Levee	277
Surprised by the Water	279

LIST OF ILLUSTRATIONS.

	PAGE.
No so Romantic as it Looks	282
Telegraphing Under Difficulties	285
Rescuing People	288
Camps on the Levee	290
Waiting for a Steamer	292
The Search Light	293
Scene at High Water	297
Negroes Moving Out	301
Stock Raft	303
Picking Up Refugees	306
Deserted Farmhouse	308
Flood in China	312
Dykes of Holland	316
Relief of Leyden	318
Breaking of the Dykes, Holland	322
Map of Conemaugh Valley	325
The Broken Dam	334
Fleeing Engine	337
Wreck of the Trains	340
Mill Creek	345
At the Stone Bridge	349
Desperate Struggle	354
The Gorge at the Bridge	358
Battle with the Waters	362
Johnstown After the Flood	371
At the Morgue	376
Conemaugh Viaduct	381
At the Summit of Popocatepetl	397
View in Active Crater	401
Crater of Orizaba	405
Eruption of Vesuvius	411
Coral Reefs	418
Destruction of Pompeii	424
Vesuvius in 1737	435
Destruction of Sodom	441
Destruction of Catania	446
Mt. Hecla	450
Jorullo	455
Geyser	457

LIST OF ILLUSTRATIONS.

	PAGE.
The Yellowstone Park	462
Cattle in Volcanic Mud	473
Convulsion on the Coast of Sumatra	478
Effect of Earthquake on Masonry	484
The Deluge	497
Ruined Roman Colonnade	500
Antioch	502
Massive Architecture Wrecked, Asia Minor	504
Ruins Near Cairo	506
Ruins Near Nineveh	507
Remains of Ancient Hebrew Masonry	509
Great Earthquake in Calabria	511
Destruction of Messina	513
Disaster of Scylla	515
Lisbon	517
Earthquake at Lisbon	520
Ruined Cathedral	522
Scene at Chio	524
Panic at Casamicciola	529
Earthquake in Andalusia	532
Wreck of the Charleston Earthquake	538
Houses Thrown into Ravine	542
Wreck on King Street, Charleston	544
Scene at Charleston	548
Old State House, Charleston	551
Charleston	554
Wreck of Factory	557
Ruined Dwelling	560
Earthquake in China	564
After the Shock	568
Scene at Caracas	571
Ruins of San Salvador	573
Fright at San Salvador	575
Shock at Lake in Honduras	577
Wreck at Mendoza	579
Great Sea Wave	583
Earthquake in Spain	586

GREAT DISASTERS

AND

HORRORS IN THE WORLD'S HISTORY.

CHAPTER I.

MYTHS OF THE WINDS.

> "Gray in his mossy cave Æolus stood
> Gazing in reverie at the distant sails,
> That skimmed the surface of the glassy deep,
> Unvexed by blasts of Eurus' boisterous whims.
> The restless winds in leash about their lord
> Full often murmuring, plucked his floating robe,
> Or stirred his tangled tresses with their breath,
> Impatient at the lack of wilder liberty."

SO sang the bard of the fabled cave of the winds. Thus the old Romans and Greeks have taught us to think and to speak of the spirits of the air. Thus the very name of "spirit" was originally identical with "breath" or "wind." Those poetic old Hellenes! They contrived to find something delightfully human in all the phenomena of nature. The woods were peopled with fauns and dryads. Around the bend of yonder rushy stream, a wary woodsman found a bathing nymph. Beyond that rock Actæon saw the chaste Diana sporting in the crystal pool. Here is the spot where baffled Phœbus found his Daphne changed into a laurel tree.

See you those stately poplars by the side of Italy's stream? There Phaëthon's mourning sisters changed their fleshly robes for those green spires. From their waving boughs the cry of the kingfisher Alcyone reminds us that

CAVE OF THE WINDS.

halcyon days may yet be in store for the most unfortunate. The response hurled back from yonder cliff warns us to drop a tear for the poor nymph Echo, whose unrequited love caused her to pine away till only a voice was left. To this day she answers every call, hoping to yet meet her love. That flaunting yellow flower is sprung from that very Narcissus who was so handsome he fell in love with himself. Ten thousand egotistic beauties of later days have not met so happy a fate.

Hark! was that the sea-shell of Triton? Neptune approaches with his Naiad train. You may see the plunge of his dolphin steeds. And see! what vision of incomparable loveliness is that? It is Aphrodite, goddess of love—sprung from the foam of the sea—as fragile as the fleecy mass from whence she came; as inconstant as the tossing wave on which she dances. How can love be otherwise, since she is its queen? In the sky above you see the beautiful Andromeda with the radiant Perseus. There Hercules yet wields his club and wears his lionskin. And there—

It is vanished. The disenchantment is complete. Modern civilization has replaced the nymph with the peasant, and the faun with the brigand. The pipe of Pan is forever silent. Marsyas is revenged, for Apollo is no more. Jupiter dethroned Saturn; Jupiter has long since been dethroned. Where are the hands that penned those beauteous fancies; the bards that sung the deeds of the gods? Dust and ashes these two thousand years.

Their works live after them. Passing centuries have not improved upon their lovely phantasies: it may be because they could not. Rome has named the months of our year: Norway has aided to name the days of our week. Easter preserves the name of Œstara, Teuton goddess of springtime, of new life, new light. So the names of the winds remain. Auster, the south wind, has his memorial in Australia. Zephyr, the gentle west wind, is still a theme for poet's song. Rude Boreas, "blustering railer," will always find a home in the north. Civilization has not driven him from his domain. Æolus, the master spirit, most powerful because most delicate and beautiful, still stirs our wind-harps with his breath. The spirits of the air are as boisterous and untamed as in the days of Æneas.

And what figures would appeal more strongly to the imagination than these simple personifications? How can too great importance be attached to the part the winds perform in the economy of nature? Without them the land would become a Sahara; the seas would be covered with a London fog. In the rustle of the breeze, as well as in the roar of hurricane, there is purpose and energy. The hand that guides one, controls the other. "He holdeth the wind in his fists."

In every age man's imagination has been strongly influenced by the mysterious or unknown. There is little play for poetic sentiment in the cold practicality of science. That which is clearly comprehended, loses half its charm. The botanist carefully plucks to pieces a flower; it is analyzed, and all its mechanism understood—but it is no longer a flower. The alchemist has produced the wonderful science of chemistry; but the philosopher's stone and the secret of producing gold are forever numbered among the shadowy myths of the past. The explorer has roamed in countless climes amid a myriad perils: a thousand treasures has he given to the world: but his El Dorado and the Fountain of Perpetual Youth have become as a dream in the night. And thus for aye will phantoms vanish as we grasp. Truth bears a magic wand at whose touch the unreal dies as a snowflake in a flame. All time has borne its legends of the risen departed, whose spirits roam the earth by night; but we have not proved that the dead have done in six thousand years so much evil as the living in a single day.

So one by one our cherished fables disappear. The steam-engine seems a thing of life; but we do not find a hidden geni therein. Electricity, one of the youngest of man's practical discoveries, has become the most easily controlled. The bolts of Jove are the prisoners of man. The river is harnessed to the mill and factory. But the winds roam as free as in the day of creation "when the morning stars sang together, and all the sons of God shouted for joy." Of all the forces of nature the wind and sea are least beneath control of man. The command "Subdue and have dominion" has not yet been fully obeyed.

Small wonder, then, that a glamour of mysticism remains about the storm and its birth. Man finds himself in the presence of a power beyond his comprehension. Of the various elements of nature, the wind, the sea and the storm are more than ever the realm of fancy and awe. One often wonders at many other ancient myths; but there seems nothing surprising in the Grecian fancy that the winds were the spirit slaves of Æolus; or in the Arabian thought, that storms were but the battles of wonderful genii, whose weapons were fire, water, and their own powerful breath. In the crash of the thunder the Arab heard their terrible strokes. The Northman beheld giants, contending now with each other, now with the giants of frost or of fire; now resting a moment in their cavern home—now chasing the clouds like frightened sheep from their realm of Mistheim. Some day all these powers would be arrayed in battle with the gods themselves, and Ragnarok, or universal chaos would follow. God made man in his own image; man has ever since endeavored to make all things in his own. So have the winds become personified in every age and land.

Charles Kingsley has given us a beautiful picture of the "air mothers," and the part they play in the realm of nature. Compare the ancient with the modern. We now know the laws and the work of the winds; but we have not found a better manner of picturing them. They are still the beautiful spirits of the air; the Peris of the upper deep, thoughtless in life, weeping repentant tears in the hour of their death.

"Who are these who follow us softly over the moor in the autumn evening? Their wings brush and rustle in the fir boughs, and they whisper before and behind us, as if they called gently to each other, like birds flocking homeward to their nests.

"The woodpecker on the pine stems knows them, and laughs aloud for joy as they pass. The rooks above the pasture know them, and wheel around and tumble in their play.

"The brown leaves on the oak-tree know them, and flutter faintly, and beckon as they pass. In the chattering of the dry leaves there is a meaning, and a cry of weary things longing for rest.

"'Take us home, take us home, you soft air-mothers, now our fathers, the sunbeams, are grown dull. Our green summer beauty is all draggled, and our faces are grown wan and thin; and the buds, the ungrateful children whom we nourished, thrust us off from our seats. Waft us down, you soft air-mothers, upon your wings, to the quiet earth, that we may go to our home, as all things go, and become air and sunlight once again!'

"The bold young fir seeds know them, and rattle impatiently in their cones. 'Blow more strongly, blow more fiercely, slow air-mothers, and shake us from our prisons of dead wood, that we may fly and spur away northeastward, each on his horny wing. We will dive like arrows through the heather, and drive our sharp beaks into the soil, and rise again, as green trees, toward the sunlight, and spread out lusty boughs.'

"They never think, bold fools, of what is coming to bring them low in the midst of their pride—of the reckless axe which will fell them, and saws which will shape them into logs, and the trains which will roar and rattle over them as they lie buried in the gravel of the way, till they are ground and rattled into powder, and dug up and flung upon the fire, that they too may return home, like all things, and become air and sunlight once again.

"The air-mothers hear their prayers, and do their bidding: but faintly, for they themselves are tired and sad, and their garments rent and worn. Ah! how different were those soft air-mothers, when, invisible to mortal eyes, they started on their long sky journey, five thousand miles across the sea.

"Out of the blazing caldron which lies between the two New Worlds, they leaped up, when the great sun called them, in whirls and spouts of clear hot steam, and rushed to the northward, while the whirling earthball whirled them east.

"So northeastward they rushed aloft, across the gay West Indian Isles, having below the glitter of the flying-fish, and the sidelong eyes of cruel sharks: above the canefields and the plantain gardens, and the cocoanut groves which fringe the shores: above the rocks which throbbed with earthquakes, and the peaks of old volcanoes, cinder-strewn: while far beneath, the ghosts of their dead sisters hurried homeward on the northeast breeze.

"Wild deeds they did, as they rushed onward, and struggled and fought among themselves, up and down, and round and backward in the fury of their blind hot youth. They tired themselves by struggling with each other, and by tearing the heavy water into waves; and their wings grew clogged with sea-spray, and soaked more and more with steam.

"At last, the sea grew cold beneath them, and their clear steam sank to mist; and they saw themselves and each other wrapped in dull, rain-laden clouds. Then they drew their white cloud garments around them, and veiled themselves for very shame: and they said, 'We have been wild and wayward: and alas, our pure youth is gone. But we will do one good deed, yet, before we die, and so we shall not have lived in vain. We will glide onward to the land and weep there, and refresh all things with warm, soft rain, and make the grass grow, and the buds burst; we will quench the thirst of man and beast, and wash the soiled world clean.'

"So they are wandering past us, the air-mothers, to weep the leaves into their graves: to weep the seeds into their seed-beds, and to weep the soil into the plains: to get the rich earth ready for the winter, and then creep northward and die there. But will they live again, those chilled air-mothers? Yes; they must live again. For all things move forever: and not even ghosts can rest.

"The corpses of their sisters piling on them from above, press them onward, press them southward toward the sun once more, across the floes, and round the icebergs—weeping tears of snow and sleet—while men hate their wild, harsh voices, and shrink before their bitter breath. They know not that the cold bleak snow-storms, as they hurtle from the black northeast, bear back the ghosts of the soft air-mothers, as penitents, to their father, the great sun.

MYTHS OF THE WINDS.

"But as they fly southward warm life thrills them, and they drop their loads of sleet and snow, and meet their young live sisters from the south, and greet them with flash and thunderpeal. Men call them the southwest wind, those air-mothers: and their ghosts, the northeast trade; and value them, and rightly; because they bear the traders out and back across the sea."

So they live, and so they die, those beautiful air-mothers—for life is evermore fed by death. And in their wayward course they bring the early and the latter rain: that so long as time shall be, seed-time and harvest and and summer and winter shall not fail. And men love them, and welcome each in their turn, whether laden with the pure white snow, or the cooling moisture of the distant sea; for man is a fickle creature, and remains constant to none. In summer he sings of the Arctic winds; and in winter, he longs for the breath of the south; for like the air-mothers, his course is ever onward, seeking that which he has not. Yet, sometimes in his discontent, he would curse the soft air-mothers: but without them he could not live. But the bard knows them all, and will sing of their deeds till the sun waxes cold with the weight of years.

CHAPTER II.

CONSTANT WINDS.

> "Up from the sea I sprang, O voyager,
> Ere Aphrodite rose from out its foam.
> I am a banned, unresting wanderer,
> Doomed o'er the surface of the deep to roam
> Without being aged, o'erwhelmed with days,
> The end of being is my only dream.
> I trod the earth ere man's ephemeral race,
> And onward flee long as yon sun shall beam,
>   Ever, forever,
>   Here, and wherever,
> Turneth the earth, must I course forever!"

THE phenomena of climate and seasons are too familiar to need especial comment or description. They are dependent, in the first place, upon the annual journey of the earth about the sun, the inclination of the earth's axis to its orbit, and the distance of any particular region in question, from the equator.

But the changes thus constantly made are greatly modified by other factors. Chief among these agencies are the form and extent of the continents, their position relative to each other and the water areas, and the currents of the air and sea.

Men usually identify climate with atmospheric conditions. A warm atmosphere is for them the whole of a warm climate: it is really but one of its factors, at most: it is often to be considered as a result, rather than a cause. On lofty plateaus, or in mountainous regions, the heat is not oppressive, even in the tropics; but here the moderate temperature is due to the elevation. France is as far north as Labrador; but there is no similarity whatever in climatic conditions, as there should be, were climate dependent only on the heating of the local atmosphere by the rays of the sun. Who would think of instituting a comparison of sunny Rome or Madrid with the city of New York? Yet the three are nearly on the same parallel: Rome furthest north. So there is little resemblance between the warmth of sunny Florida and the scorching heat of the Sahara: or between the climates in those portions of our own Pacific and Atlantic coasts that lie between the same parallels. So we find that though there is a general relation between the climate of a region and its distance from the equator, there are many other conditions to be considered. First, let us note atmospheric currents and disturbances.

"The wind bloweth where it listeth, and no man knoweth whence it cometh, or whither it goeth."

"The world do move." The illustration so full of meaning two thousand years since has lost much of its force. The truth of yesterday is the error of to-day. The fact of to-day may be the phantasy of to-morrow. So it has come to pass that in our day the origin and laws of air currents are believed to be as well understood as those of any other forces in nature. Yet scientific theorists are, after all, divided on not a few points.

Two general classes of winds are recognized: the constant, and variable. Constant winds are those that blow all the year in the same direction. The beautiful concept of Kingsley, in the preceding chapter, contains the leading points of our knowledge concerning them.

All the various phenomena of air currents are dependent upon one unchanging law: that gaseous bodies—and all but two others—always greatly expand under the influence of heat. There are two noted partial exceptions:

one of these prevents our globe from becoming a complete iceberg, and is as important as the law itself. Iron expands, till its melting point; but in its liquid state it occupies less space than when solid. Water contracts under the influence of cold, until the temperature of 39° is reached; after that it expands: and when frozen occupies about one-eighth more space than before. This wise provision of the Creator is second to none in importance, as regards its influence upon the climate of the earth at large. Had it been otherwise—did ice sink instead of float, our rivers and seas would in time become solid masses of ice; for water is so poor a conductor of heat, that its under-currents warm very slowly. Any one who plunges into a lake in mid-summer may often find the water warm at the surface, and of almost icy coldness a short distance beneath. The great Polar current comes down from Baffin's Bay, and off the coast of Newfoundland it plunges beneath the warm, lighter current of the Gulf Stream; but it is not warmed by it. Registering thermometers detect its icy coldness almost unchanged in the realms of the tropics, far beneath the surface.

Note some simple illustrations of the expansive force of freezing water. Every housewife knows that a bottle left full of water will burst when the water freezes. The same power is shown in the gradual disintegration of rocks by alternate freezing and thawing. Water freezing in the crevices bursts off small particles, or even large fragments; so that rocks long exposed to the weather, crumble more or less. Every one is familiar with the appearance presented by steep clay-banks, in late winter and early spring, of ragged masses and fragments ready to fall at any time. Still another instance of this destructive power is shown in the killing of vegetation by freezing. Plants are built of myriads of tiny cells. The moisture within freezes and bursts the cell-walls, destroying the plant life. Certain plants have cells more elastic than others, which in consequence are not destroyed by freezing. But as an expanded cell does not readily shrink to its former size, subsequent freezings, when the cell contains more water than before, may finally destroy it. So wheat is "winter-killed," by too frequent freezing. So globes of steel may be burst by this force.

To show the poor qualities of water as a conductor of heat, take a long glass tube and fill with water. Then put a piece of ice in one end. The water at the other end may now be brought to the boiling point by means of the flame of a lamp, ere the ice at the other end is melted.

Every one is familiar with the fact that heated air rises; but not all inquire why it does so. Take a foot-ball or bladder and partially inflate it; then hold it near a hot fire, and it may be swollen almost to bursting. Now, there is no more air in it than before; and if it be laid in a cold place, it will shrink to its first inflation. This shows how great is the expansive power of heat on the atmosphere. The same weight occupying a much larger bulk, we perceive that heated air is much lighter, and must rise. This, then, is the cause of what are known as constant winds.

As the earth revolves on its axis, the air is unequally heated, that nearest the equator becoming the warmest, in consequence of its receiving the most direct rays. Here, then, the air rises most rapidly; while the cooler air to the north or south must flow southward or northward to fill the vacuum. Now, the earth turning on its axis from west to east, whirls the northward and southward currents to the westward, so that they appear to blow from the northeast and southeast. The result of this loss of direction is gradual; so that when first perceptible, they are almost from a due northerly or southerly direction. As they near the equator, they are more rapid, and turn more decidedly to the west, never becoming violent, however; rarely exceeding fifteen to eighteen miles per hour.

It would appear that at the point where these meet each other, or come in contact with the ascending warm current, there must be a region of calms or light, variable winds, and occasional tempests. Such, in fact, is the case. This belt is from two hundred and eighty to four hundred miles in width, and lies along the thermal equator, or line of greatest average heat. This is not the same at the earth s equator, properly so called; for, as the land has greater capacity for absorbing and retaining heat than the sea, and as most of the land lies in the northern hemisphere, it is evident the highest mean temperature must be north of the equator. So this belt of calms must lie in the same region; and, in fact, in the Atlantic ocean it lies between 3 and 9° north latitude, and in the Pacific, between 4 and 8°. As the sun travels northward during the first half of the year, this region of calms shifts slightly, also, so as to always nearly coincide with belt of the greatest mean heat.

At first sight, it appears curious that the motion of the earth should deflect these winds to the west. It would appear that the earth, atmosphere and all, must revolve as a unit about its axis; else, if the atmosphere lose time, its speed to the westward should be constantly accelerated, and long ago should have reached a velocity that would shake the mountains themselves; while, in fact, there is no variation perceptible.

It should be remembered that at the equator the earth is about twenty-four thousand miles in circumference; and as one complete revolution is made every twenty-four hours, a point on the equator is carried eastward at the rate of one thousand miles an hour. But if a circle be drawn around the earth parallel to the equator, at some distance from it, it is at once seen that any object in this circle, having a shorter distance to traverse, is carried eastward at a slower rate; so that a point only a few yards from either pole must necessarily advance but a few feet per hour. So then, a body of air moving from either pole toward the equator, must needs advance very slowly if the friction of the upper reverse currents and of the surface of the globe are to have opportunity to overcome its relative inertia and give it the same velocity as that of any point over which it may pass.

Now, in the case of these constant winds, the inertia is very nearly overcome, as they start from a circle in which the velocity to the eastward is about 750 miles per hour. If the inertia were fully overcome, there would be no perceptible wind; as the velocity is actually but fifteen to eighteen miles per hour, it appears that the friction encountered actually destroys from thirteen-fourteenths to fifteen-sixteenths of the inertia. Hence, we find these constant air currents toward the west are, in reality, the result of the earth carrying any object on its surface a little more rapidly than the atmosphere moves; so that these winds are precisely the same in principle as the well-known fact that when you run rapidly in still air (so-called), it seems that the wind is blowing directly in your face.

In like manner, it appears that a wind from west to east is merely an air-current moving a little more rapidly than the earth revolves at that point. The relative difference between the velocity of air-currents must vary greatly; for a violent easterly or westerly wind very near the poles may equal or even exceed the speed of the rotation of that point; while the most violent tropical storms average between one-twentieth and one-eighth of the local rotation. The latter is not often exceeded. But whatever the relation of the respective velocities, it is clear that the velocity of the wind in general must depend largely on the amount of air abnormally heated, and upon the rapidity with which it is heated. So men have come to recognize that a period of unusually oppressive heat forebodes a storm of some sort. But few regard the unusual warmth as a reason of the storm. They are linked, in the popular mind, as antecedent and consequent, rather than as cause and effect.

These constant winds near the equator have been named trade-winds, because of their importance to commerce. Unknown before the first voyage of Columbus, they filled the minds of his crew with fear that they could never return home, if the wind blew always in one direction. The same gentle wind bore Magellan in his voyage around the world, and caused him to give the name of "Pacific," or "peaceful," to the great ocean on our west; and the same steady breezes made the fortune of many a noble galleon in the days when Peru was an Ophir, Mexico an El Dorado, and the Philippine Isles a Tarshish where they took shipping for the distant land of gold.

Owing to the fact that the continents intercept the regular trades by reason of their elevation and irregular conformation, and also because of their much greater specific heat, whereby they set in motion many other local currents, the trades are found to begin only a considerable distance to the west of the continents. Yet the influence of the trades is sufficient to make easterly winds the prevailing ones on the great inland plains: as in the Sahara, Arabia, Southern Siberia, and portions of North and South America.

It is clear that other nearly constant currents must exist to supply the vacuum that would be otherwise caused by the trades. These are found to the south and north of the trade belts, and, as might be expected, blow nearly in the opposite direction, being descending currents; while the trades, as before stated, are ascending. The column of hot air from the equator starts toward the poles above the trades, while a polar current sets in toward the equator; but as the amount of air displaced at the equator is by far the greatest, much of it can, of course, never reach the poles. On meeting the polar current, the two partially mingle and descend, forming what is called the return trade. This blows, most of the year, to the southeast, the equatorial current prevailing and coming from a region whose easterly rotation is more rapid. At certain seasons of the year, however, the polar current prevails to some extent, though not sufficiently to overcome the eastward trend; so the wind in this belt blows alternately to the southeast and the northeast.

Between the region of trades and alternating winds is a belt, on either side of the equator, of calms and variable winds, which shift northward or southward, parallel to the belt of calms between the trades. These two zones, however, are much less clearly defined than the great central one, and are not liable to such extraordinary disturbances.

Such is the great constant wind, with its dependents So long as the sun has warmed the earth, it has hurried on its course, subject to unceasing law, and destined to cease only when the heavens and the earth shall pass away, and chaos or annihilation shall end the things that be. A Wandering Jew of the atmosphere, it flies ever onward, bearing the merchant to his port, and the raincloud to the land; ever and anon desolating the isles with its bursts of fury; then resuming its restless course, like the remorseful Salathiel.

CHAPTER III.

PERIODIC WINDS.

> "Earth has each year her resurrection hours
> When the spring stirs within her, and the powers
> Of life revive; the sleeping zephyrs rouse,
> The blushing orchards clothe their naked boughs,
> The swallow skims above the lakelet's verge.
> Swift summer speeds with fire in every vein,
> And autumn's glories crimson hill and plain.
> Then warmth and life from Nature take their flight,
> And winter robes her in a shroud of white,
> While mournful Boreas chants her funeral dirge."

SO the seasons tread their ceaseless round in the temperate zones, and to a certain degree in the colder regions of the earth. But when we examine the change of seasons in the tropical world, we find a state of things so different that we are at once led to inquire the reason: and it will be found primarily in certain periodical winds.

When the sun is north of the equator: that is, while our northern summer is in progress, India enjoys a steady sea wind from the southwest, which bring a rainy season to the corresponding coasts of Hindostan and Farther India. When the sun returns to the south, the winds set in from the opposite direction, coming down across the great upland plateau of Central Asia, sometimes called, from its immense height and extent, the "Roof of the World." These periodic winds are called monsoons: a corruption of the Arabic word *Moussin*, season. They are in reality a modification of the trade-winds.

A glance at a map will show that the northern half of the great Indian Ocean is enclosed by land masses as no other large body of water is. Consequently, while in the southern section the southeast trade is present, the northeast trade of the northern part is so modified by the surrounding land areas as to almost entirely lose its distinctive character. Hence, most tropical regions have, properly speaking, but two seasons: the rainy, and the dry. As the clouds swept in meet with an intensely heated region, the trade never chills them sufficiently to produce snow, except in extremely elevated regions.

This is the direct cause of the monsoons: During the northern summer, southern Asia, being under the rays of the vertical sun, becomes intensely heated; and the cooler and denser air of the adjacent ocean, and of southern Africa, flows towards it, producing the southwest monsoon, which lasts from April or May to September or October. The time of its beginning and its close varies in different latitudes, according to the time at which the sun is vertical in each.

During the southern summer, southern Africa being under the vertical sun and intensely heated, the cooler air of the surrounding seas, and of southern Asia, flows towards it. This produces the northeast monsoon, which lasts from October or November to April. This monsoon is, in fact, only the regular northeast trade-wind somewhat intensified.

A similar exchange takes place between Asia and Australia, but it is less marked, owing, perhaps, to the great islands lying between these continents.

The period of transition of the monsoons, in spring and autumn, is marked by sudden and violent gales, and terrific thunder storms. Destructive hurricanes, also, are of frequent occurrence. This corresponds with the period of equinoctial storms in higher latitudes.

There are narrow monsoon belts in the Atlantic, along

the coast of Africa and of Brazil, also on the Pacific coasts of North and South America; but the phenomena they exhibit are of a much less striking character. On the African coast, in general, the winds blow from sea to land in summer, from land to sea in winter; on the Brazilian, the wind is from the northeast in summer, while in winter the southeast trade resumes its sway. The monsoons of the Pacific coast of America blow from the northwest and north during the southern summer; from the southwest and south during the northern. The regular trade-wind makes itself so strongly felt in northern Brazil, which is unusually level, that a boat can sail almost as rapidly up the swift current of the Amazon as it can row down: and Humboldt records that he found it of great strength at the foot of the eastern slope of the Andes.

Another modification of the northeast trade is found in the Etesian winds of Greece and the adjacent archipelago. This is a true intermittent trade, blowing only in the daytime, however, and lasting from July to September. The cool air of the peninsula rushes toward the extremely heated regions of the Mediterranean and north Africa.

Somewhat similar are the northers, or blizzards, of our Western States. By the laws already given, it is seen that northerly winds can prevail in any region only when some region further south is unusually heated. Now, the northern portion of America may be roughly compared to a trough. The cold polar current sets to the southward across the continent, and is turned to the east by the Rocky Mountain range, giving it a general southeast course. Hence, when the southern summer is in progress, our prevailing winds are from the northwest; and when the heated portion of the world is north of the equator, we have the return trade, giving us as our prevailing wind that from the southwest. When our return trade is unusually prolonged, we have a late fall; and if the southern summer is unusually warm, we have the polar current longer than usual, and a late spring in consequence. The polar current seldom makes its presence felt beyond the Texan plains; though occasionally it reaches the Mexican plateau, or sweeps across the Gulf to the Antilles.

A similar cold wind from Central France toward the Riviera is locally known as the Mistral. The cold winds from the south, which in crossing the plains of Patagonia, are turned eastward by the Andes, are called in Uruguay the *pamperos*, as their direction causes the popular belief that they originate in the pampas, or grassy plains. In Malta the cold wind becomes known as the *gregale*—in the Adriatic sea it is the *tramontana;* in Trieste and Dalmatia it is the *bora*. In New Zealand the corresponding cold blast comes from the south, and is known as the buster. When loaded with drifting snow, as in the blizzard of the United States, the cold wind of the Yenisei Valley, in Asia, is locally called the *purga;* in the steppes of Central Asia it is the *bura*.

Eastern Asia receives its prevailing cold current from the northwest; while western Asia and Europe receive their cold wave from the northeast, there being no range of mountains, as in America, to deflect the current, as the polar currents are disposed to follow the continents, having their origin in arctic lands; while for a similar reason the return trades reach their extremes on the ocean. Hence, lines drawn through the places which possess the same mean annual temperature reach a higher latitude at sea than on land.

These are the chief periodical winds of long periods. There is one other class to be noted: the diurnal land and sea breezes. These occur along all coasts, whether in the zone of trades or of variable winds; but the phenomenon is more strongly marked in the tropical regions, and in the summer of the temperate latitudes, because of the greater difference in the temperature of land and sea by day and by night.

During the hottest part of the day the air over the land frequently reaches a temperature of 100° Fahr., and even more, while that over the sea rarely rises above 80°. During the night the land radiates its heat with such rapidity that, towards morning, its atmosphere may be from 10° to to 15° colder than that of the sea.

Soon after sunrise, the land being warmer than the sea, a sea breeze sets in, which increases in force until about three o'clock, when the difference of temperature is greatest. It then gradually diminishes until about sunset, when, the temperature of the land and sea having become equal, the atmosphere is at rest, the calm continuing for an hour or more.

Soon the land becomes cooler than the sea, and a gentle breeze from the former sets in. It increases in force as the night advances, becoming strongest a little before morning, when the temperature of the land is lowest; after which it rapidly dies away, and is succeeded by a calm, to be soon replaced by the sea breeze.

One other species of variable wind is to be noticed: the hot, dry, dust-laden blast from desert regions. Such occur more or less periodically, and are known by different names in different localities.

Tom Moore has told us that "love's witchery" on the heart is

"Like the wind of the south o'er the summer lute blowing,
That hushed all its music, and withered its frame."

The reference is to the simoom of Syria and Arabia. One who has not experienced this wind can have little idea of its oppressiveness. Apt to come at any hour during the hottest months of the year, with a temperature so great that a piece of silver exposed to it becomes hot enough to blister the flesh, and laden with the impalpable dust of the desert, vegetation is scorched and withered by it, and animals flee from it as from the pestilence. It may last but a short time: it may endure several days.

At the first indication of its approach, people flee to their houses: doors and windows are shut and every crevice that could allow any dust to enter is tightly stuffed: while the wind lasts no one ventures out. Such unfortunate animals as happen to be overtaken by it have literally to struggle for their lives. The wind is not steady, but comes in fitful gusts, sometimes differing as much as 20° in temperature. The streets are deserted; and were they otherwise, a person could hardly be seen at a few yards distance. Hours pass: that implacable enemy, the dust, sifts in at unknown chinks. By degrees it covers everything. Valuable lace and tapestry are nearly ruined. You put on a skull-cap; yet it penetrates your hair. It finds its way beneath the garments to the skin, producing distressing dryness and roughness. The lips parch and crack. The eyes are red and inflamed. You drink as if famished, and gasp for breath. You are excessively irritable; you reach the verge of complete nervous prostration. At length the ordeal is over. You creep into the street, to find your neighbors looking like corpses; some, it may be, actually dead from nervous exhaustion. Dead birds and animals lie on the earth. It is a case of the survival of the fittest. You pluck a leaf from a neighboring tree; it crumbles to dust in your grasp.

Such are the effects of an unusually protracted wind, even when most favorably situated to encounter it. But if a caravan be overtaken by such in the desert, happy are they who escape. The camels kneel and thrust their

THE SIMOOM.

noses into the sand, against each other, into a pack of goods—anywhere to avoid breathing that poisonous blast. The men throw themselves upon the ground behind the camels, and muffle their heads in their garments. The storm is at hand; perchance attended by whirling columns of sand. You raise your head: a thick, dun-colored cloud flies at you; a heat as of red-hot iron, it seems, holds you in its choking grasp. You find your way to your water bottle, and drink deeply. The lurid sun turns the sweeping columns of sand to pillars of fire. Superstitious fear seizes your Arab comrades. Gradually the storm passes on: the men pick themselves up and endeavor to shake the irritating dust and sand from out the folds of their clothing, and the party resumes its way, happy that they are not numbered among the dead whose bones are bleaching by the way. Tales are not wanting of great caravans completely overwhelmed by the sandstorms of the desert.

These storms are met with in their greatest severity in Egypt and Arabia. In Egypt, this wind is called the *Khamsin*, or fifty, referring to the period of fifty days— the latter part of April, May, and early June—when they may be expected. They never blow through the entire season: rarely so long as fifteen days at a time. In Arabia the simoom may travel from the center of the peninsula toward any point of the compass; the Khamsin of Egypt blows from the southwest. Winds of the same character cross the Mediterranean. In Spain the wind is known as the *Solano*, or *Levanter*, or *Leveche*: in Sicily and Italy it is the *Sirocco*. The distressing dryness is somewhat modified by the journey across the Mediterranean. The same wind in Syria is called *Samiel;* and a similar wind which blows from the Sahara southwest to the Guinea coast is called the *Harmattan*. In California a similar dry hot wind blows from the interior toward the coast, during the hot season, and is called the desert wind. Such occasional hot blasts are experienced in southeastern Dakota, coming from the "bad lands," or sandy and rocky wastes along the upper Missouri river.

All these periodical or varying winds may be very properly, from their time and character, be called the season winds of the earth, as another means of distinction from the constant trades: as they in part bring changes of season, and in part are brought that way.

Into the question of climate and seasons one other element enters, of especial importance in regard to those disturbances of the regular winds, which we call storms. That factor is the quantity of moisture in the atmosphere, and the consequent rainfall or snowfall of a region. Without this element, the phenomenal disturbances known as tornadoes would hardly occur: or if they did, there would be greater difficulty in ascertaining their approach.

Water, in its vapor state, is but three-fifths the weight of the air, and in consequence rapidly rises. This evaporation, as it is called, goes on at all times: even when the water is frozen. A very thin sheet of ice, hung in the open air, will finally disappear, even though the temperature be always below freezing.

Now, all the phenomena of rain, snow, and hail, that are brought by different seasons, in different climes, depend upon a single simple law: that warm air can hold a much greater quantity of vapor than cold air. The amount of moisture that may be held in suspension at different temperatures is as follows:

Temperature of Air.	Weight of vapor in a cubic foot of saturated air.	Temperature of Air.	Weight of vapor in a cubic foot of saturated air.
20 deg. Fahr.	1.30 grains Troy.	70 deg. Fahr.	8.00 grains Troy.
32 " "	2.13 " "	80 " "	10.95 " "
50 " "	4.09 " "	90 " "	14.81 " "
62 " "	6.15 " "	100 " "	19.79 " "

This gives a second reason why storms of wind and rain closely follow extremely hot weather.

Now, as the vapor is so much lighter than the air, their mixture must also be lighter. So any unusual amount of moisture is at once detected by the barometer, an instrument for measuring the pressure of the atmosphere. If the air grow moister, and therefore lighter, the barometer falls; a storm is approaching.

Since cold air can retain but little moisture, if a warm moist current be chilled, it must lose a part of its vapor, which at once falls to the earth as rain. If the cold be somewhat greater, the moisture is crystallized into snow. Greely's observations at Fort Conger show that, varied a are the forms of snow crystals, those that fall during any particular storm are invariably of the same types, even though they may be collected from localities widely removed from each other. All crystals of snow are hexagonal in plan, but there is much variety in detail. The laws that produce one variety at one time, and a second at another, are not yet known.

The subject of hail is a peculiarly perplexing one to the meteorologist. Hailstones are more or less spherical in form, and are made of alternate layers of soft opaque ice, and hard clear ice. It is evident that they must acquire this structure by being whirled about between clouds of different temperature and density. Some have supposed that they are formed in a whirlwind, whose axis is horizontal, but for the present we must be content with Lord Dundreary's explanation, for "it ith one of thothe thingth which no fellah can underthtand."

Raindrops from a great height are larger than those from below, for they increase as they pass through the vapor-masses. As the warmest currents are also the highest, it will at once be understood why warm and tropical rains fall in large drops, while drizzling rains, mists, and fogs are characteristic of cold regions and cold seasons.

The masses of more or less condensed vapor in the upper air currents are what are known as clouds. Their various forms and appearance are shown in the cut on the — page.

The *cirrus* and *cirro-cumulus* clouds are the highest, are mostly in the altitudes of perpetual frost, and are supposed often to consist of minute ice crystals. In temperate latitudes they are usually formed in, and move with, the upper air current, or return-trade from the tropical regions.

The *cumulus* clouds are characteristic of the tropics, and of the summer days in middle latitudes, their height depending upon the relative humidity of the air. They are formed by local ascending currents, which carry a large amount of vapor into the cooler upper air. There the vapors are condensed, and are gradually heaped up into those heavy masses of sharply defined clouds,,which look like vast snowy mountains. Their base is horizontal, and marks the height at which the dew point is reached and condensation begins.

The accumulation of vapors is often so great that these clouds form a column several thousand feet high. In this case the difference in the temperature and the electrical conditions of the upper and lower portions is such that electrical discharges takes place, accompanied by condensation of a portion of the cloud, forming a thunderstorm.

Stratus clouds are most frequently seen in the morning or evening, and are always low. They are formed by the descent of the higher clouds and vapors of midday into the lower air as the temperature decreases. They are more frequent in winter and summer than in the intermediate seasons.

The *nimbus* cloud is more dense and heavy than the others, which may all be transformed into the nimbus by

PERIODIC WINDS. 45

FORMS OF CLOUDS.

a diminution of temperature. It is of a dark-leaden hue, changing into grey. This is the most common form of cloud in polar latitudes; and, during the cold season, it is the most frequent of the temperate zones.

If a moist current cross a mountain range, it loses its moisture in the cold region, and growing narrower as it descends the other slope, presents the phenomena of a warm dry wind from the mountains. Thus the wind that brings rain to Norway, gives warm fair weather to Sweden. Of the same character are the hot winds of Switzerland, called Foëhn winds, and the Chinook winds which blow from the eastward into Idaho, Washington, and western Montana. Similar winds occur occasionally in South Africa, Australia, New Zealand, and Peru. These hot winds must not be confounded with the hot and poisonous winds from desert regions described before.

Such, in fine, are the noted varying intermittent, or periodic winds. However uncertain they may appear at first thought, they are obedient to the same unchanging laws that bind the universe into one harmonious whole. No doubt the ancients, if they had been acquainted with their office, would have personified them as the nymphs of the seasons. But, knowing naught of the wonderful immutable laws that bind them, they could only say to each,

"We know not whence thou com'st, or whither goest,
When round our homes thy wizard blast thou blowest."

In eternal law and harmony they found only endless confusion and wild caprice. Man interpreted nature by man.

Yet they are the angels of the seasons, these air-spirits, sent by an allwise Providence to bring the rain and the snow, and the sunshine and storm in their season, to give seed to the sower and bread to the eater; that while man shall dwell on earth, seedtime and harvest and summer and winter may not cease. So they wander, clothing the tropics with emerald cloaks of strangest beauty, and robing the poles with ermine and crystal: painting with rainbow-tints the autumn leaves, and touching with virgin blush the orchards in spring; in all things obeying the decree of Him who hath set the seasons in order and made everything beautiful in its time.

CHAPTER IV.

TORNADOES AND CYCLONES.

> "O sad and mournful wind!
> From what wild depths of human pain and sorrow
> Could'st thou those tones of restless anguish borrow
> As of a soul that dreams of no to-morrow,
> O sad and mournful wind!
>
> O, thou art fierce and wild!
> Thy mighty chariot through the black skies lashing,
> The cloud-shapes round the mountain-summits dashing,
> The waves of ocean round the wrecked bark crashing—
> O, thou art fierce and wild!"

MEN find no difficulty in recognizing law and system in the phenomena that are of constant or frequent recurrence. That which is most difficult to explain, may pass without a serious thought so long as it manifests no stupendous or sudden power. The water may wear away the stone for centuries and its progress be unheeded by those who daily visit the pool.

So all observe and admire the beauty and order that prevails in the system of winds hitherto described. Their movements seem so simple and natural, that people take them as a matter of course. Rather, we should say, they may be depended upon with such certainty that the laws which they followed were unheeded for more than six thousand years. Relying on result, men gave themselves no concern about principle.

But in the sudden storm, the cyclone or tempest that comes sweeping the land with hardly any warning, flooding and destroying, men find mystery.

And who is not justly awed thereby? What other power so easily and frequently wrecks and ravages? Who may point out its course or stay its progress? And indeed it would seem difficult at first to find any law or system that controls the motion of the storm. If a rain storm always came from the same direction; if unusually high winds always blew from the same quarters, just as the moderate breezes of spring and summer can always be expected from the same general direction, it would appear that there was much greater subordination to definite law. But what can be more perplexing than to have a storm blow violently from one quarter for a time, and after a brief calm to blow with equal violence the other way? Can such phenomena be explained by any principles hitherto discovered?

What is a storm? Strictly speaking, it is any marked or unusual disturbance of the normal atmospheric conditions. There may be excessive wind: there may be cessation of the customary winds. Two great classes are found: cyclonic, or low area storms, and anti-cyclonic, or high area storms. The former may be accompanied by heavy rainfall or snow; the latter is usually noted for absence of either. It is with the low area storm that we must deal at present.

This term is used to designate all storms which are marked by low barometer, and therefore it is clear that such are accompanied and partially occasioned by an unusual amount of moisture in the atmosphere. The resultant commotion is usually extensive, the storm centre traveling across the country; but occasionally the effects are perceptible only for a short distance, the storm centre either breaking up or ascending to the upper atmosphere.

By a cyclonic storm is signified a storm characterized by unusually low barometer, and a wind system blowing spirally inward, as in a genuine cyclone. They usually affect only the lower strata of the air. Quite frequently they are broken up by striking low mountain ranges, such as the Alleghany system : and often pass Mount Washington without making their presence felt at the signal station on its summit. To what extent they are influenced by or are due to the upper air currents is therefore unknown, though not a few of the attendant phenomena indicate that the latter are of no little importance.

Any one who has observed the waters at the junction of two streams, is familiar with the appearance of numerous tiny eddies or whirlpools formed at the point of junction. Such are perceptible also in every rapid stream, when the current, sheering sharply from a projecting point, is made in a measure to collide with itself. This is also the principle of the many tiny whirlwinds seen during the warm summer days : and such are also observable in winter, if there be snow enough to render their presence in the air clearly visible. Their results are most readily recognized in snow-drifts, where the wind meets some special obstruction. It does not often occur that a high fence is covered with a snow-drift: a great drift will be thrown up by it, but not against it : and the side next the fence will be curved inward, or concave. The wind strikes the fence and partially recoils, curving upward to pass over the fence. The drift is then built up between the wind and the current recoiling from the fence, and its inner curve shows the direction pursued by the rebounding current.

Now, when opposing air-currents meet each other on a large scale, the immense whirlwind that is produced is called a cyclone or tornado. It follows then, that if we would find any regularity or law in these unusual disturbances, we must know if there exists any permanent condition of atmospheric currents that is favorable to their generation.

That such a state exists, we have already learned. The great belts of calms that we have found between the trade-winds and the return trades and polar currents, are more appropriately called the zones of equinoctial storms. We have in them districts of general calms, with winds infringing upon either side. It is evident then that, as in the case of the fence, whose recoil-current curves the snow-drift, a whirling current of considerable magnitude may arise here at any time: hence, violent storms do arise in these regions more or less at all periods of the year. But we have seen that these zones of calms move slightly to the north or south with the course of the sun. It would then appear that at the equinoctial period, when they return from the mean position toward the extreme northern or southern limit, there would be opportunity for unusual disturbances, especially since the heavy rainfall of those periods would unusually affect the temperature of the atmosphere.

That is precisely what occurs. The equinoxes are marked by storms of unusual severity, and the influence of the sudden falls of rain is so great that some eminent men believe them to be nearly the sole factor in the formation of these storms. In one case they doubtless are. If a very heavy rain be decidedly local, there is low barometer at that place. Now, if on either side there be areas of high barometer, the opposing currents flowing toward the center of low area are sufficient to meet all the conditions necessary for a cyclonic storm. As the zone of calms is comparatively narrow, it is apparent that the diameter of the area of any storm, owing to the pressure exerted by the incoming currents of wind, must be still less. Hence, the cyclone center, at its time of formation, seldom exceeds one hundred miles in diameter. As it travels away from the compressing currents that formed it, it is clear that its centrifugal force must increase; hence, its area increases, and its violence correspondingly diminishes.

These facts refer to the unusually violent cyclonic storms, properly known as cyclones. But all low area storms are characterized by the upward spiral motion, though not strong enough in the case of ordinary summer rains and thunderstorms to be especially noticed. We shall see, by and by, how this spiral motion may result without the intervention of any strong opposing currents.

Why and how a cyclone travels, is a question that at once propounds itself. Its motion is in accordance with a fixed law, whose operation varies only as it may be affected by unusual peculiarities in the configuration of the surface over which it travels. The reason of the motion is not so easy to explain; neither is it easy to explain why heat expands objects: but its operation is none the less certain. And so the route pursued by any storm can be readily indicated in advance. It is not a matter of mere conjecture.

The motion of a cyclone or tornado is in accordance with the same law that governs the motion of planets around the sun. It can be illustrated in a very simple manner by the spinning of a top.

Spin a top on a perfectly smooth and level surface. It will be better if the peg of the top be blunt or round, so that there will be no tendency to settle steadily into some possible hole or depression.

Now, the instant any degree of steadiness is attained, the top begins to move in small curves. If it be spun on a marble slab smoothly coated with fine flour or sand, it can be made to record its motions, which may then be carefully studied. It will be found that the form of the curve is nearly the same with every start. It will describe a parabola, pause a moment, then describe a second, and so on.

The chief peculiarity of this separate curvilinear motion is that its direction is always in an *opposite* direction to that of the rotation of the top. If the top turn from left to right, it will move from right to left, and vice versa. The same tendency will manifest itself even if the peg of the top be placed in a slight depression or socket, so that the curve cannot be made. Then the upper portion of the top will incline to one side, and begin describing a curve: but, as before, in a direction contrary to the direction of rotation.

The common toy known as a gyroscope illustrates the last peculiarity also. It consists of a wheel within a metal frame, which has a peg like a top. If the wheel be made to revolve rapidly, the whole may be balanced on the peg: when the frame will begin to slowly revolve in the opposite direction: and if placed upon a smooth level surface, like the top it will tend to describe the same course.

Still other illustrations of this principle are even more familiar than the spinning of a top. Any one who has seen the game of soldiers in a bowling alley knows that in order to make the ball turn to the left as it moves forward, it must spin the other way; that is, with the hands of a watch. To travel or curve to the right, it must spin in the contrary direction. So in our "great national game," base-ball, the pitcher curves the ball any way he pleases merely by following this law. It is not necessary to take into account, as many do, the return trades, as occasioning the travel of a whirling storm; and the fact is, that the cyclone frequently travels more rapidly than the ordinary wind moving in the same direction.

Now, the motion of the planets is similar: rotating in

one direction, they travel in the other. So we find the general law is,

All revolving bodies, left free as to direction, travel in a curve in a direction opposite to that of their rotation. This curve is usually some form of conic section: an ellipse, parabola or hyperbola. The planets, and some comets, move in ellipses. Some comets travel parabolas or hyperbolas. And the parabola is the customary path of the cyclonic storm. As the cyclone in the northern hemisphere rotates from right to left, and in the southern from

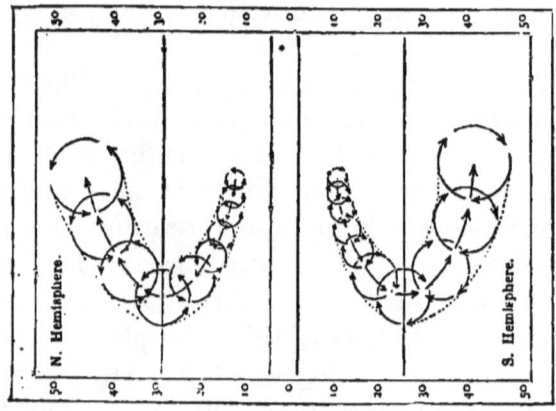

left to right, their paths must necessarily be in opposite directions, as may be seen by the accompanying diagram. So in either case, the direction of the path is always away from the equator.

As far as the United States are concerned, most noncyclonic storms originate in the Saskatchewan country, or along the southeastern slope of the Rocky Mountains. By far the greater number pass over the St. Lawrence valley. A small number are developed in the Gulf, or in the Pacific: but these are much affected, often broken up, in crossing the Rocky or Appalachian systems. The usual course is somewhat north of east; but there are a few notable exceptions. The immense amount of vapor wafted up the Mississippi valley induces some low area storms to move southward from Manitoba into the upper Mississippi valley. In like manner, the excessive moisture along our north Pacific coast causes occasional storms to move southward from Alaska to Oregon.

But the course of a cyclonic storm, we have seen, must be different.

The accompanying diagram illustrates the fact that the wind blows from all directions toward the center of the storm. As the storm revolves, the wind would come apparently from the south for any one on the eastern edge of the cyclone of the northern hemisphere. Hence, in the case of a storm of large diameter, people in Richmond or Washington may often be surprised by an apparent northeast gale, which reaches them before it strikes New York or Boston. At the center of the storm is absolute calm. So if a cyclone pass centrally over any point in the northern hemisphere, a person at that place will find the wind blowing violently from the southeast: then after an interval of calm, it will blow with equal violence from the northwest. This will be the case if the path of the storm has already turned to the northeast, so that its northeast quarter may be called its front. If on the northwest course, however, the apparently alternate winds would be from the northeast and southwest. So one in the path of a southern cyclone would find the winds proceeding from the same quarters; for though it revolves in the opposite direction, its front or path is also in the opposite direction; so in either hemisphere, the southeast or the northeast wind will be the first felt by one directly in the track of the storm.

Another result of the path of a cyclone is that the direction of its center from the stand-point of any observer

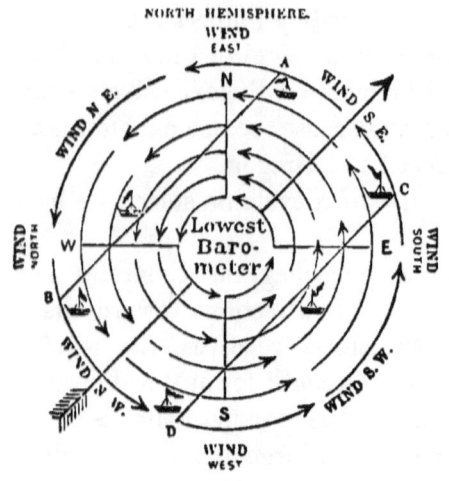

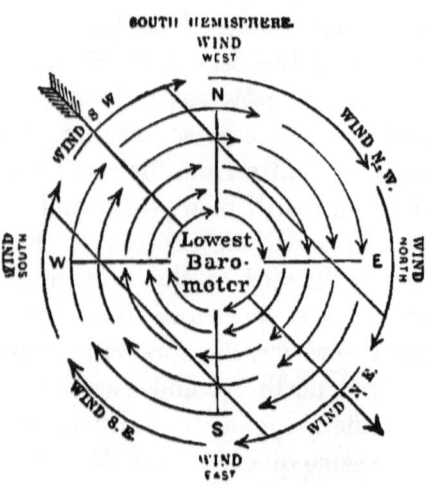

ROTATION OF STORMS.

is readily known. A glance at the diagram shows at once that if any one within the storm area of a cyclone of the northern hemisphere stands with his back to the wind, the storm center, where the barometer is lowest, is invariably on his left: but if he stand with his back to the wind of a southern cyclone, the storm center is always on his right. Hence, if a vessel be overtaken by a cyclone, the captain at once may know how to pass beyond its range, by shaping his course at right angles to that of the wind. Thus, if in a northern cyclone, he must sail to the right, supposing his back is to the wind: in the southern hemisphere, he would sail to the left.

As an example of the expansion of the storm area in its journey, may be mentioned the West India hurricane of 1839, which had, in the Antilles, a diameter of three hundred miles, which increased to five hundred at the Bermudas, and eight hundred on the parallel of 50° north latitude.

To draw again upon the illustration of the spinning top, it will be observed that the curvilinear motion is extremely slow in comparison with that of rotation, but increases as the rotation decreases. The same law applies to the movement of cyclones. The slowest motion forward is usually near the apex of the curve: and the progress on the ocean is much slower than on the land. Traveling over the latter, the irregularities of surface act in the case of the storm just as a rough surface does in the case of the top. The motion may be accelerated, but its regularity is lessened. So while at sea the parabolic path of the storm is almost absolutely perfect, but on reaching the land its motion is more rapid, and less regular, conforming somewhat to the configuration of the surface.

To illustrate, take the great cyclone of August 16th to 22nd, 1888. This started off Point Jupiter, Florida, with a rainfall of 2.2 inches in twelve hours, while the rotary velocity of the wind was sixty miles per hour. Its path across the Gulf of Mexico was a perfect semi-parabola, curving northward into western Louisiana; but rapid as was the rotary velocity, three and a half days were required for the journey across the gulf. Meanwhile, it was rapidly widening: for within a few hours of its reaching land, its eastern edge was assailing Mobile, Alabama, with a south wind of fifty-five miles an hour. Almost at the same time the western half was flooding Memphis and Vicksburg with an enormous rainfall—almost four inches in twelve hours, at Memphis. By the morning of August 21st, thirty-six hours after reaching land, it was central over middle Tennessee and Kentucky; heavy rains fell over the entire region. But by this time its eastern edge was in collision with the Appalachian chain; while a heavy local rain at the northern extremity of that chain created an additional diversion in a new area of low barometer. So it left the hitherto parabolic route, and shot away nearly at a tangent along the western Appalachian slope, passing from Tennessee to Newfoundland in thirty-six hours, thus moving nearly three times as rapidly as in the Gulf: while its violence, or rotary speed, was vastly lessened.

This storm was one of the most destructive of the recent cyclones that have swept our country, doing immense damage to crops, bridges, houses, herds—in short, everything that can be seriously damaged by wind or flood.

The damage in Louisiana alone was estimated at $500,000. But it was by no means the most destructive of the West India storms.

An examination of the areas of calms, which are the hot-beds of cyclones and hurricanes, shows that the region which produces the great cyclones of the United States lies in the Antilles and Caribbean Sea. In the Pacific the portion of the calm belt of the Tropic of Cancer causes the ravages of cyclones or hurricanes originating there to be felt chiefly in Japan and China. The storms of the Pacific arising in the equatorial calm belt, are most violent in the East Indies, and the southern peninsulas of Asia. As these regions are much warmer, and consequently the atmosphere may hold a much greater quantity of vapor, it follows that cyclones in that quarter much exceed in violence those of our own land.

Such are the general laws of these terrible disturbances of nature, as ascertained by years of careful observation. In the United States, our Signal Service, with well-equipped observatories at important localities, is able to make these principles of practical use: to detect the incipient storm and mark out its path, ere it strikes its fiercest blow.

It should be observed, ere leaving this topic, that a few would-be prophets have maintained that not only great storms, but also earthquakes, volcanic eruptions, tidal waves, etc., are due to planetary influences. Observing that the most violent hurricanes occur near the equinoctial period, they argue that the equinoxes of the planets ought to also disturb the earth. They ignore the fact that as to our own equinoctial disturbances, the change in the relative position of the earth and sun is sufficient to produce change in the location of heated air-currents and consequent storms. They seek to find in the Equinox Absolute, some strange mysterious magic, some inexplicable power or *Deus ex machina*, whose business it is to get up a disturbance here on earth at every possible opportunity, no matter in what planet he may be for the nonce located.

But it is difficult to rid any man of his hobby. In the question of the equinoxes of other planets, their recurrence is of sufficient frequency to allow the weather-crank full play for his imagination. Two of the major planets lie within the earth's orbit, and their more rapid course about

WATER SPOUTS AT SEA.

the sun results in there being an equinox in one or the other of them about once in each month. So no matter in what month a great storm may occur, the enthusiast can point out that a neighboring planet is at or near an equinox

A careful examination of the equinoxes of the inner planets for a period of fifteen years shows that the number occurring in the month of April was 22 per cent. above the average occurrence for any month: whence, it would appear that the disturbances at that period ought to be equally in excess. But as a matter of fact, storms on the earth are most numerous and violent at the time of the autumnal equinox—September and October—when no such departure from the average of equinoxes of the other planets appears.

If planetary influence were the cause of our storms, it would be reasonable to suppose that disturbances would be greatest when the planets are nearest to the earth: but the advocates of the theory do not seem to consider this a factor at all. Nor could the planetary equinox theory account for the fact that storms of peculiar character always originate in the same regions. For instance, why do cyclones always originate near the tropics and move away from the equator? If the planetary equinoxes produce violent earthquakes, why are they so partial to North America as never in our whole history to have given us a very serious shaking up? Why is it that of the hundreds of recorded tornadoes of the past century in the United States, only one has ever occurred west of Dodge City, Kansas? Clearly the adherents of the equinoctial theory will have to admit local terrestrial conditions that modify all their theories: and to make such an admission will be, in the end, to give up the fight.

The writer knew of a boy who wasted a pound and a half of bird-shot in trying to kill a small owl. The game was finally secured, and the young Nimrod discovered a hatful of feathers with the body of a robin—and of no earthly use.

Attacking the planetary theory is of little more use. But the theory is the resort of many would-be weather prophets, who needlessly alarm the ignorant with their gloomy forebodings.

In a country as large as our own, any sort of weather is a very safe prediction to make for any day in the century, as minor rains and cloudy seasons and small storms are merely local. Any sort of prediction would be nearly sure to hit some portion of the country; and one who is so disposed can easily win a cheap notoriety and gain scores of testimonials as to the correctness of his predictions. Every unusual catastrophe produces a brood of these gentry who are eager to make the trial. But those who endeavor to indicate the exact locality where any great disturbance is to take place, meet discomfiture with a uniformity that ought to be discouraging. The work of the Signal Service is as carefully done as may well be: yet its best men assert that an average of 90 per cent. of correctness in their prognostications is unusual, because of the extremely small areas covered by local disturbances. Rainy weather announced for western Missouri may be correct every time for Kansas City, but be 10 per cent. in error for Nevada, Missouri. When those whose time is devoted to the weather can not always be correct, it is useless to listen to charlatans.

A careful study of sun-spots with relation to storms has been made of late years. The fact is elicited that the spots seem to have a definite connection with electrical disturbances: but while there are numbers of coincidences between unusual sun-spots and great storms, the number of striking exceptions seems equally great. Hence, it can not be fairly inferred that there is any definite relation between them. And so far as electrical phenomena on the earth are connected with storms, they always appear as dependent upon rather than productive of atmospheric currents. Indeed, the most remarkable electrical disturbances occur at times when no atmospheric current is prevalent. The most beautiful electrical display, the aurora, appears when the air is abnormally still and unusually dry. The necessity of the latter condition accounts for the fact that it is usually observable only in cold weather and occurs with great frequency and in remarkable brilliancy in the polar regions. It results from electric currents passing through extremely rarefied and dry air, and may be produced on a small scale artificially.

Poe was right when he held that many things remain long secrets by reason of their very simplicity. Six thousand years steam hissed and fumed in men's faces, and tilted the kettle lid, before they learned its expansive power. Six thousand years the lightning flamed and roared before man realized it could be made one of his most obedient servants. Six thousand years he cudgeled his wits to discover the secret of the wind: yet when he made a fire within his house, he closed the door to prevent unpleasant draughts of air. And so he continues, constantly endeavoring to find some strange mystery in the things that are dependent on simplest laws.

There was a time when men stood aghast at small-pox, cholera, yellow fever, and many similar calamities, and spoke with bated breath of the "mysterious visitations of providence," the "scourge of God," and so on. When the Turks once besieged a plague-stricken city, a comet appeared in the sky. The pious inhabitants prayed "O Lord, deliver us from the devil, the Turk and the comet," and usually such people believed such plagues were the judgment of God on them for their sins. Modern science holds that about the only sin the Lord punishes in that way is the sin of filthy streets, or back-door cess-pools. When man has once learned the means of control and prevention, evils lose their mysterious witchery.

On the other hand, let the laws of any force in nature be every so well understood: yet, so long as they are beyond the control of man, they will retain for him an eerie uncanny fascination. The pigmy has harnessed the steam and chained the lightning: but when the storm clouds lower and the forests moan, the sea roars and the lightning glows, he stands in fear and awe before a power whose might he but vaguely comprehends. He may know of the winds, whence and whither bound; but when the Stygian darkness has passed on, leaving wreck and ruin, want and woe, desolation and despair, shattered homes and hopes, and bleeding hearts, this knowledge of law is, for the nonce, forgotten, and the hurricane is transformed, in his disordered vision, into a demon of wrath, or caprice; or he speaks, hesitatingly it may be, of the mysterious dispensation of an inscrutable providence. But in the mighty wind, as in the soughing breeze, there is only obedience to universal law. But when the Author of law displays his power, man's instinct, however unwilling his reason, acknowledges a God.

CHAPTER V.

THE LOUISVILLE TORNADO.

> " At eve along the calm resplendent west
> I marked a cloud alive with fairy light,
> So warmly pure, so sweetly, richly bright,
> It seemed a spirit of ether, floating blest,
> In its own happy empire! While possest
> With admiration of the marvelous light,
> Slowly its hues, opal and chrysolite,
> Waned on the shadowy gloaming's phantom breast.
> The cloud became a terror, whose dark womb,
> Throbbed with keen lightnings, by destruction hurled,
> Red bolt on bolt, while a drear ominous gloom
> Enveloped Nature: o'er the startled world—
> A deep alarum—burst the thunder boom
> And the swift Storm his coal-black wings unfurled!"

THERE is a perspective of news as well as of art, which requires that such features in a view as are supposed to be nearest to the observer must be given larger detail. It is a natural consequence of the fact that a small object near by may conceal from view a mountain in the distance.

So in the news world a dog run over on Washington avenue takes rank with a wreck in the Indian Ocean. A fight in a neighboring saloon gets ten inches: a strike in Germany ten lines. Your neighbor's new barn is a good item for the county paper whose editor cares nothing for the new bank in Boston. The Widow Jones gets a puff for whitewashing her fence; the refitting of the White House gets a line. A million of people who have heard of George Washington, never heard of Alfred the Great.

Now, not a few will think that there is injustice in this.

Doubtless the tendency of the time is to exaggerate perspective to obtain startling effects. Caricature is characteristic of the age. And yet, there was never before a time when so many people took interest in things that lay beyond their own narrow circle; even if that interest be from mere curiosity.

Sometimes this self-centered condition of humanity has an amusing aspect: as if one should imagine the earth terminated with his own apparent horizon. Some South Sea Islanders called the first white men who visited them, "sky-breakers." The reason is simple. Dwelling on their little islets, mere specks in the deep, and in all their myths and legends having no account of any other race, they supposed themselves to be the only people in the world. Their sky was a vast wall of blue stones raised by one of their mythical heroes. It shut in the world and could not be far away, though none of them had endeavored to reach it. So these strange white creatures were not of this world; neither were they of the race of the gods; they came from no one knew where, and had somehow broken through the blue wall that bounded the world. And white men are in some islands called "sky-breakers" to this day.

Something of the same spirit is manifested by the Chinese. The devil of their mythology is white. So our occidental sensibilities received quite a shock when we learned that we were "foreign devils." The Japanese more considerately called us "foreign beasts," as though uncertain of our status in the animal kingdom. And to this day our magnificent vessels are gravely styled "devil ships" by the Chinese.

Such are what might be appropriately styled ludicrous exaggerations of perspective. And we of the west are similarly so wrapped up in our self-sufficiency that it hardly occurs to us that we may appear as amusing to foreigners as they to us. In this respect our charity begins at home. It is the way of the world.

But there are a thousand occurrences that make us feel that the principle is just, no matter to what extremes we may foolishly carry it. It comes home to each with peculiar emphasis in the hour of distress. The famine in Asia does not weigh upon you so heavily as the death of the woman who starved in the garret across the street. A fire that burns Chicago is easier forgotten that the one which destroys the little home that represents the savings of years of your life. The cholera in India has no such terrors for you as the diphtheria or scarlet fever in your own village. The Czar of Russia is blown to pieces in his carriage; but he has no remembrance at the bedside of your sick friend. Ten thousand dead victims of a distant earthquake are hidden by the coffin in your own home.

Since the same law applies to the interests of nations, it is not necessary, in reviewing the work of destructive tempests, to apologize for giving chief place to the recent Louisville tornado, however insignificant it may appear in comparison with scores of others that have desolated the earth in days gone by. The latter shall be noticed in due time.

In the foregoing chapter we have seen that the great cyclones that occasionally visit us originate in the neighborhood of the Antilles. Of course, similar conditions may produce smaller storms of the same class in numerous localities. These small storms whose paths are but a few yards, or sometimes as much as a mile in diameter, are called, to distinguish them from the great cyclone of twenty to two hundred miles in diameter, by the Portuguese title of *tornados*, or "turning-storms." Often the broken character of the country will cause a large gathering storm to break

WHERE THE STORM ENTERED LOUISVILLE.

up into half a dozen or more of the smaller ones, which, in their narrow paths are as destructive as the cyclone.

It is the unexpected that happens. No one experiences so many surprises, or has more pet beliefs upset than that oracle of the chimney-corner, the oldest inhabitant. It was long believed that tornadoes never passed over an old Indian camp ground. Whatever the popular opinion of savage intellect, there is marvelous confidence in his instinct. Again, it was thought a tornado never would pass over a large city. The storm in question demolished both these " olde wyves' tales."

During March 27th, 1890, the Signal Service Department observed a threatening storm center gather in the southwestern portion of Wyoming, and start eastward with great rapidity. Notice was promptly given. Railway, telegraph and electric light officials were warned that on Thursday night a hurricane would blow with a speed of at least fifty miles an hour. Signal Service predictions had sometimes failed, and this last one excited no particular concern. The destroyer came and was gone in two minutes; and blocks on blocks of Louisville were a ghastly ruin.

The tornado was accompanied by a cloud and tremendous rain To an observer at the Falls, the cloud was seen to come up the gap between the hills which guard the banks of the beautiful Ohio. He described it as "balloon-shaped, twisting an attenuated tail to the earth. It emitted a constant fusillade of lightning, and seemed to be composed of a lurid, snake-like mass of electric currents, whose light would sometimes be extinguished for a few moments, making an almost intolerable darkness. It was accompanied by a fearful roar, like that of a thousand trains crossing the big bridge at once. It could be seen to strike Louisville, and then with incredible rapidity it leaped the river, churning it into white foam as it went toward the Indiana shore."

The streets of Louisville parallel to the river are named; those at right angles are numbered from east to west. The section visited may be described as a rectangle a mile square, bounded on the west by Eighteenth street, on the east by Seventh, on the south by Broadway, and on the north by the Ohio river. It comprehends the business portion of the city. Through this district the cyclone swept diagonally from southwest to northeast, crossing the river and leaving the city at the foot of Seventh street. The business houses or residences of perhaps 10,000 people lay in its path.

Two days after the storm, when there had been time for a calm survey, its track is thus described by a correspondent of the Associated Press:

"It first descended upon the beautiful little suburb of Parkland, southwest of the city, destroying many private residences. The loss of life was inconsiderable at this initial point, however. Rushing onward toward the northwest it lifted for a moment above the trees and housetops, and descended again a mile further on at Maple and Eighteenth streets. From this on its pathway is clearly marked. At no time did the base of the funnel touch the ground, and one hundred feet higher in the air, it would have passed by without doing comparatively much damage.

"The ruins as they now are often show the first, and even the second and third stories of buildings still intact, with the roofs and higher stories swept away except in places where the debris from the upper floors crushed in the lower, and brought the walls down to the ground in total collapse. From Maple and Eighteenth streets it went northward one block, then west at an angle another block; and then curving to the northeast as far as Magazine and

THE LOUISVILLE TORNADO. 71

BAXTER PARK, LOUISVILLE.

Thirteenth streets. A quick change to the north is perceptible here, and after traveling in that direction two blocks, another turn to the west. An acute angle was then made, the line turning from Fifteenth street northeast to Thirteenth street again; thence, due east to Tenth street, and north a block to Market street. At Thirteenth and Jefferson streets it swept through Baxter Park, doing great damage, and a block eastward destroyed St. John's Episcopal Church, in the rectory of which the Rev. S. E. Barnwell and his little son were crushed and burned to death, the rest of the family escaping.

"St. John's Church is in the street immediately in the rear of the ill-fated Falls City Hall. The eccentric monster went on eastward past the Falls City Hall without touching it, and then, as if suddenly recollecting, it swept around the block and started westward on the south side of Market street. Had the change of direction been made a trifle sooner or later Falls City Hall would have escaped, and the dead been numbered within thirty or forty at the most.

"As if satisfied with the work accomplished, it turned north again and struck Main street. This thoroughfare is the principal business street in the city. It runs parallel with the river from east to west, and but a block south of it. It is lined with wholesale houses, and was the solidest part of the city in point of architecture.

"The tornado reached Main street at Twelfth, and then shaped its course directly east down the middle of the broad street, sweeping away the solid stores and warehouses on both sides. From Twelfth to Seventh streets on Main it is a wholesaling district, and it was practically untenanted at that hour. Had the storm come in the daytime and taken the same direction, hundreds who were at their houses and escaped unhurt would have been killed.

"At Seventh street and Main the buildings change in their character. The big Louisville Hotel is on Main between Sixth and Seventh, and east of the hotel are restaurants, saloons and other hotels which contained thousands of people at that hour. The tornado chased down Main street, carrying everything before it, passing Eleventh street, Tenth, Ninth, Eighth, and Seventh. A block further and the Louisville Hotel, with its hundreds of tenants, would have been reached. The escape of the hotel is the strangest incident of all. Adjoining it on the west, from whence the storm came, was a three-story building used as a saloon on the first floor, and occupied in the upper stories as sleeping apartments for the hotel servants. This three-story building, right under the east wall of the hotel, was totally demolished and not a timber left a dozen feet higher than the ground. Its inmates were killed. The great hotel shook from roof to cellar with the force of the shock, but it was spared.

"The storm veered at the sharpest kind of an angle to the north again, crossed Main street, and struck for the river, taking in the Union Depot on the way. Strange to say, although the depot was totally demolished, only one person was killed there. At the point where the tornado crossed the river, between New Albany and Jeffersonville, it is supposed several small crafts were sunk.

"Reaching the opposite bank of the river, the storm turned to the east again and took off a bite from Jeffersonville. It went along Front street for a few blocks, damaging buildings, but causing no loss of life. Then it took to the river and struck the Kentucky shore about four miles east of where it left it, and outside of the city of Louisville. At this exact spot is located the Louisville pumping works, which supplies the whole city with water.

"The pumping works were destroyed, and the city is now

threatened with a water famine in consequence. The next heard of the peculiar course taken by the tornado is from Eminence, Ky., about forty miles east of Louisville, which was badly damaged by the storm. The intervening country may have suffered somewhat, but no other towns were visited, and from Eminence the destroyer probably took a final leave of the earth's surface and passed on to the Atlantic Coast at a higher and less dangerous altitude."

This outline seems to show how easily the course of a storm is modified by the irregularities of surface, even when the obstacles are such as it can overcome. It is seen that the course of a small storm over broken country, little resembles the steady curve of the storm in the open sea. Ever and anon, the obstacles below momentarily break the regular current, which is as often renewed in a moment by the powerful upward suction in the upper air. This is the phenomenon known as "jumping," which may be repeated till the widening of the center leaves the storm too weak to promptly restore the current at the ground, and the danger from the tornado is over. Some of the apparent eccentricities in the city, are doubtless due to the fact that occasional buildings were strong enough to resist; and leaving such at slight variations in its course, made it present the appearance of doubling on its track.

So many blocks of buildings, great and small, in an instant violently hurled to pieces, would seem to infer with certainty the death of nearly all the occupants. That only about a hundred should have been killed outright, was therefore a matter of astonishment no less than of gratitude. The terror and anguish of the first moments or hours could not, however, be measured by the actual calamity to human life. Members of households suddenly separated from each other in the darkness, could only fear the worst.

LOUISVILLE TORNADO—FALLS CITY HALL.

Their startled imagination saw the missing one dead or dying under the huge piles of fallen buildings. There were excited cries and calls and wailing of the living; a mad rush and frantic tugging at the ruins, from beneath which were sometimes heard shrieks for help or groans of the dying. To add to the universal terror, fires broke out in many places, threatening imprisoned wretches with a fate more horrible than the crush of falling walls, or timbers, bricks or iron, hurtling through the air. Before help could reach them the flames took hold on some and hushed their cries forever. Fortunately, the fire-alarm connections were left intact, and as alarm after alarm was sent, there was a dashing of the engines to the rescue, and the whole fire-department was presently engaged in extinguishing the flames, or recovering the living and the dead. Hospitals and morgues were suddenly improvised in sheds or shops, where the wounded were cared for, or the dead were deposited to await the recognition or claim of the living.

Falls City Hall was the theatre of the principal loss of life. It was a brick building fronting on Market between Eleventh and Twelfth. The ground-floor had long been used as a market, and contained forty or fifty stalls of gardeners and butchers. These stalls were closed and the keepers were absent at the hour of the disaster. In front on the second floor were three small rooms, one of them utilized as an office, the other two as toilet rooms. Behind these was a large hall, and in the rear of this still another hall, in which a young lady, her father, brother and sister being present, was teaching a dancing school. There might have been sixty-five persons in this room, though one witness says twenty-eight. In one of the small rooms seven men, constituting the Executive Committee of the Roman Knights, was holding a business meeting. In another room a band of musicians, fifteen in number, were going through a rehearsal. Some decorators were at work in the large hall, preparing it for some coming occasion. On the third floor were assembled the Jewel Lodge No. 2 of the Knights and Ladies of Honor, with an attendance of a hundred or more. In an adjoining hall the Humboldt Lodge No. 146 of I. O. O. F. with seventeen members was in session. The whole number of people in the building must have been nearly or quite two hundred. In an instant the fearful wrench of the cyclone had twisted the building into fragments, and tumbled it in shapeless ruin upon the inmates.

Ten minutes after the collapse might have been seen a frantic multitude hastily gathering from all quarters, among them many women clutching vainly with their fingers at the slate roof, and madly tearing at the wreck beneath which the imprisoned and wounded were crying for help. Presently, fire broke out, but it was happily extinguished. The work of rescue was now organized and speedily set in motion, but an hour elapsed before the first victim was extricated. This was a lady, found sitting upright with bruised head and broken arm. She told of her vain effort to escape, and of the position in which she had last seen her companions. Meanwhile, some were digging in the center of the debris in answer to a voice which grew fainter and fainter until it was hushed forever. The work of rescue was now shifted to the other end of the pile.

James Hassen was foremost among the workers, and on reaching the hall room of the Knights and Ladies, he took from the ruins the first body, which proved to be that of his wife, and who expired in his arms. He gently laid his dead wife aside, and hurried again to aid in recovering the rest. Presently, ten women were reached, clasped in each others arms—all dead but one. The dancing room was

AT WORK IN THE WRECK.

reached. One lady was taken out fatally hurt, and one after another her three children, unconscious, but destined to recover. While her husband was urging the rescue of his fourth child, still somewhere beneath the ruins, an under-current of air having been admitted, the fire again broke out with startling fierceness, and the furious heat compelled a suspension of the work. The groans of the imprisoned were now changed to fearful shrieks, while the watchers, helpless to render aid, screamed and ran wildly about with anxiety and horror. Three or four lines of hose were turned upon the flames, and they were subdued; but an hour, in which probably many a life went out, had been lost from the work. By twelve o'clock many dead and wounded had been removed from the ruins. The dead were largely in the majority. Many of these exhibited no outward wounds, and had been apparently suffocated by gas escaping from broken pipes.

But the reader may be spared further details of the recovery at Falls City Hall. Suffice it to say, that two days were required to remove the wreck and demonstrate the precise extent of the calamity. On this spot, about eighty persons had lost their lives.

The narratives of some of the survivors will serve to show that while the tornado comes without warning, the heaviest wind is not just at first: and a cool head may sometimes profit by the interval to escape. Sailors have a saying that the "tail" of a gale is strongest. A young man who was taken from the wreck of the hall says:

"I was dancing, when a flash of lightning, followed by a crash, made me think that the lightning had struck some part of the rear of the building. The next moment, the big doors that enter into the big hall in front flew open. I continued dancing, and cried to some of the boys to close the doors. They did so, and were bolting them, when they were again forced open with such force as to knock down everybody around them. Then the window sashes were blown in, and the building commenced rocking. I saw that the house was about to fall, and I hallooed: 'The walls will go next.' I ran to the dressing-room, and I think most of the girls followed me. I got under a table and held fast to the legs, thinking that I might be saved in that way. Then the walls began crumbling, and the lights went out, and the floor descended like an elevator. The crash stunned me for a moment, but finally a flash of lightning showed me a hole in the debris, through which I might have crawled had not my leg been pinioned between some timbers. There were people all around me, and they were crying for help; but there was no one to aid us. I tugged and strained, but I could not get loose. Finally, I heard my father's voice, and answered him; and directly he crawled down the hole. It took him three-quarters of an hour to extricate me, and then we both crawled out. If there had been help at once, we might have saved others, as I knew about where they all were, but they were more or less hurt."

That less than half of those in the building should have been killed is a matter of wonder. The manner of individual escapes can only be inferred from one or two more which we subjoin.

One of the lady members of the lodge of the Knights and Ladies of Honor relates:

"I went to attend the lodge meeting, and when all were present the calamity came. There must have been about seventy-five people in the room at the time of the tornado. None of them were able to get out before the building fell in. The first intimation we had of what was coming was the flash of lightning and the beating of hail against the windows. The wind howled, and I heard a fearful roaring noise. The people became frightened, and hurriedly gathered their wraps together. All were fearful of impending danger.

"Just at this moment I saw a round hole blown through the wall, immediately above one of the windows. The gas went out and then I saw another large round hole appear in the roof. Through this I saw the lightning play with awful grandeur. This natural light was all that relieved the gloom and darkness. I heard one of the trustees of the lodge call out to all the people to go out quickly and in a body. He cried out not to rush, as some one would be killed if they did. Then I knew no more until I became conscious, and found that I was partially imbedded in bricks and timbers. I felt blood running down my neck and became aware that I had been struck on the head by a brick or timber. I extricated myself, and by the flashes of lightning made my way over the terrible mass of debris and dead bodies toward the front. I saw a man making his way down the pile of bricks to to the street, and I followed. When I reached the sidewalk I was aided to a neighboring store by a lodge trustee. I don't know how he made his way out. I heard cries for help as I came out, but I had barely strength to move, and could not help the others."

A thrilling experience was that of another member of the same lodge. His estimate of the attendance, larger than the foregoing, is yet materially exceeded by others. He says:

"The first intimations of danger we had were two distinct rockings of the building, about which time a dormer window in the lodge room was blown from its casings, and immediately after the plastering began to drop from the ceiling. A wild rush was made for the ante-room, which carried me with it, and I had just reached the door when

MAIN STREET, BETWEEN ELEVENTH AND TWELFTH, LOUISVILLE.

the entire floor gave way, and we were precipitated to the basement, blinded and almost suffocated by a cloud of dust, and crushed and jammed by falling timbers. In some way the doorframe fell with me and maintained an upright position when it stopped, and I was enabled to extricate myself from the debris and make an exit to the street through an adjoining house, whose doors I kicked in. Meanwhile, the shrieks and groans of those still imprisoned by the wreck formed a chorus that, in connection with the howling of the storm, made my very heart sick. I was, so far as hasty examination went, comparatively uninjured, and at once returned over the ruins with several men to the rear of the place and extinguished a fire that had begun to blaze fiercely. By this time the rain was falling in torrents, and it was difficult for those who had gathered from the neighborhood, or who had been as lucky as I was to escape with life, to tell where to begin the work of rescue.

"The vivid lightning flashes only gave momentary views of the position of the ruins, and blinded everybody. Among those whom I saw and recognized as having escaped from Jewel lodge I can name only the treasurer, who was covered with dust, drenched with rain and wellnigh distracted by the probable fate of her aged father, who had attended the lodge meeting with her and who was still in the ruins. The entire building collapsed in front and rear, and of the east and west side walls nothing was standing above the second story.

"So far as I could judge when I had succeeded in escaping, there were less than a dozen, all told, who got out unhurt; and the cries for help and groans that issued from the broken and twisted heap was proof that scores were still there, unable to escape."

The Union Depot was utterly demolished. An officer of the Louisville Southern Road relates the story:

"Quite a crowd of people were present waiting for trains. Mr. Woodard, of the Monon Railroad, was near me, and I had been talking to him. The wind was blowing strong, and seemed to increase in power. We heard a dull moaning in the distance, and the glass in the windows of the depot was shattered, although the first puff was merely the advance guard of the tornado. The people became alarmed. One man started to rush into the ticket office, but the ticket-seller pushed him back. Mr. Woodard and I also started for the ticket office. Just at this moment the tornado, like a clap of thunder, struck the depot.

"The building gave way and tumbled in upon us. I was just at the door of the ticket office when it went down. I fell, and a man standing near me fell across me. A heavy girder fell on top of him. Mr. Woodard was only a few feet away. I never lost consciousness. I spoke to Mr. Woodard and he replied. We both thought we could get out alive if the depot did not catch fire. I knew that there had been stoves with fire burning in them in the depot before the tornado struck it, and I expected the flames to break out at every moment.

"I spoke to the man who was lying across me and told him that he must manage to squeeze from under the girder. I thought that if he was off me I could manage to get out. After many desperate efforts he managed to get from under the girder, but in doing so his bowels were torn so terribly that the doctors do not think he can recover. He was a brakeman, who had come here to be a witness in some case. I do not remember his name.

"After the brakeman got off me, I was able to use my strength. Then I got out, and so did Mr. Woodard. I was under the wreck just thirty-five minutes. I was slightly bruised in the arm and leg, but that amounts to nothing."

UNION DEPOT, LOUISVILLE.

Though forty or fifty persons were in the depot at the time, only one, a restaurant boy, was killed. Twenty-one passenger coaches were more or less wrecked. On following days the impression of the ruins upon the beholder was peculiarly gloomy. Instead of the stir of life, the brilliancy of electric lights, the scream of whistles and the rumbling of trains, there was a scattered wreck, and comparative silence. A few chickens, liberated from their coop, crept at dusk to roost on a timber, and in subdued tones seemed to be discussing with each other the mournful situation.

CHAPTER VI.

INCIDENTS OF THE TORNADO.

> "O cold and savage wind!
> It racks my soul to hear the wild lamenting
> Of wounded hearts whose grief knows no relenting,
> Can not their woe e'er sway thee to repenting?
> O cold and savage wind!
>
> O melancholy wind!
> Hast thou no requiem for the dead and dying?
> Art thou some fierce despairing spirit sighing
> O'er a lost Paradise behind thee lying?
> O melancholy wind!"

TOO frequently in the confusion of great disasters the woes of the poorer classes are forgotten in the attention given to their more oppulent neighbors. There is only too often good cause given for a slight modification of Shylock's speech, "Hath not a Jew eyes?" etc. There is no sadder record than that so frequently given in a single line: "Dead—a woman, name unknown." What fearful heart-aches often end in the Potter's field!

Adjoining the Louisville Hotel was a saloon and cigar store, the rooms over which were occupied by the hotel laundry girls. These were hurled into the cellar, and so tightly wedged that death could not have been long delayed. One was found sitting upright, the pallor of death on her face, and agony in every feature. Another lay upon her back, with hands outstretched above her head, as though she tried to thrust destruction back. A third was sitting, dead; while near by another lay upon her face, as though refusing to behold that which she could not shun.

> "Nor you, ye proud, impute to these the fault,
>   If memory o'er their tomb no trophies raise,
> Where through the long-drawn aisle and fretted vault
>   The pealing anthem swells the note of praise."

Poor laundry girls! Let their dead dust be mentioned with reverence. Had they been spoiled daughters of wealth and fashion, press reporters would have waxed eloquent of their birth, their history, their beauty, their accomplishments, their heritage. We should have heard in detail the names of their wealthy and mourning friends, and of their impressive obsequies. Magnificent monuments would have risen to mark their sleeping dust. These five laundry girls were taken up tenderly, and two or three days later, together borne without pomp to humble graves. But is not honest industry in useful avocation toiling for bread a more royal thing than silks and diamonds, bedizzening frivolty and idleness? Is there not in America many a haughty heiress, less worthy of our tears, than these?

> "Let not ambition mock their useful toil,
>   Their homely joys and destiny obscure;"

and when we say, Peace to their ashes! will not the reader add a fervent Amen!

On Seventeenth street was a pathetic sight. One blackened and charred wall stood swaying in the wind. Just over the door was a sign—"Plain Sewing." An old woman had been the sole tenant. Here, any day for years past, it may be,

> "With fingers weary and worn,
>   With eyelids heavy and red,
> A woman sat in unwomanly rags,
>   Plying her needle and thread:—
> Stitch—Stitch—Stitch,
>   In poverty, hunger and dirt,
> And still with a voice of dolorous pitch,
>   She sang the song of the shirt."

Her charred body was dug from beneath the ruins. Tragic end of a life of poverty and toil! But when we reflect on the lot of many another sewing woman, who still survives, we may, with Solomon, feel inclined to "praise the dead who are already dead, more than the living who are yet alive."

About Thirteenth and Walnut dwelt a peddler with wife and child. He knocked a hole in the side wall of his wrecked home, and dragged out his little family over a seemingly impassable pile of debris. Then he thought of another woman and two helpless children imprisoned up stairs. He rushed to their rescue, and dragged them out just in time to save them from the flames, which two minutes later were licking up all that would burn.

Society must think more of its lonely toilers; even of its peddlers and publicans and sinners. It was the keeper of a brothel in Memphis, who, during the awful yellow-fever visitation, turned her house into a hospital, and ministered to the suffering till she fell a victim herself. Jesus was looking at some very nice people when he said, "The publicans and the harlots go into the kingdom of God before you." To those good people, such a thing would be one of the "mysteries of Providence."

"Mysteries of Providence" are continually ferreted out on such occasions. Reporters, to whom everything that can be written is news, gather up a hundred items and give them to the public; often grouping items in a manner that is strikingly grotesque. There is no grimmer humor than the apparently matter-of-fact statement that during a great Italian earthquake, wherein lofty cathedrals were shaken to pieces and hundreds of people killed, statues of the Virgin escaped uninjured. Sober-minded people are prone to wonder what is the relative value of a human life and a graven image. One might, if such things were of constant occurrence, consider them as meant by Providence as a very sarcastic punishment for the violation of the second commandment.

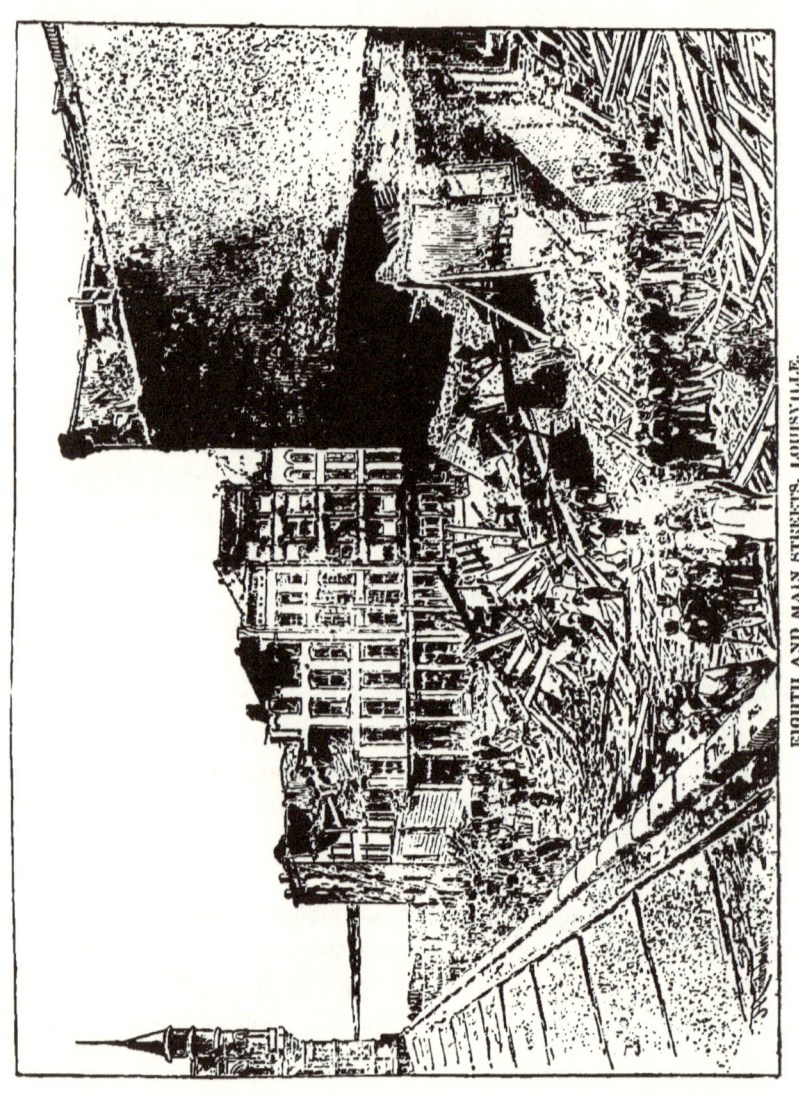

EIGHTH AND MAIN STREETS, LOUISVILLE.

It is related that at the time of the massacre of St. Bartholomew, a Romish captain secured a number of fugitives, among whom he felt satisfied there were some good Catholics. Not being able to distinguish them readily, he referred the perplexing case to a fanatical priest. The response came promptly: "Kill all; the Lord will know his own!"

Interpreters of the inscrutable ways of Providence might find such the only solution for many particulars of the storm. The pious but superstitious folk who believe that all such visitations are for the sins of a people, instead of the result of laws that send the rain alike upon the just and the unjust, might find some perplexity in conning the following cases.

On the next street back of Falls City Hall stood the St. John's Episcopal Church. The rector, with his little four-year-old boy, was in the study. The rectory and the church were completely destroyed, and the rector and his child were killed. In an adjoining building, ten or eleven men were playing cards. The house was demolished, but not one of the players was seriously hurt. The preacher perished; the idlers were saved—herein is food for reflection.

Tierney's saloon was on Eleventh, between Main and Market. The ice-box saved him and four other men from being crushed. They crowded beside it, and crawled out uninjured. The pastor and the useful laundry girls perished; the saloon-keeper and his patrons survived.

The Catholic buildings at Seventeenth and Broadway were Father Desney's residence, the Sisters' Home, the Church of the Sacred Heart, and the parochial school. All these were wrecked by the wind, and Sister Pius was killed. There is a story that, amid' utter ruin, the image of the Virgin was left standing, untouched by harm.

Let the devout remember that a saloon-keeper obtained an equal deliverance.

Elmer Barnes and several others ran into Eckerle's saloon, 1001 West Market, and securely closed the door. The building fell with a crash, and the men were buried in the ruins. Barnes and Eckerle were overwhelmed by the falling bricks and timber. Eckerle was fearfully injured; Barnes was drawn from the ruins, and died a few hours afterward. The other men were only slightly hurt. If we have had occasion to mention the destruction of one church and of several saloons, it is probably only because saloons are more numerous than churches.

At a grocery store at the corner of Sixteenth and Magazine streets the owner and five others were standing at the bar in the back part of the store. A dreadful roaring sound was heard, and the house rocked back and forth. The owner's wife and children screamed and ran out the back way. Almost instantly the rear wall of the building fell. The six men rushed to escape by the front door, but the wind closed it with such force that it could not be opened. The floor beneath gave way, and three men were dropped into the cellar and pinned among the ruins. The other three escaped through a side window. Instantly a fire kindled and took hold on the imprisoned men. Their cries were awful, while their escaped companions witnesssd the horrible cremation and were powerless to render aid.

We record but a few of the multitude of deaths, experiences, incidents and escapes. Doubtless, there is many an untold tale—something of personal interest connected with almost every one of the hundreds of buildings partially or wholly wrecked. The press at first exaggerated, and perhaps finally minimized the loss of life. There is reason to think that not all the names of the dead were given to the public, while subsequently several died of their wounds. To the list of those who were killed outright, or died in a few hours, better information might have added several names, and possibly subtracted or corrected others.

The public may find in the press reports lists of the dead and numerous records of persons injured or killed by the fallings of walls, or by flying missiles; but these, after all, must be regarded as exceptions. There can be no very correct estimate of the number of people who were in the down-town district at the time of the accident. Yet, it would be safe to say only a very small portion of those in the path of the storm suffered any injury.

That a storm of such magnitude and fury should have swept through the heart of a city of 200,000 people, to destroy outright no more than five or six score lives, may excite our wonder. The most obvious reason of the low mortality will be found in the hour and place of the principal visitation. The place was the business part of the city, and the hour between eight and nine P. M., when the wholesale houses and the streets in their vicinity were comparatively deserted. Another fact is also to be noted. The cyclone seems to have reached the ground scarcely at any point at all. Its principal fury was probably expended in the region above the housetops. The roofs and tops of walls were removed; the damage below resulted principally from their fall. Humbler buildings sheltering human lives were sometimes crushed by the fall of the upper portion of the wall of some contiguous building; as notably, in the case of the house occupied by the laundry girls, and which was smashed by the fall of the wall from the top story of the Louisville Hotel; or the case of a colored family whose house was crushed by the wall of the Falls City Hall. But in any case of cyclonic visita-

CORNER MAIN AND CLINTON STREETS, LOUISVILLE.

tion the escapes will probably amaze us more than the deaths; for when it will seem that nothing living could have escaped, the majority will not only probably be found alive, but absolutely unhurt. Of numerous cases, a few specimens will suffice:

Peter Speth and family were seated in the parlor when the cyclone arrived. The family huddled together in the hall, doubtless to avail themselves of the protection of the side walls not far apart. The walls of the second story fell in with a crash. The building and furniture were destroyed, but the family escaped without injury.

Eleven men were in a barber shop at 1803 Broadway. The roof was blown off; the walls fell in, but all the men escaped through the windows without a scratch.

At 329 Eleventh street, on the upper floor of a two-story brick, a lady lay at the point of death; watched by her son and daughter. She begged them to flee for their lives, but they refused to forsake her. The roof was stripped clean off, but the devoted children with their mother escaped injury.

In one cottage on Chapel street dwelt a family of five. At once all were in the house, when the storm demolished it, and four escaped unhurt.

Major Galt, of the Louisville and Nashville Road, lived in a two-story brick. He apprehended no danger till the walls fell. His wife was buried under a pile of bricks. Her husband with difficulty extricated her, and carried her unconscious to the house of a neighbor. Save for the shock, she was not seriously hurt.

Now, were such cases the exception—had not such instances happened in a hundred other places similarly visited—there would certainly be cause for perplexity. But the phenomena of the Louisville storm tend only to establish the truth of a fact long suspected: that the **most**

LOOKING EAST FROM TENTH AND MAIN, LOUISVILLE.

destructive effects of a tornado are not always attributable to the direct force of the wind. A number of interesting incidents of the Louisville storm will serve to illustrate a now clearly established fact.

Mrs. Fitzpatrick and her family were in a two-story brick, 1433 Seventeenth street. They were all in an upper room and could not get out. The walls fell outward, while the floor still remained in its place. They climbed down unhurt.

James Smith (colored) lived with his wife and seven children in Congress Alley, in the rear of Falls City Hall. Himself, his wife and three children were crushed beneath the mass of bricks and timbers; the remaining four children were taken out more dead than alive. Yet, the house was not in the least moved from its place. The building was crushed by the wall of the hall, which fell outward. Similar was the fate of the laundry girls. The house in which they were was crushed by the top of the wall of the Louisville Hotel, which fell outward, toward the wind.

The colored Odd Fellows were holding a meeting in their hall at Thirteenth and Walnut. The two upper stories were blown entirely down. Several large circular holes were blown through the brick walls; one of these in the side away from the storm. Several received more or less injury, but not one was fatally hurt.

At 1315 Eighteenth street, was a magnificent new brick cottage. The roof remained, but in the west wall were made "six holes, round as a dollar, and large enough to admit a flour barrel." It is added that the missing bricks were nowhere to be found.

Finally, take the experience of a grocer on West Market street:

"I was inside of my store, and my clerk was there, too. Standing on the pavement outside were policeman Harlow, a man named Charles Taylor, who said he lived in Jeffersonville, a negro whose name I do not know, and Carl Rice, an eight-year-old boy who lived with his parents in the rooms above my store. When the wind grew high and the hail began to pelt, Mr. Harlow attempted to open the front door of the store, which was closed, to come inside for shelter. At that moment the tornado came in all its fury. No one who was not in it can conceive of its terrific force. The suction from without, as the full force came, was so great that it was impossible to get the front door open. My clerk at work on it on the inside and Mr. Harlow on the outside, were as powerless against the wind as babies would have been in attempting to move a stone wall.

"But their efforts were not of long duration. The tornado forced its way in the rear of the upper stories of my building, and with impetuosity unequaled forged through the apartments against the front wall. This wall popped out and fell to the pavement below, upon those standing there, burying them in the debris. The front is entirely gone, as you see. Mr. Harlow and the little boy Carl Rice, were close up to to the front door, and only a small portion of the wall struck them. Taylor and the negro were out on the pavement further, and they fared worse. Taylor's leg was broken at the ankle, and he was internally injured. The negro had a hole knocked in his skull larger than a silver dollar, and was used up generally. Mr. Harlow was bruised, but fortunately has no bones broken, and is not dangerously hurt. The little boy's head was pretty badly cut and bruised, but he is not in a serious condition."

Now, in all of these cases is noticeable the same peculiar feature of walls falling outward, sometimes even against the wind: or of holes being burst in walls, the bricks being

INCIDENTS OF THE TORNADO. 99

CORNER JEFFERSON AND TWELFTH STREETS, LOUISVILLE.

thrown so far that they could not be found, or distinguished from those of other houses. This might seem inexplicable—that the windward walls often fall outward. But it must be remembered that all storms with a wind system blowing spirally upward and inward are characterized by low barometer, signifying a diminution in atmospheric pressure at the storm center; and the lower the barometer, the more violent the storm. Now, it is clear that if a storm advance slowly, and be widely diffused, the air in the regions through which it moves has time to accommodate itself gradually to the change, and expanding slowly to equalize the pressure in all directions, its rarefaction is not perceptible to the ordinary observer: and the denser air within a dwelling expands so gradually that all the surplus can escape through chinks and crevices, if the doors and windows be closed.

But the narrow-path tornado comes so rapidly as to produce little atmospheric change beforehand; while directly at its center the barometer may stand as much as two inches lower than in the surrounding region. Now, a fall of two inches means, in round numbers, a lessening of pressure of one pound to every square inch, or one hundred and forty-four pounds to the square foot. As the air normally presses equally in all directions, the passage of a storm of this sort may mean a sudden change from fifteen pounds pressure to the inch on each side of a wall, to fifteen pounds on the inside and fourteen only on the outside. When such a sudden change is brought to bear on every square inch of the interior of a house, it necessarily amounts to an explosion.

Suppose that in the case of the door which the men were unable to open, that the pressure had been as great as one pound to the inch. Then an ordinary seven-by-three door would be held in place by a force of a ton and a half. This same power has been observed to burst the weather-boarding from frame houses, leaving the frame and inner surfaces intact.

The reader will wonder why, in such cases, the windows do not burst out, leaving the walls unhurt. This often occurs. But very great pressure would evidently act just as does powder in a blast: the rock is rent ere the tamping is torn out, though the latter has far less resistive power; while very violent explosives do not even need any tamping in order to utilize their force.

It would seem, then, that a house with open doors and windows has a better chance of weathering a tornado, whether in respect to direct impact of wind, or to the expansive force of air within, than a house which is shut up. Here, again, quite a number of instances can be adduced of houses caught suddenly thus by tornadoes and escaping unhurt, while houses upon either side were demolished.

But that the direct force of the wind on the Louisville occasion was very great is abundantly evidenced. Numerous are the apparently curious freaks that were noticed. A city paper, four days after the storm, contained the following:

"There are hundreds of the most interesting and miraculous incidents connected with the tornado, showing the queerest sort of freaks of the wind. A block of iron casting, weighing over one hundred and fifty pounds, was blown into the second story of the Chesapeake, Ohio and Southern Railway building, near the Union Depot. Nobody knows where it came from, and the nearest building from which it could have come is nearly one hundred yards away. Great sheets of tin roofing were dropped upon Dr. Barry's farm near Turner's Station, forty miles from the city, on the Short Line. In the ruins of a house on West Main street a clock was found clinging to the wall. It was a large

ON NINTH STREET, LOUISVILLE.

office clock, but no one in the vicinity had ever seen it before, and no one knows where it came from. It was badly broken, but the hands still pointed to 8:20 p. m. A large slab of marble was found in a residence on West Madison street which was never there before. It will weigh over one hundred pounds. At Baird's drug store on Market above Ninth, two bird cages with the birds were blown in through the skylight. The cages were not injured, and the birds are as full of song as ever. When the building occupied by Brand & Bethel, the tobacco men of Green street, went to pieces, a portion of the frame-work dropped through the roof of a little cottage just east of the factory. It consisted of a heavy timber, to which were mortised four upright pieces of timber. When this came through the cottage the family were sitting around the table in the dining-room, and the four uprights simply pinned them in but did not hurt them in the least. It was one of the most wonderful escapes yet heard of."

To the unexperienced reader some of these items seem almost apocryphal. But when it is remembered that a tallow candle may be shot through a deal board, or that an ox may be killed by a putty-ball fired from a gun, or that a revolver loaded with water instead of ball is a deadly weapon, it will not seem preposterous that a cage may be hurled through a skylight without seriously discommoding the birds. The writer has seen soft pine shingles driven endwise through oak boards an inch thick by a Missouri tornado. Other similar cases might be given.

The carrying of objects to a distance depends as much on the upward current as the horizontal motion. One of the simplest illustrations of the inevitable spiral course that an upward or downward current pursues may be seen in the ordinary wash-bowl with hole in the bottom. As soon as the plug is drawn and the water commences to

RUINED TOBACCO WAREHOUSES.

pour out, it begins to assume a spiral course; and, long before the water is out, there is a circular hole in the fluid, reaching to the bottom of the basin. This last illustrates also that the air is rarest at the center of the storm. Pouring liquids through a funnel will show the same spiral tendency. So an object borne away by a tornado rises in curves much like those of a hawk or eagle in flying.

Other peculiar feats of the wind were noticed. Some persons caught by the storm, had no especial trouble in keeping on their feet; while others were knocked about severely. One man was killed by having his throat cut by a piece of flying glass. A frame house, standing near the corner of Eighteenth and Maple, was shot full of holes by flying bricks from another house a hundred yards away. A lady standing in the doorway was picked up by the wind and hurled against a telegraph pole at a distance of sixty feet. Another lady and her nephew, at the first shock rushed into the street. They were caught up by the wind and hurled some distance against a fence. They were found unconscious and both badly hurt.

A frame house on Sixteenth street looked as if it had suffered bombardment. Holes were cut in the weatherboarding by planks evidently driven through the air endwise, and pieces several feet long had penetrated and stuck hard and fast.

The building of the Louisville City Railway at Twelfth and Jefferson streets was scooped through the middle, while the ends were left standing. This was, perhaps, due to the explosive force of the air within, which burst out the weaker portions. In a building of any considerable length, the points most easily overthrown by lateral pressure would naturally be found in the middle portions of the longer walls.

At a stone-yard on Walnut, between Thirteenth and Fourteenth, the immense iron "traveler," with its locomotive—the whole weighing many tons—mounted on an elevated track and used for transferring immense blocks of stone from one side of the yard to the other, was blown into the street and smashed to pieces, while close by, three small brick buildings and one frame were left unharmed. Such cases show how the larger obstacles cause the storm to somewhat overleap the smaller ones, producing the "jumping" motion mentioned before. The narrow path of the storm may be judged from the fact that no small portion of the good people of Louisville were not aware of the ruinous tempest till they read of its deeds in the morning papers.

The total damage done to property is estimated at $2,000,000. Much the heaviest loss was among the great tobacco warehouses.

There has been some discussion as to whether any sort of buildings are safe in a storm: but so long as the most violent tropical cyclones leave many houses unhurt after a protracted gale, there is little fear that the walls of our large buildings may not readily be made massive enough to withstand any atmospheric storms.

The chief damage done to business houses was along Main, Jefferson and Walnut streets; the damage to dwellings being greatest along Broadway. The havoc on all the crossings in the limits of the tornado was remarkable.

It was observed that the buildings on the north sides of the streets parallel to the river suffered most. These more nearly faced the advancing storm, while the open street in front of them gave the wind an increased advantage. This will be better comprehended if the reader will recollect that the tornado of the northern hemisphere rotates in a direction contrary to the hands of a watch. So in the case of one moving eastward or northeastward, the wind on the front edge is blowing directly northward or northwestward. So the current, slightly broken in passing through a block, regains its strength somewhat in slanting across the next street, and assaults the next block with renewed force.

Louisville, though the principal sufferer by the storm, was not the first. The tornado formed some distance to the southwest of the city, and on its devastating march toward Louisville mowed clean a wide swath through the woods, and fell upon the beautiful suburb of Parkland. The Mayor's two-story brick residence parted with its roof at the first shock. The Mayor's wife was up-stairs in bed, ill of pneumonia. Her husband and another man seized the bed and carried her into the yard. Scarcely was this accomplished when the full force of the storm prostrated the building.

It may be noticed in this connection, that the most destructive wind is never in the first shock, the parting gust being usually the most damaging. Doubtless this is because the expansion of the atmosphere within the house at the moment the center of calm passes over it weakens the building to such an extent that the rear of the tornado, striking the house from the opposite direction, readily overthrows it. No such peculiarity is observable in a forest. The trees, containing no vast quantities of air, are usually felled by the first stroke, if at all.

The track of the storm through Parkland was one-eighth of a mile wide. From the rate at which it spread, it is clear it could be but short-lived. Within its path, it was more destructive in Parkland than in Louisville. The frame school-house was lifted from its foundation, carried a few feet away, and then torn to fragments. The Daisy Line depot was totally demolished. The Masonic

Temple parted with its upper story. Thirteen houses in the village were completely wrecked, and several others more or less damaged. It will be remembered that in Louisville the upper stories suffered most: but here the storm was fresh, and almost every building struck was razed to the ground. The total damage was about $20,000.

CORNER OF FRONT AND MULBERRY STREET.

VIEW AT JEFFERSONVILLE.

Passing through Louisville and crossing the river, the cyclone struck Jeffersonville, on the Indiana side. Here, upwards of eighty houses were seriously damaged, and quite a number totally destroyed. Two days later, the press gave the loss at $500,000—probably a great exaggeration, as the particulars given did not tally at all with the general statement. Singularly enough, not a life was lost, and only one or two persons were materially injured.

INCIDENTS OF THE TORNADO.   109

The damage was mostly to roofs and top-stories, and the people were doubtless indoors and below. This, however, does not account for the deliverance of a number of persons in buildings which were completely destroyed. Possibly some of these may be accounted for by sudden explosions of buildings, such as has been noticed heretofore. The fragments would be much more apt to injure persons just outside than those within. The largely increased percentage of damage done to roofs and upper sto-

CORNER WALL AND FRONT STREETS, JEFFERSONVILLE.

ries only shows how rapidly the storm was weakening. It could not go very much farther with its devastation. The old Orphans' Home was wrecked; one old lady injured; a pastor's house demolished, while two men in the upper story in some mysterious way escaped unhurt. At the foot of Front street, a shanty occupied by a man with wife and three children was lifted bodily and thrown into the river. The family would have been drowned had not some car-works employes rescued them, at the peril of their own lives. A number of guests, and some who came for shelter, were in a house at the corner of First and Spring streets. The shock of the tornado was followed by a hail of bricks and tumbling walls, but no one of the entire assembly was seriously hurt.

The average American worships no god but Mammon. He may go to church and bow his head to Jehovah, but it is Mammon who keeps his heart. Between his devout

THE STOUSS HOUSE

WRECK AT JEFFERSONVILLE.

amens he is thinking of the main chance. He can be converted and made religious; it is a great deal harder to make him honest. He is willing to sing the praises of the Lord, but he doesn't like to foot the bills. Amid the sorrow and bereavement of a stricken city, the American was true to himself. Those who had lost house and friends, were asked to pay ten dollars for a carriage in which to follow the corpse to the grave. As about thirty victims of the storm were buried on Sunday, it may be inferred that the carriages in each procession were none too numerous. A sad sight was that of the four laundry girls, and the chamber-maid, all being borne together to their long home. Hardly less impressive was the burial at half-hour intervals of ten members of the I. O. O. F., killed in Falls City Hall. It was a profitable day for undertakers.

Nor did the officers of the Louisville and Southern Railroad forget their interests. They had for some time been desirous of regaining possession of their property controlled by the Monon Route. This they did in the confusion, dismay and darkness, immediately following the storm.

The writer does not wish to do any injustice to his people. Such items present but one side of the American's character. He is a strange mixture of grasping greed and warm-hearted generosity. The latter is an inborn trait; the former in-drilled. We live in a rushing age. We are no more in a hurry about being rich than we are about a score of other things. Haste is a national characteristic.

Further, our people are brought up with peculiar ideas of success in life. Everything is reduced to a basis of cold cash. A man may be learned, talented, industrious; but all these things are counted for naught if he is not also wealthy. So our young people are brought up to think that money-making is the one business of life; and as a result the business world is full of those who resort to sharp practice and questionable methods, merely because they have been taught to subordinate honor and equity to gain-getting. Yet, the warm sympathies and native generosity of our people are continually coming to the front, in a way that, in view of the other traits, is sometimes amusingly inconsistent. Men who will haggle almost

LOUISVILLE TORNADO—CORNER TENTH AND MAIN STREETS.

about the price of a pin, or make their living by wild or fraudulent speculation; nay, even professional gamblers, or worse characters, are prompt in responding to the wail of a distressed city or state. After all, we are brethren. Yet, our good and bad qualities are so thoroughly mingled that we must continually rob Peter to pay Paul.

The American has another prominent trait—independence. He does not accept aid, as such, when he feels he can do without it: nor does he wait for demands of help, when he hears of great misfortunes that have befallen his fellow countrymen. Leigh Hunt once asked a very ragged and forlorn Irishman, " Why don't you ask for alms?" " Alms, is it? Sure and isn't it begging I am with every bone of my body?" The average American is generally quick to recognize a case that speaks for itself. To Louisville, in the hour of her calamity, came tenders of help from many quarters, and these offers would have been greatly multiplied, had not the citizens declined the proffered assistance. They felt that the resources of the city were equal to the necessity. They were grateful, but self-reliant.

CHAPTER VII.

OTHER TORNADOES.

"From the dark earth impervious vapors rise,
Increase the darkness and involve the skies.
At once the rushing winds, with roaring sound,
Burst from th' Æolian caves and rend the ground;
With equal rage their airy quarrel try,
And win by turns the kingdom of the sky.
But with a thicker night black Auster shrouds
The heavens, and drives on heaps the rolling clouds,
From whose dark womb a rattling tempest pours,
Which the cold north congeals to haily showers.
From pole to pole the thunder roars aloud,
And broken lightnings flash from every cloud.
Now smokes with showers the misty mountain ground,
And floated fields lie undistinguished 'round.
Where late was dust, now rapid torrents play—
Rush through the mounds, and bear the dams away.
Old limbs of trees, from crackling forests torn,
Are whirled in air, and on the winds are borne."

A CASUAL glance at the papers during the last days of March would have satisfied any one that the storm which passed over the country was anything but insignificant. So far, we have given only the story of a single neighborhood; while a score of others suffered more or less. A brief account of some of these will be of interest, and will give us a far better idea of the character of great storms and tornadoes.

The farthest point west touched by a tornado on that memorable day was a strip near the line between Missouri and Kansas, some fifty or sixty miles south of Kansas City. Here, a small tornado made its appearance about five o'clock in the afternoon, demolishing some fences and

LOOKING WEST FROM TENTH AND MAIN, LOUISVILLE.

barns, and breaking down a few trees: but, so far as known, no one was hurt. Meanwhile, the main storm had passed eastward much earlier in the afternoon.

Shortly after the storm reached St. Louis, violent cyclonic movements were excited in southeast Missouri, upwards of a hundred miles away. At 3 P. M. the little town of Bloomsdale was struck, and five houses were instantly prostrated. The occupants of four of them were, at the time, in the Catholic church, and the family who occupied the fifth escaped unhurt. Two sides of their house were blown away; while one side was blown inward, and would have crushed them but for chairs and tables which sustained its weight. The church suffered the loss of its steeple, and was otherwise damaged. A stable containing seven horses was blown away, and not one of the horses was injured.

A cloud gathered, and a cyclone seemed to form at, or over, Charleston. It followed the Cairo branch of the Iron Mountain Road eastward. Four miles from Charleston it struck the flag-station known as Hough's, having on the way demolished one or two farm-houses, and made havoc of the forest. The little hamlet of Hough's was razed from the earth, not a house being left intact. One dwelling was blown two hundred feet across the railway track and smashed. The owner, his wife and son were killed, and another son was badly injured. The three-year-old baby was taken up unharmed. Another family lived near by in a log house. It was blown away, and they were left sitting on the floor, wondering.

Such a case as this is by no means rare. It is one of the many freaks of the wind not easily understood. In the great cyclone of forty or fifty miles in diameter, the wind comes in gusts or waves, and such effects might be readily understood; but in the case of the tornado, of at most but a few hundred yards in diameter, its passage is too rapid for those in its path to learn definitely whether it be uniform or not.

Other peculiar feats were noticed at Hough's. A girl seventeen years old was blown one hundred and fifty yards into a pond, but was rescued in time to save her from drowning; and it is said that a man and woman were blown across a sixty-acre wheat field, and picked up insensible. The further statement that the bark was peeled clean from the trees, though seemingly most incredible of all, is very probably true; for the writer has a vivid recollection of precisely the same phenomenon on the theater of the Marshfield cyclone in southwest Missouri. In that instance the bark was peeled from hundreds of hickory saplings, almost from the roots to their topmost twigs. This effect was inconceivable from any cause that could be thought of. It was done by missiles flying through the air, or the trees were bent over and threshed against the ground, or there was some unknown force prevalent in the storm, similar, perhaps, to that which shatters the bark or body of a thunder-smitten oak. To an observer on the ground the first two suppositions seemed to be excluded. Is this peculiar power of the tornado to be sought, like that of Keely's Motor, in some occult force?

From Hough's Station the tornado may have bounded above the tree-tops and descended again a few miles further on at Bird's Point, opposite to Cairo, Illinois. Anyhow, a tornado struck the former place at 4:35 P. M. It was first seen above the trees, it showed a yellowish cast, and had the usual funnel shape. About three hundred yards from the town it came to the ground and commenced its work of destruction. Eight or ten houses were blown to pieces, or badly damaged; a roof was carried two hundred feet into the air; a yearling calf was thrown forty

VIEW IN THE RESIDENCE DISTRICT, LOUISVILLE.

feet into a big ditch filled with water, and—nobody was hurt.

At Cape Girardeau, on the Mississippi, fifty miles above Bird's Point, there was a tremendous hail, which broke thousands of windows, and a gale lasting far into the night, with damage to timber, fences, and buildings.

Illinois suffered far worse than Missouri. The southern part of the state fared badly; and the further south, the worse. The storm which struck St. Louis at 3 p. m., was, a few minutes later, giving the Illinois towns on the other side a lively experience. Edwardsville, O'Fallon and Centerville received a heavy gale. At Coulterville, buildings, barns, and orchards suffered severely, and several persons were injured. Sparta was struck about 3:15 p. m. From the second story of the public school building, observers watched the approach of the storm. Two black clouds from opposite quarters of the heavens came together, as by attraction, and mingled with a rotary motion. The tornado passed within a mile of the town on the northeast, and mowed a swath through the heavy timber. No such rain, hail and wind, mingled with fire, had ever been seen before. Many barns were destroyed; several houses were blown to pieces; three or four persons were seriously hurt. A traveling man was whisked out of his buggy by the wind, carried some distance, and sustained severe injuries; the horses were thrown down, and the buggy was completely wrecked.

At Grand Tower, on the Mississippi, forty miles above Cape Girardeau, there was a terrific tornado at 4:30 p. m. It came from the west, and swept houses, trees, trains—everything, in its course. Its track is described as one of "extreme desolation." Four or five persons, at least, were killed, and as many injured. Twenty-seven dwelling-houses were completely demolished, and a great many others unroofed, or otherwise damaged.

At Murphysboro, Illinois, many windows were broken by the great hail; while there came an unverified report of fifteen or more persons killed about Shiloh, and to the north of Campbell Hill. South of Murphysboro, several houses were blown down; two children were killed.

At Centralia, two and one-fourth inches of rain fell in twenty minutes, changing later into snow. Farm buildings west of town suffered considerable damage.

At Carbondale, the dreaded funnel appeared, and two blocks of houses were unroofed.

Five miles southwest of Xenia, many out-buildings were blown down and several houses destroyed. A schoolhouse on the prairie was blown away, and one of the sills carried nearly a quarter of a mile.

In the southern part of Union county, seven miles southwest of Anna, a tornado swept a track about half a mile wide and four miles long, over the richest farms, destroying stock, orchards, forests and houses. One or two persons were fatally hurt. At Mt. Pleasant, twelve miles east of Anna, there was extensive destruction of property.

At Braidwood, a number of houses and out-buildings were blown away; trees were torn up, several persons severely injured, and two or three children are said to have "disappeared." The writer remembers an instance that occurred some years ago, when a fourteen-year-old boy was carried five miles and dropped into a stream: but such a case does not occur in this country once in many years. One of the freaks told of the wind at Braidwood is, that it rolled a man in the road and whisked a watch out of his pocket. It does not appear that any funnel-shaped cloud was seen here.

At Cairo, out of a fleet of shanty-boats, thirteen were destroyed, and an old cripple was drowned.

The storm struck Nashville (Ill.) at 4 P. M. The rain,

RUINED DWELLINGS.

changing to furious hail, fell so fast that one could scarcely see ten feet. The wind blew with terrific force. The Prohibition Tabernacle and a two-story brick cooper shop went down. Beginning six miles southeast on Little Prairie, the damage was fearful, and ranged through a sweep, to the northeast, of twenty miles. Not less than thirty houses were destroyed, and twice that number badly damaged. Of numerous casualties, one or two will illustrate the force of the wind at this place: One family of seven were sitting in their house as the storm drew near. Two of the little girls becoming frightened, ran out, when the wind caught them up, carried them across a field a quarter of a mile wide, and dropped them uninjured, save from violent pelting of the hail. As the remaining members of the family were in the act of forsaking the house, it fell, and all were more or less hurt.

This case would seem to indicate a lack of uniformity in the strength of the wind; it being powerful enough at one point to carry away children, while the house, only a few feet away at most, was still standing. One or two other cases of persons being carried a considerable distance were reported from Nashville.

All such instances show the powerful upward current of the tornado; for wind of greater horizontal velocity is often observed, which produces no such effects. To the uplifting force must be in some degree attributed the fact that in many cases only roofs or upper stories are damaged. This same force is responsible for not a few showers of objects that do not pertain to the upper air: such as the occasionally reported showers of fish and frogs.

A tornado swept up Bay Bottom in Pope county, accompanied by "rain and hail in floods and volleys." A partial report shows a school-house dashed against a bluff a hundred feet away and reduced to kindling-wood. A number of residences were destroyed, and several persons were killed.

In all the cases hitherto noted, the tornado, when seen, is reported as about one-eighth of a mile wide. The next one on the list, while powerful, is much smaller.

The southwest part of Olney was devastated by a cyclone at 5:35 p. m. Its track was about a hundred yards wide and a mile long. It shattered or destroyed the homes of, perhaps, five hundred people. Strange to relate, only two or three persons were badly hurt. John Bourrell was voted the wisest man. His house was blown to atoms; but he and his wife were safe in their "cyclone cellar," and absorbing much comfort from a $600 cyclone policy on their building.

But the climax of ruin for Illinois was reached at Metropolis, a town of 4,000 people, situated on the Ohio River, thirty-eight miles above Cairo, and eleven miles below Paducah. A greenish tinge of the approaching cloud was the only unusual portent. "Suddenly there came from the southwest a rolling, apparently born of the union of two clouds, which met in mid-air, and in a moment swooped down into the Ohio river, now at flood-tide, and on lifting, there followed it a column of water, estimated all the way from fifty to two hundred feet in height." This curious phenomenon swept onward, striking the river front like the hammer of a Cyclop. In an instant, down went a large number of buildings, including principal business houses, and the finest residences of the city. A few persons were seriously hurt, and two or three were killed. Of course, there were wonderful escapes. One gentleman had a numerous array of little children; the house was swept from over the family, and not a soul was hurt. In the country the devastation was even more appalling. Residences, out-buildings, churches, even gravestones were wiped from the face of the earth.

A relief committee was organized. In their dispatch of two days later, addressed to the St. Louis *Republic* newspaper, and praying for help, they say: "Hundreds of homes, the result of a life of labor, have been swept away in less time than it takes to record it. All kinds of property have been destroyed. The damage is estimated at over $200,000."

Such is a partial list of the more important casualties

PATH OF TORNADO—OLNEY, ILL.

of the great storm. Space is lacking to give detail to all the minor visitations and incidents. Such storms only attract the attention of the public when some thickly-settled region is visited. Numerous hamlets and small towns might be named, of which nothing but the bare fact that a tornado passed through is recorded. The rural districts are, of course, far more frequently swept; but the narrowness and short path of the tornado preclude its doing much damage among them.

Now, we have noticed a dozen different localities, all experiencing much the same sort of storms. The unthinking person might deem all this devastation the work of a single storm. Such is the case: but a distinction must be made between the storm itself, and the tornadoes produced by it. That there were various tornadoes entirely distinct, or independent of each other, the reader may clearly perceive, by examining the foregoing pages. It will be noticed that in several cases the tornado was seen to form near the spot devastated; and further may be noted the hours at which the whirlwinds appeared. For instance, the one which passed near Shawneetown, Missouri, came later than most of those in Illinois; yet all moved toward the northeast. A brief review of the main storm will be of interest, and show how the various tornadoes were produced.

It has already been stated that the storm originated somewhere about the southwest corner of Wyoming. Here, as early as Wednesday morning, the Signal Service observed an area of very low barometer. It moved rapidly eastward, with a trend toward the south, passing in the vicinity of Denver, Kansas City, and St. Louis, thence northeast through the central part of Indiana to Lake Erie. The central path of the storm was a violent and progressive movement of the air, doing in its passage trifling damage in some localities. The cyclonic movements which did the principal mischief, were all to the south of the storm center, and were local and violent motions of the air about an axis, while yet there was a progressive movement from southwest to northeast.

Now, these lesser whirlwinds are produced in exactly the same way as the great cyclones of many miles in diameter, which we have already seen do not originate on land often, because of the irregularities of surface that hinder.

But the local currents of wind, in meeting, produce the whirling motion. Compare with the moving of a current of water. Every river forms eddies along the bank, which move a short distance down and toward the main current, and then break up. Consider the great area of low barometer moving eastward, and it will be seen that the local tornadoes, suddenly forming and moving but a few miles, are simply eddies on its edge. It is easy to watch these

SCENE AT OLNEY, ILL.

produced on a small scale; for nature's principles are the same in small and great: when we have mastered the atom, we have mastered the whole object.

Let one observe a great fire in a forest or prairie. On the outskirts of newly burned areas, when the air has been rarefied by heat, may be seen sudden and violent movements about a point, as though there was a spirit in the wind. In a moment it has lifted the ashes and scorched stalks, and whatever light matters were in its way, and circling, perhaps, wider and stronger for a time, has borne them onward and upward toward the heavens, where at length its force was dissipated, and it mingled with the surrounding air. Similar movements were excited along the southern limits of the storm area, which we are describing; and hence, not one cyclone, but more properly speaking, a multitude of little cyclones—tornadoes independent of each other, but dependent on the main current,

WHIRLWIND FROM BURNT PRAIRIE.

or great eastward traveling storm center—swept through points in Illinois, Missouri, Tennessee and Kentucky; all rushing toward the line of the lowest barometrical depression, the actual and advancing storm center. Not since the Signal Service had been established had the barometer at St. Louis stood so low as 28.46, which, reduced to sea-level, means 29.08. Toward this region of rarefied air—this partial vacuum—the cyclonic movements from the south rushed with inconceivable fury, and as the nucleus of the storm was rapidly moving eastward, the cyclonic movements were turned from a north to a northeast course. All these varied movements simply result from the effort of a disturbed atmosphere to restore an equilibrium.

The illustration of the fire used above also affords a good example of the way rotation may result from rising air. Any one who has watched a great fire in calm weather knows that sparks and smoke do not rise straight up, but in spirals and whirls, the warmer centers rising faster, just as the middle of a stream flows faster than the edge.

But the powerful winds and the damage done were not all the work of the marginal whirlwinds. A storm center moving so rapidly must necessarily have carried a steady high wind. Leaving Wyoming, by Wednesday evening the storm was in the middle of Colorado; on Wednesday night, it moved well into Kansas; on Thursday, it crossed States of Missouri and Illinois, and Thursday night it was passing over Indiana.

The climax of energy was apparently not attained until the storm reached Illinois. In Missouri, more or less damage was done to fences and buildings, from Sedalia to St. Louis. At the former place, a roof or two was blown off, and the teachers in one of the schools were so alarmed that they dismissed the children. Jefferson City, sixty miles further on, made a record of damaged roofs and shattered windows. At St. Louis, there was a deluge of rain at three o'clock in the afternoon, lasting a half hour; and the wind blew with fury during the evening and greater part of the night. It drove in and smashed some plate-glass windows, blew off an occasional roof, and from the top of the corner of St. Patrick's School, hurled to the sidewalk a stone weighing, probably, four hundred pounds.

The story of the Louisville tornado serves to well illustrate all the peculiar features of the local whirlwinds produced by great storms. They seldom travel more than thirty miles; usually much less. Sometimes as large as two miles in diameter, they seldom exceed five hundred yards; and one of but fifty yards in diameter may be powerful enough to wreck a house.

Often it is possible to trace the path of a tornado through the forest a century or more after its passage; for the reason that trees once destroyed are usually replaced by different varieties. But the tornado usually originates in the open country, though after its formation it may sweep through heavy timber.

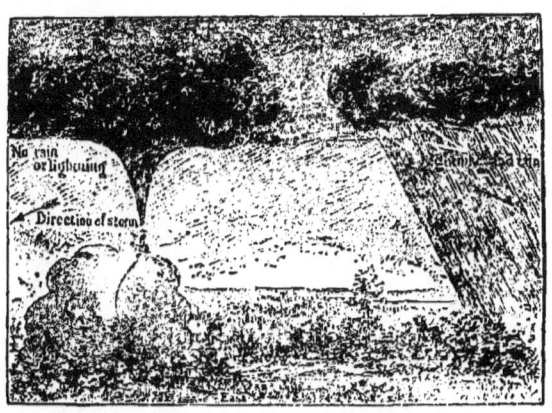

TORNADO FOLLOWED BY RAIN STORM.

So far as loss of life is concerned, the tornado is much more to be feared than lightning. About two thousand people have been killed in this country within ten years by these rotary storms. Yet, all over the land, people put up rods that are expensive, and often worse than useless, as a precaution against lightning, when a small "cyclone cellar" could be dug that would be far more useful, and less expensive. While intense electrical displays accompany the tornado, there is no authentic record of lightning striking during one; and as will be seen in another place, the amount of electricity present seems to be rather an effect than a cause: for rapid motion of gases may be made to produce powerful electric currents.

While the tornado is justly feared in this country, yet, as a destructive agent, it is far surpassed by a number of

Instantaneous View of a Tornado.

others whose ravages are less dreaded. It would be comparatively easy to show, we think, that more persons have been killed in one way or another by railways in ten years past than by tornadoes.

The one that has been so carefully examined must not be considered as the worst our country has known. An examination of records of the past century will show a number that were more destructive to life and property. Doubtless, an account of some of these would interest the reader. Place is given to a few.

The tornado has been observed, to some extent, in this country for more than a century: but only when our central states were well peopled did it attract very great attention. It is not common in the eastern states, and but one has ever been recorded west of Dodge City, Kansas. It is not unknown in Europe, though far less common than with us, having been noticed a few times in France. In general, it is so rare that a tornado that passed through Monville in 1845 attracted such attention as to be noticed in French text-books on physics. To the American, there is nothing unusual in the conduct of this storm.

Perhaps the earliest detail of a storm of this sort among us is that of a double one in South Carolina, on the afternoon of May 2, 1761:

"The tornado crossed the Ashley River and swooped down upon the shipping at Rebellion Wharf with such fury as to threaten the destruction of the entire fleet. From the city, it was seen coming at first rapidly toward Wappo Creek, like a column of smoke, with a very irregular and tumultuous movement. The quantity of vapor which composed this column, and its prodigious velocity, produced such intense commotion that it agitated Ashley River to its depths and left the channel bare. The ebb and flow made the shipping float off to a great distance. When it struck the river, it made a noise like continuous thunder; its diameter, at that moment, was estimated at fifteen hundred feet, and its height, as seen at Charles-

TORNADO AT MONVILLE.

ton, at twenty-five degrees. It was met at White Point by another whirlwind, which descended Cooper River, but was not equal to the first. When they came together, the commotion in the air was much greater still; the foam and the vapor seemed to be thrown to the height of forty degrees, while the clouds that hurried from all directions toward that point seemed to rush thither and whirl about at one and the same time, with incredible velocity. The meteor then darted on the shipping in the roadstead, and reached them in three minutes, although the distance was nearly six miles. Out of forty-five vessels, five were sunk on the spot; the state ship, Dolphin, and eleven others were dismasted. The damage, estimated at more than £200,000, was done in a moment, and even the vessels that sank were swallowed up so rapidly that the people who were below had scarcely time to scramble up on deck. The whirlwind of Cooper River changed the course of the one that came from Wappo Creek, which, had it not been for that, would, proceeding in the same direction, have swept away the city of Charleston before it like so much straw.

"This terrible column was first perceived about noon, at more than fifty miles southwest of the roads. It destroyed everything in its way, making a complete avenue when it passed through the woods. The loss of the five ships was so sudden that it is not known whether it was the weight of the column of wind, or the mass of water driven upon them that made them go down."

The tornado occasionally originates at sea and whirls up a heavy column of water for a few feet, which, meeting the dark funnel from above, presents the appearance of a pillar of water reaching the clouds. Not a few ignorant people once imagined that all rain originated from the water thus sucked up. These columns, or "water-spouts," are generally a few feet in diameter, and may sometimes be broken by firing a cannon-ball through them. They are not ordinarily considered dangerous: but there are some exceptions, and it is not improbable that many a ship that left port, never to be heard of again, has been overwhelmed by some gigantic water-spout.

Of the most destructive tornadoes in the United States, Mississippi records the two leading ones. The first came on May 7, 1840, and Natchez was the principal sufferer, though other portions of Adams county were swept. The day began warm and cloudy, with the wind south, veering to east. At 2:15 P. M., the sky became a lurid yellow; the storm striking the river six or seven miles below the city, did not reach it until 2 P. M. The rush of the wind did not last five minutes, and the destructive blast only a few seconds. Houses were burst outward; three hundred and seventeen persons were killed in the city and on the river. Sheet tin was carried twenty miles, and windows thirty miles. One hundred and nine persons were badly injured, and property to the value of $1,260,000 destroyed. Most of the deaths resulted from drowning; two steamers and sixty flatboats were sunk, while the city was flooded with nine inches of rain. Enormous hail-stones fell. A desk fastened with three locks, was blown open by the explosive force of the expanding air within. Another curious freak of this expansive power occurred in a tornado at New Brunswick. A towel hanging on the wall was found apparently blown nearly through it. The expanding air had driven the towel in a large crevice which opened in the wall behind it; and the crevice closed as the storm passed on, holding the towel to puzzle the neighborhood.

The next great tornado visited Natchez, June 16, 1842, and killed five hundred people.

Next to these, in destruction of life, is the famous

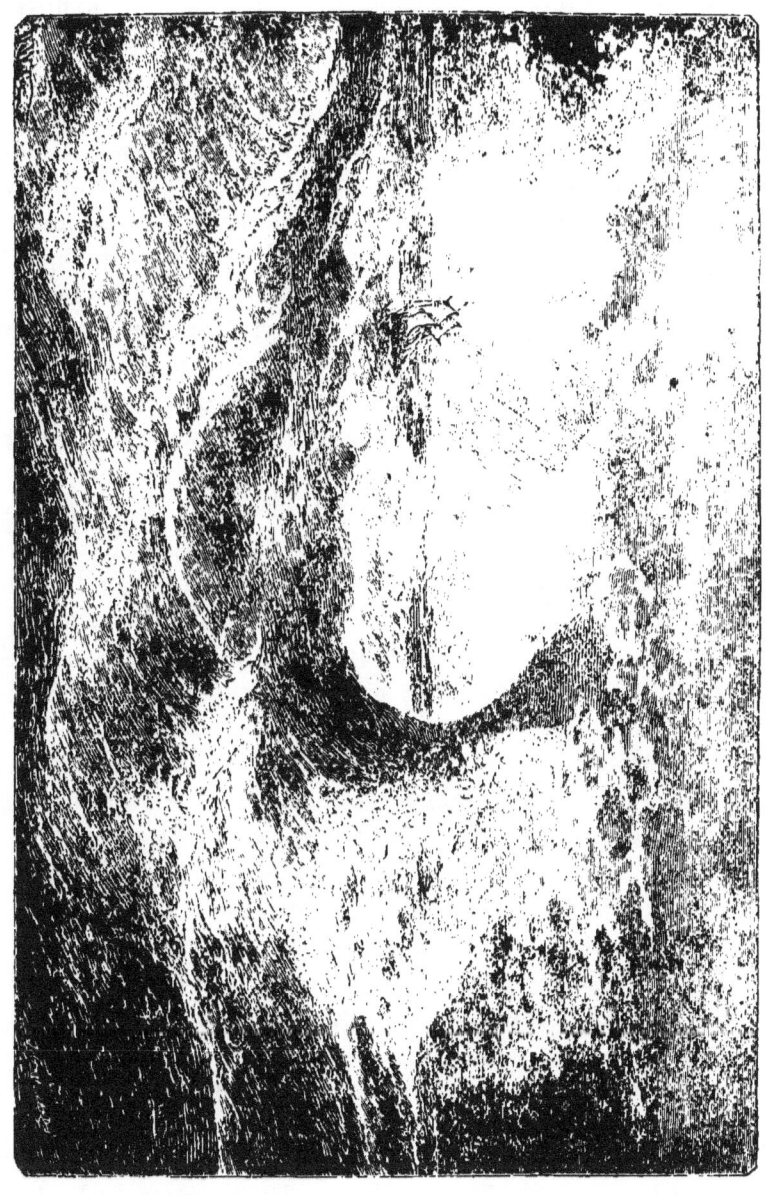

WATER-SPOUT AT SEA.

Marshfield tornado of April, 1880, in which one hundred and one persons were killed, and six hundred injured. The town of Marshfield was literally wiped off the earth. This tornado is notable for its unusually wide path, and the large area traversed. Four counties were swept; and though the country was sparsely settled and comparatively little improved, yet the damage to property was estimated at more than $1,000,000. Gen. Greely, of the Signal Service, pronounces it one of the most remarkable in the history of the United States. It formed at the junction of two streams, a few miles southwest of Marshfield; and, like the South Carolina tornado of 1761, owed its immense power to the union of two lesser storms that had traveled down the valleys of the respective streams. Such a tornado passing over a great city would equal the earthquake in disastrous effects. Perhaps a better idea of its power may be gathered from a comparison with the New Haven storm of 1878, which killed but thirty-four people and destroyed $2,000,000 worth of property—as much as the recent storm at Louisville. The remarkable feature about every tornado—the very small destruction of life—may be better understood when it is stated that, excluding the two Natchez tornadoes, where the number of houses wrecked is not known, and the Louisville storm, the twenty most destructive tornadoes in the United States have killed six hundred and thirteen people, and destroyed over three thousand houses. This brings us to the peculiar fact that but one person is killed in every five houses. As the average house may be counted as containing four persons, it appears that the chances that any single individual in a wrecked house will not be killed, are nineteen to one. While the mathematical calculation may be encouraging, yet few will care to take the risk of a tornado, even though the odds be vastly in their favor. People place little dependence in arithmetic as a life preserver. The recent Louisville storm presents a high average, as about fifty of the victims were taken from a single building. The lowest average is shown by the tornado that struck Camden, New Jersey, August 3d, 1885, when five hundred houses were destroyed, and but six persons killed: one for every eighty-three houses. In general, there seems to be a prevalence of a one to ten rate: but a storm in a city usually vastly increases the death rate by reason of the number of brick houses, which, when wrecked, fall much more compactly than frame buildings.

MINNESOTA TORNADO, FORMING LATERAL SPURS.

The greatest destruction of property has been in Ohio, where the aggregate now amounts to about $9,000,000. Next is Minnesota with $7,000,000, and Missouri and Mississippi with about $4,000,000 each. Missouri is first in respect to loss of life, and Mississippi next. The months most liable to tornadoes are May, April, June, and July, in order; and the time of day the hottest; that is, from 3 to 5 P. M.

These data suffice to show the peculiar acts of the tornado in our land. There is one case of a great storm attended by tornadoes on its southeast border, that is even more noteworthy than the great one so minutely detailed in the preceding pages. A storm center passing over a wider region, on February 9, 1884, produced, after ten o'clock that day, over sixty tornadoes in Mississippi, Alabama, Georgia, South Carolina, Kentucky and Tennessee, and North Carolina. Over ten thousand buildings were destroyed, eight hundred people killed, and twenty-five hundred wounded. The damage done by any single one was small, while the aggregate was fearful.

The tornado is occasionally seen in Europe: but in the few instances recorded, it has been much smaller, and moved much slower than the same sort of storm in America, though quite as powerful within the territory traversed. One that was very formidable, was observed near Boulogne, in 1822. It moved about irregularly for an hour, tearing holes in the ground, snapping off trees, and twisting down houses; yet, it was not twenty-five feet in diameter. Another one in 1872, swept through a little town in Italy, and was so powerful as to twist iron balcony railings together like so many skeins of thread. Several persons were killed.

In some portions of the Sahara and of Arabia, very numerous small whirlwinds accompany desert storms, whirling up the fine sand in dense columns, presenting the appearance of clouds in a region where clouds are unknown. So many writhing columns, swaying like dancing serpents, present a peculiarly terrifying aspect to the superstitious Arab, who has only too good reason to fear them. Strange tales of their destructiveness are rife. It is said that the army of Cambyses was overwhelmed by one of these desert storms. This story must, however, be taken "with a grain of salt." But there is no doubt that a sand storm is quite as dangerous as a Dakota blizzard.

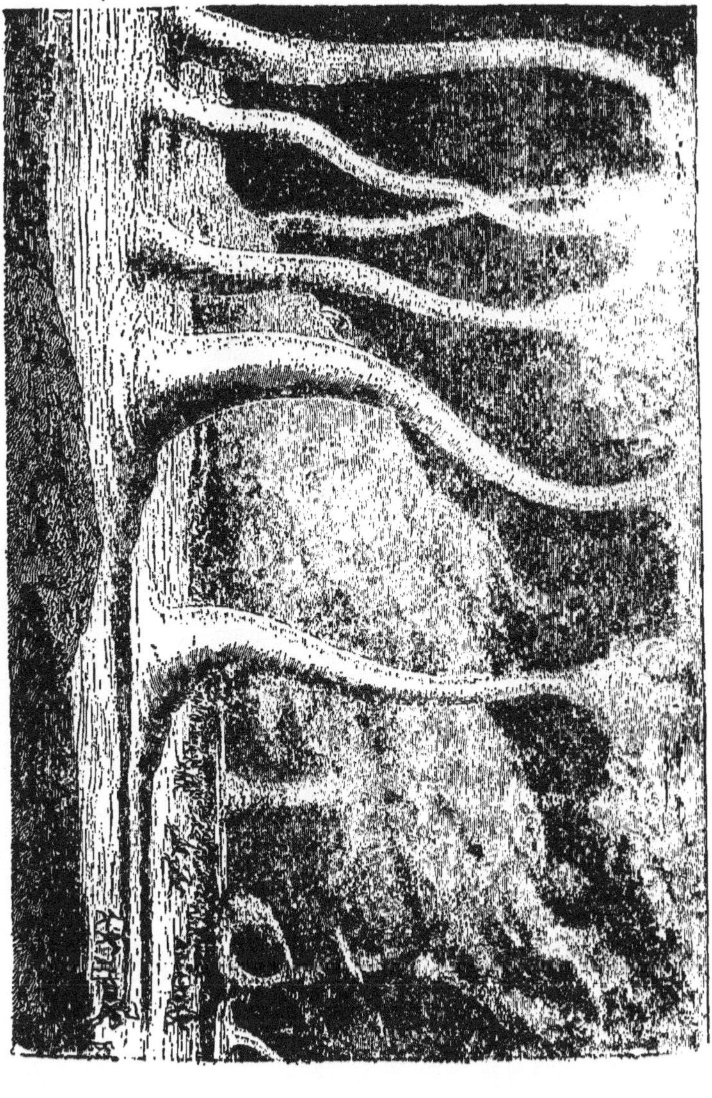

OTHER TORNADOES. 139

SAND SPOUTS IN THE DESERT.

In tropical regions the tornado or "land-spout," as many Europeans call it, gives place to the great cyclone. Still, it appears occasionally. One which swept the suburbs of Calcutta, in 1838, was but a few yards in diameter; but in its march of sixteen miles, it killed two hundred and fifteen persons, wounded two hundred and thirty-three, and destroyed one thousand two hundred and forty-five houses: thus displaying quite as great power as any tornado observed in our own land. The speed of rotation was so great that a bamboo cane was driven through a mud wall five feet thick, faced on both sides with brick; as great penetrative power as is usually given to a six-pound cannon-ball.

CHAPTER VIII.

TROPICAL CYCLONES.

"The Storm is on his way!
With a lightning sword and a thunder shout,
And his robe on the night-wind floating out,
The Storm is on his way!

The Storm is on his way!
He smites, and the death-swept valleys groan,
The ocean writhes, and the forests moan,—
The Storm is on his way!"

THE preceding pages show only the destructive power of the small tornadoes of our land. We are fortunate in that the great cyclone is, comparatively, a rare visitor among us. A moment's consideration of this ravager, as he appears in the tropics, will show how trifling are the storms that have swept over our own land. A few examples will convince the most skeptical.

Of the great cyclones which have traversed our country in recent times, we may mention the hurricane of October 21-24, 1878. Gen. Greeley says: "It first damaged buildings and sank vessels at Havana. It entered the United States near Wilmington, N. C., and moving due north, passed over Washington and eastern Pennsylvania, after which it curved eastward, and crossing New England, left the coast near Portland, Maine. In Philadelphia, over seven hundred substantial buildings were totally destroyed, or seriously damaged, bridges injured, twenty-two vessels sunk, several persons injured, and eight killed, entailing a loss variously estimated from one to two millions of dollars. Other loss of life and great damage by freshets and winds occurred elsewhere in Pennsylvania. A large number of steamers, ships and coasting vessels were dismantled, wrecked or sunk along the New Jersey, Virginia and North Carolina coasts, entailing loss of life and enormous pecuniary damage. The wind reached seventy-two miles per hour at Philadelphia, and eighty-eight along the coast." Another cyclone the next year ruined one hundred large vessels and two hundred yachts and smacks. Another, in 1881, destroyed four hundred persons along the Carolina coasts, and damaged property to the extent of $1,600,000.

But these are exceeded by the great Nova Scotia cyclone of 1873. The property damage alone is estimated at nearly $5,000,000. The Signal Service report says that "one thousand and thirty-two ships, of which four hundred and thirty-five were small fishing schooners, are known to have been destroyed during the 24th and 25th of August, in the neighborhood of the Gulf of St. Lawrence and the Atlantic shores of Nova Scotia, Cape Breton and New Foundland. On the other hand, over one hundred and ninety vessels were destroyed by this hurricane in its passage over the ocean before it reached Nova Scotia, making a grand total of at least one thousand two hundred and twenty-three vessels destroyed within a few days by its power. Two hundred and twenty-three lives are definitely reported to be lost, and the moderate estimate of the numerous cases in which whole crews have been lost swells this number to nearly five hundred; and if to this is added the loss of life on land, and the loss in the earlier history of the cyclone, the grand total amounts to at least six hundred lives."

Had the famed Shah Jehan ever visited the West Indies, it is probable that he might have pronounced many of its lovely islets fit rivals for that beautiful creation of his fancy, which bore above the gateway:

> "If there be Paradise upon the earth,
> This it is, this it is, this it is."

Among the loveliest groups are the beautiful Virgin Isles, and loveliest of these is the famed island of St. Thomas. A lofty mountain girdles the island, leaving an opening between two hills into a wide oval harbor, while the pretty little town lies around the inner side of the port, sloping up the mountain behind, the queen of a vast natural amphitheater. Such a fine harbor has rendered St. Thomas almost the mistress of West Indian commerce; and one would not suspect, in looking at the sunny slopes and green-clad ranges around the azure harbor, that in this region is the birthplace of the Storm King. Yet, not a spot on earth has been more frequently visited by great cyclones.

One of the most notable of its visitations during this century occurred August 2, 1837. The barometer fell rapidly during the forenoon, and by noon the storm began. In a short time it increased to a tremendous gale. At about three o'clock, the wind suddenly ceased. In a few moments it blew from the other direction, roaring and rolling black clouds before it, raising up immense sea-waves, covering the island with intense gloom. Six hours it blew, ever increasing. Tiles and slates whizzed through the air, to be shattered on the rocks or driven into timbers: great trees were whirled about, often dashing away houses that seemed about to weather the storm, while the terrible roar of the wind was such that even the crash of the thunder could hardly be distinguished. One authority tells us that the great guns at the fort were blown through the air and tossed about the beach like chaff! This must be taken with allowance. It is more probable that the great guns on the beach were washed up from the wrecks of some old pirate vessels or ships of war.

About 10 P. M. there was a slight cessation of the storm, and the people were congratulating themselves that the worst was over, when there came a violent earthquake, which laid in ruins almost everything that was left. The wreck took fire in two or three places: at once the hurricane began with renewed vigor: and ere the wretched people had fully comprehended the magnitude of the calamity, the whole ruined town was a sea of flame. Buffeted by the wind, blinded by the smoke and the pelting spray whirled up from the raging sea, the people ran for the slopes of the hills: the light of the funeral pyre of their hopes and labors rendering the gloom more horrible, and seeming to rival the gleams of Tartarus.

Day broke at last. The storm was gone. The earthquake staggered the miserable folk no longer. The warm and brilliant sun of the West Indies smiled upon the scene. "The whole country round was strewn with large trees, uprooted or snapped off, and all plantations were destroyed. In the town the fire was dying out, and it was only here and there that the ruins were still smoking. The hurricane had swept away nearly all the wooden houses; those which had been lightly placed upon beams, just above the soil, being carried off as they stood, while the larger ones, which had resisted the hurricane, were overturned in an instant by the earthquake. The whole town was strewn with wrecks that told of the violence of the catastrophe. The port, so gay and animated the day before, was dreary and deserted, a few masts here and there emerging from the water: while all along the shore, and even upon the slope of the hills, were scattered wreckage and corpses of sailors."

While we have noticed only the destruction wrought at

CYCLONE, FIRE AND EARTHQUAKE AT ST. THOMAS.

St. Thomas, this storm was general throughout the Antilles. In the Bahamas, it was less violent, they lying on the outskirts of the storm. Millions of dollars worth of property—merchandise, vegetation, houses, and vessels—were destroyed, and thousands of lives lost.

Thirty years later, St. Thomas again suffered from the combined forces of storm and earthquake; and the damage was greater, because the earthquake, with its sea-wave, came a few days after the storm, as the work of restoration was well under way, and so involved a second prostration of the resources of the people. Moreover, the town had grown considerably in thirty years, and there was much more valuable property to damage. Fifteen large steamers and many smaller vessels were driven on the shore by the storm : while the sea-wave, a few days later, found the port again filled with vessels of different nations. It overleaped the sentinel hills at the entrance of the bay, and swept with tremendous force upon the city, drowning with its terrible roar, the despairing cry of the sailors; then suddenly retired with the wreck of the city to its dark abyss. The batteries of heavy guns at the entrance of the harbor were swept away. A few injured vessels wallowed on the waves, but most had been swallowed up and left no trace behind.

While there is always deep sympathy for those who suffer such calamities, yet it must remain of the type bestowed upon sufferers in Arctic expeditions. The character of the climate is well known, and the whole matter resolves itself into a question of the risk one is willing to run. There is no blind chance in control of these movements. The cyclone frequents only certain regions, and its habit and power is understood. While we pity the sufferers, we can not assert that the scourge is mysterious or unaccountable, any more than we find mystery in the fact of eternal snow in the Polar world.

"DROWNING, WITH ITS TERRIBLE ROAR, THE DESPAIRING CRY OF THE SAILORS."

But there have been storms in the West Indies far more destructive than either of these, or both together. One of the most noted of the century is the famous Barbadoes storm of 1831, which an eye-witness thus describes:

"On the morning of the 10th of August, the sun arose without a cloud; at 10 A. M. a breeze that had been blowing, died away; towards 2 P. M. the heat became oppressive; at 5 P. M. thick clouds appeared in the north, rain fell, and was succeeded by a sudden stillness and a dismal blackness all around except towards the zenith, where there was an obscure circle of imperfect light. Till 10:30 P. M., however, there was no sign of change; then lightning appeared in the north, and very unusual fluctuations of the thermometer were observed. All this time the storm was only approaching.

"After midnight the continued flashing of the lightning was awfully grand, and a gale blew fiercely from the north and northeast, but at 1 A. M., on the 11th of August, the tempestuous rage of the wind increased as the storm suddenly shifted and burst from the northwest and immediate points. The upper regions were illuminated by incessant lightning, but the quivering sheet of blaze was surpassed in brilliancy by the darts of electric fire which exploded in every direction. At a little after 2 A. M. the astounding roar of the hurricane can not be described by language.

"About three o'clock the wind abated and the lightning ceased for a few moments at a time, when the blackness in which the town was enveloped was inexpressibly awful. Fiery meteors were presently seen falling from the heavens; one in particular of a globular form and a deep-red hue, was observed by the writer to descend perpendicularly from a vast height. On approaching the earth it assumed a dazzling whiteness and an elongated form, and on reaching the ground splashed around in the same manner as melted metal would have done, and was instantly extinct." (It is evident that the coincidence on this occasion with the day on which the earth is known to pass through the August belt of meteors, rendered the effect of this great storm at Barbadoes more striking. It is not safe to assert that there was any relation between the phenomena.) "A few minutes after, the deafening noise of the wind sank to a solemn murmur, or rather a distant roar; and the lightning which from midnight had flashed and darted forkedly with but few momentary intermissions, now for nearly half a minute played frightfully between the clouds and the earth with novel and surprising action. The vast body of vapor appeared to touch the houses, and issued downward flaming blazes, which were nimbly returned from the earth upward.

"The moment after this singular alteration of lightning the hurricane again burst forth from the western points with violence prodigious beyond description, hurling before it thousands of missiles, the fragments of every unsheltered structure of human art. The strongest houses were caused to vibrate from their foundations, and the surface of the very earth trembled as the destroyer raged over it. No thunder was at any time distinctly heard. The horrible roar and yelling of the wind; the noise of the ocean, whose frightful waves threatened the town with the destruction of all that the other elements might spare; the clattering of tiles, the falling of floors, and walls, and the combination of a thousand other sounds, formed a hideous and appalling din.

"About 5 A. M. the storm abated; at six o'clock the wind was at south, at seven o'clock, southeast, at eight o'clock, east-southeast; and at nine o'clock, the weather was clear.

"The view from the summit of the cathedral tower, a few hours later, was frightfully grand. The whole face of the country was laid waste; no sign of vegetation was apparent, except here and there small patches of sickly green. The surface of the ground appeared as if fire had run through the land, scorching and burning up the productions of the earth. The few remaining trees, stripped of their boughs and foliage, wore a cold and wintry aspect; and the numerous seats in the environs of Bridgetown, formerly concealed among thick groves, were now exposed and in ruins."

One peculiarity noticeable, was that in some places trees, timbers, and many other objects, presented a scorched appearance, as though subjected to intense heat. The reason of this is not clear, as unusual heat was not perceptible after the beginning of the storm by any one. It may be that this was produced by unusual quantities of electricity escaping through imperfect conductors,: for we learn, from other phenomena, that during this storm there was an unusual state of electrical tension in the atmosphere. Sparks occasionally leaped from the heads of persons out of doors. Vast numbers of trees that were not blown down, speedily died: and it has been suggested that an excess of electricity killed them.

The total loss in this storm is not definitely known. Some further idea of its fearful violence may be gathered from the fact that at the north end of Barbadoes, the waves broke over a cliff seventy feet high, and the saltwater spray was carried inland in such quantities as to kill all the fresh-water fish in ponds far in the interior. As for the tremendous roar of the wind, the commanding officer of the thirty-sixth regiment sought protection by getting under the arch of a lower window outside his house. He did not hear the roof and upper story of the house fall, and only found it out by the dust caused by the fall.

Far more destructive was the great hurricane of 1780.

TROPICAL CYCLONES. 151

HURRICANE IN THE TROPICS.

The French and English were at war. Admiral George Rodney was in the West Indies with an English fleet in several divisions. The French had sent a convoy of five thousand troops to Martinique. The storm was of immense width, extending from Trinidad, on the extreme southwest, to Antigua. The evening of October 9th was red and lowering. By ten o'clock next morning, the wind was high, and by one o'clock, vessels in the harbors were dragging their anchors. The water was driven on shore with such force at Barbadoes, that it was four feet deep in the Government House. The family took refuge under the cannon, only to find that they were moved about by the wind. By morning not a building in town was standing; every tree was either blown away, or stripped of branches and leaves.

The sunny islands were suddenly become as bleak and bare as a Siberian steppe.

As to the loss, ten thousand perished at Martinique; six thousand at Santa Lucia; four thousand five hundred at St. Eustatia; three thousand five hundred at Barbadoes. Scores of smaller islands were devastated, but the loss in detail is not known. Of the British fleet, the greater part was destroyed; only one vessel out of nineteen at St. Eustatia survived. A score of other ships of war and numerous transports were sunk. Of the French convoy, with five thousand troops, the governor wrote laconically that it "had disappeared." Several English vessels at Barbadoes were carried far in shore and converted into dwellings. Doubtless, fifty thousand would hardly be too great an estimate of the total loss of life in this storm. In a similar one in 1813, the hurricane drove back the Gulf Stream, piling up the water thirty feet deep in the Gulf of Mexico. The ship *Ledbury Snow*, endeavored to ride out the storm, and when it was over, found herself high and dry. She had let go her anchor among the tree-tops of Elliot's

Key. The Barbadoes region suffered another severe gale in 1782, when the prizes captured by Admiral Rodney were sunk, a number of merchant vessels and two English war-ships foundered, and three thousand lives were lost at sea alone.

The temperate zone has its occasional hurricanes, though they are by no means as powerful or as frequent as those of the tropics. It is stated that in the year 944, one thousand five hundred houses were destroyed by a tempest in London. In the year 1090, it is recorded that a violent storm overturned six hundred and six houses in London alone.

Terrible as is the destruction of the cyclone in the western world, its fury here can not give a fair idea of the awful havoc it makes in Oriental regions. All through the Malay archipelago, along the coasts of China, Japan, the Phillipines, Hindostan, and Farther India, the ravages of the Storm King have been appalling, far exceeding even the terrible hurricanes of the West Indies.

Hindostan affords peculiar facilities for destructiveness of cyclones. Both its great rivers flow, for the latter part of their course, through low alluvial plains, and their deltas extend into the ocean directly toward the region of monsoons; so that a hurricane may send a great tidal wave up the river: while the low rich plains for miles around are but few feet above tide-water, and teem with a population atttacted by the amazing fertility. So a sudden great storm may totally submerge, without any warning, hundreds of square miles of these fertile tracts, with all their inhabitants. Even when the sea-wave is not added to the horrors of the storm, the losses are fearful. A cyclone at Calcutta in 1867, destroyed thirty thousand houses, wrecked or sunk six hundred ships and smaller vessels in the river, and killed ten thousand persons in the city alone. When to this is added the havoc committed by the storm—one hundred miles wide—in the rural districts, as it traveled on toward the foot-hills, it is clear that every reader may be devoutly thankful that such terrible visitants are altogether unknown in our land.

Terrible as this storm was, there was a greater one on the 5th of October, 1864. About one hundred ships were lost; and over sixty thousand persons perished; forty-three thousand in Calcutta alone. It was accompanied by a "bore" on the Hooghly, the water rising thirty feet, which is ten feet higher than the highest spring tides; whole towns were nearly destroyed. It indicated its approach for several days, and Capt. Watson, of the *Clarence*, seeing the barometer falling, knew a cyclone was approaching, and saved his ship by steering out of its range.

Compare this with the storms of our own land, that thrill the country with horror if but one hundred people are killed, and remember that the cyclone of India destroyed six hundred lives where one was destroyed in this region. Compare with the most terrible storms recorded in the West Indies, and the latter must yield.

Coringa, on the Coromandel coast, has been several times desolated by these terrible storm waves. In December, 1789, three immense rollers came ashore during a single storm; the town was destroyed; the neighboring country inundated. Ships were torn from their anchorage and thrown high on the land: twenty thousand people were lost; and the heaps of sand and mud rendered search for bodies and property useless.

In May, 1833, the region at the mouth of the Hooghly was inundated by a cyclone. Three hundred villages and fifty thousand people were destroyed. In June, 1822, Burisal and Backergunge, at the mouth of the Ganges, were overwhelmed, and fifty thousand persons drowned.

But Hindostan has far greater horrors to report. A

terrible flood in 1887 was driven by the cyclone over the Ganges delta. The victims numbered many thousands: exact figures not at hand. But in 1876, a cyclone swept the Backergunge district, and rolled in a storm wave over the eastern edge of the fertile delta, covering it with from ten to fifty feet of water. When the storm had subsided, it was found that more than one hundred thousand people had perished!

Finally, a great cyclone in 1737, October 11–12, swept the Ganges delta with a wave thirty feet deep on the land. Three hundred thousand people perished in this storm! The mind can not grasp the appalling magnitude of such a disaster.

These cases are the most destructive cyclones on record, and in each case the destruction is due largely to the character of the region traversed, though the winds of Bengal are not surpassed in violence by those of any country in the world. Were the harbor an open seaport, instead of a large river, no ship could live through such a storm.

Other regions in the east suffer much from tempests. The whole Malay archipelago, with the Moluccas and Philippines, are visited quite as frequently as the coasts of Hindostan. A cyclone that swept the Philippine Islands, November 6, 1885, destroyed ten thousand people, and millions of dollars worth of property.

The same character of storms is frequently met with in the Japan and China seas, where it is known as the "typhoon," our Anglicised spelling of the Chinese title, "tei-fun." With one example of the power of this storm, this chapter must close. In the narrative of Commander Hall, of the British Navy, is found this description of a typhoon that occurred at Hong Kong, July 21–22, 1841:

"For days previously large black clouds appeared to

COAST OF INDIA SUBMERGED BY A STORM.

settle on the hills on either side; the atmosphere was extremely sultry and oppressive, and the most vivid lightning shot incessantly along the dense threatening clouds, and looked more brilliant, because the phenomena were most remarkable at night; while during the day, the threatening appearances were moderated considerably, and sometimes almost entirely disappeared. The vibrations of the mercury in the barometer were constant and rapid, and though it occasionally rose, still the improvement was only temporary; a storm was therefore confidently predicted. Between seven and eight o'clock in the morning, the wind was blowing very hard from the northward, or directly upon the shores of Hong Kong, and continued to increase in heavy squalls hour after hour. Ships were beginning to drive, and the work of destruction had commenced on every side; the Chinese junks and boats were blown about in all directions, and one of them was seen to founder with all hands on board. The fine basin of Hong Hong was gradually covered with scattered wrecks of the war of elements; planks, spars, broken boats, and human beings clinging hopelessly for succor to every treacherous log, were tossed about on every side; the wind howled and tore everything away before it, literally sweeping the face of the waters. From half-past ten to half-past two the hurricane was at its highest, the barometer at this time having descended to 28.50. The air was filled with spray and salt, so that it was impossible to see anything that was not close at hand; the wind roared and howled fearfully, so that it was impossible to hear a word that was said. Ships were now drifting foul of each other in all directions, masts were being cut away, and from the strength of the wind forcing the sea high upon the shore, several ships were driven high and dry. The Chinese were all distracted, imploring their gods in vain for help;

such an awful scene of destruction and ruin is rarely witnessed, and almost every one was so busy in thinking of his own safety, as to be unable to render assistance to any one else. Hundreds of Chinese were drowned, and occasionally a whole family, children and all, floated past the ships, clinging in apparent apathy (perhaps under the influence of opium) to the last remnants of their shattered boats, which soon tumbled to pieces and left them to their fate. On the 26th another typhoon occurred, but not so severe as the first."

The storm at sea presents a class of peculiar dangers and a variety of thrilling experiences, such as the landsman never knows. The stories of great shipwrecks and other purely naval disasters form some of the most interesting narratives in history: and doubtless the reader will be pleased to notice in detail the perils of the deep, and to learn of the precautions taken and the means in common use for averting, as far as possible, the disastrous results of the tempest. Certainly, the brave tars who peril their lives on the ocean to bring us the luxuries of a foreign land deserve especial attention, and no apology need be given for devoting a portion of this volume to the story of their perils and daring.

CHAPTER IX.

PERILS OF THE SEA.

"Daughter, the night was made for sleep;
Why dost thou moan, why dost thou weep?
Wherefore thy mournful vigil keep?
　　Daughter, daughter, my daughter!

Mother, to me the night wind cries.
Cold on the sands thy lover lies,
With none to close his glazed eyes;
　　Nello, Nello, my Nello!

THE Storm at Sea! From the days of David to the present, the poet and the novelist have taxed their energies to portray the perils of those who go down into the deep in ships. The ravages of the hurricane on shore are confined largely to those portions of the world unknown to the ancients; but the treacherous deep has been sung in every age. We may hardly choose which of the myriad wrecks to describe. St. Paul's perilous voyage to Rome is familiar wherever the gospel is preached; Jonah has furnished a comparison for the unlucky for centuries, Virgil has sung of the perils of exiled Æneas in his search for a foreign home.

The sea has dangers peculiarly its own, and likewise charms possessed by nothing else in nature. Every one may have heard of the little earnest woman who at her first sight of the ocean sighed: "Ah—at last here is something there is enough of!" The sailor knows the ocean's every mood, and may sing with Barry Cornwall:

"HE SINKS INTO THY DEPTHS, WITH BUBBLING GROAN,
WITHOUT A GRAVE, UNKNELLED, UNCOFFINED, AND UNKNOWN."

> "I love, oh, how I love to ride,
> On the fierce, foaming, bursting
> When every mad wave drowns the moon,
> Or whistles aloft his tempest tune,
> And tells how goeth the world below,
> And why the sou'west blasts do blow!"

Or if his mind be better adapted for homelier ditties, he may hum:

> "The wind it blew a hurricane, the sea was mountains rollin',
> When Barney Buntlin' turned his quid, and said to Billy Bowlin':
> 'A strong sou'wester's blowin', Billy; don't you hear it roar now?
> How I pity all unhappy folks as lives upon the shore now!'"

Or if becalmed, and forced for days to lie beneath a scorching tropical sun,

> "As idly as a painted ship
> Upon a painted ocean,"

the inevitable dreariness of the wide waste of scarcely heaving water will oppress the mind till the sailor may murmur:

> "So lonely 'twas that God himself
> Scarce seemed there to be."

It is beyond dispute that the sea has been one of the most important factors in civilizations ancient and modern. Greece was no longer supreme in power when her naval supremacy was gone; Rome was not mistress of the world till she became mistress of the Mediterranean. Not a single great system of civilization has originated in districts far inland. The great centers—Greece, Rome, Asia Minor, Egypt, Spain, England—all that have wielded unusual power—are sea-coasts, peninsulas or islands. The Jew became prominent as a trader from the day Jewish vessels sailed from Tarshish. To some extent, these facts must be considered as results of position only, however powerful the tendencies or traits of any particular stock.

It is not merely as a highway for commerce and ready intercommunication that the seas have enriched mankind.

The submarine world presents views as strange and weirdly beautiful as the ancient myths of nymphs and naiads.

> "Deep in the wave lies a coral grove,
> Where the purple mullet and goldfish rove;
> Where the seaflower spreads its leaves of blue,
> That never were wet with falling dew;
> But in bright and changeful beauty, shine
> Far down in the green and glassy brine."

And thousands of the human race depend entirely upon the products of the sea for a livelihood. The fish taken as food would be an enormous item in any year: but the billows that surge over the deep conceal far more treasure than these.

> "Full many a gem of purest ray serene,
> The dark unfathomed caves of ocean bear."

All our pearls, nearly all our amber, sponges, and as beautiful and delicate as spun glass, corals of infinite number and variety—all these, and more, we must obtain from the depths of the sea. Yet, while eagerness for gain leads men to brave countless perils to obtain these treasures, thousands of sad hearts will deem them dearly bought, and recall the more precious treasures of the deep.

> "Yet more! the billows and the depths have more!
> High hearts and brave are gathered to thy breast!
> They hear not now the booming waters roar;
> The battle thunders will not break their rest.
> Keep thy red gold and gems, thou stormy grave!
> Give back the true and brave!
>
> "Give back the lost and lovely! those for whom
> The place was kept at board and hearth so long,
> The prayer went up through midnight's breathless gloom,
> And the vain yearning woke 'midst festive song!
> Hold fast thy buried isles, thy towers or throne —
> But all is not thine own.
>
> "To thee the love of woman hath gone down;
> Dark flow the tides o'er manhood's noble head,
> Or youth's bright locks, and beauty's flowery crown;
> Yet must thou hear a voice—Restore the dead!
> Earth shall reclaim her precious things from thee!
> Restore the dead, thou sea!'

Like the atmosphere, the ocean has its great constant currents, which play an important part in the economy of

CAST ASHORE.

nature. These flow steadily on, one beneath another, and are little affected by atmospheric disturbances. The presence of submarine currents is often shown by icebergs moving steadily onward against a surface current and moderate wind. But there is nothing in the sea, so far as known, that corresponds to the variable winds or local currents of the atmosphere: for as water is so much heavier than air, its equilibrium is not so easily disturbed by unusual heating: and moreover, it does not expand under the influence of heat to an extent in the least approaching the expansion of the air. Hence, its currents are steady and slow-moving, and, however much they affect climate and winds by the heating or cooling of the air above them, they offer no obstacle worthy of note to the sailor. The latter must then fear only the power of the storm: and were submarine vessels readily constructed and navigated, the storm would lose its terrors: for

>"When the wrathful spirit of storms,
> Has made the top of the wave his own,
> And when the ship from his fury flies,
> When the myriad voices of ocean roar,
> When the wind-god frowns in the murky skies,
> And demons are waiting the wreck on shore,
> Then far below in the peaceful sea,
> The purple mullet and goldfish rove,
> Where the waters murmur tranquilly,
> Through the bending twigs of the coral grove."

It should be said, however, that the sea and storm are not responsible for all the disasters at sea. For years the greatest losses of life and property were due to the greed of conscienceless owners, who sent rotten tubs to sea, fearfully overloaded and heavily insured, certain to make a good profit whether they perished or no. As for the sailors, they were not worth considering: there were plenty to be obtained. Human life is the cheapest commodity in any market. By a liberal spending of this currency men become Alexanders or Cæsars, or Sullas, or Marii: henceforth they are "Great."

These abuses were especially prevalent in England, the

greatest of maritime powers; nor were they corrected till Mr. Samuel Plimsoll, in 1870, began a series of earnest efforts to have a systematic inspection organized. He made a startling arraignment of the atrocious methods of the land-sharks. He wrote, in 1873, "No means are neglected by Parliament to provide for the safety of life ashore; and yet, as I said before, you may build a ship in any way you please, you may use timber utterly unfit, you may use it in quantity utterly inadequate, but no one has any authority to interfere with you.

"You may even buy an old ship two hundred and fifty tons burden by auction for £50, sold to be broken up, because extremely old and rotten; she had a narrow escape on her last voyage, and had suffered so severely that she was quite unfit to go to sea again without more being spent in repairs upon her than she would be worth when done. Instead of breaking up this old ship, bought for 4s. per ton (the cost of a new ship being from £10 to £14 per ton), as was expected, you may give her a coat of paint—she is too rotten for caulking—and to the dismay of her late owners, you may prepare to send her to sea. You may be remonstrated with, in the strongest terms, against doing so, even to being told that if you persist, and the men are lost, you deserve to be tried for manslaughter.

"You may engage men in another port, and they, having signed articles without seeing the ship, you may send them to the port where the ship lies in the custody of a mariner. You may then (after re-christening the ship, which ought not to be allowed), if you have managed to insure her heavily, load her until the main deck is within two feet of the water amidships, and send her to sea. Nobody can prevent you. Nay, more, if the men become riotous, you may arrest them without a magistrate's warrant, and take them to prison, and the magistrates, who have no choice (they have not to make, but only to administer the law), will commit them to prison for twelve weeks with hard labor; or better still for you, you may send a policeman on board to overawe the mutineers, and induce them to do their duty! And then, if the ship is lost with all hands, you will gain a large sum of money and you will be asked no questions, as no inquiry will ever be held over those unfortunate men, unless (which has only happened once, I think), some member of the House asks for inquiry.

"The river policeman who in one case threatened a refractory crew with imprisonment, and urged them to do their duty (!) told me afterwards (when they were all drowned) that he and his colleagues at the river-side station had spoken to each other about the ship being dreadfully overloaded as she passed their station on the river, before he went on board to urge duty (!) and that he then, when he saw me, 'rued badly that he had not locked 'em up without talk, as then they wouldn't have been drowned.'"

He also found that some ship-builders put together mere floating coffins, using "devils," or dummy bolts, or bolt-heads without any shaft, to present the appearance of a staunchly built vessel. The old shell would founder in the first strong breeze. Hundreds of examples came in his way of entire crews lost in these hulks. What such losses meant to the poor dependent families at home we may imagine, but may not readily portray.

Another prolific source of disaster was the neglect to supply captains with the proper charts. There are notable instances of great vessels so lost. One ship and cargo, value $350,000, was lost near Boulogne, because the captain's chart had not the lights properly marked on it

The great steamer *Deutschland*, having a large number

WRECK OF THE MINOTAUR.

of German emigrants on board, ran on an unmarked shoal near the mouth of the Thames, December 30, 1875, and was lost. The vessel was fourteen hours on the shoal in in the winter storm, ere her signals of distress were perceived. Fifty-seven of her passengers had been lost in the heavy sea ere help reached her.

Ship after ship has left her port, never to be heard of again, whose crews might have still been in peace and comfort with their families, had the owners had the least trace of humanity, or regard for simple justice. A single example will illustrate.

In a hovel, Plimsoll found a young wife, scrubbing for a living, trying to support herself and three children. "She had a loving husband but very lately, but the owner of the ship on which he served, the S—— n, was a very needy man, who insured her for £3,000 more than she had cost him. So if she sank he would gain all this. Well, one voyage she was loaded *under the owner's personal superintendence;* she was loaded so deeply that the dockmaster pointed her out to a friend as she left the dock, and said emphatically, 'That ship will never reach her destination.' She never did, for she was lost with all hands—twenty men and boys."

Under the owner's personal superintendence! Could cool calculating villany go any further? Yet this is but one out of many scores!

Yet, despite the apparent frequency of complaints from those who suffered most by these practices, the abuses had grown up so gradually that the masses of the people had come to accept them as almost a necessary concomitant of naval matters. While holding out stoutly for the difference of a penny more or less in wages, there was no effort at concerted action for better treatment. Men accustomed to risking their lives daily came to look upon the matter as of no great consequence. Only the worst possible vessels were very seriously objected to; and these usually had little difficulty in obtaining crews of men long out of employment, who would accept any risk rather than remain a burden to their friends and families, however the latter might object to the proceeding. So thousands went to a watery grave. Official records of the period showed that one-half the losses at sea were the result of sending out rotten hulks. Yet, when reforms were suggested, the promoters were frequently told that if such things did not properly regulate themselves as a matter of political economy, there was no use striving for a change. Cool weighing of human life against gold!

Even in staunch ships the accommodations provided for the sailors were of the meanest sort. Men might wade to their bunks through water, or be packed in a filthy forecastle like herrings; they were fed on "salt horse" and moldy biscuit; they might rot with scurvy—if the ship got to port with her cargo, it made little difference how the crew fared.

Our own ships and the Russian and French vessels the investigator found far superior in treatment of the sailor: and the majority of English owners did well by their crews; but Plimsoll's efforts induced great improvement. Compulsory survey and no overloading were his main remedies for the prevention of the terrible loss of life in the mercantile marine. He cites two cases of great firms—the first engaged in the coal carrying, and the second in the guano trade—who do not permit overloading, and the first, in fifteen years had not, out of a large fleet of steamers, lost a single vessel, although they made from fifty to seventy double trips per year. The second case deserves particular mention. About the year 1860, the firm of Anthony Gibbs & Co., of London, took a contract from the Peruvian Government to charter and load ships from the Chincha Islands with guano, and as many as three or four hundred ships left those islands annually for different parts of the world. At first they were allowed to load and proceed to sea without inspection or surveying, and were permitted to load as deeply as the masters thought fit. What was the result? Accidents and losses were reported every few days, and many of their ships foundered at sea, some with all hands on board. When the head of the house at Lima, Peru, introduced proper surveying before loading, to discover what repairs were needed, etc., allowing no overloading, and not permitting the ships to go to sea without full inspection of her pumps and gear, a sudden and wonderful change took place, and for years after not one of these ships foundered at sea.

There is no sadder record than that which has been made of many a gallant vessel, sailing with the best prospects—"Missing," or "Never heard of." Occasionally the mysterious fate of some of these vessels has been revealed by the picking up of sealed bottles containing brief records of the disastrous end of the missing ships. But such cases are rare in comparison with the vast majority of the disasters; for the greatest peril to a vessel in a storm is the vicinity of a reef or shoal. In the open sea there is comparative safety, even in a considerable gale, for good seamen; but a shoal or rocky coast may be fatal to the vessel striking, even though the wind be but moderate. So nearly all disasters occur along shore; and the time is past in which it is possible for a vessel to be lost on an unknown or uninhabited coast. Hence, soon or late, the lot of nearly every vessel is known. Occasionally a vessel has been abandoned as unseaworthy or unmanageable, and has surprised those abandoning her by drifting around for months in the path of other vessels and occasionally fouling with some of them, to their serious injury.

PERILS OF THE SEA.

The polar seas present peculiar perils to the navigator. Almost every one has heard of the ill-fated Franklin

WRECKED ON A ROCK.

expedition, even though others may not be familiar. The attempts to find a northwest passage have long ceased, it being indisputable that it is useless though found. The great expeditions of later years have been equipped purely from a scientific standpoint. No conceivable benefit to commerce can result therefrom.

But the vast majority of fatalities in the polar seas have not been among the great exploring expeditions, any more than the majority of disasters in warmer climes are among first-class passenger steamers. The world over, it is the coasting vessels, the fishing smacks, the second and third-class freighters that swell the lists of losses at sea. And in the polar seas the most numerous disasters are among the whaling and sealing vessels, which visit the regions season after season. Many a vessel has been crushed like an egg-shell amid the enormous masses of ice. Often a vessel seemingly hopelessly imprisoned has been abandoned by the crew, only to be freed by some caprice of the winds and picked up by some other crew. And again there have been instances of vessels seen resting in masses of ice far above the water, raised by continual tilting and piling of ice-cakes beneath. Sometimes a vessel has floated about thus for a considerable period. Comparatively speaking, losses of life have been small in proportion to the dangers and property losses. Where so many vessels are in the same region at a time, the crew of a crushed ship can generally reach another vessel without great difficulty. But years ago, when the whaling fleet was smaller, and steam had not been called to the seaman's aid, the peril of life was greater; and many is the vessel that sailed away never to be heard of again.

One of the best stories illustrating this class of dangers is that of the whaleship *Rufus*. A whaling vessel in 1774 found an abandoned ship; and on boarding her, found the crew scattered about in the postures assumed when they first yielded to the fatal sleep. The tale, in verse worth

PERILS OF THE SEA 173

CASTAWAYS ON A RAFT.

remembering, but seldom or never seen, was told many years ago by an unknown author. The distinctness and simplicity of the style render the poem worth preserving, aside from the interest of the story.

THE SHIP RUFUS.

Sing not, my Muse, of brightening fields
    Of ether, fair displayed,
Of whispering bowers, where Zephyr yields
    His fragrance to the glade

But haste thee to the frozen throne,
    The starry blue domain
Where Winter, monarch dread and lone,
    Asserts his iron reign.

Now Europe's northern cape recedes,
    And Iceland's utmost shore;
The sailor turns his face and heeds
    Those viewless forms no more.

For mountains, distant yet, but bright,
    Edging the arctic tide,
'Neath spiry flames of dancing light,
    At masthead are descried.

For see! in glittering points, the coast
    Divides; the mountain chain,
On waves afar in silence tossed,
    Trembles athwart the main.

Anon, the mariner looks forth,
    And scans with cheerless brow,—
Borne onward by the angry North,
    An arctic navy now.

"How shall the good ship Rufus speed?
    How live?" the master cried;—
"God send us help in time of need,"—
    "Amen!" the crew replied.

Each ice-built crag and snowy cliff
  Chases the foaming spray;
And, 'mid those moving Alps, the skiff
  Must find her destined way.

Her destined way?—Her destined fate!
  Now drops the needful gale;
The waves become a glassy plate;
  The bark forbears to sail.

Prisoned of God; by mountains pent,—
  Fuel and food consumed;—
Ask not of me the dire event,
  Nor why they thus were doomed.

* * * * * *

Again, borne forth by waves and wind,
  Men spread a venturous sail,
'Mid rocks of massy ice to find
  The scarce less massy whale.

The optic tube now aids the eye,
  And scans the distant sea:
A distant speck they now descry;
  A speck—what can it be?

"What can it be?" inquire the men—
  "An iceberg, or a sail?"
As yet the crew inquire in vain,
  And doubt must yet prevail.

Yes, doubt prevails, and strengthens still,
  Though fast the object nears.
"Sure 'tis no sail which at the will
  Of winds and billows steers!"

Fancy still limns out forms uncouth,
  Yet scarce herself persuades;
But fancy now gives place to truth
  More startling than her shades.

A dreary hull, with shattered mast,
　　And sails of strangest guise,
And cordage fluttering in the blast,
　　Now meets their wondering eyes.

The bark they hail;—in many a groan
　　The bellowing shrouds reply;
But bellowing shrouds respond alone;—
　　No voice returns the cry.

Strange!—for, as near with curious haste
　　They ply, and glance within,
Lo! at the cabin window placed,
　　A form is dimly seen.

They mount the floating ruin now—
　　Her deck is overlaid
Man's height in crusted ice and snow,
　　Which shows no human tread.

To find the hatch beneath the drift,
　　They all their efforts lend,—
Its frozen planks at length they lift,
　　And fearfully descend.

Now pause they at the cabin door;—
　　Now enter, as they will;—
Its quiet inmate, as before,
　　Sits unconcerned and still.

With pen in hand, and half reclined,
　　Like those in thoughtful moods;
To noises deaf, to visions blind,
　　He cares not who intrudes.

No!—for a filmy mold invests
　　His long untroubled brow;—
His eyeballs green sought not his guests,
　　Nor can he turn them now.

PERILS OF THE SEA.

SINKING OF THE LONDON.

A crumbling page before him lay,
  Which told the unspoken woe ;—
"Our cabin fire went out to-day—
  Food spent five days ago ;—

"Locked in the ice three weeks,—our crew
  All dead,—all hope is o'er ;—
Ship Rufus—1762—
  One hour, and I'm no more !"

Now horror on the souls sunk down—
  On all who viewed the scene ;
Twelve arctic winters then had flown,
  Since this a corpse had been !

Twelve years on polar surges tossed,
  By northern blasts conveyed—
Destroyed—preserved, by iron frost,
  Her crew were statues made.

Perchance this fate-directed prow
  Had crossed 'neath cloudless skies
The pole, which jealous Nature now
  Shuts out from human eyes.

Perchance the dreamed of Northern Way
  This guileless keel had plowed,
While billows with the helm did play,
  And wild winds trimmed the shroud.

Say when, Stern Spirits of the North,
  They found their watery grave?
Or do ye still in awful mirth,
  Toss them from wave to wave?

CHAPTER X.

LIFE-SAVING MEASURES.

"'O father, I hear the church-bells ring,
O say, what may it be?'
'Tis a fog-bell on a rock-bound coast,'
And he steered for the open sea.

'O father, I hear the sound of guns,
O say, what may it be?'
'Some ship in distress that can not live
In such an angry sea.'

'O father, I see a gleaming light,
O say, what may it be?'
But the father answered not a word,
For a frozen corpse was he.
* * * * * * *
At daybreak, on the bleak sea beach,
A fisherman stood aghast,
To see the form of a maiden fair,
Lashed close to a drifting mast.

The salt sea was frozen on her breast,
The salt tears in her eyes.
And he saw her hair, like the brown seaweed,
On the billows fall and rise."

ONE of the most destructive storms on record, and certainly the most terrible ever known on the whole English coast is the great storm of 1703. It is the only storm which has ever been made the subject of a Parliamentary memorial. It raged for a week over nearly the whole of England. Scores of vessels were driven on shore and perished. At Bristol, the in-driven sea filled the merchants' cellars, destroying sugar, tobacco, and other produce, to the value of hundreds of thousands of dollars. Eighty people were drowned in the river and adjacent marshes, fifteen thousand sheep were drowned by the overflow or backing up of the Severn. At London, the

STORM ON THE SHOALS, 1703.

river was filled with vessels, the crews of which were nearly all on shore. The storm tore them from their moorings, and drove them into a bight on the opposite side of the stream. It was a strange sight they presented after the storm. Defoe says that "there lay, by the best account he could take, few less than seven hundred sail of ships, some very great ones, between Shadwell and Limehouse inclusive; the posture is not to be imagined but by them that saw it; some vessels lay heeling off with the bow of another ship over her waist, and the stern of another upon her forecastle; the boltsprits of some drove into the cabin windows of others; some lay with their sterns tossed up so high that the tide flowed into their forecastles before they could come to rights; some lay so leaning upon others that the undermost vessels would sink before the other could float; the number of masts, boltsprits and yards split and broke, the staving the heads and sterns and carved work, the tearing and destruction of rigging, and the squeezing of boats to pieces between the ships, is not to be reckoned; but there was hardly a vessel to be seen that had not suffered some damage or other in one or all of these articles."

In the city itself, the streets were covered with tiles, slates, bricks, and fallen chimneys. Common tiles rose to nearly six times their usual price. Numbers of people were killed by crumbling roofs or falling houses. In Gloucester, six hundred great trees were prostrated in a space of five acres. The Bishop of Bath and Wells, and his wife, were among the more noted dead. The total loss of life has been estimated at from eight to thirty thousand. The former is Defoe's, but as he only counts those of which he obtained direct personal information, this estimate is certainly too low.

A single item of this storm will give some idea of the peculiar dangers once incurred by shipwrecked sailors. Mr. Whymper writes, "The townspeople of Deal, in particular, were blamed for their inhumanity in leaving many to their fate who could have been rescued. Boatmen went off to the sands for booty, some of whom would not listen to poor wretches who might have been saved. Many unfortunate shipwrecked persons could be seen, by the aid of glasses, walking on the Goodwin Sands in despairing postures, knowing that they would, as Defoe puts it, 'be washed into another world' at the reflux of the tide. The mayor of Deal, Mr. Thomas Powell, asked the Custom House officers to take out their boats and endeavor to save the lives of some of these unfortunates, but they utterly refused. The mayor then offered, from his own pocket, five shillings a head for all saved, and a number of fishermen and others volunteered, and succeeded in bringing two hundred persons on shore, who would have been lost in a half an hour afterwards. The Queen's agent for sick and wounded seamen would not furnish a penny for their lodging or food, and the good mayor supplied all of them with what they required. Several died, and he was compelled to bury all of them at his own expense; he furnished a large number with money to pay their way to London. He received no thanks from the Government of the day, but some long time after was reimbursed the large sums he had expended."

One not versed in the tales of the past might be astounded at such inhumanity; yet the case cited is comparatively a mild one. People acquainted with the history of pirates and buccaneers know that coasts everywhere were once more or less infested with land-sharks, more merciless than any shark of the deep, who enriched themselves by the misfortunes of others: and drowning sailors would be disregarded in the race for plunder. Yet this is but a shadow of the fearful tragedies often enacted.

Picture a richly laden vessel, homeward bound, with

scores of eager anxious hearts on board, and other scores in port eagerly waiting them. The captain smiles thoughtfully, as he murmurs, "We shall be at home to-morrow!" The mother with child in arms repeats, as she thinks of the waiting husband, "We shall be home to-morrow!" The bronzed wanderer, returning after years of adventure, wonders if his boyhood's home is changed, as he thinks, "I shall be home to-morrow!"

There is but the faintest indication of storm. On shore, cruel, sinister faces scan the sky and the distant ship as the twilight settles down, and whisper together, and scowl as they recall past disappointments. They will take care that they are not disappointed again. Their grizzled old leader will see to that.

Night gathers apace. The storm bursts—the ship is far off shore, and in safe quarters. It is time to act "Now, in the pitchy darkness of the night, with bowed head, and faltering steps battling against the storm, the old man leads a white horse along the edge of the cliff. To the tip of the horse's tail a lantern is tied, and the light sways with the movement of the horse, and in its movements seems not unlike the masthead light of a vessel rocked by the motion of the sea. A whisper has gone through the village of a chance of something happening during the night, and most of the men and many of the women are on the alert, lurking in the caves beneath the cliff, or sheltered behind jutting pieces of rock.

"The vessel makes in steadily for the land; the captain grows uneasy, and fears running into danger; he will put the vessel round, and try and battle his way out to sea.

" The look-out man reports a dim light ahead. What kind? and whither away? He can make out that it is a ship's light, for it is in motion. Yes, she must be a vessel standing on in the same course as that which they are on.

It is all safe, then; the captain will stand in a little longer; when suddenly, in the lull of the storm, a hoarse murmur is heard—surely the sound of the sea beating upon rocks!

ON A LEE SHORE.

Yes! look! a white gleam upon the water! Breakers ahead! breakers ahead! Oh, a very knell of doom! The cry rings through the ship, 'Down, down with the helm—round her to!' Too late, too late! A crash, a shudder from stem to stern of the stout ship, the shriek of many voices in their agony, green seas sweeping over the vessel, and soon broken timbers, bales of cargo, and lifeless bodies scattered along the beach, while the shattered remnant of the hull is torn still further to pieces with each insweep of the mighty seas as they roll it to and fro among the rocks. Fearful and crafty the smile that darkened the face of the willing murderer who was leading the horse with the false light as he heard the crash of the vessel and the shrieks of the drowning crew! Fearful the smile that darkened the faces of the men and women waiting on the beach as they came out from their places, ready to struggle and fight among themselves for any spoil that might come ashore! A homeward-bound ship from the Indies! Great good fortune—rich spoil! Bale after bale is seized upon by the wreckers, and dragged high upon the beach out of the way of the surf. But, see! a sailor clinging to a bit of broken mast! With his last conscious effort he gains a footing on the shore, staggers forward, and falls. Is he alive? Not now! Why did that fearful old woman kneel upon his chest and cover his mouth with her cloak? Dead men tell no tales—claim no property!"

No fiction of the fancy, this! Only the last great day will ever reveal how many souls have perished at the hands of those who should have succored them. Think of a man and his wife reaching the shore after an exhausting struggle; the man leaving his wife in a sheltered nook while he goes in search of human habitations, and returning after a few moments to find his wife, a plundered, naked corpse! And yet, such practices were tolerably common, even within the range of a century past!

In striking contrast with the heartless wreckers are those known on the British coast as "hovellers." These put out to sea in stormy weather to ascertain if vessels in the offing are in need of anything, or are otherwise crippled: and many a ship have they saved from wreck by their timely aid.

It appears strange that, among a people so dependent upon the sea as the English, no regularly organized methods of diminishing the losses by wreck existed till within the present century. Yet such is the fact. A hundred years ago, there was no boat that could safely venture in a heavy sea; and if, perchance, some humane people wished to succor a vessel in distress, few were the means and terrible the risks. The graphic pen of Dickens, in this abridged narrative, will illustrate the case. The scene is Yarmouth, England:

"In the difficulty of hearing anything but wind and waves, and in the crowd, and the unspeakable confusion, and my first breathless efforts to stand against the weather, I was so confused that I looked out to sea for the wreck, and saw nothing but the foaming heads of the great waves. A half-dressed boatman, standing next me, pointed with his bare arm (a tattooed arrow on it, pointing in the same direction) to the left. Then, O great Heaven, I saw it, close in upon us!

"One mast was broken off short, six or eight feet from the deck, and lay over the side, entangled in a maze of sail and rigging; and all that ruin, as the ship rolled and beat—which she did without a moment's pause, and with a violence quite inconceivable—beat the side as if it would stave it in. Some efforts were even then being made to cut this portion of the wreck away; for, as the ship, which was broadside on, turned towards us in her rolling, I plainly descried her people at work with axes, especially one active figure with long curling hair, conspicuous among the rest.

"But a great cry, which was audible even above the wind

LIFE-SAVING MEASURES. 187

HOVELLERS RELIEVING A VESSEL.

and water, rose from the shore at this moment; the sea, sweeping over the rolling wreck, made a clean breach, and carried men, spars, casks, planks, bulwarks—heaps of such toys—into the boiling surge. The second mast was yet standing, with the rags of a rent sail, and a wild confusion of broken cordage flapping to and fro. The ship had struck once, the same boatman hoarsely said in my ear, and then lifted in and struck again.

"As he spoke, there was another great cry of pity from the beach; four men arose with the wreck out of the deep, clinging to the rigging of the remaining mast; uppermost, the active figure with the curling hair. There was a bell on board; and, as the ship rolled and dashed, like a desperate creature driven mad, now showing us the whole sweep of her deck, as she turned on her beam-ends towards the shore, now, nothing but her keel, as she sprung wildly over and turned towards the sea, the bell rang; and its sound, the knell of those unhappy men, was borne towards us on the wind.

"Again, we lost her, and again she rose. Two men were gone. The agony on shore increased. Men groaned and clasped their hands, women shrieked and turned away their faces. Some ran wildly up and down along the beach, crying for help where no help could be. I found myself one of these, frantically imploring a knot of sailors whom I knew, not to let those two lost creatures perish before our eyes, when I noticed that some new sensation moved the people on the beach, and saw them part, and Ham come breaking through them to the front.

"I ran to him, held him back with both arms and implored the men with whom I had been speaking not to listen to him, not to do murder, not to let him stir from off that sand! Another cry arose on shore, and, looking to the wreck, we saw the cruel sail, with blow on blow, beat off the lower of the two men, and fly up in triumph round the active figure left alone upon the mast.

"Against such a sight, and against such determination as that of the calmly desperate man, I might as hopefully have entreated the wind. 'Mas'r Davy,' he said, cheerily grasping me by both hands, 'if my time is come, 'tis come. If 'tain't, I'll bide it. Lord above bless you, and bless all! Mates, make me ready! I'm a-going off!'

"I don't know what I answered, or what they rejoined; but I saw a hurry on the beach, and men running with ropes from a capstan that was there, and penetrating into a circle of figures that hid him from me. Then I saw him standing alone, in a seaman's frock and trousers, a rope in his hand, or slung to his wrist; another round his body, and several of the best men, holding, at a little distance, to the latter, which he laid out himself, slack upon the shore, at his feet.

"Ham watched the sea, standing alone, with the silence of suspended breath behind him, and the storm before, until there was a great retiring wave, when, with a backward glance at those who held the rope which was made fast round his body, he dashed in after it, and, in a moment was buffeting with the water. Now, he made for the wreck, rising with the hills, falling with the valleys, lost beneath the rugged foam, borne in towards the shore, borne on towards the ship, striving hard and valiantly.

"The distance was nothing, but the power of the sea and wind made the strife deadly. At length, he neared the wreck. He was so near that with one more of his vigorous strokes he would be clinging to it—when a high, green, vast hill-side of water, moving on, shoreward, from the beyond the ship, he seemed to leap up into it with a mighty bound, and the ship was gone!

"On running to the spot where they were hauling in,

THE LIFE-BOAT.

I saw some eddying fragments in the sea, as if a mere cask had been broken. Consternation was in every face. They drew him to my very feet—insensible—dead—beaten to death by the great wave; and his generous heart was stilled forever."

Such things weighed heavily upon the humanely disposed; and when a century ago Mr. Greathead, who had a great heart, stood at Newcastle-on-Tyne, and saw man after man drop from a great wreck into a raging sea without the possibility of rescue, he set himself to work upon the problem of the life-boat. Noticing that the half of a circular wooden bowl invariably turned concave side upward, when thrown in the water, it occurred to him at once that a boat with a curved instead of straight keel would always right itself. Wouldhave, at the same time was advocating padding the boat heavily with cork: and the first life-boat was constructed from these ideas. A year or two later, a minister in the Orkneys suggested that all boats could be made self-righting by fixing an empty water-tight cask in either end. So the idea of air-chambers developed: and later the curved keel was made of iron, to aid in ballasting the craft: so that the modern life-boat, with curved iron keel, cork padding, air chambers, and tubes to permit water to flow out, cannot be sunk, or made to float bottom up. The men may sometimes be washed out of it, or a side stove in, but the boat will always be found right side up.

Strange as it may appear, though the first life-boat, with its crudities, saved hundreds of lives within a few years, the Government took no steps to institute a general system or life-saving service. To the average American, this seems striking; but governments a century ago were more concerned about the success in war than about the welfare of the masses; they studied destruction of life more than its preservation: and if perchance, some ruler affected peculiar concern for the welfare of "the State," it was generally the case that the definition of Louis XIV was applicable; "The State—that's *me!*"

But Sir William Hillary and Thomas Wilson made earnest appeals to Parliament for the establishment of a national life-saving institution; and Hillary added the more effective argument of many deeds of personal daring in the venturous work. Between 1821–1846, no fewer than one hundred and forty-four wrecks occurred on the Isle of Man, and "one hundred and seventy-two lives were lost; while the destruction of property was estimated at a quarter of a million. In 1825, when the *City of Glasgow* steamer was stranded in Douglas Bay, Sir William Hillary assisted in saving the lives of sixty-two persons; and in the same year eleven men from the brig *Leopard*, and nine from the sloop *Fancy*, which became a total wreck. In 1827–32, Sir William, accompanied by his son, saved many other lives; but his greatest success was on the 20th of November, 1830, when he saved in the life-boat twenty-two men, the whole of the crew of the mail steamer *St. George*, which became a total wreck on St. Mary's Rock. On this occasion he was washed overboard among the wreck, with three other persons, and was saved with great difficulty, having had six of his ribs fractured."

So the British institution arose, small at first, but mighty in its work since. Ten years after, in 1850, it was reorganized, and improved life-boats secured. The importance of the work may be imagined when we record that from 1852 to 1871, the wrecks on British coasts alone averaged one thousand four hundred and forty-six per annum! When we add the work of our own life-saving service, and the service of life-boats in many other lands, we may realize how inestimable is the value of such an institution.

THE LIFE-BOAT AT WORK.

Among the earlier measures to prevent loss of life are fog-bells, fog-horns, and lighthouses, to warn the sailor of dangerous shoals. In earlier days, wreckers sometimes silenced the fog-bell. Southey has given us a ballad upon the poetic justice said to have been meted out to a famous pirate who removed the bell placed by the abbot of Arberbrothok upon the Inchcape Rock, off the Scottish coast. One year later, with a rich booty, the pirate nears home once more,

> "They hear no sound, the swell is strong;
> Though the wind hath fallen they drift along,
> Till the vessel strikes with a shivering shock,—
> 'Oh, Christ! it is the Inchcape Rock!'
>
> Sir Ralph the Rover tore his hair;
> He curst himself in his despair;
> The waves rush in on every side,
> The ship is sinking beneath the tide."

With this notice of the extent to which man may be responsible for disasters, the subject must be dismissed. Ere leaving the topic of storms, the reader shall know of one of the most notable naval disasters of the century, which will illustrate the difficulty with which even powerful war ships face high winds at sea.

CHAPTER XI.

GREAT SAMOAN HURRICANE.

"Roll on, thou deep and dark-blue Ocean, roll!
Ten thousand fleets sweep over thee in vain.
Man marks the earth with ruin: his control
Stops with thy shores: upon the watery plain
The wrecks are all thy deed; nor doth remain
A shadow of man's ravage, save his own,
When for a moment, like a drop of rain,
He sinks into thy depths with bubbling groan,
Without a grave, unknelled, uncoffined, and unknown."

DURING the fall of 1888, no little interest centered in one of the little inland groups of the Pacific. In 1887, German officers in the Samoan group conceived that the king, Malietoa, was so prejudiced toward their interests that he should be deposed. So without much ceremony they laid hands upon and carried him into exile, placing him on an island some thousands of miles distant.

There seems no reason to doubt that Germany's ultimate design was to formally occupy the islands. It is the old story of the civilized man's dealings with the savage; of the man who has ten talents, obtaining the property of the man with one.

Methods have changed somewhat, however, since the day when our pilgrim fathers kindly relieved the Red man of such encumbrances as he had in the way of real estate, and established quit-claim deeds and perfect titles in their flint-lock muskets. It is not now considered "good form," as it was in the days of olden Spanish America, to declare one's self Marquis of this or Duke de that, with several thousands of Indians as slaves or tributaries, without consulting them. The modern method is that of the European guide who attaches himself to your person willy-nilly, in order that he rifle your pockets as the need of his divers imaginary services. It is a less expensive method, and none the less sure. So the colonizers of our day kindly establish a "protectorate" over Naboth's vineyard. Naboth, however, fully understands the process, as some civilized races have found to their cost.

The Samoans were in high dudgeon at the action of Germany; and when the foreigners coolly proceeded, without consulting the wishes of the natives, to select and establish a new king, whom they thought would be favorable to their own interests, open hostility resulted.

The Samoans had no way to bring back their former king, Malictoa; but they promptly deposed the creature of the Germans, Tamasese, and chose instead Mataafa, a relative and personal representative of their exiled king. The few American residents and frequenters of the islands approved this, deeming the act of the Germans one of unjustifiable aggression.

Civil war resulted. At the outset, Tamasese's strong personal following, and the fear of German interference, gave him a very large party. But in the half-dozen fierce battles that were fought he was decidedly worsted, and, forced to flee from the capital, Apia, he shut himself up in a native fortress eight miles distant.

The Germans had in the meantime actively espoused his cause, and went so far as to bombard several native villages. Still they did not come into direct personal collision with the natives until December, 1888. A body of Germans landed a few miles from Apia, and assaulted Mataafa's forces.

The island blood was up. The battle was stubbornly

contested. The Germans were utterly routed and driven back to their vessels with a loss of fifty killed and wounded.

This is precisely the sort of pretext a "protecting" power desires. In great indignation at the pesky people who had failed to allow themselves to be thrashed, the Germans formally declared war, and began a series of high-handed seizures and aggressions. The interests of other nations in Samoa were endangered. There was but one American man-of-war in the harbor.

As soon as the War Department learned of the state of affairs, reinforcements were sent out, and it seemed highly probable that a collision between America and Germany might be precipitated at any moment. Thus, there were collected in the harbor the American warship *Trenton*, the flag-ship of Rear-Admiral Kimberly, and one of the largest vessels in the navy, N. H. Farquhar, Commander: the *Nipsic*, Commander D. W. Mullan; and the *Vandalia*, Commander C. M. Schoonmaker. The Germans were represented by the warship *Olga*, and the cruisers *Eber* and *Adler*. England had sent the man-of-war *Calliope*. In addition, there were in the harbor ten or twelve schooners and trading vessels. Such was the force assembled at Apia, March 15, 1889.

The news does not travel rapidly from that portion of the world. During the spring a report reached America that the looked-for collision between the assembled forces had occurred, and that the *Nipsic* had been sunk by the *Olga*. There was much suppressed excitement; but as the report was not officially confirmed, this soon ceased.

No one was prepared for the actual occurrence, or the magnitude of the calamity.

The town of Apia, the Samoan capital, lies around a small circular bay. Across the mouth of the harbor, two miles in width, extends a coral reef, which is visible at low water. A break in the reef a quarter of a mile in width forms the entrance to the harbor. Only a small portion of the latter is available for anchorage, as the eastern part is quite shallow, and on the west the bay has a small fringing reef well out from the shore. It will be seen that the crowded condition of the harbor rendered it peculiarly perilous. The war vessels were anchored in the deep water, the *Eber* and *Nipsic* being nearest the shore. The schooners and lighter craft were in the shoal water next to the fringing reef on the west side of the harbor.

The town is composed of cottages, built after the native pattern: low, of elastic materials, and bound well together; so that the low houses, swaying easily with the wind, are not so easily blown away as structures of stiffer and more pretentious build. The American consulate, facing the harbor, lies about the center of the town, with a long strip of sandy beach before it.

For some weeks the weather had been gloomy and capricious. The time of the vernal equinox was at hand, and a low area storm of unusual violence might be expected at any time. During the afternoon of March 15, the wind began to increase: the war ships lowered their topmasts and secured their spars; one or two prepared storm-sails for emergencies. The anchors were all out, and steam was raised lest the anchors should not hold.

The wind increased steadily, blowing from the same quarter continuously. Though the only recorded observations are at this one point, its proximity to the equator, the steadiness of the wind and the length of time it blew indicate a cyclonic tempest of unusual violence.

By 11 P. M. the wind was a strong gale: not too strong in the harbor for small boats, however; for the crews of nearly all the schooners, divining what was coming, put out their spare anchors and went ashore, leaving the vessels to their fate. Mayhap the anchors would hold; but on their lives they would take no risks.

An hour later immense rollers were coming in from the ocean, finding the coral reef only a partial check. Ordinarily a reef insures a harbor from the force of the waves, and leaves only the direct fury of the winds to be encountered. But the reef at Apia is a lower barrier than such harbors usually possess, and may not be seen at high tide.

At midnight, rain was falling. The wind still increased. The vessels were pitching fearfully. At this time the *Eber*, nearest the shore, began dragging her anchors, and was compelled to aid them with her engines. At one o'clock the *Vandalia*, also, was compelled to use her engines. Should the wind increase, their case was truly desperate.

The rain poured in torrents; fiercer grew the gale. By three o'clock every vessel in the harbor was dragging her anchors. There might be a collision, or a wreck, at any time. Every able-bodied man was required, that any emergency might be met. Neither officer nor private could think of sleep.

Those on shore realized the peril of the situation. Accustomed to heavy gales, the natives slept soundly for a time in their low huts. At length, the crash of falling trees and the tearing away of roofs began to be heard in the storm. Little knots of people crept about in the darkness, seeking shelter from the tempest. Sand and pebbles, gathered up from the beach, were hurled by the wind with cutting force. The tide was rising, and the gale brought it into the streets, a hundred feet above the usual high water mark. The spray from the dashing surf sprang high in the air, and beat into the windows of houses nearest the shore. It was a memorable night.

Long before dawn the natives were huddled in little groups about the shore, gazing at the shifting lights of the tossing vessels. Their houses were being wrecked, their crops and trees destroyed, but they themselves were measurably safe. But those in the harbor!

There was little need of conversation; and, indeed, did one wish to speak to his neighbor, he was compelled to shout in his ear. As each peered into his fellow's face in the uncertain light, he saw the shadow of a terrible fear and a desperate resolve that spoke plainer than any words. Explanations were useless; that tacit understanding was enough. For the time, thrones, principalities, feuds and hostilities were forgotten. The followers of Tamasese and Mataafa were shoulder to shoulder. No longer was there thought of the foeman who had exiled their chief and bombarded their villages. Out in that seething caldron were scores of human beings, battling for life with wind and wave. That was enough.

As the day drew near, the white men on the shore began to join the little groups of natives. Through the gloom could be seen the lights of the plunging ships, and ever and anon there came on the gale the sound of shouted orders, like a distant echo. The wavering of the lights showed that, despite steam and anchor, the vessels were slowly dragging about, crossing and re-crossing each others' paths. The breathless watchers on the beach listened for the crash of collision that would be the death-knell of scores of gallant marines. Some shielded their faces with bits of tile, and endeavored to distinguish the position of the respective ships. Less hopeful than the whites, the natives saw no chance of escape. Which vessel would strike first? Would any be saved?

GREAT SAMOAN HURRICANE.   201

Between five and six o'clock, it began to grow light. The position of the vessels was completely altered. Forced

BOW OF THE EBER, CAST ASHORE.

from their moorings, they were drifting toward the inner reef. Each contended stubbornly with the storm. Volumes of black smoke poured from the furnaces of the quivering hulls. A number of the sailing vessels were already on the reef. Fragments of wreckage began to be tossed ashore. The *Trenton* and *Vandalia*, being farthest out in the harbor, were scarcely visible through the mist and spray. The large iron hulls were tossed about like corks. Wave after wave dashed over their decks. The men swarmed about the masts and the lower rigging, clinging to anything they could grasp. The *Eber*, *Adler* and *Nipsic* were within a few yards of each other and close on the fatal reef. Each vessel seemed as though endowed with a life of its own. They struggled like wild creatures; as the stag might struggle in the clutch of a panther.

The *Eber* slowly retreated toward the reef, contesting every inch. Suddenly she paused, recovered, and dashed forward into the teeth of the furious storm.

It was her last desperate sally. The current bore her to the right. In a moment she collided with the *Nipsic*, her bow carrying away a boat and several feet of the post-quarter rail. Falling back, she fouled with the *Olga*, and her rudder was carried away. This left her helpless. Swinging broadside to the wind, she lay a few moments rolling heavily in the trough of the sea. Over her deck the surf foamed and roared.

At length, a gigantic wave lifted her up and hurled her with awful force upon the reef. Striking fairly on her keel, she heeled over toward the sea. No further trace of her was seen. Every timber must have been shattered. Doubtless more of her crew were crushed than were drowned.

The horror-stricken natives, accustomed to the sea from infancy, dashed into the surf, struggling with death for the lives of their late oppressors. They were but savages; they knew no better.

For a few moments, not a hand was raised from the site

of the wreck. At length, a few faintly struggling forms appeared in the surf. They were grasped by eager hands, and safely reached the shore. Another was seen clinging to the piling of a small wharf, beaten half senseless by the furious waves. He was drawn ashore. It was a handsome boyish-faced lieutenant, the sole surviving officer. Out of a total force of seventy-six men and officers on the *Eber*, five only were saved. The young lieutenant was the officer of the watch at the time of the wreck. The others were all below, and must have been crushed to death. This occurred about six o'clock in the morning.

Finding no other survivors, those on shore turned to the remaining vessels once more. Their position had changed again. The situation rapidly grew more perilous.

The *Adler* had fouled with the *Olga*, and was close on the reef, some two hundred yards from where the *Eber* struck, and like it, was approaching the shore broadside on. The suspense was prolonged and painful. For nearly half an hour she lay thus swept by the waves.

Finally, a huge roller tossed her on top of the reef and turned her over on her side, throwing those on deck into the water. They struggled to regain the vessel; those who succeeded clung to guns, tackling, spars and masts; but twenty were drowned. The vessel lay with her keel to the sea and nearly her entire hull out of water; so those who clung to the rigging were fairly protected.

During the day the natives succeeded in getting a line to the wreck, and a number of the sailors escaped. But the line parted while some were still on the vessel, and could not be replaced. The remainder of the crew clung to the wreck through all that terrible day and night, and were finally gotten off when at the verge of exhaustion.

While the *Adler* was drifting toward the reef, the *Nipsic* was battling with fearful odds. Facing the wind, she was

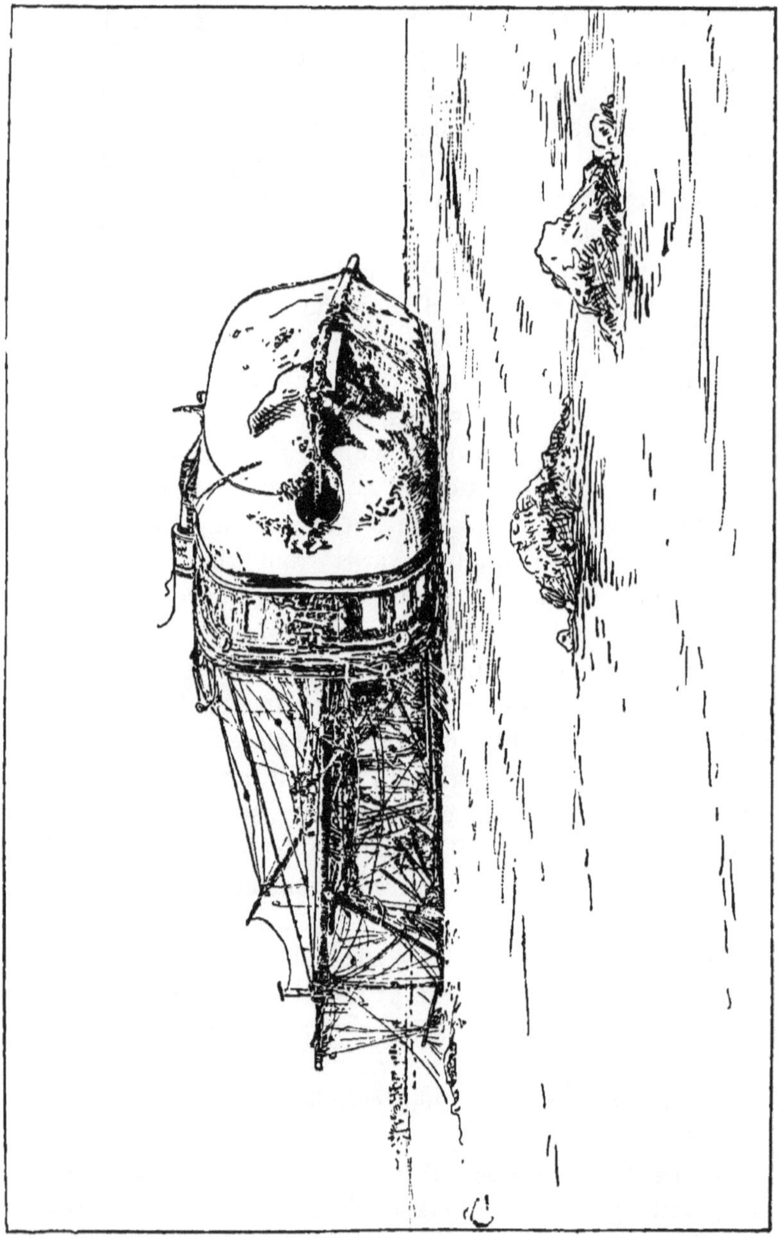

THE ADLER ON THE REEF.

nevertheless dragging her three anchors, and receding toward the reef.

But her chief danger lay in another source. The gigantic *Olga*, which had crippled the two vessels already wrecked, threatened to crush her also. While the *Nipsic* endeavored by skillful use of steam and rudder to avoid the *Olga*, a little schooner, the *Lily*, fell in her way and was cut down in an instant. There were but three men on board; two of whom succeeded in reaching the *Olga*.

Just then it occurred to the commander of the *Nipsic* to reinforce the anchors by attaching a hawser to one of the heavy eight-inch rifles and casting it overboard. Ere this was accomplished the *Olga* struck her a terrible blow directly amidships. Her smoke-stack was overturned and fell on the deck with a terrible crash. One of her boats was carried away and the rail splintered. No one at first knew the extent of the damage. The frightened crew clambered into the rigging, thinking the ship was sinking. The lumbering smoke-stack dashed from side to side with the roll of the ship.

It was a frightful moment. Only a few yards away the *Eber* had disappeared. The *Nipsic* had swung around and was rapidly nearing the spot. Only promptness and most skillful management saved her officers and crew from the fate of the *Eber*.

Captain Mullane was on the bridge at the time, and took in the situation in an instant. With the smoke-stack gone it would be impossible to keep up steam; without steam the reef could not be avoided. At once the smoke-stack was chocked to prevent its rolling about the deck, and orders were given to beach the ship while a small head of steam was still available. Two hundred yards away lay the sandy beach before the American consulate.

A great throng awaited anxiously the result of this

manœuvre. The vessel's course was parallel to the terrible reef, and but a few feet from it. Her crew were gathered about the bow, and those on shore recognized many a familiar face or personal friend in the driving spray, on whom they might be looking for the last time. One or two of the crew had been on shore during the night, and now stood watching the fate of their comrades.

Barely escaping the reef, the steamer plunged into the sand a few yards from the shore, and swung around diagonally to the storm. The breakers dashed furiously upon her stern, and it seemed as though she would be beaten to pieces in an instant. Those who escaped must do so at once.

Five sailors dashed into a boat; but the falls did not work properly, and one end of the boat dropped. The men fell into the sea and were drowned. The surgeon and five sick men were placed in another boat: no sooner launched than capsized. But the natives had formed a chain by grasping each others hands; and dashing into surf where a white man would have perished at once, they seized the men and passed them to the shore. Several of those on the *Nipsic* took advantage of the opportunity and sprang overboard. But two of these were lost.

Meanwhile, all those remaining on board had crowded into the forecastle. The natives in the surf, under the direction of two of their chiefs, Seumanu Tafa and Salu Anae, had succeeded in getting lines to the vessels, and double hawsers were quickly stretched to the shore. Scores of eager hands were outstretched to assist in the work. The waves broke high on the beach, and the undertow was so strong that even the natives narrowly escaped being carried out into the bay. The white men on shore scarcely dared venture into the surf. The rain poured more heavily. The clouds of flying sand grew thicker and more

GREAT SAMOAN HURRICANE.

SAMOANS SAVING THE LIVES OF AMERICAN SAILORS

cutting. The hoarse shouts of the officers mingled with the roar of the storm, and the stricken vessel quivered in every fibre. Fragments of wreckage were ever and anon hurled amongst those in the surf. The gloom of the awful tempest combined with all these things to produce a tableau of chaos itself.

Yet, throughout the whole fearful scene, the natives never faltered, but sang and shouted words of encouragement to each other as they stood at their chosen posts. The white men on shore rendered all the aid in their power; but the posts of danger and need were filled by the natives. An eye-witness of the scene says:

"To one who saw the noble work of those men during the storm, it is a cause of wonder that they should be called savages by more enlightened races. There seemed to be no instinct of the savage in a man who could rush into that boiling torrent of water that broke upon the reef, and place his own life in peril to save the helpless drowning men of a foreign country.

"While the Americans and Germans were treated alike, it was plain that their sympathies were with the Americans, and they redoubled their efforts when they saw an opportunity to aid the men who represented a country which had insisted that their native government should not be interfered with by a foreign power."

The coolness of Captain Mullane had mastered the frightened crew. There was no longer confusion. The officers stood by the rail and directed the movements of the men. Time after time the rolling billows dashed the men from the hawser; but the gallant natives succeeded in saving all. By eight o'clock the *Nipsic* was deserted. The three smallest of the war ships were wrecked.

The four large men-of-war were well out in the harbor, and for the time measurably safe.

But near ten o'clock, the situation became alarming again. Masses of floating wreckage struck the *Trenton*, as it was lifted by a heavy wave, and carried away the rudder and propeller. Her anchors, unaided, would not keep her from the reef, or from fouling with the other vessels in the harbor.

The *Vandalia* and the *Calliope* were drifting toward the wreck of the *Adler*. As the *Vandalia* endeavored to steam away, the iron prow of the Englishman arose high in the air and fell with full force upon the *Vandalia's* port-quarter. The *Calliope* lost her jib-boom, and the heavy timbers of the *Vandalia* were shivered. Every man near the point of the collision was thrown from his feet by the shock. Water was rushing through a great rent in the cabin. It seemed that the *Vandalia* had received her death blow. The frightened men swarmed from the hatches, but presently returned to their posts.

At this crisis the Englishman essayed a bold manœuvre. Seeing that to remain where he was would be, in a few more moments, ruin to the *Vandalia*, he resolved to take all risks himself, and letting go all anchors, swung around to the wind and endeavored to put to sea. For a moment the vessel seemed stationary. Then the tremendous power of the propeller began to tell, and the vessel moved slowly forward in the teeth of the storm. Volumes of smoke poured from her funnels, and the ship groaned in every timber. Gradually it became clear that she could escape from the harbor.

This is one of the most daring feats in the naval annals. It was the one desperate chance to save the *Calliope* and her crew from certain death. An accident to the machinery at this moment, or a slight change in the direction of the wind as she neared the narrow gate-way of the harbor, would have been fatal. Down in the fire room, the men

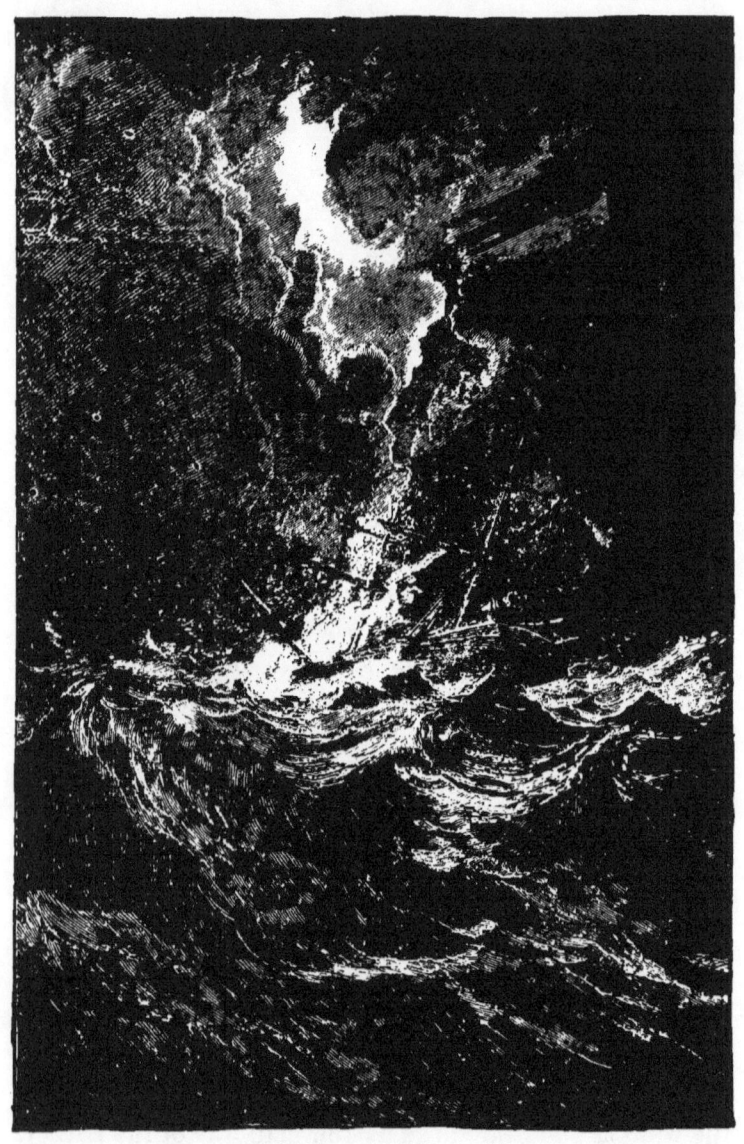

THE CALLIOPE PUTTING TO SEA.

worked as they never had before. The *Trenton* lay close to the reef, and the *Calliope* was compelled to pass between the two. The flagship's fires were out, and she could do nothing to save herself. Every man felt that a few moments longer would find him a grave in the coral reef. Those on shore were watching with intensest anxiety.

Just then a strange sound came, borne on the wind; a wild ringing cry from the four hundred and fifty on board the *Trenton*. The Americans were cheering the *Calliope*. Expecting death for themselves, they rejoiced that their friends might yet escape, and the heart of every Englishman went out to the brave Americans who gave their parting tribute to the Queen's ship.

There is something peculiarly touching in this incident. It is far above the *morituri te salutamus* of the gladiator in the arena. It was an expression of immortal courage; the dying saluting the victor; the doomed saluting the saved; manhood distressed greeting manhood triumphant. The English seamen returned the cry. The *Calliope* safely reached the sea. Her commander afterward said: "Those ringing cheers of the American flagship pierced deep into my heart, and I will ever remember that mighty outburst of fellow-feeling, which I felt came from the bottom of the hearts of the gallant admiral and his crew. Every man on board the *Calliope* felt as I did; it made us work to win. I can only say, God bless America and her noble sailors."

Meanwhile the *Vandalia*, seeing her doom certain, endeavored to reach the beach, but being a much larger vessel than the *Nipsic*, she could not come so near the shore. A blow from a terrific wave in the night had hurled the captain across his cabin and so injured him that he was unable to control his vessel. His executive officer, Carlin, was in command, but the captain stood by his side to the last. Carlin's coolness and nerve were wonderful. He had been on duty thirty consecutive hours, and had not tasted food all that time.

In order to reach the beach, the *Vandalia* was compelled to execute the same perilous feat that had been performed three hours before by the *Nipsic*. Slipping her anchors, she crowded on all steam and skirted the edge of the reef, finally dashing into the soft sand two hundred yards from the shore and eighty yards from the stern of the *Nipsic*. The engines were stopped and the fires put out; all hands were ordered on deck, and the vessel swung around broadside to the waves.

At first, her position being supposed safe, it was thought the two hundred and forty men on board might well remain until the storm was over. The men were scattered about the deck and forecastle, clinging to the guns, the masts, rigging and sides of the ship. Within half an hour her real danger became apparent; she wallowed lower and lower in the yielding sand; more and more frequently the seas dashed over her, flooding the hatchways with water. Her boats were dashed from the davits and torn to pieces. It was attempted to fire lines to the shore, but all her powder was ruined. The spray and mist arose in such masses from the sides of the ship, that those on shore could hardly distinguish her position.

At this moment a brave sailor volunteered to swim through the surf with a line, in the hope that his comrades might be rescued. It was a perilous task, as the water was filled with floating wreckage. Fastening a cord to his body, he sprang overboard: an immense wave hurled him against the side of the vessel and struck him senseless. He was drowned almost within touch of his comrades. Gradually the men were driven from the gun-deck. By noon it was under water. The heavy billows that swept over the ship hissed the men from their feet and dashed them against the sides. The sea water intensified the pain of their bruises. Soon all of the men sought refuge in the rigging, and a few officers only remained on the poop-deck. The waves grew more violent.

For once the best men on shore were powerless. No boat could live in the surf, and there was no fitting apparatus on shore, that a line might be conveyed to the vessel. The scenes on the land were desperate, but the Vandalia's doom was sealed.

Finally, they resolved on bolder efforts than had hitherto been made. Three natives fastened a cord to their bodies, and, passing around the side of the bay a quarter of a mile above the wrecked war ship, endeavored to take advantage of the powerful current setting toward the shore, and so reach the vessel. Powerful swimmers as they were, they were hurled to the beach without being able to get within one hundred yards of the vessel. Urged by their chief to try again, effort after effort was made, but without success.

Seeing no other chance, those on the Vandalia one by one dropped into the sea, in the faint hope that they might yet reach the land in safety. Some succeeded in reaching the wreck of the Nipsic, only a short distance away, but many were too weak to draw themselves up to its deck. As they clung to the ropes, the violence of the waves, in some cases, tore the clothing from their bodies.

The captain, sick and feeble, was growing weaker every moment. The brave Carlin stood by him endeavoring to hold him on, and speaking words of encouragement. He had not sufficient strength left to clamber into the rigging and refused a life preserver, insisting that it should be given to some of the others. At length an immense roller plunged toward the vessel, and the captain bent forward to receive the shock. A heavy machine gun was torn from its fastening and hurled full upon the captain. His body passed overboard and was never more seen.

THE BOW OF THE SUNKEN VANDALIA.

One by one others of the officers were beaten from the deck. The suffering was not only with those on the vessel. The brave fellows who labored on the shore and in the surf were cut and bruised by flying sand and the floating fragments. Exposure to the sea water was making them stiff and sore. The natives sought occasional shelter and rest behind an up-turned boat or the masses of drift, and then returned to the battle.

Finally, as by common consent, nearly all of those left in the rigging dropped into the sea. It was an easy matter to reach the *Nipsic*, and a few succeeded in clambering to her deck; but many were too weak and exhausted to hold on long enough to receive assistance from their comrades, and too far off to be reached by the natives.

By three o'clock the hull of the *Vandalia* had almost disappeared. A few men were still in the rigging, lying exhausted on the small platforms or clinging to the ratlines or yards with the desperation of dying men, expecting every moment to be their last. Their arms and limbs were bruised and swollen and cut by holding on the rough ropes. For twenty-four hours they had been without food, and cold and exposure were doing their work. At this moment the rear of the *Nipsic* swung to the sea, so that but fifty yards separated the two vessels. A successful effort was made to stretch a line between the two; but before all in the fore-rigging could be rescued, the line parted and could not be replaced.

Meanwhile the *Trenton*, without steam or rudder, lay with her head to the wind, while volumes of water dashed through the hawse-pipes and flooded the engine room. Had the vessel gone down suddenly, none below could have escaped. They stood at their posts till waist deep in the water and the fires were extinct. The berth-deck was flooded. Lieut. Allen and a portion of the men made repeated efforts to close the hawse-pipes, but the force of the waves tore away every plug. Still they labored on, far beneath the decks, momentarily expecting the last.

The admiral and his officers stood on the bridge directing the movements of the vessel. When almost on the eastern shoals a bold coup was suggested by Lieut. Brown. Every man was ordered into the port-rigging, and the compact mass of bodies was used as a sail. The vessel was brought into the center of the bay again. Then she commenced to drift back toward the *Olga*, which had been holding up in the gale more successfully than any of the other vessels. The stars and stripes were flung to the breeze. If she were doomed, she would go down with flying colors. The *Olga* endeavored to steam out of the way, but her bow struck the starboard quarter of the flag-ship, shivering the heavy timbers, carrying away several boats, and throwing the flag to the deck. Again it was flung from the mast-head. The *Olga* reached the mud-flat on the east side of the harbor. Not a life was lost, and a few weeks later the vessel was hauled off and saved.

The struggle of the *Trenton* was almost ended. It was five o'clock and daylight was fading as the immense war ship bore down upon the *Vandalia*. When she struck the latter, all would be over.

That was a memorable scene. The night was coming on the wings of the storm. Those in the *Vandalia's* main-top still clung, bruised and bleeding. Their eyes were blinded by the salty spray. They looked on the black waters below knowing they had no strength for further battle with the waves. The final hour was upon them. The great black hull of the *Trenton* could be seen through the gloom, about to dash upon the stranded vessel and grind her to atoms. Those on the beach ceased their efforts in despair, and stood waiting the last act of the tragedy.

At this moment there came over the waves a renewal of the wild cheer of the morning. Four hundred and fifty voices were heard above the roar of the storm, "Three cheers for the *Vandalia!*" A cheer in the morning had animated the British; perhaps another cheer now would encourage the despairing seamen of the *Vandalia* to hold on a little longer. A response went up, feeble, quavering and uncertain, so faint it was scarcely heard by those on shore. With death staring them in the face, they sent up a cheer for the flagship; a cheer more pathetic than any lamentation. That was the saddest cry ever heard. Every heart on shore was melted to pity. "God help them!" they murmured.

Darkness hid the scene. The last cheer had died away. As those on shore listened for the crash, another strange sound came up from the deep. It was a wild burst of music in defiance of the storm. The *Trenton's* band was playing the "Star Spangled Banner." Never before had the thousand men on sea and shore heard such strains at a time like that. The feelings of the Americans on the beach were indescribable. The power of the music vied with the howling of the storm.

Men who during that awful day had exhausted every means of rendering some assistance to their comrades, now seemed inspired to greater effort. They dashed at the surf like wild creatures; but they were powerless. There was nothing left for them to do but wait; and, if they dared, to hope.

The *Trenton* proved the *Vandalia's* salvation. She bore lightly against her without a shock, and swung around in the sand broadside to the sunken ship. Those who remained quickly escaped to the *Trenton's* deck.

By ten o'clock the beach was deserted, and all that tempest or man could do had been done. A few watchers patrolled the beach all night in hope of rescuing some one who might not have escaped to the *Trenton*. But one person was found—a young ensign.

One hundred and forty-four persons had perished. Ninety-one were from the German vessels; fifty-one from

AFTER THE STORM: TRENTON IN THE FOREGROUND; VANDALIA'S BOW IN RIGHT CENTER; OLGA IN THE DISTANCE.

the Americans; two from a little trading schooner. Not more than one-third of the bodies were recovered.

The storm died away. It was a strange scene which

the morning sun beheld. The shore was strewn with drifted wreck. The shattered schooners lay about the reef. The streets were crossed with fallen trees, and roofless houses stood amid the groves. A fragment of the *Eber's* bow was high upon the beach. Far up the western reef the *Adler* lay. The *Olga* stood unharmed upon the eastern shoal. Before the consulate, the *Nipsic* was fast in the sand. Only the bow of the *Vandalia's* hull could be seen. By her side was the *Trenton*, grand though in ruin. And above the desolation floated the Star Spangled Banner, triumphant over the storm.

CHAPTER XII.

ELECTRIC STORMS.

"Far along,
From peak to peak the rattling crags among,
Leaps the live thunder! Not from one lone cloud,
But every mountain now hath found a tongue,
And Jura answers through her misty shroud,
Back to the joyous Alps, who call to her aloud!

And this is in the night:—Most glorious night!
Thou wert not sent for slumber! let me be
A sharer in thy fierce and far delight,
A portion of the tempest and of thee!
How the lit lake shines, a phosphoric sea,
And the big rain comes dancing to the earth!
And now again 'tis black—and now, the glee,
Of the loud hills shakes with its mountain mirth,
As if they did rejoice o'er a young earthquake's birth."

WHO has not quailed before the storm? Few, indeed, are they whose spirits kindle with the flash of the lightning, and joy in the roar of the thunder, that fills the heavens like the voice of many waters. Bold is the heart that in such scenes can mount with a Byron, and say to the Avernian gloom that wraps the frightened world,

"Let me be
A portion of the tempest and of the!"

Only that fiery, untameable spirit, fearless of man or demon, dare so approach the King of the Storm, or pat the mane of Ocean in his wrath. A thousand plaudits has he won—but not a follower: for when the lightning flames and roars, the cheering rabble slink away in fear, nor dare to emulate that genius, strange and wild as chaos as itself.

ELECTRIC STORMS. 221

THE LYSE FIORD.

The fear of the tempest belongs to every age. The ancient Greeks, from whom the Romans borrowed and modified the myth, told how Hephaistos toiled in his volcanic forge to form the bolts of Zeus, great father of gods and men. These flaming weapons could none oppose. By them rebellious giants were overturned. And the bold Goth, rugged and vigorous, heard the voice of the war-god, Thor, shout to him:

> "Mine eyes are the lightning,
> The wheels of my chariot
> Roll in the thunder!"

The Arab saw the wild combat of genii, whom the great Solomon had not subdued. Woe to the luckless wight who should arouse their ill-will! The Arabian Nights tell us of a contest between one of these spirits of fire and a beautiful princess, versed in magic. The swarthy Moor beheld the hand of God, waving on his angels to contest with the hosts of evil; and the same idea of wild combat in the spirit world is found in the myths of the Caribs and Lapps. In the Hindoo cosmogony, the lightning and storm are the chief weapons of Siva, the destroyer, who will one day blot the world out of existence. Only in the red man's tales do we find the idea of the Christian world, of one Great Spirit who rules all nature. In the Persian mythology, lightning and gloom represent the contest between the forces of Ahriman, prince of evil, and Ormuzd, the great creator and preserver of good. And among the old Etruscans, from whom the Romans borrowed many rites and ceremonies, the lightning was one of the chief objects in their system of augury and divination. A favorable flash of lightning outweighed all portents of ill. The thunder was the voice of the gods, communicating their will to men.

And so the ancients were content to pass the mystery

by, unsolved. Now and then a Pliny, a Seneca, an Aristotle, ventured a timid speculation upon the origin and cause of lightning, but as electricity was an unknown force to them, their conjectures were as wild as the chimerical tales of Cimmerian darkness in ultra-Scythian realms, or of the Utopian haven of bliss, where the Hyperboreans dwelt. But one of their various conjectures is worthy of note, as it contains an element of truth. It was, that the lightning was produced by mutual friction or violent concussion of the clouds.

Since electricity has been recognized as the agent in the phenomena of thunder storms, inquiry as to whether it is a cause or a result of the formation of clouds, has produced evidence in favor of the latter fact (though clouds differently charged have mutual attraction for each other), for rapid motion of gases may be made to generate electricity. A natural sequence would be that thunder storms are most violent where clouds are heaviest. Hence, thunder storms are naturally most frequent and violent in the tropics, where the greater heat produces immense masses of vapor, and are unknown in the polar world, where the comparative dryness of the atmosphere is unfavorable. The unusual amount of electricity in dense clouds in rapid motion is shown by the tremenduous electrical displays attendant upon tornadoes and cyclones. Another illustration of lightning resulting from cloud agency, rather than controlling them, may be found in the cloudless Sahara, where evidences of electricity are sometimes to be observed in the time of the Khamsin, while the thunder storm is unknown. One notable exception to the rule that thunder storms are violent and frequent in all tropical regions is to be found in Peru, with its cloudless skies and eternal sun, where a rainfall or a thunder storm would be as great a curiosity as a palm tree at the north pole. The mere fact of elevation renders the thunder storm more violent in mountainous regions, in both temperate and tropical worlds.

Knowing the character of this mysterious power, we may not enter upon a lengthy discussion of the changes, chemical, physical and otherwise, that may be produced by it. Within the scope of this work, only its rank as an agent of destruction and a historical factor may be considered. Is electricity to be greatly feared ? to be put on a par with the flood, the hurricane, and the earthquake? Has it ever figured in the history of nations sufficiently to directly affect their destinies?

The first and most familiar aspect of its power is the thunder storm, which needs not a word of description. It results merely from the discharges passing between two bodies oppositely charged. There is one comparatively rare form of lightning, in which it appears as a globe of fire slowly descending, with wayward and unexpected dashes to the side, sometimes coming down a chimney and playing about the floor like a kitten, much to the discomfiture of the inmates, till it at length explodes with immense force, hurling zig-zag lightnings all about. This peculiar freak, several times observed, is as yet unexplained.

The lightning seems throughout most civilized nations to be the most dreaded of all natural agencies, if we may judge from the many precautions taken against it. And in truth it is a terrific power, cleaving the hardest rocks, rending the mighty oak, and fusing the most refractory substances. Darting into the soil it frequently forms tubes of vitreous appearance by fusing the earth and stones as it passes. The writer has seen masses of straw fused in in the same way. And when we remember that French savants have, with the most powerful of batteries been able to produce tubes only an inch in length and one-fiftieth of an inch in diameter by passing shocks through powdered glass, we may well stand in awe at the terrible power that produces tubes thirty feet long and four inches in diameter in the far more obstinate feldspar and quartz.

There are numerous cases of death by lightning; but the instances in which more than one person has been killed by a flash are comparatively rare. The freaks

IDEAL SUBTERRANEAN STORM.

played far outdo those of the wind, and puzzle the wisest. March 20, 1784, about four hundred people were assembled in the theatre at Mantua, when lightning struck the building, and killed two persons, injuring ten. But many who were not hurt found the bolt had melted their watch-keys, earrings, and split diamonds they were wearing. How such feats could be performed without in the least harming the possessors is a mystery.

June 11, 1819, while a large assembly were attending

divine services in the church of Chateau Neuf les Montiers, in France, lightning struck the building, killing nine persons and wounding eighty-two. In 1715 the lightning fell into the abbey of Noirmoutiers, near Tours, and killed twenty-two horses, but did no further harm to the one hundred and fifty monks at supper than to turn over their one hundred and fifty bottles of wine. In 1855, lightning struck a flock of sheep in France, killing seventy-eight of them and two dogs, and sparing the old shepherdess. A French author relates the case of a priest who was killed by lightning, while the horse on which he rode was unhurt, and quietly continued homeward with the stiffened corpse. A somewhat similar case has come within the knowledge of the writer: a man on horseback being killed, and the saddle perforated; yet the horse remained apparently unhurt. I remember another instance of a man who was struck, and escaped unharmed; but one of his boots was torn to shreds and some of the hobnails melted: and I myself have been struck upon the foot, with no other result than a peculiar numbness, lasting nearly half an hour.

In many instances a livid streak is the only mark left upon the dead body; and again it may be torn almost to atoms; while in some cases not the slightest trace is perceptible. The greater number fall in the first class. In 1838, some cattle were killed by lightning near Nymnegen, in Holland. Their bones were shattered to a thousand fragments, as though by nitro-glycerine; while externally there was no particular token visible. Some sheep killed in Bohemia, in 1718, were similarly served. The fragments of bone were driven so thoroughly throughout the flesh that the carcasses were unfit for food.

In 1869, the mayor of Pradette, France, was killed by lightning, and all his clothes, with the exception of one shoe, were torn from the body. "August 11, 1855, a man was struck by lightning on a road near Vallerois, and entirely divested of his raiment, only a few remnants of which could afterwards be found. Ten minutes after the stroke he was restored to consciousness, complained of the cold, and asked how he came to be without any clothing. No doubt, he would have more easily consoled himself for the loss of his apparel had he known of the case reported by Sestier, of a man whose whole right side was burnt, as if he had been held for some time over a fire-pan, while his shirt, his drawers and the rest of his dress bore no marks whatever of combustion." Sometimes the clothing is found unstitched; again, it is burnt, and again, in some mysterious manner, seems to be annihilated.

Prof. Tyndall relates his sensations upon having a powerful electric discharge pass through him: " Life was absolutely blotted out for a very sensible interval, without a trace of pain. In a second or so consciousness returned. * * * The *intellectual* consciousness of my position was restored with singular rapidity, but not so the *optical* consciousness. * * * The appearance which my body presented to myself was that of a number of separate pieces. The arms, for example, were detached from the trunk and suspended in the air. In fact, memory and the power of reasoning appeared to be complete long before the optic nerve was restored to healthy action. But what I wish chiefly to dwell upon here, is the absolute painlessness of the shock; and there can not be a doubt that to a person struck dead by lightning the passage from life to death occurs without consciousness being in the least degree implicated. It is an abrupt stoppage of sensation, unaccompanied by a pang."

There is another class of peculiar freaks performed by this subtle force, which the following instances illustrate.

Prof. Perty tells of a thunder storm in Switzerland, when "the lightning sprang from a pear tree upon the verandah of a house, where it killed a boy and wounded his mother. The pear tree and the house were burned down. On the arm of the wounded woman a remarkably elegant impression of twigs and leaves, like a photographic copy of part of the pear tree, was found."

There are several cases noted of persons sitting near windows when lightning flashing near by has produced an exact likeness of the person, as though engraved on the glass.

"In 1825 the lightning fell upon the brigantine *El Buon Servo*, which lay at anchor in the bay of Armiro, at the mouth of the Adriatic Sea. The superstitious Ionian sailors generally fasten a horseshoe to the foremasts of their ships, probably fancying that this simple means affords them protection against the evil intentions of wizards and witches. Of course, the *Buon Servo* was not without its horseshoe. Antonio Teodoro, of Scarpanto, was sitting near the mast, when it was struck by lightning. He was killed at once. No marks of combustion were found on his body, nor were his clothes torn; but on his back was found the distinct impression of a horseshoe of the same size as that which was nailed to the mast."

In the records of the Academy of Sciences, we find that "the Signora Morosa, a lady of Lugano, who sat near a window during a thunder storm, received a shock which did her no further injury; but a flower which stood in the passage of the electric fluid was distinctly pictured on her thigh." She carried the mark to her grave.

Lightning is one of the most useful purifiers of the atmosphere. There can be no doubt that large quantities of noxious exhalations are destroyed by electrical discharges. Its beneficial effects in this respect have been long noted. "Both Hippocrates and Galenus remark that the water which falls during a thunder storm is more healthy to drink than that which proceeds from a uniformly clouded sky: and Plutarch mentions that the rain from a thunder cloud is considered as more favorable to vegetation, and communicates to plants a particular flavor." There are also on record a number of instances in which persons long in poor health, on receiving light shocks, have greatly improved in health and appearance. Similar results have been noticed in plant life. Doubtless such cases as these gave rise to the belief of the ancients, that to be struck by lightning was to be favored by the gods.

This opinion was especially noted in the case of Mithridates. Slightly wounded in the forehead by lightning when a child, he escaped unhurt later in life, when his sword was totally destroyed. These facts caused him to be held in superstitious fear by the Romans. And Quinitus Julius Eburnus became consul, B. C., mainly because of a similar mark of divine favor. Those who were killed by a flash were believed to be not subject to decay, and were robed in white and buried where they fell. So also those whose tombs lightning struck were peculiarly honored of Heaven. Lord Byron alludes to this in his stanza upon the bust of Ariosto on the poet's tomb at Ferrara, which had been struck by lightning:

> "The lightning rent from Ariosto's bust
> The iron crown of laurel's mimicked leaves,
> Nor was the ominous element unjust,
> For the true laurel wreath which glory weaves
> Is of the tree no bolt of thunder cleaves,
> And the false semblance but disgraced his brow;
> Yet, still, if fondly superstition grieves,
> Know, that the lightning sanctifies below
> Whate'er it strikes—yon head is doubly sacred now."

The identification of electricity with lightning is a comparatively recent occurrence. The story of Benjamin

Franklin, patron saint of the devout lightning-rod agent, is too familiar to require repetition. Yet, the idea was first broached in the latter part of the seventeenth century by two students of the new force, more than fifty years before Franklin's experiments.

Thunder clouds usually float from two thousand to five thousand feet from the earth; but there is one case on record of two priests being killed by lightning from a cloud only thirty yards from the ground; while another thunder storm is noted as having occurred eighteen thousand feet from the earth. As sound travels about one thousand and ninety feet per second, any one may ascertain the distance of a flash by noting the time that elapses ere the thunder is heard. All existing records fail to tell of thunder heard more than four miles; while the cannonading at Paris in 1871 could be heard one hundred and five miles; and Waterloo could be heard one hundred and fifty miles.

The action of lightning is instantaneous, and when near by the report is at first a single sharp crack; but it is always followed by a long rolling, so characteristic that every name given the thunder in a measure endeavors to imitate it. The reason of the continued roll from a single flash is simple, and is to be found in the fact that a flash usually travels several miles; and as sound travels as stated above, the sounds generated at different distances come to the ear in rapid succession, resulting in a continuous roar.

As the flash is due merely to the attraction between two bodies charged with opposite kinds of electricity, the discharge may pass either up or down. Cases are on record of persons on a mountain side being killed by lightning from a cloud below them, and of people on the ground killed by lightning dashing from them toward the sky.

Among the more notable fatalities resulting from lightning may be mentioned the terrible thunder storm of 1793, at Buenos Ayres, when the lightning struck thirty-seven times within the city, and killed nineteen people. A number of persons were killed on June 18, 1872, in England, at different places; and numerous others perished within the month from similar discharges.

Electricity seems to kill by destroying nervous power. Cardanus tells of eight reapers being killed while taking their meal under an oak. When the witnesses of the occurrence ran to the spot, they saw a strange sight. The victims "seemed to be still busy with their frugal repast. One of them held his glass, another was putting some bread into his mouth, a third had his hand in the dish. The angel of death had struck them so violently that the whole surface of their bodies bore the marks of his black wings. They seemed so many statues sculptured in black marble."

"In another case where ten reapers were killed under a hedge, one of them had a dog on his knee at the time when he was struck. The unfortunate man was caressing with one hand his little companion, and with the other giving him a piece of bread. Both master and dog were merely inert masses of rigid muscle and stiffened sinew, and yet the bread was still held by the lifeless hand. The dog, with his mouth expressively open, seemed still to beg for the proffered morsel."

A peasant woman in the suburbs of Nancy was struck while gathering flowers. She was found standing, holding in her hand the daisy she had been plucking. A French soldier took refuge under a tree during a storm; a peasant sheltered himself in a copse near by. The soldier was killed by lightning. The storm over, the peasant crept out and called to the soldier to come on. Receiving no answer, he

HARVESTERS KILLED BY LIGHTNING.

went up and touched the erect, motionless figure. It at once melted away. Only a little dust remained. A similar result occurred not long since in a powerful electric light plant. A large rat endeavored to cross some of the machinery, and at once became rigid, as though an image of stone. One of the employes, taking a stick, endeavored to push the carcass off; it at once disappeared in a cloud of impalpable dust.

Terrible results have followed from lightning striking into powder magazines. August 18, 1769, the powder vault in the tower of St. Nazaire, at Brescia, was struck. The explosion destroyed one-sixth of the city completely, and damaged all buildings more or less. Three thousand persons were killed, while the property ruined amounted to over $3,000,000. June 26, 1807, the lightning struck a magazine in the fortress of the Luxembourg, ruining the lower town, and killing or wounding two hundred and thirty people. In 1856 the powder vaults in the church of St. John, in the island of Rhodes were struck. More than two hundred people were instantly killed.

The lightning often shows in itself a sort of explosive power. Every one is familiar with the blasting of trees, and the throwing of fragments to a great distance. Some unusually violent effects of this class have been noticed. In 1762, stones weighing one hundred and fifty pounds, were flung from a church in Cornwall, to a distance of one hundred and eighty feet. In the Shetland Isles, during the last century, a rock of mica schist, one hundred and five feet long, ten feet broad, and from three to five feet thick, was in an instant torn by a flash of lightning from its bed, and broken into three large and several smaller fragments. One piece twenty-six feet long, ten feet broad, and four feet thick, was merely inverted. A second, twenty-eight feet long, seventeen feet broad, and five feet thick, was hurled over a high point to a distance of fifty yards: another mass, forty feet long, was hurled still further in the same direction, quite into the sea.

Certain localities seem to have peculiar attractive power for lightning. On the Norwegian coast is a narrow channel between two dark rocky headlands, where the lightning seems often to play almost incessantly. The gloomy chasm, so frequently reverberating with the roll of the thunder, is viewed with superstitious fear by ignorant sailors; and the boldest heart is filled with awe in the forbidding presence of the Lyse Fjord. By many he is thought a venturesome captain who will dare take his vessel through this frowning gateway.

But after a careful consideration of the topic, it is clear that lightning is less to be feared than almost any other of the atmospheric phenomena. Comparatively rare are the cases where more than one or two persons are killed at once. Statistics hitherto collected show that scarcely one death in two thousand is occasioned by it. And yet no force seems to be so universally feared. Every people in every age have taken precautions against it, while the hurricane and the flood pass almost unheeded.

The ancient Thracians were wont to shoot their arrows at the sky during a storm, to remind the fire-gods to be a little more careful in their sport. A similar practice is found among certain South African tribes: while the South Sea Islanders, far more fearless, tell of Ina, a woman whom the moon stole for his wife, while she was beating bark-cloth. She may be seen in the moon to-day—the figure we call the "man in the moon." Continually at work, she spreads out her cloth on the sky to dry—(clouds)—fastening it down with blue stones, of which the sky is built. When done, she gathers it up, throwing down the stones, which, falling upon the earth, produce the sound of thunder. The lightning is the torch the moon holds to aid her in her work.

Augustus was wont to retire to a subterranean vault during a storm, and it is said the Japanese emperors had a similar custom, having the additional precaution of large reservoirs of water over the grottos. When away from home, Augustus usually wrapped himself in sealskin, believed, not only by the Romans, but by many others, to be lightning-proof. In some portions of France, the peasants believe snake skins to be an efficient anti-lightning charm. And among not a few of the ancients there was a belief prevalent that lightning never injured a person in bed.

In the passage quoted from Byron on the bust of Ariosto, allusion is made to the belief that lightning never strikes the laurel—plant sacred to Apollo. Firm in this opinion, Tiberius, during thunder storms, put on a laurel crown; and similar virtue is to-day ascribed by the Chinese to peach and mulberry trees. Not a few persons to-day believe glass to be a safeguard, and that a person is safe beside a closed window. Seamen, and not a few of the peasantry of different regions, believe the firing of guns will break up a thunder storm. Tolling of church-bells is another powerful protection against the fires of the sky, which has cost many a bell-ringer his life; a tall steeple being unusually liable to be struck, and a damp bell-rope forming a good conductor. One authority tells us of three hundred and eighty-six steeples struck within thirty-three years, and one hundred and twenty-one bell-ringers killed. The preventive was all right; but these tollers had sinned away all right to protection, and perished as victims of Divine wrath, instead of an absurd custom.

Such are some of the many illusory modes of protection in vogue in times past, and existing to no small extent in the present. Comment upon them is unnecessary. We know to-day that the higher objects are most liable to be struck, and that metals are the best conductors; and on these facts the whole system of lightning-rod protection is based.

But in regard to even the best conductors, a witty German has found much room for ridicule. "While I am writing this, symptoms of dysentery are showing themselves with us in Gottingen. Six persons are said to have died of this complaint—that is more than twice as many in a few days as the lightning has killed in our town in half a century—and yet the public seems remarkably easy upon the subject. I do not even find that the cheapest *dysentery conductors* have been resorted to. People still go about in light clothing, although the wind is already blowing over the stubble, and I have even perceived, within the last few days, that some persons sleep with open windows, which are very carefully closed during a thunder storm, and yet there is not a single instance known that lightning has ever made its way through an open window, while dysentery very easily strikes into a bedroom, particularly when, after a warm day, it makes its appearance in company of rain and a cool wind. Is not this singular? How would people conduct themselves in these days if the dysentery was to rise above the horizon in the form of a low black cloud, changing day into twilight, and whenever it selected a victim, explode with a violent thunder clap, which made the house shake? I believe there would be no end of singing and praying. And yet this storm is now impending on our heads—but without thunder claps and black clouds, which are, after all, only accessories—and we go about our affairs as if nothing were happening."

The fact that objects reaching much above the general

surface are most liable to be struck, places ships at sea in a peculiarly dangerous position; and considering the relative number of the two, ships are more frequently struck than houses. The packet boat *New York*, was struck some years since: the chain which was attached to the mainmast as conductor was entirely volatilized, not being large enough to act as conductor.

The fact that electricity passes most readily from elevated points, renders the ship the scene of the most beautiful of the more common electric phenomena. Any one who has visited an electric plant knows how sparks and flashes of light accumulate on the brushes; and a similar spectacle may at times be seen on the wires of electric lights at night. So at sea during cloudy weather, the yards, masts, spars and other more prominent points often glow with pale lambent flames, of greenish or bluish tint. One who clambers up to them may find upon near approach that they almost disappear; while to one a short distance away they are as distinct as ever. A hand plunged into the flame glows with the same spectral light. This phenomenon is popularly known among sailors as "St. Elmo's fire;" but there is much difference of opinion as to what it may forebode. Some sailors believe the ghost of a dead comrade is accompanying the ship. Others consider that St. Elmo has taken the ship under his protection. A more common, and the rational view, is thus given by Longfellow:

> "Last night I saw St. Elmo's stars
> With their glimmering lanterns, all at play,
> On the tops of the masts, and the tips of the spars,
> And I knew we should have foul weather to-day.
> Cheerily, my hearties!—yo-heave-oh!
> Brail up the mainsail and let her go,
> As the winds will, and St. Antonio."

This phenomenon has been noticed from the earliest

times. Shakespeare wrote three centuries ago, in "The Tempest:"

> *Prospero.*— "Hast thou, spirit,
> Performed, to point the tempest that I bid thee?"
> *Ariel.*— "To every article.
> I boarded the King's ship: now on the beak,
> Now in the waist, the deck, in every cabin,
> I flamed amazement: sometimes I'd divide,
> And burn in many places: on the topmast,
> The yards and bowsprit would I flame distinctly;
> Then meet and join."

When Lysander was about to set sail from Lampsacus to attack the Athenian fleet, "Castor and Pollux" appeared upon each side of the Lacedemonian admiral's vessel, greatly encouraging him. Such were the names of the strange lights among the ancients: and ever and anon we find record of their appearance.

This title needs explanation. This peculiar halo is not confined to the sea, nor to inanimate objects. The electric aureole has been frequently observed upon persons, and has always been considered a good omen. The Spartan Gylippus on his march to raise the siege of Syracuse, saw a star upon his lance and rejoiced at the token of divine favor. Nearly every tyro in Latin is familiar with the tale that Servius Tullius, when a child, was found asleep in his cradle with flames playing about him, and was in consequence educated like a prince, and became king of Rome. Stories of halos about Constantine the Great, and the Visigoth emperor Wamba, are also told. It is said that during Cæsar's African war, flames sprang from the standards of the fifth legion during a stormy night: and at a time when Rome, almost in despair at the triumphs of Carthage and the death of two Scipios in Spain, was seriously meditating the abandonment of the contest, Lucius Marcius ventured upon a harangue to encourage the dispirited legions. While he spoke, a flame rested upon his helmet. Roused by the wonderful mark of divine favor, the Romans went forth yet again, and gained one of their greatest victories. What might have been the fate of the world if Carthage, not Rome, had prevailed? Who dare assert that an electric flame has not changed the destinies of the universe?

But the earliest story of this sort comes from the famed expedition of the *Argo,* in search of the Golden Fleece. During a fearful storm Orpheus invoked the gods of Samothracia; and immediately divine lights appeared upon the heads of Castor and Pollux, two members of the party, and the storm ceased. So after death the two mythical heroes were promoted a place among the demi-gods, and became the especial patrons of sailors: and the strange lights on shipboard were supposed to indicate their presence. A single light, however, was supposed to bode evil, and to be the work of the mischief-making Helena.

Since the extension of travel and scientific research, this phenomenon has been so frequently observed as to be no longer considered remarkable; and it is supposed to be due to electric clouds or currents coming in direct contact with objects, so that instead of the flash of lightning from a distance, there is a steady discharge, often with some hissing or crackling sound, noticeable at the brushes of any electric machine; in fact, the noise is seldom absent. It almost invariably appears before or after a thunder storm: and has hardly ever been observed during one. To this same cause must be attributed the occasional showers of luminous rain and dust.

But no amount of science can rob such appearances of their terrors for the uninitiated. Of scores of instances we might name, a single one will suffice. Prof. Siemens tells of an unusual electric disturbance during a Khamsin, while his party and his Arab guides were upon the summit of the great pyramid. Hearing a hissing noise as the wind rose, he at length concluded it must be due to electricity: and "holding up a full wine-bottle, the head of which was coated with tin foil," the same hissing was increased. The bottle was then wrapped with moist paper, to increase its capacity. Even before this, a severe shock could be obtained from the head of the bottle.

"The Arabs, who for some time had been looking on with astonishment at our proceedings, came to the conclusion that we were practicing magic, and insisted upon our leaving the pyramid. Their remonstrances being of no avail, they now wanted to use the right of the stronger, and to make us descend by force. I retreated to the highest stone block and loaded my bottle as strongly as possible, while the leader of the Arabs seized me by the other hand and was endeavoring to drag me down. At this critical moment, I touched him with the neck of the bottle, and the effects of the shock it produced were such as to surpass my keenest expectations. The son of the desert, whose nerves had never before felt a similar commotion, fell flat down upon the ground, as if struck by lightning; and then springing up with a dreadful howl, soon vanished out of sight, followed by all his comrades."

These cases of halos and electric aureoles thus far mentioned, have clearly played a far more important part in the history of nations than the more frequently occurring lightning stroke, merely because of the wonderful hold they have had upon the superstitious tendency of man. Leave Servius Tullius out of the history of Rome, or leave out the speech and aureole of Marcius, and who can say how different the face of the earth might be?

More frequently observed, and because of its frequency, comparatively unheeded in northern climes, is the aurora, which in the temperate zone has frequently inspired terror equal to the earthquake, though absolutely harmless. The writer recalls that a bright aurora not so very many years ago caused not a few superstitious folk to believe the end of the world was at hand. They believed the red streamers to be the chariot of fire in which the Lord was speeding earthward. This was the great aurora of September 3, 1859, which was visible from the United States to Siberia, from the Cape of Good Hope and Australia to the north of Europe. It was the most tremendous ever known, and well calculated to terrify the superstitious.*

Humboldt, and others since, have supposed the aurora to be light emitted by the earth itself; but to-day its electric character is proven beyond a doubt. Electric discharges passed through a tube containing greatly rarefied dry air produce the same effect on a small scale; and every aurora produces a powerful disturbance of magnetic instruments. In most cases, they are attended by a hissing, crackling noise: so the Siberians are wont to say that "the raging host is passing."

We find occasional references to the aurora among ancient writers, but little attempt to explain it. So we have even few myths, it not being common enough in warmer climes to hold a place in popular tales. But in Iceland, and more northern regions, it is of constant and brilliant occurrence, merely because it requires dry air, and the coldest air is the driest. So among Scandinavian races appears the myth embodied by Longfellow in the "Saga of King Olaf." The war god, Thor, speaks:

---

*And even so late as 1872, the brilliant aurora which was seen as far south as Alexandria, was believed by the intelligent Parisians to forebode terrible wars, and the speedy overthrow of the hated Germans, who had so lately trampled their capital and their pride. And in earlier days the northern light had been deemed the harbinger of war, famine or pestilence.

> "The light thou beholdest
> Stream through the heavens
> In flashes of crimson,
> Is but my red beard,
> Blown by the night wind,
> Affrighting the nations."

And Scott has told us of the belief in Scotland and the northern isles, of spirits abroad in the upper air:

> "The monk gazed long on the lovely moon,
> Then into the night he looked forth:
> And red and bright, the streamers light,
> Were dancing in the glowing north.
> So had he seen, in fair Castile,
> The youth in glittering squadrons start,
> Sudden the flying jennet wheel,
> And hurl the unexpected dart.
> He knew by the streams that shot so bright,
> That spirits were riding the Northern light."

The light emitted by the aurora varies much in intensity. Ordinarily it is not greater than that of the moon in her first quarter; but a few instances are recorded where it was powerful enough to make itself perceptible by day; and on one occasion it was strong enough at night to cast a shadow in the midst of a Newfoundland fog. As the phenomenon has been carefully studied only within a century, it is not safe to affirm with certainty what records of the past three hundred years have induced many to believe; that it is of special frequency at periods of one hundred and fifty years. This can only apply to the temperate zones; for in the polar world it is to be seen on almost every clear still night.

M. Martins has given us a striking picture of the auroras. "At times they are simple diffused gleams or luminous patches; at others, quivering rays of pure white which run across the sky, starting from the horizon as if an invisible pencil were being drawn over the celestial vault. At times it stops in its course: the incomplete rays

LAND OF THE AURORA.

do not reach the zenith, but the aurora continues at some other point; a bouquet of rays darts forth, spreads out into a fan, then becomes pale and dies out. At other times long golden draperies float above the head of the spectator, and take a thousand folds and undulations, as if agitated by the wind. They appear to be at but a slight elevation in the atmosphere, and it seems strange that the rustling of the folds, as they double back on each other, is not audible. Generally a luminous bow is seen in the north; a black segment separates it from the horizon, its dark color forming a contrast with the pure white or red of the bow, which darts forth the rays, extends, becomes divided, and soon presents the appearance of a luminous fan, which fills the northern sky, and mounts nearly to the zenith, where the rays, uniting, form a crown, which in its turn, darts forth luminous jets in all directions. The sky then looks like a cupola of fire: blue, green, red, yellow and white vibrate in the palpitating rays of the aurora. But this brilliant spectacle lasts only a few minutes; the crown first ceases to emit luminous jets, and then gradually dies out; a diffuse light fills the sky; here and there a few luminous patches, resembling light clouds, open and close with an incredible rapidity, like a heart that is beating very fast. They soon get pale in their turn; everything fades away and becomes confused; the aurora seems to be in its death-throes; the stars, which its light had obscured, shine with a renewed brightness; and the long polar night, sombre and profound, again assumes its sway over the icy solitudes of earth and ocean."

In the presence of such brilliancy and beauty, both poet and artist may despair. It may be copied only by the master hand that sent it flaming through the heavens. There is naught under the sun whereunto to liken it, and it is the electric flash which men may least fear; and yet, even it has wrought evil at times; for its magnetic power disturbs the compass; and the electric storms it betokens have more than once in the past caused electric wires to set objects near them on fire. I well remember the powerful electric disturbances that attended a magnificent aurora in 1884, which was visible as far as southern Arkansas. Depots were fired in many places by electric switch-boards; one in Pennsylvania taking fire four times. During this electric storm, telegraphs and telephones were temporarily useless.

Such are the phenomena presented in the atmosphere by this most mysterious power. Dreadful in the lightning's leap, strange and uncanny in the aureole's glow, wildly and weirdly beautiful in the flickering flash and flow of the Northern Light, we have seen that, though it has played an important part in the history of the world because of its appeal to man's superstition, it is notwithstanding the occasional bolt of death, to be considered, while one of the most powerful and universal, one of the least to be feared of all the forces of nature; and is practicably responsible for few great disasters.

CHAPTER XIII.

RAIN, HAIL AND SNOW.

"I bring fresh showers for the thirsty flowers,
    From the seas and the streams,
I bear light shade for the leaves when laid
    In their noonday dreams.
From my wings are shaken the dews that waken
    The sweet birds every one,
When rocked to rest on their mother's breast,
    As she dances about the sun.
I wield the flail of the lashing hail,
    And whiten the green plains under,
And then again I dissolve in rain,
    And laugh as I pass in thunder.

I am the daughter of earth and water,
    And the nursling of the sky,
I pass through the pores of the ocean and shores,
    I change, but I can not die.
For after the rain, when with never a stain
    The pavilion of heaven is bare,
And the winds and sunbeams with their convex gleams,
    Build up the blue dome of air,
I silently laugh at my own cenotaph,
    And out of the caverns of rain,
Like a child from the womb, like a ghost from the tomb,
    I arise and unbuild it again."

THE cloud is well worth Shelley's admiration; for though it be but a vague oppressive mist when it enwraps, yet afar it assumes either beauty or gloom, as its seeming whims may dictate. Few are they who have never paused in silent admiration of some beautiful fleecy spirit of the upper deep, changing every instant like the shifting figures of a kaleidoscope, or presenting fantastic likenesses of natural objects, or ever and anon presenting pictures of strange monsters, such as only the superstitious and timid can imagine. Often in times past have nations stood aghast at the portentous signs observed in season of some great calamity. A lurid beam of light from the hidden sun, darting through a rift in the clouds, has been reported as a flaming sword. Shortly before the destruction of Jerusalem, the sky was filled with horses and chariots, rushing to battle. After the siege the wretched survivors recognized too late what was the purpose of the warning.

Wordsworth speaks of these bizarre fantasies:

> "Lo! In the burning west the craggy nape
> Of a proud Ararat! and thereupon,
> The Ark, her melancholy voyage done.
> Yon rampant cloud mimics a lion's shape,
> There combats a huge crocodile—agape,
> A golden spear to swallow! and that brown
> And mossy grove, so near yon blazing town,
> Stirs and recedes—destruction to escape,
> Yet all is harmless—as the Elysian shades
> Where spirits dwell in undisturbed repose,
> Silently disappear and quickly fades,
> Meek Nature's evening comment on the shows
> That for oblivion take their daily birth
> From all the fuming vanities of Earth."

And naught can present so sombre and terrifying an aspect as those phantoms of the air, when mailed with the lightning and flying with the storm.

Yet, upon the cloud the welfare of the human race is dependent, as much as upon any other force in nature: for rain or drouth, famine or plenty, snow or flood, all follow in its path. More than once has rain or storm decided the destiny of nations. Far different might our own lot have been, if that bitter storm of Christmas night, 1777, had not given Washington an opportunity of surprising the carousing Hessians in Trenton, and so reviving the drooping spirits of his countrymen. Hardly would he have escaped, but that the sudden frost hardened the ground and enabled him to steal away by night with his artillery, leaving the chafing Cornwallis the privilege of attacking the deserted camp on the Assanpink in the morning. It was a winter storm that enabled the bold Vermonters to surprise the frowning fortress on the upper Hudson. Napoleon could invade Russia, and drive the Cossack pell-mell before him; no mortal power could control the elements; and his splendid hosts melted away like snow in the breath of the icy storm; and once more the Cossack sang to his steed:

> "Now fiercely neigh, my gallant gray; thy breast is broad and ample.
> Thy hoofs shall prance o'er the fields of France and the pride of her heroes trample."

Again the "Man of Destiny" was conquered by the elements.

> "There was a sound of revelry by night"

as the dread combat of Waterloo prepared. The plan of the "Genius of War" was superb. But all his contests were problems of artillery. "The Lord is on the side of the strongest battalions and heaviest artillery"—bold manner of saying that "when one seeks for the reason of the successes of great generals, one is surprised to find that they did everything necessary to insure them." But he who would insure success must have the clouds at his beck. That night it rained. The mud crippled his artillery and left the contest to the rifle and bayonet. Waterloo was lost. A shower of rain changed the face of Europe—the history of the world.

Scriptural narrative and the sage Josephus tell us how the Philistine host were cut down by the motley rabble of almost unarmed Israelites, routed mainly by a terrific thunder storm that beat in their faces, flamed upon their weapons, and transformed the disciplined army into a panic-stricken multitude. What might have been the future of Israel and the Jewish faith, but for the intervention of that storm? We need not multiply instances. The causes that produce the different phenomena of

condensation in rain, hail and snow, are not known. Rainfall is the most indefinite of all the atmospheric phenomena in location, quantity, frequency, and distribution. The winds do not vary greatly, one year with another; but such is not the case with the rain. Sometimes the condensation is slow and the moisture falls on the earth as mist. Some suppose that the rainfall is due merely to the cold of great elevations: and this would seem to be well supported by the prevalence of fogs on the Newfoundland banks, where the constant cold current and the occasional icebergs produce a similar degree of cold at sea level, condensing the moisture from the warm seas southward. Others urge that two masses of saturated air of different temperature combine, necessarily condensing the surplus; and the Newfoundland banks are again referred to as an illustration.

Light on fog-banks often presents peculiar and beautiful illusions. The writer remembers having seen a whole town apparently wrapped in flames, the effect being produced by the lights from many windows shining through a light mist that was curling and twisting before a light breeze. Similar causes produce the peculiar halos and mock-suns and mock-moons not infrequently seen in the sky. These, and the beautiful rainbow, all depend upon the reflection and refraction of light in passing through vapor masses. These curious spectacles once had no little terror for the ignorant and superstitious. Shakespeare doubtless alludes to some such case in the dialogue between Hubert and King John, making Hubert narrate an exaggerated version of the facts, as the superstitiously inclined rabble reported it:

> *Hubert.*—" My lord, they say five moons were seen to-night;
> Four fixed; and the fifth did whirl about
> The other four with wondrous motion."
>
> *King John.*— " Five moons?"
>
> *Hubert.*—" Old men and beldams in the streets
> Do prophecy upon it dangerously;
> Young Arthur's death is common in their mouths."

Sometimes an appearance more terrifying to the uninitiated is seen. The traveler in Germany may hear strange myths of specters that frequent the mountains. It was long said that spirits dwelt on the summit of the Matterhorn. Gigantic phantoms roamed the Harz Mountains. One of the best known of all these apparitions is the famous "Specter of the Brocken." The wanderer on the lonely height at sunrise may see upon a neighboring summit a gigantic shadowy figure, moving about, and mimicking every motion of the traveler. Of course, it is but his shadow on a neighboring fog-bank; but the solution remained a mystery long enough to terrify many a simple peasant into needless invocations of the saints. But similar appearances are occasionally observable in many localities. The Spaniard Ulloa records that on the mountain Pambamarca, in Peru, he saw his shadow on the cloud surrounded by three complete circular rainbows. The same peculiarity has been frequently noticed elsewhere, but never on so grand a scale. We find no peculiar myths concerning halos in general, it being generally considered that they announce the approach of rain; and the fog-bank is of no especial danger save to the seaman, or the traveler overtaken and blinded by one in mountain fastnesses; though their depressing influence has led one writer to exclaim:

> "Fly, fly, profane fogs! fly hence far away,
> Taint not the pure springs of the springing day
> With your dull influence; it is for you
> To sit and scowl upon night's heavy brow."

And the fog, though not ornamental—unless we except that dry haze, the Indian summer—may be useful in preventing a frost, or in keeping a parched earth from drying too rapidly. But for this last, all the world prefers the rain, and sings with Longfellow:

SPECTER OF THE BROCKEN.

> "How beautiful is the rain!
> After the dust and heat,
> In the broad and fiery street,
> In the narrow lane,
> How beautiful is the rain!
> How it clatters along the roofs
> Like the tramp of hoofs!
> How it gushes and struggles out,
> From the throat of the overflowing spout,
> Across the window pane it pours and pours,
> And swift and wide,
> With a muddy tide,
> Like a river, down the gutter roars
> The rain, the welcome rain."

Not always welcome; for we find the same poet moaning:"

> "The day is cold, and dark, and dreary,
> It rains, and the rain is never weary."

And certainly, the farmer who looks through the driving rain at his ruined crops has little sentiment left to expend upon its beauty. But the world over, after a rain every feature of a landscape stands out with singular clearness; the haze commonly prevalent has for the nonce disappeared.

The amount of rainfall varies so vastly in different countries, that it would be tedious to the reader to enter upon a detail of the different amounts. In general it is greatest upon those portions of the land first reached by regular incoming sea winds. So in South America, Peru and southern Ecuador are practically without rain, as the Andes and the Amazon forests deprive the trade winds of their moisture ere they reach the Pacific coast; while southern Chili seldom sees the sun; lying in the track of the return trades, whose moisture is at once precipitated by the Andes. So in India the monsoon which pours deluges of water along the southwestern coasts, brings but twenty-three inches a year to the central plateau; and by the time Central Asia is reached, it is so dry the steppes of

Tartary must remain almost a desert. And in our own land, we find in general the heaviest rain from the eastern coast to the central region: while the western plateau along the eastern slopes of the Rockies is unusually dry, and liable to protracted drouths: and in the Mojave desert, and in southeastern California, the rainfall is less than two inches per year. On the North Pacific coast the rainfall increases rapidly, as in the southern Andes; but in general our highest mean rainfall is in the southern portion of the Gulf States. The highest average in the world is so far credited to Sumatra, one hundred and thirty inches. This, of course, refers to tracts of considerable size; for a small tract in Assam, on a mountain slope, where is the town of Cherrapungee, has a rainfall of four hundred and ninety-three and two-tenth inches per annum—more than forty-one feet! Twenty-two feet of rain have fallen there in a single month! A better idea of this may be obtained by observing that our average rainfall, from Missouri eastward, is about three feet a year. The rains of the Amazon and Congo basins are enormous, and would suffice to swell our Mississippi to as great volume as either of them. On the other hand, the lowest recorded rainfall for a large tract is that of Greenland—fifteen and five-tenth inches; while Australia, with fifteen and seven-tenth inches, is but little better off. It may be mentioned here, that the term "mean rainfall" includes snow also: ten inches of snow being ordinarily estimated as one inch of rain.

A point long mooted, now considered as definitely settled, was, the influence of forests upon rainfall. There was no doubt that forests retarded the descent of water into the streams, and so lessened the danger of floods; and observations of late years has shown that the forest also increases the amount of rainfall, aiding in the work of condensa-

RAIN, HAIL AND SNOW. 255

tion. In the northern lumber regions, the rainfall in the cleared tracts is less than in the time of the forests, while floods are more sudden and dangerous.

These general features being noticed, mention of a few extraordinary rainfalls may be of interest. The most remarkable rain in one day occurred September 13, 1879, at Purneah, in Bengal, when thirty-five inches fell; about as much as Illinois gets in a year. At Nagina, thirty-two and four-tenth inches fell. Some extraordinary showers have been recorded in our own country, the most rapid being one and one-half inches in five minutes: the most rapid long one, ten inches in three hours; but no record of a day in anywise approaches the Bengal rain.

A peculiar phenomenon of occasional occurrence in the Western States is that of "cloud-bursts," or "water-spouts" as they are sometimes called, when immense masses of water fall in a few minutes. As the entire amount of moisture that can be held by the atmosphere at ordinary temperature would make but two inches of rain, it must follow that to produce such downpours as are here recorded, immense quantities of moisture from a wide area must be drawn in and condensed rapidly at a single point. Perhaps this is done by a reverse cyclonic movement, the atmosphere rapidly descending in a "spout," instead of ascending.

August 11, 1876, a tremendous downpour occurred at Fort Sully, Dakota: "and on the opposite side of the Missouri River, the water draining from a canon was reported to have moved out in a solid bank three feet deep and two hundred feet wide." Two others of nearly equal violence occurred during the same month: one in Utah, and one in Kansas. "June 12, 1879, on Beaver Creek, ninety miles south of Deadwood, Dakota, there was a cloudburst, which, without a gradual rise of water, in a few minutes covered the country and drowned eleven persons." A cloud-burst in June, 1884, sent a torrent eight feet deep from the hillside into Jefferson, Montana, drowning several persons. Another one in June, 1885, destroyed a town in Mexico, drowning over one hundred and seventy of its eight hundred inhabitants. Cloud-bursts near Pittsburg, on the night of July 25, 1874, destroyed $500,000 worth of property, and drowned or crushed in the wrecks, one hundred and thirty-four persons. A cloud-burst in Arizona, August 6, 1881, changed the Hassayampa River from a dry ravine at sunset to a river a mile wide and from two to fifteen feet deep by 11 P. M.; by noon next day the river was again dry. Two days later a downpour at Central City, Colorado, suddenly left from four to six feet of water in the two principal streets.

Snow is practically unknown over two-thirds of the land surface of the earth, and the damage done by it is confined largely to the inland regions of the temperate zone. And even then heavy snowfalls do no great injury unless followed by extremely cold wind. The blizzard laden with "icy sand" is fearful.

> "The night sets in on a world of snow,
> And the air grows sharp and chill,
> And the warning roar of a fearful blow
> Is heard on the distant hill.
> And the Norther! See! On the mountain peak,
> In his breath, how the old trees writhe and shriek!
> He shouts on the plains, Ho-ho! Ho-ho!
> He drives from his nostrils the blinding snow,
> And growls with a savage will."

The extreme ranges of temperature produced suddenly by high area or anti-cyclonic storms are the most dangerous features of the blizzard; while the only damage done by snow is to blind the person caught away from home, and cause him to lose his way. The past ten years have been marked by severe storms in our own winter season, the most terrible being that of January 11, 1888, when the wind blew from thirty to fifty miles an hour, and large numbers of persons in the west were frozen, and thousands of cattle perished. At Helena, Montana, the thermometer fell fifty degrees in four and one-half hours. The snow-laden wind reached a speed of forty miles an hour at Galveston, Texas. At Brownsville, Texas, the temperature fell forty degrees in eight hours. Two months later came an exceedingly heavy snow attended by high winds, in the eastern Middle States. This is popularly known as the "New York blizzard." Snow drifted in many places ten or fifteen feet deep.

> "The fence was lost, and the wall of stone,
> The windows blocked, and the well-curb gone,
> The haystack had grown to a mountain lift,
> And the woodpile looked like a monstrous drift,
> As it lay by the farmer's door."

The chief damage in all snow storms results from the temporary obstruction of roads and cessation of business. No very great destruction of human life has ever resulted, save in case of armies overtaken by the storm. Napoleon lost four hundred and fifty thousand men on his Russian expedition. Both armies suffered terribly in the recent Russo-Turkish war, as they lay facing each other at Shipka Pass.

The constant accumulations of snow in the colder regions of the earth produce those immense rivers of ice known as glaciers, the fragments breaking from which as they enter the sea are known as icebergs. These, borne by currents to the southward, have no small influence in modifying the climate. In mountainous regions the accumulations of snow and ice produce snow-slides and avalanches; but owing to their entirely local character, the damage wrought by them is comparatively insignificant, not even approaching the lightning in the total.

Hail has been far more destructive. As stated elsewhere, the cause of hail is hitherto unexplained. The storm usually travels in narrow belts. Many are the wonderful tales told of it. It is said that May 8, 1802, a mass of ice weighing eleven hundred pounds fell in Hungary. Again, we hear of an ice-block the size of an elephant, which fell near Seringapatam, in the reign of Tippoo Sahib. The good father Huc, in his travels in Tartary, reported the fall of an ice-block the size of a millstone, which, in very warm weather, required three days to melt. And we are told that in the time of Charlemagne, there fell hailstones fifteen feet long, eleven feet wide and six feet thick. All these we steadfastly do not believe.

Yet, there are well authenticated records of many disastrous hail storms and enormous hailstones. A storm in France, in 1788, traveled in two bands: one, four hundred and twenty by ten miles; the other, five hundred by five miles. Five million dollars worth of property was destroyed. In 1865 a severe storm swept a wide path from Bordeaux to Belgium, accumulating in such masses that it was not all melted in one or two localities for four days. One bed was one and one-fourth miles long and two-fifths of a mile wide, containing twenty-one million cubic feet. Doubtless similar accumulations in depressions, adhering together, gave rise to the tales of enormous blocks mentioned above.

An enormous hail storm in India, in 1853, is said to have killed eighty-four persons and three thousand cattle. During a storm at Naini Tal, in 1855, hailstones weighing one and one-half pounds fell. Our own land has had a number of severe hail storms within the past ten years, that have done immense damage to crops, and occasionally killed cattle, while smaller animals have perished by hundreds. Frequent are the records of hailstones as large as oranges, goose-eggs, and occasionally as large as a fist, with gathered drifts two or three feet deep. Europe has also had several of her smaller towns nearly destroyed by combined flood and hail. Yet, none of these equal in fatality the great hail storm of two years since at Moradabad, India.

It smashed in windows, glass doors and the lighter roofs, "The verandas were blown away by the wind. A great part of the roof fell in, and the massive pucca portico was blown down. The walls shook. It was nearly dark outside, and hailstones of enormous size were dashed down with a force which I have never seen anything to equal. * * * There were long ridges of hail one or two feet in depth. * * * Not a house in the civil station that did not receive the most serious injury.

"Two hundred and thirty deaths in all have been reported up to the present time. The total number may be safely put as under two hundred and fifty. Men caught in the open and without shelter, were simply pounded to death by the hail."

Spain and southern France have on record some showers of extremely large hailstones. In 1829, masses of ice weighing four and one-half pounds fell at Cazorta, Spain. Houses were stove-in by them. During a hurricane in the south of France, in 1844, there fell ice-masses weighing eleven pounds.

Mysterious and ominous to those ignorant of their cause have been the many showers of "ink, blood, sulphur," falls of red or green snow, and similar phenomena. Such things were believed to betoken the wrath of God, and to forebode war, famine, pestilence, flood, and other dire calamities. Of course, the good people knew exactly what any shower meant—after the calamity occurred. When it didn't occur, the shower was simply a warning.

That such phenomena are readily explained goes without saying; and not a few of the wise of days past have refused to be seriously alarmed, though they could not find a correct solution of the mystery. Some of the philosophic minds of other days endeavored to explain these occurrences by supposing blood vaporized from battle-fields was mingled with rain, not knowing that the red portion of the blood can not evaporate.

The microscope has solved these mysteries. The rains of blood are merely stained by earthy matter: sometimes organic, gathered by the wind; sometimes volcanic dust, thrown out by eruptions; and in one case, where numerous blood-spots appeared on houses and fences in Provence, in 1608, and the priests asserted it was the work of the devil, the spots at length proved to be the excrement of butterflies. Rains of melted sulphur have been found to owe their color to the yellow pollen of pine trees. Ink is merely sooty rain-water. Showers of this character are more frequent than might be supposed. More than a score have occurred in Europe in the present century; and a number in this country. Red and green snow owe their color to microscopic vegetable life, and are quite commonly met with in the Arctic world. One bold headland has long been known as Crimson Cliff, from the extensive deposits of red snow there.

CHAPTER XIV.

FLOODS IN THE SOUTH.

"'Mother dear, the water's coming after!
   Mother, 'tis between us and the hill!'
Looking down, they see the flood, with laughter
   Lapping idly 'neath the window sill.

     *   *   *   *   *   *

'Mother, in the water we are wading!
   Mother, it grows deeper as we go!'
'Hasten, children! hasten—day is fading!'
   Higher creeps the river, black and slow.

     *   *   *   *   *   *

'Mother, 'tis so deep, and we are dripping!
   Mother, we are sinking! Haste, oh haste!'
In her arms uplifting them and gripping,
   On she plunges, wading to the waist.

     *   *   *   *   *   *

Flowers the river snatches, while it calls so—
   Flowers its lean hands never snatched before,
Will it snatch these human flowers also,
   Where they cling, sad creatures of the shore?"

EVERY country is confronted with a serious problem in its great rivers. In some lands the only problem is, how to get rid of flood-water as quickly as possible: in others, comes the additional question of securing sufficient water for irrigation during the dry season. Egypt occupies an anomalous position, the latter question being the the only one of any practical interest. Without rains, she depends on the rise of the Nile for her existence, and no one dreams of such a thing as endeavoring to check the overflow. During seed-time the fellaheen may be seen sometimes in mud knee-deep, busily planting their fields; and in summer they may be seen hoisting water from the stream and emptying it into their irrigating ditches.

In our own land, we have hitherto had no need of irrigation, except in those districts where there is no fear of a flood; such as the arid regions of our southwestern states. In China, the people are contending with both sides of the problem; and their success in the second feature has not greatly surpassed their achievements in the first. In most other lands, the flood problem is the chief one. The Amazon at flood time rises from sixty to one hundred feet, and its volume is almost inconceivable. But since the larger part of its course lies in an almost uninhabited region, the high water gives no concern to the people. The Orinoco rises so high, and is in such a level region, that during part of the year one of its upper tributaries flows backward and reaches the Amazon.

The great length of the Mississippi and Missouri present the gravest difficulties. The sources of each lie in regions where heavy snows fall during a considerable part of the winter; and all the melting snows of the central portion of the country—from western Pennsylvania to Colorado, Montana and central Dakota—must find their way to the sea by way of the single stream. By reason of the difference in latitude and altitude, the melted snows of the head-waters usually swell the lower river in May and early in June, after the spring rains are over. But it quite often happens that after unusually heavy winter snows the warm weather sets in in the mountains very early; so that the great floods of the upper valleys reach the lower river just when extremely heavy rains are prevalent in the central and southern regions. This forms a combination that is terrible to combat, and is the cause of all the trouble. The present system is effective in ordinary cases; but for the occasional great exceptions it has hitherto proved insufficient. We do not seem to be any nearer a practical solution of the problem than when it first presented itself. Yet, the government of the United States spends millions of dollars every year in attempts which have, so far at least, proved totally futile to confine the great river within its banks, and so avoid the perils which every spring threaten an area larger than all New England and the Middle States.

The wonderful and often terrible changes that come with the changes of season, and which produce such effects as the illustrations show, are simply inconceivable to one who has not seen them. That a stream so quiet and comparatively small as the Mississippi is at low water, should become a raging torrent of twenty miles average width, and ten feet average depth from shore to shore, throughout the eleven hundred miles from Cairo to the sea, is simply incredible until one has seen it. This river, however, did that in 1882, when the great general overflow occurred. Unnumbered lives were lost that year, and the damage to property was never even estimated. Details were hard to get when communication was so nearly cut off as it then was; and after the floods were over, no effort was made to reckon the extent of the disaster.

Since that spring the reports have not indicated any flood equal to the present one; and the only reason why this year has not proved as disastrous as 1882, is that the levees have been strengthened since then. The fact, however, that the levee system has, as a whole, successfully withstood the pressure of the highest water known for many years, is by no means as reassuring as it seems on first consideration; for there is grave reason to believe that the levees themselves serve to increase the very danger against which they are a guard.

The planters of the earlier days made efforts to protect themselves by means of "levees:" a name given by the

TROPICAL FLOOD.

French to dykes, or artificial banks, and meaning simply "raised places." But of later years, both state and national resources have been spent freely in endeavoring to curb the restless giant. More than $25,000,000 has been spent in this way since the war. The Mississippi River Commission, organized in 1879, under the supervision of the War Department, as the Signal Service has been, had nominally in view the increasing of facilities for navigation; but as the methods employed for the two objects have necessarily been much the same, no little has been done for protection.

The character of the lower Mississippi and its valley gravely increase the difficulties of the case. Its bed has been worn for ages through a somewhat elevated region, and at present the resultant valley has a width varying from twenty to one hundred and fifty miles. The result has been that the channel of the river shifts continually, and is extremely crooked, literally turning time and again to every conceivable point of the compass. These curves present the most vexatious features the levee system must contend with; for it is easily perceived that the levee on the convex side of the bend in the river has the current directed full against it, adding the great eroding power of the water to the weight it must sustain.

"The levees are relied on as the chief aid to the work of the commission, but the commission does not construct them, or even work directly to strengthen them. These levees are nothing more than artificial banks or heaps of soil shoveled up along the line of the natural banks. The commission is working to narrow the wide places in the river, so as to secure a uniform width of three thousand feet. This is done by constructing revetments, consisting principally of mattrasses of wire and brush, which are secured by rubble-stone. In other places great quantities of stone are

MAKING MATS FOR LEVEE FRONTS.

dumped, and various similar means are used to encourage the scour in the shallower parts of the river, and also to prevent the undermining of the natural or artificial banks.

"On a convex shore, where the water is shoal, the levee has been carried along the river edge as near as possible, as there is no danger, under such conditions, of a caving bank. Where the bank is liable to give way, the levees are placed further back, and where a break in the levee itself has occurred from the caving of the bank, loops are made, joining the two broken parts. It must be borne in mind that the banks proper along the river are about forty feet high above low water, and as the river rises five to seven feet over these banks, the levees are constructed of sufficient height to restrain the waters within their proper limits. The material is found on the spot, either clay or sand, as the case may be. A so-called "muck" ditch a few feet wide is dug along the center line of the projected levee, down to where the earth is comparatively free from all organic matter, such as grass and roots of trees. By this method some adhesion to the ground is gained, and the artificial construction is not easily swept away. The earth is taken from the front of the levee line as near the water as the circumstances will permit. Standard levees have a "crown," or width at the top, of eight feet, except in the case of a very low levee, when the "crown" is not less than its height. The side slopes are one vertical to three or three and one-half horizontal. Present levees are carried up from two to three feet above the high-water mark of their position."

The river channel, in general, in the upper danger region, adheres to the right side of the valley, and on the left the danger lies chiefly at a few points where the bluffs recede considerably from the river. Throughout the middle and lower flood districts the bends of the stream are so numerous and capricious that the danger lies equally upon either side of the stream. Hence, the levee system is not uniform. The whole alluvial front of the river is leveed on the left bank, the principal line extending from Horn Lake, just below Memphis, to Vicksburg, covering the great Yazoo Basin. On the right bank of the river there are four principal sections which are liable to be overflowed. The first is known as St. Francis front, which runs from Commerce, Missouri, to the St. Francis River. The White River front is the second, extending from Helena, Arkansas, to the mouth of the White and Arkansas Rivers. The third and fourth, known as the Tensas and the Atchafalaya fronts, run respectively from the Arkansas River to the Red River in Louisiana, and from the Red River to New Orleans. The first two sections have received no government work except in limited localities, where it was merely incidental to the work of river improvement undertaken by the commission; and those fronts are everywhere exposed to the overflow, except where private enterprise has done the work. The Social Circle Levee, near Laconia, Arkansas, is an example, and a notable one, of what has been done by the residents. These uprotected tracts have all been submerged, and the low lands turned into an enormous lake.

The overflow waters that pass over the upper part of this section spread over the northeastern part of Arkansas as far back as the high ground, reaching their greatest width about opposite Memphis, and then pass back into the Mississippi by way of the St. Francis River. The overflow below Helena is carried back by the White River. From Arkansas City down, the river, comprising the third and fourth sections, is completely leveed.

Throughout all the lowland districts are hundreds of farms and valuable plantations, the soil being built up by ages of alluvial deposits. Most of the towns are built on high ground; there being a few notable exceptions. A general flood in this valley means that millions of acres of land are submerged, and such crops as are in the fields are destroyed. More frequently, the land is flooded just

STRUGGLE TO HOLD THE LEVEE.

at planting time, and the land remains wet too long to allow certain crops to be planted in season. Thus, the water in the flooded districts may abate in time to allow a fair cotton crop; while the chance for corn is lost. Fences and small outbuildings are floated away, and often large numbers of stock are drowned; but, after all, the chief damage is usually indirect: the evil of hindrance rather than of destruction. Further, the retiring water leaves numerous pools and marshes that are rank breeders of malaria, adding vastly to the unhealthiness of the country.

In many places there are marshy or timbered tracts adjacent to the river that are not available for cultivation. In these districts the levees are often erected at the border of the cultivable land, so that the river has a large area of waste land over which to spread the surplus water without doing any injury. Such areas really aid to reduce the high-water level. In some cases, a second or third levee is built some hundreds of yards to the rear, to serve as a sort of reserve, in case the river break through the first.

Doubtless the reader has pictured to himself a flooded district as something like a stream in a mountain gorge; an immense torrent of water rushing at race-horse speed, uprooting trees, tearing away huge boulders, sweeping away houses in an instant, without a moment's warning, and drowning young and old by scores. If such be his idea, he will find it necessary to remodel it; or, rather, to cast it away entirely. Let him follow a guide to the scene of danger. A great levee, the protection of thousands of acres of rich lands, and perhaps millions of dollars worth of property, is announced unsafe. Sometimes it is decided to abandon the river line, weakened for long distances, and erect a new levee some hundreds of yards to the rear.

But if the design be to hold the line already established, then the scene is an animated one. All along the narrow ridge of earth patrolmen are watching the work at every point. Hundreds of men work day and night throwing up and strengthening the levees, upon which the salvation of the district depends. Break after break occurs,

and it is as fast mended. The waves caused by the rough March winds send great volumes of water splashing over the weak embankment, almost washing the men off their feet. The work is continued all day, force relieving force at night. Thousands of lanterns flashing in the darkness, as the men pass to and fro with wheelbarrows filled with sacks of earth and lumber, present a scene weird and ghostly. At intervals during the night the sound of steam whistles tell of some new break, some new danger to face and overcome. Often the negroes seem little disposed to work, even at good wages, preferring to sit on the levee and fish. But when the danger is fully upon them, they can work furiously. Sometimes, in leading the forlorn hope, some energetic old fellow may shout to his terrified, pious brethren, "Dis is no time for prayin'--go to work!" Out on the border districts where help not easily obtained, even the wives and daughters of planters—ladies of culture and refinement, it may be—sometimes turn out and toil in the mud and rain, contending with the foe that threatens their homes. If the levees before a great city be threatened, as frequently occurs, the scene becomes still more exciting. Business is almost entirely suspended in the city and the clerks in the dry goods stores, the lawyers, the merchants and the common laborers stand shoulder to shoulder with picks and shovels fighting the common enemy. What the outcome will be no one knows. All are alarmed. Hundreds of boats are moored to back-doors, ready for use when the worst shall come. Merchants have placed their goods high up in their stores, hoping the waters will not reach them when they rise. Housekeepers have packed up their goods out of the way of the water and laid in stores enough to last for weeks, in case it becomes necessary to stay indoors for that length of time. All railway communication with the outside world is cut off, nearly all the tracks being several feet under water. The mails are sent miles away, by boat.

Such cases were frequent in the recent floods. Greenville, Mississippi, is one of the towns that suffered much.

"NO TIME FOR PRAYIN'; GO TO WORK!"

The water from crevasses above came down upon the town, and were stopped by a levee around the city. But while the enemy in the rear could be held in check, it was not so easy to repel the attack upon the river front; and here the water won the day. All efforts were in vain. The forlorn and miserable city appeared as though some savage caricaturist had endeavored to perpetrate a burlesque upon Venice. A few skiffs crept about the muddy currents that answered for streets. On outhouses and fences occasionally might be seen a few melancholy looking fowls. Here some grocer paddled about to see if his patrons wanted aught; yonder went a funeral party in a single boat. Many a weary mile would have to be traversed to reach a dry grave. The lower floors of most houses lay beneath the water, and from the second-story disconsolate people looked out upon the turbid waste, wondering what the end would be.

If the scene upon the levee is exciting when efforts are made to avoid breaks, still more so is it when a small break is being closed. The scurrying to and fro; the hoarse shouting of orders; the wild cries for aid from threatened points; men plunging up to their necks in the rushing flood, driving stakes, dragging sacks of earth, heaving in boulders and rubble stone; others bringing timbers and planks from hundreds of yards away; the dim, smoky glare of countless torches; the burly figures of wearied men begrimed almost beyond semblance of humanity—such a picture is more like a strange nightmare that one never forgets.

Then suddenly there is a general melting away of hundreds of feet of the sodden levee. The fight is lost. Scores of the laborers leave for their homes to save what they can of their property. From farm to farm the news spreads. In the dead hour of the night, when all is serene, the dread cry comes, "the levee is broken," and then comes a wild stampede for safety, many in their night clothes, women dragging their babes, husbands carrying their wives, and the poor negroes, wild with terror, unable to do anything but stand and view the scene of the waters rushing to bear them to their doom. Magnificent planta-

FUNERAL DURING THE FLOOD.

tions of yesterday are to-day seas of rushing, foaming water. Here and there in the shallows stand a few shivering, half-starved cattle; and occasionally is seen a family, still hoping that the flood may not be disastrous, clinging to their residence.

The view of a crevasse in an inland levee, miles away from the channel, is strikingly grand; but for those in its path the grandeur is lost in a feeling of despair and danger. The ocean presents a different spectacle, for the ocean has no swift current, and its waves are greater. The foaming mountain torrent can not compare with it, for the mountain torrent is at best but a few yards in breadth. But in the swollen river is found an apparently illimitable expanse of water, heaving restlessly under the swift foot of the wind, or foaming and dashing at the roar of the storm, hurling itself in billows upon the toilers on the levee, and striking them into the ditch beyond, yet, with all the fury expended laterally, rushing seaward almost with the speed of a train. For miles between the levee and the main channel the stream pours through a great forest, or canebrake, or cypress swamp.

The fearful noise of a crevasse may be heard for a long distance. No need to tell the planters far inland the meaning of that distant hoarse murmur. Approaching the break, the murmur swells to a deep sullen roar. The water comes tearing through the dense forest at race-horse speed, not in a broad belt, but closing in from every direction, pouring into that break as into an immense funnel. As far as the eye can penetrate into that dense, gloomy forest, it is raggedly carpeted with a heavy, tossing sheet of snow-white foam. It breaks over stumps, snags and the upturned roots of fallen trees, flinging white clouds of spray up among the branches of trees overhead, mounts in snowy billows over piles of driftwood, it snarls, hisses and roars like some mad monster at everything in its path, and then plows in one solid foaming mass into that raging maelstrom between the ragged, frothy jaws of the crevasse.

"Nearest the break, just as it sweeps into the crevasse, it curls on either side, and huge breakers mark the line where it chafes the crumbling ends of the levee. Once beyond the broken barriers, it plunges into a wild, lonesome-looking swamp, that still shows the tracks of the former disaster. Here, for the first time, the real power of this tremendous flood begins to assert itself. Supple young trees, eight or ten inches in diameter, are bent and stripped of every leaf, their naked branches and twigs whipping the foaming surface of the rustling cataract.

"It sweeps into the standing timber with a hoarse roar, foaming around sturdy trunks, and here and there one sees a tall tree swaying to and fro like a drunken man: then caught in some fierce eddy, it is twisted from its roots, and reeling around and around it falls into that tremendous current and is swept away to swell the tangled dams of drift beyond."

As far inland as the eye can reach there is nothing but flood to be seen, the currents opening out and racing away in every direction. At some distance away may be seen a flooded settlement, the water washing the windows of fifteen or twenty abandoned cottages. On a huge mound some five or six feet out of the outflow, is a group of disconsolate horses and mules who have taken refuge from the rising flood, and other hungry-looking brutes wander over the levee.

But once out of the immediate neighborhood of the break, the character of the scene changes. The current slackens, as the water spreads out like an immense fan, and at length becomes almost imperceptible. It may come in the night, giving no warning of its approach. It steals through the grass-lands like a serpent. The slumbering family hear no sound. The water creeps stealthily around the house, like the Red men in the olden days.

The morning sun finds it lapping uneasily in the breeze against the threshold. The wakening family find it crawling across the floor toward their beds. They look upon a region that appears a vast marsh; grass tops,

SURPRISED BY THE WATER.

bushes, little islets and tall trees, everywhere rising out of the water. In the barnyard the drowsy cattle chew their cuds in peaceful unconsciousness of the wily foe. The pig in the lower corner of the lot grunts contentedly to find his wallow freshly moistened. The quacking duck paddles complacently about the fields. The farmer watches anxiously the progress of the flood, trusting that there may be no necessity of leaving. Valuable property that can not be removed is taken to the second floor, if there be one. A boat, if there be one, is carefully overhauled to be ready for an emergency.

Noon comes. The flood has risen but a few inches. The cattle eye the water curiously. The negroes in their cabins speculate upon the future, and each tells his tale of "hair-breadth 'scapes and ventures" in other days, and one and all agree that "*dis* ain't no flood—sho! no! You orter hab seed the big high water way back in seventy-four. *Dat* was sumfin' like;" and in humble submission to the opinions of some old granny of unknown age and grizzled wool, it is unanimously allowed that "we ain't got no cause to be skeered *dis* time; not much!" So the happy-go-lucky fellows sit and chat, while some oily skinned picaninnies wade to deeper parts of the water, cast in their hooks and begin to swap tales of the wonderful fish their progenitors had caught in other floods, and to wonder if more brilliant achievements may not be recorded of them.

The wind rises. The great crevasse, miles away, has widened till it is hundreds of yards in extent and many feet in depth, pouring upon the land millions of cubic feet of water every minute. With the swelling breeze, the flood goes surging inland in long, low, lazy waves. The planters who have not already taken flight, conclude it is useless to endeavor to remain. If the way is open, the cattle are driven inland to the hills. Some of the negroes straggle after their employers; others cling to their rude log cabins— all they have to lose—it may be that the flood will not be serious. So long as corn meal and bacon abound, they may enjoy an endless picnic. They can fling their lines from time to time into the stream, and perchance vary their repasts with fish-fry or turtle stew.

Evening comes. The lazy waves now nearly reach the window-sills upon the lower floors. The cattle left behind low uneasily as they move about in water knee-deep. No one is near to feed them, and the udders of the cows are swollen with milk. Here and there a mule is seen, stamping impatiently and braying mournfully for lack of feed. The water displays a decided but wayward current, swirling now this way, now that. All the land is covered. Here and there numerous snakes have crawled into the bushes to escape the yellow flood. Out in a lowland tract a deserted shanty bobs idly along, now grounding a moment, now floating lazily around a great tree, finally becoming an item of the great mass of drift that has lodged at the edge of the forest, and swarms with small animals flying from the clutch of the crawling water. The game of the canebrakes and swamp regions has fled to the uplands, and from time to time some needy refugee family, heedless of game laws, adds venison to its scanty store.

The night wears away. The negro cabins are deserted: most have floated away with the growing current. The simple folk have abandoned them. Some have made their way to the levees, hoping for a passing steamer. Others, dwelling above the crevasse, have little to fear from currents; and as the water rises around them, they take to hastily constructed rafts, transferring their few household effects thereto, and dwelling for days in a floating camp, sheltered from the rain by a wagon-sheet or old quilts stretched over a low ridge-pole. Mooring the rafts to trees, they lead, to others a romantic, to themselves a precarious existence.

NOT SO ROMANTIC AS IT LOOKS.

A whole village deserted by its people wears a singularly melancholy aspect. Let the reader row with a press correspondent through the little town of Bayou Sara La, as it appeared during the recent overflow. The town lies on rolling ground, dotted here and there with low hills or drifts of sand and alluvial deposits, left there by the floods of ages ago.

"Even over the center of the roadway back from the front street, which is just behind the levee, it is unusual to find less than four feet of water, while in many places a nine-foot oar can not be made to touch bottom. In some of what, in times of low water, are beautiful residence streets, the boat as it went gliding on the shining moonlight flood would pass so close under the spreading branches of the great live oaks, which interlock their boughs over the roadway, that her occupants would be compelled to bend down almost level with the gunwales to avoid being swept off the thwarts. The freaks of the currents wandering through the flooded streets seem wholly unaccountable. Sometimes they would run parallel with, and at others directly at right angles to the streets. Often progress would be blocked by long sections of wooden-plank sidewalks, gates, doors and cisterns that had formed barriers across the street, while at every turning the boatman would be compelled to dodge huge floating masses of drift in which out-houses, timbers, sections of roofs and other heavy wreckage inextricably commingling were slowly floating on the lazy current.

"The air was soft and balmy as that of a midsummer night, and the mellow light of the young moon that was already hanging low over the great sand hills to the westward, spread a soft pale light of deep blue on the bright spangled sky. There were faint night breezes waving the topmost branches of the great shade trees, but they did not touch the rippleless, shining flood which gleamed in long narrow paths. The white moonbeams that, like ribbons of burnished silver, but slept inky and motionless under the black shadows of the trees, and the rounded outlines of each great shade tree was sharply reflected in the mirror-like surface of the water and bordered by a dainty rim of silver. Houses with snow-white walls were faithfully mirrored in that motionless, glittering flood. While to the eastward of each lay a long, deep shadow—a starless night—huge shapeless masses of wreckage drifting past black opaque shadows that grew longer and more intense as the young moon sank so low that her lower horizon was dipping behind a great hoary-crested sand hill in the west. The scene was exquisitely beautiful, but at the same time weird and uncanny. Not a human voice was heard, but near at hand between the lower whispering of the softly dipping oars came the ever varying chorus of the frogs mingling with the low musical murmuring of the mighty river and the deep sullen roar of the crevasse on the far off southern shore. There the sides of the skiff would brush the perfumed shrubbery of a submerged lawn; there could be seen the tree-tops of a splendid orchard just rising out of the flood, their lower limbs swaying and bending with the current. In all this scene of beautiful ruins there was a sense of utter loneliness that was strangely oppressive. Of those who a week ago filled this bright and hustling little town to overflowing, only six families remain. The others have all fled to the adjoining hills, leaving their houses to their fate till the water shall have subsided."

Such villages as are not deserted have little to do with the world beyond. The post-offices are often exhausted, in addition to the fact that the nearest points not blockaded are miles away; so that **the telegraph only brings** news from beyond, or tells the world how fares the little hamlet. The operator may be driven to the upper story, or to the roof, there to dispute possession with stray turtles or snakes, or to listen to the hoarse remonstrance of some

TELEGRAPHING UNDER DIFFICULTIES.

old bullfrog whose nocturnal rest is broken by the clicking of the key. All around is a dreary waste of water, on which the gleam of the moon appears like a ghostly foot-path, and the dark shadows of the naked-limbed trees menace like gaunt spectres. From his elevated position the operator may see the flash of the search-light of a steamer miles away, as the vessel flits along the stream, collecting refugees from the shores; and ever and anon the deep harsh bray of the fog-horn breaks the stillness. Save for these distant tokens of life there is

> "Death and silence! death and silence!
> Death and silence all around!"

At the great crevasse itself the spectacle is exciting. The fight is not abandoned. Desperate efforts are made to secure the ends from further washing. That once done, there is hope of closing the gap. At the extremity of the break a floating pile-driver is fiercely hammering heavy timbers into the spongy soil. There a tiny, fussing tug is engaged in trying to float a mat of brushwood against the broken bank, while a score of anxious men are watching an opportunity to peg it down. Others endeavor to weave pliant branches among the driven piles to afford a better hold for the guano sacks of earth that are being thrown into the break. From these moist earth is often washed out by the powerful current as though it were melting sugar; while now and then some timber, undermined by the steadily deepening current, leaps upward as though endowed with a life of its own, and dashes away on the foaming stream. After hours of the fierce contest, the ends are at last secured. The pigmy has stopped the giant. The work progresses more easily, now that the workers are sure of their ground. The stubborn creatures contest every inch of space. The roar of the battle goes up incessantly. One fights for life, the other for liberty—such liberty as the tyrant asks of his subjects; such liberty as the wolf asks of the sheep, or the hawk of the doves; such liberty as the strong has always demanded of the weak and defenseless.

By and by the voice of the struggling monster grows weaker. The persistent creatures that swarm about him assault him with renewed vigor and pertinacity. The roar of the conflict dies away by degrees. Step by step the two bands of men approach each other. Only a narrow channel remains. Presently the forces clasp hands over the chasm. In a few moments there remains but a tiny, remonstrant, murmuring trickle of water. Another stroke and it is finished. The pigmy has conquered the giant. The ant has chained the elephant.

But what, in the meantime, has been the fate of the district along the levee front? Here the water does not rise slowly and stealthily as in the regions far inland, where the force of the current is lost. The planters and all their available forces, it may be, have been busily fighting the rising floods, but have been finally vanquished momentarily by wind and wave. Hoping to hold the levee, few, perhaps, have removed their families, goods, or chattels, or livestock. Then when the break comes, the raging flood rushes in over the fields and woods, demolishing outhouses, shaking cottages, drowning stock, hurling masses of drift against dwellings that might otherwise stand— seeming as though a living genius of destruction.

Here a family, carrying only a few changes of clothes, and a purse but too scantily filled, hurry wildly toward the river front, in hope that a passing steamer may pick them up; there a planter who has saved his family is hurrying a drove of cattle to the levee, vaguely wondering, in the mean time, how he shall feed them if the flood lasts long; here a negro family, chattering noisily like frightened crows, trudges through water and mire knee-deep or waist-deep, bearing on their heads bundles of dirty bedding, or old clothes—one or two lugging sacks of meal and flitches of bacon, with a blind confidence that they

RESCUING PEOPLE IN INLAND DISTRICTS.

have made sufficient provision for every emergency.
There a forlorn squatter is punting a rude raft with his
few belongings slowly athwart the restless flood. Yonder
a band of negroes, unaware of the break in time to reach
the river, have congregated in an old gin house, and swarm
upon its roof, yelling and gesticulating wildly in their terror, for aid, which they fear will never reach them; and,
as the water rises higher, roofs, barns, hen-coops, and carcasses go floating past or lodge against their frail support, increasing their peril every moment. Some moan
and cry; others pray vigorously, confessing their misdeeds with voluble freedom; occasionally there is some
old crone who terrifies her auditors with the assertion that
"de Lord is sendin' another 'varsal flood on men for deir
wickedness," at which the wicked groan and cry, and the
pious clap their hands and shout, trusting to shortly see
the salvation of the Lord. In the distance appear a few
figures perched in trees, seeming like enormous crows;
over yonder, some unfortunate has shinned up a telegraph
pole, which creaks and sways with the rush of the water,
threatening constantly to return the trembling refugee to
the flood beneath. The last unfortunates have straggled
to the levee. The rest must wait for relief. Here and
there a few cattle stand lowing in water half over their
sides; a restless, snorting horse plunges impatiently about.
A floating tree-trunk strikes them from their hillock, to
swim aimlessly about till other drifting masses ride them
down. A hen-coop floats past, on which a hungry chanticleer is perched, occasionally challenging the flood, and
in the meantime, with sidelong glance eyeing the confusion and in undertones discussing the case with his half-starved, feathered harem.

It is a motley throng that huddles along the levee.
That narrow strip of earth, but eight feet wide at best, is

CAMPS ON THE LEVEE.

all that is left as a footing for hundreds. The waves swash heavily at their feet; or sometimes, as the wind blows stronger, they leap clear over the frail embankment. Trudging wearily back and forth on the clayey, slippery dykes are planters, once well-to-do, with families of culture and refinement; others of a middle class, and occasional specimens of a type denominated by the "man and brother" as "po' white trash" are to be seen among the throng. The "man and brother" is usually in the majority in the lowland districts, and adds greatly to the picturesqueness of the levees in time of flood. Some rear their tiny excuses for tents along the bank, and spend the time in uneasily watching the turbid water. Occasionally some Dinah or Chloe, who has been on the levee for a week, goes through the motion of washing clothes in the surging stream, gaining thereby the approval of conscience over a duty performed, whether the garments be improved or not. Here there is little concern, these being wandering roustabouts who had nothing to lose; there some grizzled Uncle Tom bemoans the loss of his two scrawny mules, and the few pigs and fowls, and his favorite cow, which represent the savings of years from his toil in his little patch of corn and cotton; and he feels even sorer over his losses than the rich planter who has lost a hundred times as much. So the little bands assemble, mingle and disperse, comparing notes, and all waiting in painful anxiety for some steamer to pick them up before the sodden levee shall dissolve beneath their feet and leave them struggling in the stream. At length the government relief boat appears, and gathers the throngs by hundreds, to transport them to higher lands. Beyond the levee skiffs and flat-boats move about the submerged region, picking up the people who have taken refuge on the house-tops, among the trees, or on piles of drift. None on the levee fear being passed in the night, for the powerful search-light illuminates every straggling group.

On reaching a place of safety from the waters, scores of the refugees are almost penniless, and the question of food

WAITING FOR A STEAMER.

is a pressing one. The liberal contributions of scores of generous souls suffice but for a short time. The government must again come to the front, and issue rations, or a money equivalent, sufficient to maintain the destitute till the falling of the waters allows them to resume labor upon their lands. After that, the crop-lien system in vogue in

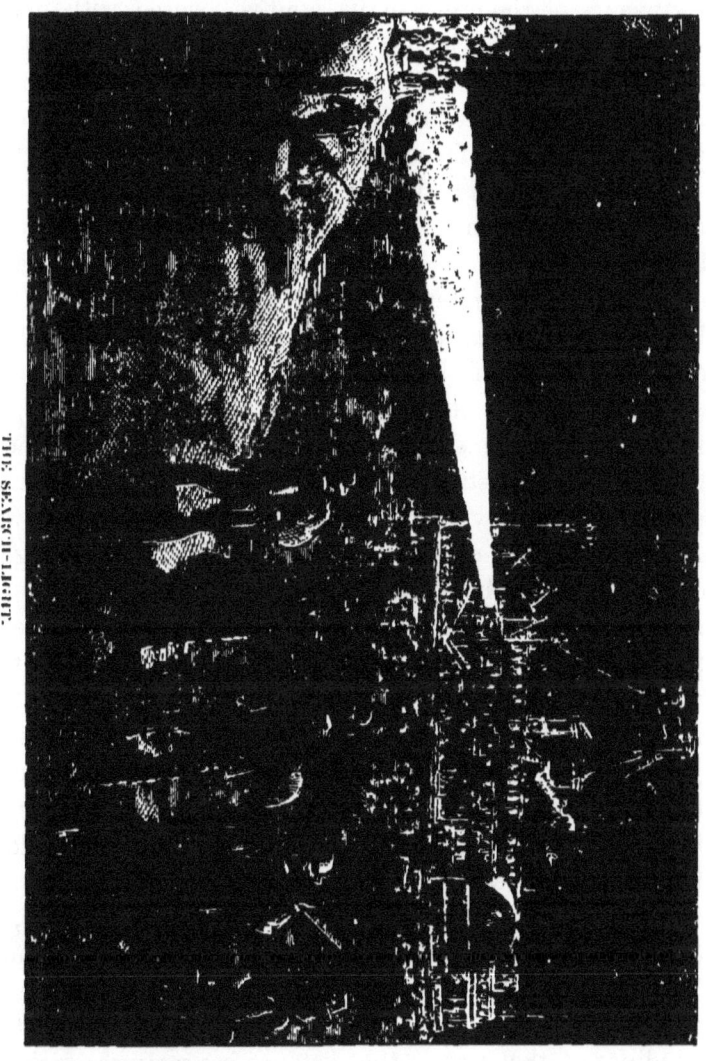

THE SEARCH-LIGHT.

the South enables the people to get credit of their merchants until the cotton-picking or corn-gathering.

When the waters subside, and the people return, it is

often difficult to find old landmarks. In one place huge trenches may be washed out; but away from the immediate vicinity of the crevasse the land is covered with mud, varying from a few inches to four or five feet in thickness—sufficient guarantee of amazing fertility, when the ground becomes dry enough to work. In the numerous little depressions in the surface are stagnant pools that linger for a month or two. The larger ones, if not before filled, are converted into ponds or marshes, which only thorough draining will destroy. The air is tainted by the hundreds of carcasses that are entangled in the heaps of drift. The hot dank soil, steaming under the summer sun, brings disease in the wake of the flood.

Louisiana, from its character, is usually the principal sufferer: the Arkansas borders fare little better. All along the course of the stream the land is dotted with lakes and pools and marshy lands, created by former overflows. Along the lower portion of the river bayous or sloughs open from either bank, and meander lazily toward the gulf. As showing the character of the country may be mentioned the Little and St. Francis Rivers, which flow southward from southeast Missouri, nearly parallel to the Mississippi, and but forty miles from it at their furthest points. In flowing one hundred and twenty miles south they double and twist, expanding into sluggish bayous as broad as the Mississippi itself, or into shallow island-dotted lakes; and the total length of the numerous bends and whimsical curves of the main stream, St. Francis, is over two hundred miles. In like manner, Pine Bluff, Arkansas, is but fifty miles from the mouth of the sluggish sandy Arkansas as the crow flies; but to follow the windings of that stream the distance is nearly three times as great. The backwater of the Mississippi finds its way into these sluggish channels, and renders comparatively useless any levees on the banks of the great river near their mouths: and from the northern border of Arkansas to the gulf the old Father of Waters pursues a course as intricate in its windings as the St. Francis. It is asserted by many that the mouth of the stream was once perhaps not far below Memphis, and that all the land to the southward has been produced partly by slow upheaval of the sea-bottom and partly by the alluvial deposits of the river and the gradual extension of its delta, which now projects many miles into the gulf This would account for the low and swampy character of the land in the entire region.

The writer has endeavored to give an accurate general view of southern floods. While differing in some features from floods in other lands, they themselves are much alike. The description of a flood of to-day would answer with but little adaptation as a narrative of fifty years ago: and further details of particular flood scenes are unnecessary. Such great overflows are not common, the levees holding the river in check on ordinary occasions. Yet, one flood season deserves more than passing notice.

CHAPTER XV.

THE FLOOD OF 1890.

> " And rearing Lindis backward pressed,
> Shook all her trembling bankes amaine,
> Then madly at the cygre's breast
> Flung up her weltering walles againe,
> Then banks came down with ruin and rout,
> Then beaten foam flew round about,
> And all the mighty floods were out.
>
> So farre, so fast the cygre drave;
> The heart had hardly time to beat,
> Before a shallow, seething wave,
> Sobbed in the grasses at our feet.
> The feet had hardly time to flee,
> Before it broke against the knee,
> And all the world was in the sea."

THE great flood of 1874 is remembered as the most destructive of human life in the history of the Mississippi valley. It came almost without warning. The rolling river rose rapidly, and the levees broke in many places before the masses suspected danger. Hundreds of people were drowned; and as for the losses of property, no attempt was made to estima'e the amount. Certainly it amounted to many millions. Perhaps only the Chicago fire could compare with it in this respect. Another great year of high water was 1882: but the damage done was smaller, as the levees had been heightened and strengthened.

But the floods of this year, in area submerged, in long duration, in height of water, and in the pertinacity with which they were contested, eclipsed all records. There is no measuring the extent of the calamity. There is nothing in the recorded history of the Mississippi valley

THE FLOOD OF 1890.

THE SCENE AT HIGH WATER.

to compare with it. In some places the gauges were completely overflowed. Levees that had withstood former waters, and had been strengthened since, snapped like whip-cords, under the tremendous strain.

Early in the present year, the Signal Service warned the people of the lower Mississippi that very high water might be expected, as the snows of the upper Ohio region had been very heavy, while the unusually early spring would bring the flood water into the lower river at the time of heavy spring rains. There the levees were carefully examined, and every precaution against high water taken. But the people, though expecting high water, had not reckoned upon such a flood as came. The river rose above the great flood of 1874, passing all previous records by two feet, and reaching a foot higher than the levees had been built to sustain.

On January 1, Cairo reported eighteen feet and rising, while the river was falling from Louisville up the Ohio, was falling at St. Louis, and stationary on the lower Mississippi. From the first day of the year the river rose at Cairo, and in ten days the river had risen thirteen feet.

From Cincinnati down the Ohio increased in volume for four days, and on January 16, at Cairo, it passed the danger line (forty feet) by three-tenths. The rise in sixteen days had been one and three-eighths feet a day. At that time the river was rising slowly from Evansville down, and falling above. A few days later came another rise in the Ohio, aided by the Tennessee and Cumberland, and by the 1st of February the water at Cairo was almost a flood. The volumes of water continued till the lower Mississippi was bank full. By the latter end of February, the danger point had been reached at Memphis, Shreveport, Vicksburg, and New Orleans. Cairo was already in trouble.

On March 12, Cairo reached its maximum, 48.9. The Signal Service Office had given out a prediction of fifty-one feet, but the failure of the upper Mississippi to rise, prevented that stage being reached. The river at St. Louis had then but five feet of water.

On March 14, Chief Signal Officer A. W. Greeley sent out a warning from Washington to the people living on the lower Mississippi. He told them that the rain they had had for four days had been drained into the tributaries of the great river and would swell it considerably. The greatest flood ever known might be expected within a few days. All stock and valuable movable property should be taken to the hills. New Orleans had then higher water than ever before.

The river was then rising in the lower Missouri, and St. Louis was reporting rapid increase in the stage of water. Cairo had fallen, but the upper Ohio and lower tributaries brought back the upper line of the flood to near the maximum stage.

The lower Mississippi tributaries began to swell. The Arkansas and Red Rivers overflowed their banks. Low levees grew weak and succumbed. Low lying towns and plantations were flooded.

Then came the nights and days of terrible struggle along lines of levee that protected vast tracts of lands. Men were pressed into service whether they liked the the work or no, and the shotgun patrol was established for the protection of the safer levees from being cut. The upper Mississippi swelled rapidly, and while not reaching a dangerous stage itself, it added enormously to the peril below. Then came floods in Arkansas, Tennessee, Mississippi, and Louisiana.

The first serious trouble from the Mississippi in Arkansas occurred in Phillips county, above the mouth of the

White River, where some five hundred people were driven from their homes to the highest points by the backwater, and the cattle, gaunt, wild-eyed, starving, were forced to subsist on cane, twigs of cotton wood and other trees felled for them. Three times the backwater and heavy local rains flooded this region, while the retiring flood left a deposit of mud from one to five feet in depth, precluding the possibility of turning the hungry cattle upon the land for two or three weeks, and rendering it impossible to raise a crop of corn or more than half a crop of cotton. At Cairo, the rivers were one hundred miles in width, covering fifty miles of Missouri lowlands, and extending to the hills in Kentucky; while Cairo itself was partially flooded. The railroads in that section were forced to stop, and the people fled to the hills for their lives. Steady rains fell in Arkansas, Ohio and lower Missouri River valleys, and by the time these began to subside, the floods in the streams below had passed previous records.

The greatest danger and trouble was in the valley from Arkansas City southward. Heavy rains produced a break in the levee at that place. March 28, the levees broke at two points on the eastern shore, between Arkansas City and Memphis, Tennessee, submerging many thousands of acres of land, and sweeping southeastward to the Yazoo River. Greenville, Mississippi, a city of 10,000, is partially protected by a high ridge through the city; but there was no means of holding back the enemy in the rear. The town is situated at the extremity of a sharp eastward curve, and a violent storm at length aided the rapid current in cutting away the front defense, and the town was forced to yield. Strenuous efforts to close the breaks above completely failed; and all that could be done was to secure the ends of the crevasses to prevent their widening. Cattle were herded for a time on the levees and embankments, but these gradually yielded, and the animals were drowned in droves. Defenses yielded where least expected. By April 3, there was two feet of water in the streets of Greenville. There was nothing left but to make the best

NEGROES MOVING OUT.

of the situation. People took to the upper floors, and appeals for state, national and individual aid were sent out. The telephone lines leading out of the city were destroyed, and communication with the outer world was greatly hindered. Occasional reports of destitution and suffering came from Greenville, but these were contradicted by meetings of leading citizens, who said, "there is no destitution here that home people can not relieve. If the negroes want to wait for government rations and refuse from $1.50 to $2.50 per day to work on levees, their starving arouses no sympathy. While all these sensational reports of destitution are traveling about, the steamboats are running into Memphis and Vicksburg begging for levee hands, and the native negro is sitting on the levee fishing."

The water swept rapidly southward, submerging almost the entire region between the Yazoo and Mississippi. Meanwhile, the trouble in Louisiana was just beginning. The banks began caving near the levee in Madison Parish Front, compelling the erection of a new levee in the rear of the old one. But the fight went on stubbornly for three weeks, both along the river front and along the bayous in the interior. Atchafalaya River was forty-five feet above low water. The contest for the levees there was as bitter as along the main stream. Occasional breaks occurred, but they were closed or kept from spreading by the twenty thousand men who labored day and night along the stream between Bayou Sara and New Orleans.

Ere long it appeared that the greatest danger was along the Concordia and Pointe Coupee parish fronts. (A parish in Louisiana coincides with what is known as a county elsewhere). Considerable appropriations were made, and the head of the third district levee system, Captain D. C. Kingman, conducted the fight on the Pointe Coupee front in person. The battle ended here in disastrous defeat. The men held their ground manfully till April 20, no serious breaks having then occurred. All that day the men were compelled to work in a drenching rain storm that was beating fiercely against the already overburdened and sodden levees on the west bank of the river. The danger at the great Morganza bend grew appalling. It was hoped that during the night the storm would cease, or at least

that the wind might shift to some other quarter, but when the morning broke there were the same leaden skies overhead, with darker masses still scurrying to the westward before a fierce easterly gale that was as fresh and strong as ever.

and which hurled storms of white-capped waves upon the rain-soaked earthworks. Bags of earth and sand were piled up along the levee, to prevent the waves from washing over. Wilder and more furious raged the storm: higher and higher beat the waves, as the day passed. "In the teeth of drenching surf and blinding rain, the battle with rising flood went bravely on. Sacks were piled upon sacks and revetments of plank and jute bagging were carried up till the superstructure upon the crown of the levee looked like a fair-sized levee itself. Not only the men, but even the women and children fought bravely for their homes in the teeth of that wild furious storm.

"As Monday night closed in, the situation was more gloomy than ever. The heavy leaden sky was deeply shadowed by low hanging clouds of dull slaty black, driven before the fierce gale that was sweeping up the reach, thrashing it into long ribs of foam that every now and then broke clear over the levees all along the New Texas system, and beat savagely against the great Morganza, just below them.

"A nightfall dark and wild with wind and storm was followed by a night black and tempestuous, and still the desperate fight went on. Here and there ruddy, flaring torches struggled with the murky gloom, but within their dim halos could be seen the big breakers hungrily licking the tops of the sodden barriers that throbbed and quivered beneath every cruel blow.

"Planters' wives and daughters stood ankle-deep in mud, filling sacks and helping to lift them upon the shoulders of the men who were carrying them to the levee. Two bold Creoles stood at one weak place, though they felt the levee dissolving beneath their feet. They sank to their knees in the mud and water, but still they stood stubbornly on the sinking dike, piling sacks in the breach, though again and again the flood seemed to be in the very act of overpowering and sweeping them away in the very center of a crevasse. It was a bloodless battle, but many a man has won fame on a gory battle-field who never turned a more steadfast, unflinching gaze into the very jaws of death than did those brave defenders of their homes during that terrible night."

Suddenly there was a wild outcry and a hurried mustering of forces at the old Morganza levee. But men and materials were no longer of any use. The dull yellow flood poured through the gap like a mighty cataract. Four hundred feet of the embankment were gone in a few moments.

At once there was a *sauve qui peut*. The volunteer forces of the neighborhood hurried away to save what they could. As the Morganza levee was backed by a wide uninhabited swamp, there was little danger of any lives being lost by the sudden breach, though the people had clung to their homes to the last.

Meanwhile, numerous other breaks were occasioned by the storm. The first occurred at Bayou Sara, and others followed so rapidly that within twenty-four hours fifteen huge crevasses were pouring their torrents upon the land. Two other breaks occurred in the Morganza; and so vast was the volume of water drawn out by the three that the river at Bayou Sara, a few miles below, fell a foot in twenty-four hours, while the decline above was but an inch or two. Despite the gloomy outlook, the men toiled wearily on and finally succeeded in closing most of the breaks; but the great Morganza crevasses defied every effort. Then came breaks in the Atchafalaya, and the turbid waters united and swept southward one hundred miles to the sea. Some towns were abandoned to the snakes and frogs; in others the people put false floors in their dwellings and prepared for a siege. Government steamers plied up and down the country, picking up the refugees and all accessible live-stock. The effort to keep back the water was at an end,

PICKING UP REFUGEES.

and all that could be done of any especial use was in the way of salvage. The only remaining question was that of providing for the destitute. Appropriations from the State treasury were made, and corporations and private individuals contributed liberally. On April 24, two great breaks occurred in Concordia Parish, north of Pointe Coupee, thus much increasing the submerged area. From the items given, and the fact of breaks in east Baton Rouge, and the Nita crevasse, and twenty or more below New Orleans, the reader may see that a large portion of eastern Louisiana lay more or less under water. By the end of April there was no fear of further danger, simply because there was little harm left to do. The continual east wind added to the distress on the lower river by sweeping Lake Pontchartrain and the gulf water across the land, up to the levees on the river.

The one peculiar feature of the recent flood is that but few lives were lost—perhaps not a dozen, all told. The warning of the Signal Service put people on their guard, and there was no occasion for surprise.

The damage to property can not be estimated. Three thousand square miles of land were more or less flooded in Louisiana alone; and while much of this was useless swamp land, the larger part comprised some of the most valuable sugar plantations in the State. Fifty thousand people were directly affected by the flood in this region. All the railroads in this district suffered severely from wash outs and loss of time and custom. Any estimate of the damage done to planters should include not only real estate and personal property, but also the amount of loss from inability to raise the customary crops. This single item would be very large. But when we consider the terrible havoc committed in other lands and attended by fearful loss of life, we may be devoutly thankful that things were no worse with us.

The levee system is attended by peculiar perils. There must be constant watching and repairing. At seasons of danger, patrols are needed, even when the levees are

DESERTED FARMHOUSE.

sound; for human nature is full of rank selfishness, and people who find their property endangered are apt to cut the levee upon the opposite side above them, to relieve themselves by flooding others. Hungry wolves will eat a wounded companion; but man is almost the only animal that seeks an opportunity for wounding his fellow that he may have a pretext for devouring him.

The craw-fish is another persistent enemy of the planter, undermining levees with his numerous tunnels, and even penetrating the low lying fields at a distance from the river, not infrequently damaging the roots of growing crops. The ground becomes like a sponge, and water oozes from the levees in countless places.

There are other objections to the levee system; and while the Mississippi River Commission, and a majority of engineers endorse it, there are not a few equally capable men who denounce it as false in theory, and mischievous in practice. The problem remains a puzzling one. If the floods are unrestrained, a large portion of the river bottom becomes uninhabitable a considerable portion of each year. As to controlling them, a man of much experience said at the time of the flood in 1882, " I have lived on the river for thirty years, and I have studied it, for it was my business to do so. I have been steam-boating all that time. I am now certain that I don't know anything about it, or about what ought to be done to it."

Another said, "When God put the river into this valley, He told it to go wherever it pleased, and it always has done so, and always will."

Yet, the problem can not be considered hopeless, though mere experiments are dangerous. There is little doubt that the levees would have withstood the unprecedented high water of the present year, had it not been aided by the severe and protracted easterly storm. But the levees must remain a constant expense. More than $90,000,000 have already been spent upon them, and the question is an even more vital one than ever.

The chief opponents of the levee system advocate the increase of outlets. A glance at a large scale-map of Louisiana will show the reader how very narrow the mouths of the river are in comparison with its breadth above; and when it is remembered that these passages required deepening ere large vessels could reach New Orleans, it is clear that the outlet men have good reasons for asserting that the proper thing to do is to open as many outlets to the sea as possible. Yet, the majority of engineers declare this to be unscientific, and radically wrong. The levee men propose to narrow the channel and to rely upon the "scour" of the water to keep the river bottom free enough to afford a clear passage to the sea. The "scour" is aided as far as possible by clearing away obstructions where it is desired to maintain a channel, and by placing other obstructions in places where natural shallows have been formed. This is the work carried on by the commission, and is one in theory with that executed by Captain Eads in the South Pass of the Delta. He claimed that if the water flowing through the pass should be confined within comparatively narrow banks, it would scour out the bottom, and so deepen its own bed. The primary result was exactly opposite to this. The water refused to do the work expected of it, and following the law of nature, sought the line of least resistance. Finding the South Pass obstructed, or rather narrowed, much of it turned aside and poured through the Southwest Pass and the Pas a l'Outre, and instead of scouring out the South Pass, scoured the other two to the depth of two feet below where their beds had formerly been. As soon as this was discovered, the two passes were partially dammed up, and the water thus forced through the South Pass.

It is evident, at a glance, that the amount of "scour" will only be as much as will permit ready exit of the water at ordinary stages. The moment that point is reached, the "scour" ceases, and does not again act unless the river be still further narrowed. Hence, this plan, while increasing facility of navigation, only robs Peter to pay Paul, so far as protection is concerned; for what is gained in depth and speed, is necessarily lost in breadth. The "scour" system has even failed to hold its own, and has had to be reinforced by dredging machines.

This last fact tends to confirm the arguments of the outlet advocates. They urge that the immense amount of silt carried by the river is destructive to the entire scheme. During flood time this silt is nearly equally distributed throughout the water. When an overflow occurs, the immense quantity is shown by the vast alluvial deposits left in the submerged region.

According to the believers in the anti-levee theory, if overflows are prevented, the earth held in suspension, instead of being deposited where it will enrich the land, will gradually sink to the bottom of the river. The result will be that the river-bed will be steadily raised until the surface of the water at ordinary stages will be as high as the present floodmarks. Levees will have to be built higher and higher, the river will be raised far above the adjacent country, and should a break occur at any point, the consequence will be disastrous in the extreme. As an example of the effect of confining a silt-bearing alluvial river to its bed, the Hoang-Ho in China is cited. By constant dyking the bottom of the stream has been raised above large tracts of the adjacent country and some of the most ter-

FLOOD IN CHINA.

THE FLOOD OF 1890. 313

rible catastrophes in the history of floods have resulted from a break in the dykes during floods.

The natural result of the continual raising of the bottom is that where any serious breach occurs, it is simply impossible to repair it. So the great river has changed its channel entirely several times in the past two thousand years. In 1852 it burst through its banks three hundred and fifty miles from the sea, and cut a new channel through the northern part of the province of Shantung to the Gulf of Pechili, where it emptied nearly two hundred and seventy-five miles north of its former mouth in the Yellow Sea. The sharp angle at which it turned off is noticeable on the maps. This region being almost unknown to foreigners at that time, no one can say how many thousands or millions of lives were destroyed by "China's Sorrow."

But the greatest disaster of this sort occurred in 1887, when the heavy fall rains of the northwest provinces swelled the streams, and the Yellow River finally broke its banks at a sharp bend in the Ho-nan province, where the town of Cheng Chou is situated. Frantic efforts were made to close the gap, but in vain. It rapidly grew to a width of one thousand two hundred yards. Some distance away the yellow torrent turned into the valley of a small stream known as the Luchia, down which it rushed in an easterly direction, overwhelming everything in its path.

"Twenty miles from Cheng Chou it encountered Chungmou, a walled city of the third rank. Its thousands of inhabitants were attending to their usual pursuits. There was no telegraph to warn them, and the first intimation of disaster came with the muddy torrent that rolled down upon them. Within a short time only the tops of the high walls marked where a flourishing city had been. Three hundred villages in the district disappeared utterly, and the lands about three hundred other villages were inundated.

"The flood turned south from Chungmou, still keeping to the course of the Luchia, and stretched out in width for thirty miles. This vast body of water was from ten to twenty feet deep. Several miles south of Kaifeng the flood struck a large river which there joins the Luchia. The result was that the flood rose to a still greater height, and pouring into a low-lying and very fertile plain which was densely populated, submerged upward of one thousand five hundred villages.

"Not far beyond this locality the flood passed into the province of Anhui, where it spread very widely. The actual loss of life could not be computed accurately, but the lowest intelligent estimate placed it at one million five hundred thousand, and one authority placed it at seven million."

The inundated provinces were under water four months. Two million survivors were left destitute. The mind quails at the appalling magnitude of such a catastrophe.

Such is the warning given by the Yellow River. It is urged that if the Mississippi is heavily leveed, the same results will follow. The Po is another instance. The bed of the stream has been raised by dykes until it is higher in many places than the tops of the houses, and such disasters as have befallen the dwellers near the Yellow River of China, have only been avoided because of the fact that the Po is a comparatively diminutive stream. It is said that the same state of affairs exists on a smaller scale still on the Tiber. But the opponents of the outlet theory ascribe the China floods to ignorant engineering—a charge that can not be easily made to stick, when it is remembered that the Chinese have some of the most remarkable specimens of engineering skill in existence.

THE FLOOD OF 1890. 315

In support of the outlet theory, a number of experienced river captains and pilots assert that the bed of the river has been slowly rising during the past thirty years; that levees are needed at points where none were years ago, while at the same time there is less water in the channel at those points than formerly. At the time of this writing Captain Condon is urging that an outlet be made through Lake Borgne, from a point ten miles below New Orleans. His company is to assume all costs, only asking that if successful, they shall be paid $500,000 for every foot of reduction of the high water level. He asserts that one-fourth of the flood waters can be readily drained off by this means. This Lake Borgne idea, commendable as it appears, has been agitated, more or less, for forty years, without being tried. A noted government engineer, Charles Ellet, urged it at the time of the flood of 1853, without avail.

Whatever be the result of present deliberations, we must hope that no effort will be spared to thoroughly test the merits of any system agreed upon. But the long deliberations and the slow movements of the governmental committes are vexatious to those most vitally concerned. A prominent Louisianian says: "If the government and the people had raised $500,000, placed a larger force, and held that Morganza levee, it would have cost less than the mere relief expenditures, to say nothing of the millions of total loss of the flood." And *Harper's Weekly* affirms that "in one respect the casual observer is moved to sarcastic reflections. When a flood does come, like the present one, or even one of much less dimensions, the work of the commission is of necessity suspended, and at first sight it seems extremely ridiculous to see engineers waiting for the water to subside before they can place confines many feet below the present surface, which confines are intended, in part at least, for the purpose of preventing similar overflows in the future."

THE HOLLAND DYKES.

Holland, the land of windmills, is another region which has a continual struggle with this levee question. The native name of the country, "Nederlands," or Netherlands, refers to the character of the region, which lies as an average, about on the sea level; while a great portion is even somewhat lower. The thrifty people who settled here, erected dykes to keep back the sea, and built windmills to pump out the water, thus reclaiming a fertile tract from the bottom of the sea. But the great dykes need incessant watching and repairing; and the expenditures upon them up to the present time, have been greater than would have been required to build them outright of solid copper. As the safety of the dykes involves all that pertains to temporal life and welfare, the people have learned not to trust to a single line of defenses. Second and third lines are erected in the rear of the first; and many large towns are completely girdled with defenses of their own.

Since the population of this region is nearly five hundred to the square mile, while our own land does not average over eighteen to the same area, it is at once clear that the breaking of the dykes is a far more serious and terrible matter than the rupture of our levees. Some fearful disasters in Holland are recorded. In 1421, the dykes gave way at Dort, and more than one hundred thousand people perished. In 1530, there was a general failure of the dykes, and the people, not dreaming of danger, were suddenly overwhelmed; four hundred thousand perished, and the loss of property was proportionate. Two great floods have occurred within this century, doing terrible damage.

The Dutch, though peaceful and phlegmatic, are a liberty-loving people, and have often shown themselves ready to sacrifice everything for their freedom. They have found more than once its safety in the loss of all else.

One of the most thrilling and memorable incidents of the sort occurred in 1574. Under the leadership of William the Silent, one of the noblest of men, the Dutch

THE RELIEF OF LEYDEN.

were struggling to throw off the yoke of Spain. Leyden was besieged. The town was well fortified. The Spaniards endeavored to starve the city into surrender. They swarmed about the outworks and taunted the famished people as "beggars." The outlook grew daily more hopeless for the besieged. Hundreds were dead of starvation. But the survivors hurled defiance at the Spaniards. They were digging up every green thing, devouring roots of grass, old leather, offal, anything that could in the least aid to sustain life. But "so long as a dog barked in the city, the Spaniards might know they held out." A few faint-hearted ones pleaded with the burgomaster to yield. But the brave Van der Werff, gaunt, pale, wearied with care and watching, told them they could only surrender when they had eaten him; so long as he lived, the city should not yield.

It was a terrible time. Women crept into out-of-the-way places to die, that their misery might not be seen by their friends. The Dutch without wished to help their friends within—but the lines of the enemy were too strong. As the last resort, the "Silent Man" ordered the dykes cut. It was done. The country folk abandoned their homes. A fleet of two hundred vessels sailed in over the land fifteen miles. They reached the Landscheiding, a great dyke five miles from the city. Three quarters of a mile nearer the town was a second dyke, the Greenway; within that was the Kirkway.

The rising water frightened the Spaniards. But at ten inches, it stopped. The Spaniards renewed their taunts. Again it rose two feet; the vessels drew nearer; then they lay aground in sight of the famished citizens. There arose a strong northwest wind—and after days of weary waiting, the fleet was close on the last lines of fortification. It was the first of October. In the morning the "beggars" of the sea would make a desperate attack upon the Spanish hordes.

In the night there came a terrible crash. The sea had undermined the wall. The citizens were filled with panic, fearing an immediate irruption of the enemy. They stood under arms through the weary night.

The morning came. Not a Spaniard was in sight. Fearing a sortie of the hunger-maddened people, they had fled in the darkness. The city was saved by the drowning of the land.

A story is told of Frederick the Great, illustrative of the same indomitable spirit. After establishing the supremacy of Prussia, he was suspected of designs upon the independence of the Netherlands. The Dutch envoy at his court, newly appointed, Frederick endeavored to overawe by a display of his power. A great military review was held; and Frederick, who took a peculiar delight in tall men, caused troop after troop of his gigantic grenadiers to file before the weazened little Dutchman, and asked his opinion. Of each one the envoy said: "Very good, *but not tall enough.*" Frederick, much nettled at this oft repeated criticism, asked the ambassador what he meant by it. "I mean," he retorted, "*that we can flood our country twelve feet deep!*" Frederick left the Dutch in peace.

Though the most terrible calamities of any kind—whether from flood, famine, or earthquake—are to be found in the history of China, yet other nations have shared in disastrous floods. We mention a few:

A notable flood occurred on the coast of Lincolnshire, England, A. D., 245. It seems to have been a high tide, aided by the wind. Three thousand people and many cattle were drowned by a flood in Cheshire, A. D., 353. Four hundred families were drowned in Glasgow, A. D.,

758, by an overflow of the Clyde. A tidal wave destroyed several English seaports in A. D., 1014. The Severn leaped its banks in 1483, submerging the adjacent lowlands, and drowning hundreds. Fifty thousand people perished in Catalonia, Spain, during a flood in 1617. In Yorkshire, England, occurred a remarkable outburst of subterranean waters in 1686.

"In September, 1687, mountain torrents inundated Navarre, and two thousand persons were drowned. Twice, in 1787 and in 1802, the Irish Liffey overran its banks and caused great damage. A reservoir in Lurca, a city of Spain, burst in 1802, in much the same way as did the dam at Johnstown, and as a result one thousand persons perished. Twenty-four villages near Presburg, and nearly all their inhabitants, were swept away in April, 1811, by an overflow of the Danube. Two years later, large provinces in Austria and Poland were flooded, and many lives were lost. In the same year a force of two thousand Turkish soldiers, who were stationed on a small island near Widdin, were surprised by a sudden overflow of the Danube and all were drowned. There were two more floods in this year, one in Silesia, where six thousand persons perished, and the French army met such losses and privations that its ruin was accelerated; and another in Poland, where four thousand persons were supposed to have been drowned. In 1816, the melting of the snow on the mountains surrounding Strabane, Ireland, caused destructive floods : and the overflow of the Vistula, in Germany, laid many villages under water. Floods that occasioned great suffering occurred in 1829, when severe rains caused the Spey and Findhorn to rise fifty feet above their ordinary level. The following year the Danube again overflowed its banks, and inundated the houses of 50,000 inhabitants of Vienna." The Saone

BREAKING OF THE DYKES, HOLLAND.

overflowed in 1840 and poured its turbulent waters into the Rhine, flooding one hundred square miles of land, and drowning thousands. Another great flood in France occurred in 1856. In 1875, still another drowned a thousand people near Toulouse; while India, the same year lost many through floods.

But no such destruction of life ever visited our own land till within a year past, and the event is more to be deplored, in that it was caused by unexcusable negligence. That flood we must next consider.

CHAPTER XVI.

THE JOHNSTOWN FLOOD.

"A sullen hoarse murmur, and nameless fear!—
A sound like the tread of a hurrying host!—
A roar like the storm, as the wild waters near,
Like the dash of the sea on a crag-bordered coast!

A wave like a mountain sweeps swift through the vale
Ten thousand wrecked homes tossing dark in its spray,
Wild cries of death-anguish echo mocks with her wail—
And the fiend of the flood now has claimed his prey!"

INDIA, profiting by long and sad experience, has provided, as far as may be possible, against the contingencies of drought and famine, by the establishment of a magnificent system of storage reservoirs, to furnish water for irrigating when rain is wanting. Some of these tanks are fine specimens of engineering, and so far as records go, no disaster has ever attended their establishment. But to be ready and efficient for purposes of irrigation, the water must be above the level of the surrounding country: hence, the only practicable plan has been to dam up the courses of streams and ravines in the hills. As nearly all Bengal is comparatively low and level, this method is not applicable there; hence, the terrible famines consequent in a comparatively small decrease of the average rain supply. But in the Deccan, in the Madras presidency, and in Ceylon, the reservoir system has been carried to an extent astounding to the white man, who depends with tolerable certainty upon the rain, and who is accustomed to consider other races as universally indolent and improvident. In fourteen districts of the Madras presidency

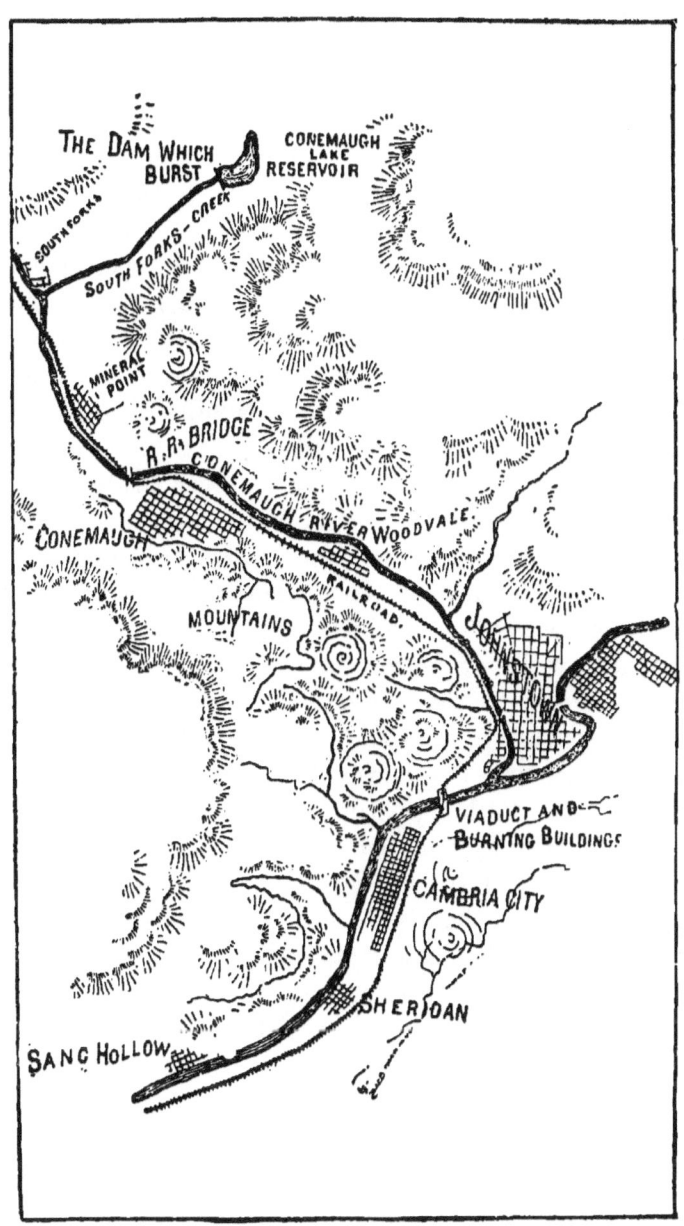

MAP OF CONEMAUGH VALLEY.

are nearly fifty-five thousand irrigation reservoirs, four-fifths of which are in regular operation. Their size may be estimated by the fact that the retaining dykes average half a mile in length. One ancient reservoir, now broken, had a dam thirty miles long, shutting in an artificial lake of eighty square miles. The Veranum tank covers fifty-three square miles, has a dam twelve miles long, and produces $55,000 per year. In Ceylon may be seen a gigantic dam of cemented stone, fifteen miles long, one hundred feet wide at the base, and forty feet wide at the top.

The same plan is of late years being extensively operated in our western tracts for the reclaiming of extensive tracts otherwise not cultivable. With these exceptions no great use of the reservoir system has been made in this country. Every saw-mill, grist-mill or factory in our land usually has its dam in an adjacent stream to insure a fair supply of water: but none of these can be properly considered general precautions against drought. The only prominent public works of the sort are the Croton storage reservoirs, by which New York is supplied with water. There are eighteen reservoirs, with a total capacity of fourteen thousand millions of gallons. China has a great canal irrigation system, which is, perhaps, safer in some respects than the Hindoo system, but which can not command as large an increase of supply in time of drought, the water being drawn from the rivers, and thus having comparatively little fall. But the canals so thoroughly intersect the whole country as to serve as public highways: and in many sections there are no other roads.

Doubtless the methods of construction in India have been learned by long experience. Certain it is that for many years, at least, no serious trouble has ever arisen from defective retaining dykes. The public welfare is so intimately connected with these pools that they are carefully inspected and repaired. The destruction of the system might at any time precipitate a terrible famine.

Not having a similar condition of things to contend with, the average American is not concerned about the few dams scattered about the land, not one in a score of which would cause any serious loss were it to break: and even were such death-traps scattered over every county, it is doubtful if a race who will crouch behind a Mississippi levee and refuse flight till the last moment, could ever be brought to a proper realization of the danger, or their culpable negligence. The American is in a hurry: and so if speed be obtained, trains may wreck, vessels collide, or boilers burst, and the coroner's jury will obligingly render a verdict of "nobody to blame." Since he also wants things at the bottom market price, he encourages the production of countless unsafe buildings, dams, and similar structures, merely because they are cheap.

The most terrible lesson ever given to cheap dam builders in the history of our country is one, which, with the reader's indulgence, we shall endeavor to narrate.

In southwest central Pennsylvania, among the foot-hills of the Alleghanies, lies the peaceful and picturesque valley of the Little Conemaugh. Here, in 1889, within a stretch of a dozen miles, lay five industrious and thriving towns: South Fork, Mineral Point, Conemaugh, Woodvale and Johnstown. The last of these, embracing as it did, Cambria and Conemaugh Borough, was a city of thirty thousand people. The population of South Fork was two thousand, Mineral Point had eight hundred, Conemaugh and Woodvale about two thousand five hundred each. The total population of the valley within the distance named could not have been far from thirty-eight thousand.

Johnstown was the center of interest as of population. Thither came on May 30th—"Decoration Day"—people from Altoona, Hollidaysburg, Somerset, Latrobe, Ebensburg and Wilmore, and from the four other towns already mentioned. There was a great concourse, a long and impressive procession of soldiers and secret orders, with bands of music, flags, regalia, banners, bunting and devices. With solemn pomp the cemetery was visited, and flowers were strewn on the graves of the patriotic dead. This sad but pleasing duty ended, the procession turned again toward the city, and entering the Opera House, listened to an eloquent oration. It was a day of more than ordinary interest and elation for Johnstown. The city stood happy and unsuspecting on the very brink of an awful doom.

During the day the sky had been overcast, and there were occasional light showers. At nightfall the clouds lowered more heavily, and seemed to descend nearer to the earth. At nine o'clock there was a gentle rain; at eleven, a tremendous down-pour, which continued with little interruption during the remainder of the night. It seemed as if the windows of heaven had been opened.

The site of Johnstown is at the Junction of Stony Creek with the Little Conemaugh. Before eight o'clock on the morning of the 31st of May, both streams were bank-full. As the day advanced the lower parts of the town were inundated. By eleven o'clock there was a depth of five feet at the corner of Main and Market streets, and at the Cambria Iron Company's store.

Still higher the waters rose. In the houses most exposed, carpets were removed from the floors, and pianos and organs were lifted on chairs and tables. Soon the two angry streams were mingling their waters in the business center of the town. Both streams had been as high before, but never both at the same time. Some thought the Cambria Iron Company, which had narrowed the channel below the stone bridge, was responsible, and should be required to widen it again, and so make a free exit for the waters.

By two o'clock the water was two to ten feet deep all over the city proper, and the people had retired to their houses. There was inconvenience and cessation of business, but no one apprehended serious danger. They surveyed the providence of God without fear: little thinking of the destruction that, swifter than the avalanche, would presently come through the heedlessness or the greed of man.

Twelve miles up the river, eastward, and at an elevation of four hundred and fifty feet above the city, lay Conemaugh Lake. This was an artificial reservoir, covering four hundred, or perhaps four hundred and fifty acres of land, and having an average depth of thirty feet. Across the south fork of the Conemaugh, about two miles above its junction with the main stream, had been built a dam, sixty-two feet high in the center, and eight hundred and fifty feet long. The valley, narrow at the dam, widened above into an extensive basin. Proposed in 1836, and authorized three years later, this reservoir had been finally constructed in 1852, as a feeder to the Pennsylvania canal, fourteen miles below. A culvert at the bottom of the dam contained five iron discharge pipes, each two feet in diameter, which could be opened at low water thus sending the contents of the reservoir to the canal at Johnstown. In 1857, the Pennsylvania Railroad Company, having bought the canal, abandoned it, and the reservoir was thenceforth disused. In July, 1862, the culvert beneath it gave way, owing to some imperfection of the foundation. The depth of water in the reservoir was, at the time, not greater than forty feet; hardly more than half its actual capacity. The breach widened into a chasm, and the water of the reservoir was discharged, with the exception of about eight feet at the bottom; but so slow was the process, owing to the substantial character of the dam, and the resistance it presented, that little harm resulted.

From 1862 to 1880, the reservoir was empty, and the property, containing something more than five hundred acres, was a waste. In 1875 it was bought by Congressman John Reilly, and was by him, four years later, transferred to the South Fork Fishing and Hunting Club. This was an association of three gentlemen; suggested and organized by Colonel B. F. Ruff, a successful railroad and tunnel contractor. All these parties had ceased from membership in the club prior to the great disaster.

The original dam, constructed with care and solidity, had involved an expenditure of $240,000. It was built in regular layers and solidly rammed, and when finished was higher in the middle than at the ends, having a spillway cut through rock in the side of the hill. The cost of reconstruction was no more than $17,000. No engineer, good or bad, had charge of the work. The material used was, for the most part, not more substantial than shale and earth and straw. The pipes at the bottom were permanently closed, and as the dam advanced, the water was discharged through a board flume over the top. It was at first intended to raise the new dam to a height of no more than forty feet, but it was presently discovered that to cut down the spill-way through rock would cost more than to construct the dam to the original elevation. This was accordingly done, though not perfectly, as the dam was two or three feet lower than the old one, and had, besides, a sag in the middle. A fatal mistake, if once the water should begin to flow over the crest.

Another mistake was the obstruction of the spill-way

with an iron grating placed to retain the fish, without taking the precaution at the same time to enlarge the passage. This would have been expensive; and here, as in the construction of the dam, it is apparent that economy was consulted.

The sum of the mistakes made in the summer of 1880, and which culminated in the disaster of 1889, were, according to the report of a corps of engineers, who made a careful survey, "the lowering of the crest, the dishing, or central sag of the crest, the closing of the bottom culvert, and the obstruction of the spill-way."

The people of the towns below had often discussed the possible rupture of the dam, but they scarcely feared it. Had it not been built by men who understood their business; and might not these be trusted, as men trust their lives to the doctor and their souls to the priest? Had it not resisted the flood of June, 1887—the highest ever known—and why then should it yield to any other? It is certain that in the towns below some were not thinking of the reservoir at all; while, in case it should give way, few had formed the remotest conception of the possible disaster. On the very day of the awful calamity, when the streets and sidewalks of Johnstown were already under water, a leading citizen, to the question, "How much higher do you think the water will rise if the reservoir should burst?" answered quietly, "About two feet;" and we have not heard that any ventured to correct the estimate.

Unsuspecting souls were they, and yet wholly like other men. Those long resident by the volcano have ceased to fear its fires. Familiarity, even with danger, breeds contempt. The evil which still delays, we fondly believe will never come. And as to the consequences, if those who build dams know so little, why should simple townsmen be expected to know more? Had they guaged that reservoir, and did they know that up there in the mountains were six hundred and forty millions of cubic feet of water, enough to make a veritable Niagara, for more than half an hour, ready to rush down upon them? Had they calculated the awful energy of twenty millions of tons of water falling four hundred and fifty feet in a progress of a dozen miles; and this progress down a pent-up valley, in some places not more than three hundred feet in width? Had they considered that the flow of a mountain of water, sixty feet high at starting, must be far more rapid on the top than at the bottom? That the base, entangled among obstructions, and overspreading them, would furnish to the water above, an inclined plane, smooth as glass, along which it would shoot with the speed of an arrow, to fall over the edge of the retarded water beneath, and furnish in its turn a ready passage for the water above and behind? That in consequence of this law, the flood would come not by a gradual rise, giving time for escape, but like a rolling mountain, to smite with the impact of a falling asteroid, and crush in an instant everything in its way? Had they reflected that such a body of water would outrun the swiftest Paul Revere who might mount steed to fly with the warning to the towns below? That to the doomed, the first announcement of danger would be the stroke of the destroyer? That to the living there would be absolutely no more time for flight than to the sinner, of preparation for judgment after Gabriel shall have blown his trumpet? It is safe to say that few, if any, had even remotely con-conceived the possibilities in the case. Men learn by experience, and even from experience they fail to learn; for the lesson of to-day is forgotten to-morrow: and human heedlessness is perpetual.

The crest of the dam stood four or five feet above the

spill-way. Towards noon of the 31st, persons on the watch saw the water of the reservoir rising at the rate of a foot an hour. Meanwhile a rumor had spread that the dam was leaking, and this attracted other observers. Some declared that jets of water were leaping from the lower side to a distance of thirty feet. Somewhere about half-past two o'clock water began to run over the top. The structure was then evidently doomed; for, though riprapped with stone on both slopes, no rampart of earth could long withstand the abrasion of a torrent running over its crest, and down its lower face. A South Fork pastor reached the spot at ten minutes before three. A foot of water was then running over the dam. A few minutes later a break was made "large enough to admit the passage of a train of cars;" then presently the whole thing dissolved almost instantly, like a phantom. A breach was made four hundred and twenty-nine feet wide clean down to the bottom, and with the noise of seven thunders and a tread that shook the hills like a young earthquake, out rushed a mountain of water "tree-top high." At such a sight the awed spectator could only gasp, "God have mercy on the people in the vale below." Rushing onward a mile in three minutes, or as some have claimed, twice or thrice as fast, in an instant down went a mill, two houses and some barns, up went an iron bridge tossed like a thing of straw, and a moment later the flood was at South Fork. Two trains, a passenger and a freight, detained by a wash-out further up the road, were standing at the station. Warned by the awful roar, the passenger train sprang out just in time to save the lives of the people on board. The engineer of the freight, seeing it impossible to move with his heavy train, unhitched the locomotive, opened the throttle-valve, and with the fireman, flew for life. The seething mountain leaped on the train and dragged it away, regard-

THE BROKEN DAM.

less of two brakemen, who surrendered their lives. The village of South Fork, standing in the angle above the junction of two streams, and on high ground, was comparatively unharmed, though two lives and considerable property were destroyed.

On rushed the river down a valley, having from the lake to Johnstown an average grade of more than thirty feet in a mile. A mile and a quarter below South Fork the river strikes at right angles a projecting cliff. The baffled stream makes a detour of two miles and returns almost into itself, having accomplished an absolute advance of no more than seventy-five feet. A railroad cut no longer than this quits the river above, then regains and crosses it by a viaduct below. The railroad bed at the upper end of the cut is twenty feet above the stream, while at the lower end it is seventy. Here the torrent divided; a part of it, twenty feet deep and forty feet above the river-bed, flowing through the cut, the other part following the channel around. When this latter portion returning struck the cliff at the lower end of the cut, the water rose to the enormous height of one hundred and twenty-five feet. From this point the monster, towering to heaven, and like a "wild beast dreadful and terrible and strong exceedingly," and ravening for prey, sprang upon Mineral Point, a little more than a mile below. The town was instantly "wiped out," forty houses being swept away and sixteen persons drowned. The rest doubtless were saved by clinging to the wreck; or warned by the ominous roar, they had fled to the neighboring hills. The Methodist church, lifted from its foundation and tossing on the torrent, solemnly, and for the last time tolled its bell, as if recognizing the end of its days and usefulness; and continued to toll until its burial was accomplished beneath the waters.

Two miles and a half below Mineral Point the flood encountered another bend of the river, with a cut and viaduct in all respects similar to that which has been described. Here again was enacted the grand and terrific scene which took place above. Then from this augmented height the torrent swept down upon East Conemaugh and Franklin, a mile below. These villages standing on opposite sides of the river, constituted the first of that series of boroughs known by the name of Johnstown.

An engineer, backing up the road, and pulling at the nose of his locomotive a train of freight cars, had proceeded a third of a mile above Conemaugh. Here the roar of the coming flood broke upon his ears, and looking up the river he saw the descending avalanche. Instantly reversing his engine and drawing the throttle, his whistle all the while shrieking a wild alarm, he pushed at utmost speed the obstructing cars back to the yard of the Pennsylvania road. Then leaping from his engine, and leaving his whistle still to sound its warning, he ran to his house near by, and with his family escaped to the hill just as the rolling torrent dashed its billows at his feet.

Three passenger trains and one freight had been standing on the side-tracks some hours, detained by the washout already mentioned. The passengers were reading, writing, conversing, worrying, walking up and down the tracks in the rain, or watching the driftwood and the constantly rising river, but conscious of no danger. Something was said about a reservoir somewhere up the road, which might burst and come down upon them, but they gave the matter no second thought. Twice was one of the trains compelled to move, as the water undermined the track, and caused it to fall into the river. Once they were startled by the crash of a bridge, which yielded to

FLEEING ENGINE.

the rushing waters, and was swept away. It was near the hour of four in the afternoon, and they were still wearily waiting. Suddenly they were startled by the long, shrill shriek, close to their ears, of engineer Hess' whistle, and looking out of their windows up the river, they saw an enormous mass of wreckage, roots, trees, and driftwood borne aloft on the back of the torrent, and rushing toward them. With one impulse, the most of the passengers leaped from the trains and fled for their lives. Those in the first train had to run round, or creep under the second in order to reach the town, and thence the hill. Between the trains and the town there was a ditch ten feet wide, and five and a half feet deep, and filled with water. Into this, many plunged—nine women and girls together. A gentleman who had leaped across tarried a moment to give a helping hand, and all were rescued, save one, an aged woman. She was apparently dazed; for, refusing the proffered hand, she said, "I will go this way," walked toward the maddened waters, and was lost. The rest fled amain to the rising ground near by, with the raging torrent not ten feet behind them. Gaining the hill they turned to behold a grand and awful scene—the crashing, tumbling buildings lifted from their foundations and hurled against each other; the shrieks and cries and screams of agonizing, despairing, dying men and women, and all Conemaugh going down in the fierce river. The round house sprang from its seat like a toy tossed from a giant's hand, and more than thirty great locomotives were rolled along "like so many pebbles." All the trains were carried away. In some of the cars the passengers could yet be seen, while on the top of one car, loosened from the rest, were two men struggling desperately to keep their hold as it rolled from side to side. The whole four trains drifted down about five hundred feet, when they were stopped in a singular manner. Some inexplicable movement of the water lifted the head of one train and threw it across that of the other. Engines from the round-house were rolled down and piled against these, a mass of trees and drift were added, and the whole four trains, with the exception of two or three cars, were arrested and anchored in the midst of the flood.

But, though the whistle was a warning, and the hills were a refuge to the people of East Conemaugh, the lives of twenty-four were lost; while of the passengers on the trains, twenty-six are known to have perished.

One family were carried down in their house, which held together till it drifted against the steep hillside, some distance below, where it was arrested long enough for them to make their escape.

Two sisters, clinging to driftwood, were being swept past the woolen mill in Woodvale, when a rope was thrown to them and they were saved.

One man was carried on a drifting log clear through Johnstown and over into Kernville, to find deliverance at the end of a wild, three-miles ride. Another, overtaken at the fair grounds, climbed on the ticket shed, and thence upon a telephone pole. This being quickly broken down by the impact of some solid body, he mounted a passing log and dashed ahead all the way to the stone bridge, a distance of more than two miles. Here he took hold of some wreckage, and by the backwater was carried to Main street, near the Presbyterian church, whence he worked his way to final safety.

A quarter of a mile below East Conemaugh was the town of Woodvale. The story of its calamity has few details, since all its five thousand inhabitants were either drowning or engaged in a mad struggle for their lives. Every one of its eight hundred houses was lifted in a minute—not one

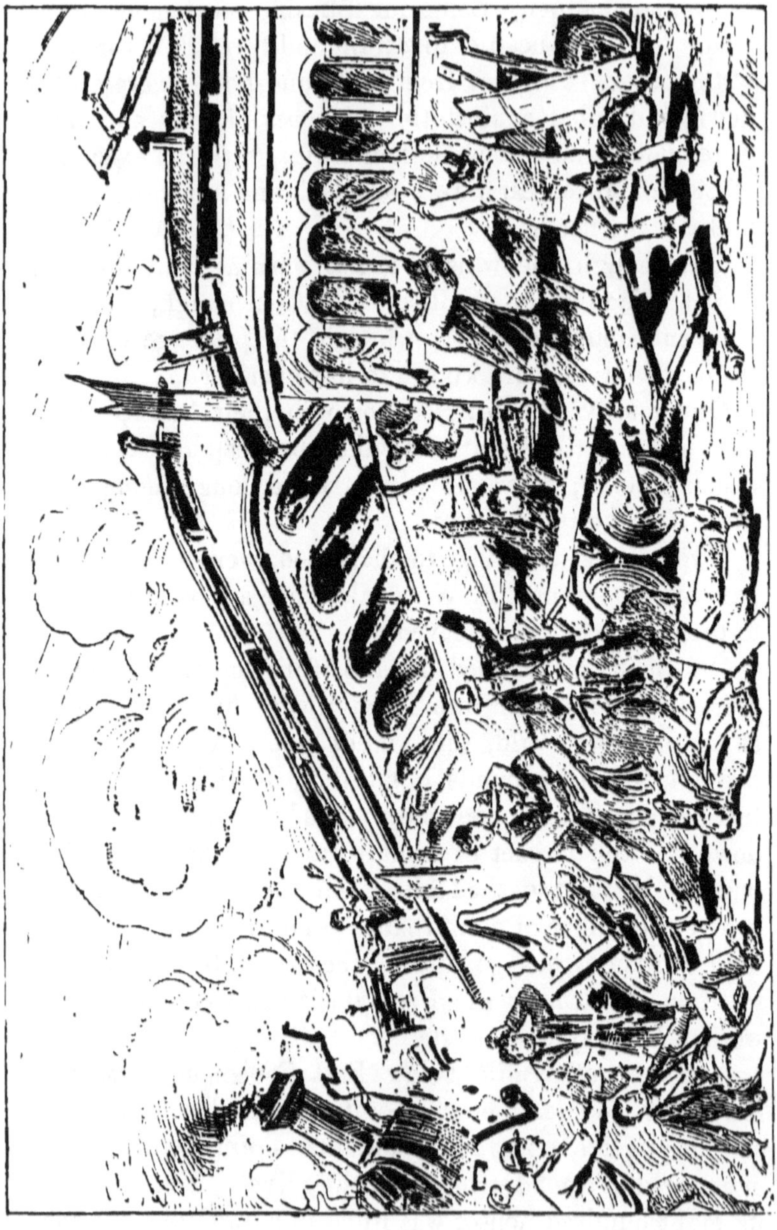

WRECK OF THE TRAINS.

remained; nothing but parts of the walls of the large woollen and flour mills. To the hills forty or sixty rods distant, not many succeeded in escaping. Relatively but few attempted it, for when the whistles sounded the alarm, the hills were too distant and the flood was too near. Such as fled were overtaken by the raging waters, and, to make destruction doubly sure, a freight train was standing between them and the hill, and this at the supreme moment, began to move. Thus many perished when there was but a step between them and deliverance. The houses were mostly frames, and the people were commonly swept away with their shattered dwellings. We know there were thousands of wonderful escapes, the recital of which would fill a bulky volume; but more than one-third of the total population were quickly counted with the dead.

Laden with corpses and debris gathered from five towns: with cars and trees and all the nameless accumulation from a valley twelve miles long, the torrent now swept down on Conemaugh Borough. This in turn was quickly swept away, though more of the inhabitants succeeded in escaping to the hills. At the lower end of the borough were the Gautier Mills, a part of the great Cambria Iron Company's plant. These occupied perhaps ten or twelve acres of ground. When the flood struck them with their hundreds of fierce fires, there were thunderous explosions that shook the hills, and the whole seemed to rise up at once and slide forward on the slanting flood. One or two experiences from this part of the town must suffice for hundreds more. One lady drifted far down across the Seventh Ward and lay all night among the wreckage, within easy reach of seven dead persons, while the luxuriant hair of a dead woman drifted frequently across her face, half buried beneath the water. A wealthy German lady, a prominent member of the Lutheran church, said. "My son Henry and his wife, my son Charles and my son-in-law were all drowned; my pastor and his wife and four nice little children were lost; there is not one brick of our good, big church left on top of another; and here is the key, which alone remains. I think my heart must break from overmuch sorrow." A few days later she sank into the grave.

CHAPTER XVII.

INCIDENTS AT JOHNSTOWN.

> "They shall sleep
> Where death may deal not again forever,
> Where change may come not till all change end.
> From the graves they have made they shall rise up never,
> Who have left naught living to ravage and rend.
> Earth, stones and thorns, of the wild ground growing,
> While the sun and the rain live, these shall be,
> Till a last wind's breath, upon all these blowing,
> Roll the sea.
>
> *   *   *   *   *   *
>
> And till in his triumph, where all things falter,
> Stretched out on the spoils that his own hand spread,
> Like a god self-slain on his own strange altar,
> Death lies dead."

THE Johnstown flood has no parallel in suddenness and destructiveness, save in the convulsions of the earthquake and volcano, agencies which will be noticed shortly, but which have never wrought such serious havoc in our own land as elsewhere. But the most deplorable feature of this terrible calamity is, that it might easily have been averted. It was due entirely to the culpable carelessness of a club of wealthy pleasure-seekers. It would be senseless to prate of "mysteries of Providence" in this connection.

Nothing can give so clear an idea of the exact character of the terrible flood—totally different from the overflow of a river—than the personal narratives of survivors. A chapter devoted to these will be of interest, and serve also to illustrate the breaking up of family and social ties that are an inevitable consequent of great calamities of every kind.

The flood was slightly less sudden at Johnstown proper than higher up the valley. Yet, to the inhabitants, in every part of the city, it was almost instantaneous. All narrators agree in the statement that they were taken completely by surprise. Few of them, whether by sound of whistle, or sight of cloud, or of coming torrent, had so much as a minute's warning. Mr. Rose seems to have had the longest notice of any. He reckons less than three minutes after he looked from his window and saw the flood a mile above, before his house fell, and himself and family were struggling beneath the water. His carriage-house was broken, perhaps three minutes in advance of his dwelling. The water which overthrew it was a sort of advance guard preceding the main body. This partial division of forces was doubtless due to the two great bends in the river, which have already been described, or rather to one of them, since one would have nearly the effect of two. The upper bend was two miles round, while the railroad cut across the neck was only seventy-five feet. The smaller portion of water pouring through the cut got nearly two miles the start of the main body, which had to flow round the bend. The water which got the start at the first cut had to flow round the second bend, not being high enough to command the short way through the second cut. Practically, therefore, the distribution of water made at two bends and cuts was only a little more than that which was made at one. Had there been no bends and railroad cuts between Conemaugh Lake and Johnstown; had the flood been confined for the entire distance to a single channel, then the towns below would have recognized no previous swell whatever; a single gigantic wall of water would have struck Johnstown as distinctly as it struck South Point; the inhabitants, in most cases, would not have had time even to reach their

MILL CREEK.

upper stories; the wave, even more than it did, would have crushed as with the single blow of a mighty hammer, and the number of survivors who could tell a tale of wonderful deliverance would have been correspondingly diminished. The lesson of these facts is for those who dwell below dams or reservoirs. If there be nothing in the nature of the channel to distribute the water, and the rupture be instantaneous, the destruction of life and property will be awful to contemplate.

At the Gautier Works, the flood, while extending over all the valley, was yet parted into three principal divisions. One of these, following the course of the Conemaugh, rushed down against the foot of the hill, just above the Stone Bridge, and would have instantly swept away that magnificiently solid structure, had it not stood parallel to, rather than at right angles with the torrent; another turning to the left, swept across Conemaugh Borough and the upper wards of Johnstown, destroying hundreds of stone buildings, the German Lutheran church, and the Hulbert House; while the third swept straight down through the middle of the city, demolishing the Y. M. C. A. Hall, the Municipal buildings, and scores of the finest residences. This last, turned into a reverse current by the damming of the water at the bridge, was presently rolled back, to ensure the destruction of whatever had escaped in its downward course.

Thousands of people, drifted from the towns above, were dead already, or still struggling in the water; and to these were now quickly added many thousands more. Of the people of Johnstown, it may be said that not a soul had time to fly. We hear nothing at all about escapes to the hills. At the scream of the warning whistle, some were startled, and looked up the river. According to their place in the town, they saw, at the distance of a mile, half a mile, or only a hundred yards away, an ominous and inexplicable dark cloud, which might be smoke or spray, hanging upon the surface of the water. They felt that something unusual had taken place, but of its nature they were not well aware. Those who saw it at the greatest distance had hardly time to scramble to the upper stories of their dwellings, before, even there, they found themselves struggling in the water; while the vast majority, on looking forth, saw buildings, not a half block above them, already leaping from their foundations. Simultaneous with the roar and rush of the torrent, came the crash of houses, the shrieks and cries of men, women and children, the revolution of everything as in a kaleidoscope, and then, driven with the speed of a race-horse, houses, furniture, cars, locomotives, railroad tracks, the Gautier plant, animals alive and dead, trees, lumber and infinite wreckage were rushed onward to be jammed and piled at the railroad bridge in a maze of ruin fifty feet high and covering forty acres of ground. Here the laboring waters finding no ready exit, were in part turned to the left up Stony Creek, and in part rolled swiftly backward across the center of the city, bearing the drift on their bosom, and in some instances droping shattered houses within a square or two of their former places. The wreckage above the bridge, entangling and holding fast, hundreds, if not thousands, as well of the living as the dead, presently caught fire, thus adding, through all the long awful night, to the horrors of flood, the fiercer horrors of flame. From the roaring conflagration, a sickly baleful gleam was thrown through a mile radius of surrounding gloom; but like the Miltonic fires of perdition, from those flames

> "No light, but rather darkness visible,
> Served only to discover sights of woe."

Some say they saw hundreds throw themselves backward into the flames, to perish, and the record of the morgues, showing how often a charred arm or leg or half a body was interred, prove that upon many, dead or alive, the fire did its awful work, while in many cases, doubtless, it was done so effectually that not a remnant could be found.

As the night drew on, St. John's Roman Catholic church which had successfully withstood the angry waters, was seen to be on fire, driving out the miserable creatures that had taken refuge in it, and with its fierce heat scorching those on the surrounding drift, till they were fain to relax their hold and drop into the water. Those flames, as they climbed the beautiful spire and seized the emblem of Christianity on its lofty top, seemed to mock the confidence of those who in their last extremity were still clinging to the cross. In the tower of the Lutheran church, near to Stony Creek, the town clock was still sustained far above the raging waters. The flood had struck the city at four, and as the hour of five drew on, when drifting corpses were now everywhere, and thousands clinging to the wreck lay at the mercy of the flood or flame, the mechanism of the clock serenely moving brought the hands to mark the hour, and slowly five times the ponderous hammer smote the massive bell, tolling the knell of thousands which that hour had rushed into eternity. On the ears of the living, the sound of those slowly beating strokes fell with a horrible sensation; for at the end of another hour would be tolled a dirge for them. There was something terrible in the calmness of that clock, faithfully telling the flight of Father Time, reckless whether he had brought joy or woe to mortal men.

But not engulfing flood, nor burning temple, nor holocaust of victims at the bridge could shake the steadfast confidence of many in their God. One little boy, when **his mother** and the rest were clinging in the drift at the

AT THE STONE BRIDGE.

bridge, asked, "Mamma, where is that God that Mr. Beale and Mr. Moore told us about, and said that he would save us?" but another little boy, despairing of temporal deliverance, was heard closing his prayer with the beautiful words of the 23rd Psalm: "Though I walk through the valley of the shadow of Death, I will fear no evil; for thou art with me; thy rod and thy staff, they comfort me." A son asked his mother, "Will we die?" She answered, "I can not tell; but one thing I *do* know, that God does all things well, and if he wants us to-night, he will take us; if not, he will find a way for our escape. We will go and sit down and see what the Lord will do." A pastor, just escaped with his family to the third story, and waist-deep in water, before he could reach it, instantly opened and read from the family Bible, which he had caught up in his flight: "God is our refuge and strength, a very present help in trouble; therefore, will not we fear, though the earth be removed, and though the mountains be carried into the midst of the sea; though the waters thereof roar and be troubled; though the mountains shake with the swelling thereof." One of the sweetest singers in the city had retreated with her family to the attic; the house was lifted and apparently moving to destruction, when, to soothe her children and her husband, she calmly sang, "Jesus, lover of my soul." While she continued to sing, the end of a large tree, having great roots, was driven through the house, anchoring it firmly just in the edge of Stony Creek River. A man who was carried over the Stone Bridge, saw a lady on a piece of wreckage shooting down the valley of death, and heard her singing those same immortal words of Charles Wesley, written by him at night, by a feeble spark, in a spring-house, where he was hiding from a raging mob:

> "Jesus, lover of my soul,
>   Let me to thy bosom fly,
>   While the raging waters roll,
>   While the tempest still is high."

A venerable man was seen upon his knees, with clasped hands, gazing steadfastly at the cross above St. John's Roman Catholic church; while another, converted the previous winter, full of faith, and always rejoicing in hope, was last seen kneeling upon the roof of his house, riding with the torrent, and shouting, "Glory to God."

The narratives of the survivors, whether from the upper, middle, or lower portions of the city, all alike serve to show that the suddenness of the doom could only be equalled by its awful horror.

The Hulbert House, built of brick, and one of the finest hotels in Johnstown, stood in the upper portion of the city. There were about sixty persons in it at the time of the catastrophe, and of these, the lives of forty-nine were lost. Many of these were in the office, when an unusual whistling of engines was heard. Imagining a fire had broken out in the midst of the flood, they all ran to the upper stories, except the proprietor, the clerk, and one guest. Two or three minutes later, the clerk walked to the window, and looked across the Conemaugh in the direction of Prospect Hill, and seeing what he mistook for a great cloud of dust, exclaimed, "My God, the hill is falling!" At that, the proprietor ran to the door, and looking up the street, realized at once the situation. Directing the other two to hasten upstairs and spread the alarm, he ran to the kitchen to warn the girls; then fleeing to the fourth floor, he reached it just as the building fell. One of the few survivors declares that the catastrophe overtook nearly all the guests no further advanced than to the foot of the stairway on the third floor, and as yet unapprized of the nature of their danger.

Rev. D. M. Miller, pastor of the Presbyterian church in East Conemaugh, had his home in Johnstown. To him and his family the deluge came without a moment's warning. They were in an upper room, fearing, suspecting nothing, till they saw houses not half a square away starting from their places, reeling and crackling onward over fences, telephone poles and fruit-trees, and jostling against each other. Before they could fly in any direction, they were waist-deep in water. Beneath the lower sash which was raised, Mr. Miller sprang out upon some floating timbers, urging his wife to follow. She, however, mounted the bed, which being instantly forced up to the ceiling she was almost smothered. The water had closed the opening beneath the sash, and up to her neck in water she now set herself desperately to effect an opening at the top of the window, but she only tore her hands in the vain attempt to wrench away the slat. Mr. Miller, by this time recovering from his first plunge, with one hand caught hold of the spout beneath the eaves, and with the other, battered through two panes of glass, cutting himself badly. Drawing up one foot, with it he now kicked out the sash, when his wife dived out under the lintel, expecting to reach footing on the roof of a small porch below. The porch, however, was gone, and she disappeared deep beneath the turbid flood. A moment later, by some violent ebullition of the water, she was thrown to the surface, and at once laid hold on the spout. Meanwhile, the house was drifting rapidly toward Stony Creek. When the vast number of houses adrift struck the hill beyond the stream there was a fearful rebound; many houses were crushed to splinters, many were upset, and scores of clinging wretches were mangled, killed, or plunged into the water and drowned. The current, arrested by the hill, divided; a part turned to the left up

Stony Creek, carrying many houses nearly a mile; part turned to the right, to add its freightage of life and ruin to the already tremendous gorge above the bridge, while between these currents a central portion was rolled back in the direction whence it came. On this portion Mr. Miller's house was carried, till wandering round and having described two-thirds of a complete circle, by the subsidence of the water it found rest at last not more than a hundred yards from its original position. During much of this journey the pastor and his wife, up to their necks in water, and battered and bruised incessantly by the terrible drift, were clinging to the spout. At last two of their neighbors being in some manner, incomprehensible to themselves, thrown upon the roof and sitting on the comb, after a time espied beneath the eaves the heads of the unfortunate couple. To creep down to the edge of the steep roof, slippery through incessant rain and recover the pastor and his wife was an undertaking fraught with extreme peril, yet these men, as did hundreds more in this awful hour, freely risked their lives in the effort to save others. A little later a woman and a boy were recovered, and brought to the same roof, on the comb of which six persons now sat until nightfall, when the house having ceased from its wanderings, they managed to creep into the attic. This being unfinished, there was no floor on which even the sick could lie; so, in the dark, in their torn and wet and filthy garments, through all the long, dreary hours of an endless night, through the forenoon of the following day, and until the middle of the afternoon, on a narrow board, they sat together until the rescuers came. Then there was a laborious clambering over broken houses and great piles of wreck, a tramp of half a mile through mud and water, when they found at last rest and refuge and friends. Twenty-eight hours they

DESPERATE STRUGGLE FOR LIFE, JOHNSTOWN.

had passed without a wink of sleep or a morsel of food, while their wounds and bruises were such as for a time to render doubtful their recovery.

Mr. Calliver, a machinist, had his dwelling in one of the upper wards of the city. His wife, an invalid, had not walked for seven years. He was watching the flood, and telling his neighbors that the worst was already past, when, looking up the river, he saw houses bounding from their places and skurrying towards him. He shouted to his family at once to flee to the attic, but, before they could reach it they were knee-deep in water. The house was floated, and borne swiftly away, but fortunately did not turn over. It drifted out of the main current, struck upon something, and was held fast, while other buildings were drifted onward. Union street school house was near, and to this place, late in the afternoon, by clambering over the accumulated drift, it became possible to escape. Here they found themselves in the company of nearly two hundred others rescued in various ways. Some were crippled, some were shivering with cold, and all had lost their nearest and dearest friends. Many were in awful suspense concerning the fate of loved ones. A sleepless, endless night dragged its slow hours along, and when at last Mr. Calliver, watching anxiously from the roof, saw the first gleam in the east, he cried out in an ecstasy, "It is morning! it is morning!" After deliverance came, being curious to know what it was that had so opportunely arrested his floating house, he made examination, and found that, of several open cars that had drifted into the neighborhood, one had dropped endwise into a cellar, and his house driven upon the end that was elevated had been penetrated with the shaft of the brake-wheel, and securely held in that place.

Rev. David J. Beale, D.D., pastor of the Presbyterian church, to whose authentic and thrillingly interesting book

"Through the Johnstown Flood," we are principally indebted for our statement of facts, and to which the reader is referred for a fuller account, records an experience, which, like those already narrated, serves to show that the visitation was as sudden as it was awful. His first intimation of the coming ruin was a roar, increasing like that of an approaching train, and a moment later the torrent had struck his residence. Urging in advance of him his family and two neighbors who were present, he rushed up stairs, and reaching the second floor found himself already waist-deep in water. At that instant, a man was shot by the force of the current through the window, and to the sudden interrogatories, "Who are you? Where did you come from?" breathless and strangling, he could only answer, "Woodvale." He had been carried on a floating roof a mile and a quarter, and as it violently struck the parsonage, he was pitched from his hold and dashed through the window. In another minute the whole company were in the third story, witnesses, blanched and mute, of the awful scene of destruction and death.

They recognized many acquaintances and friends riding on to death. They saw two little children, almost nude, clinging to one roof; four young ladies, in agonized embrace, clinging to another; houses for squares north and west torn from their places, and the whole drawn onward, to be crushed and jammed in the gorge below. Meanwhile, Capt. A. N. Hart, his wife and two children, were seen struggling in the wreckage which had drifted near the parsonage, and Mr. Beale, descending into the water in the second story, assisted them to enter through the window. Their arrival in the garret increased to fifteen the number of persons there collected.

The parsonage now began to show evident signs of giving way, and it was decided to abandon it. After an unsuccessful attempt to gain the roof, the whole party were safely passed by means of a rope from the highest window to a floating roof below. They had hoped to reach the church, which still stood secure, a short distance away; but, on making the attempt, they found themselves confronted with fifty feet of water which could not be crossed. They now began a perilous journey over wreckage to Alma Hall, half a square away. This was a four-story building, the largest and strongest in the city. Their way lay over logs and roofs and houses, fixed or moving box cars, and various debris which often concealed them from one another. One of the young ladies, crossing open water on a scantling, fell and disappeared, all but her floating hair, by which she was caught and recovered. About dark they gained the hall, and found no less than two hundred and sixty fortunate unfortunates like themselves, rescued in wondrous ways from ghastly death.

Then followed the long night of sleepless horror, unillumined, save from the burning church, and from the horrible holocaust at the bridge. The suppressed moans of those with bruised bodies and broken limbs, the crying of little children, cold and wet and hungry, and without a place to lay their heads, the anxiety for loved ones, the mourning for them that were certainly lost, the momentary dread lest the building should give way and yet overwhelm all with sudden death, conspired to make it a night never to be forgotten. Morning came at last, and then, as the sun rose above the hills, might have been seen a curious and mournful procession. Descending through a window, they walked and jumped, and crawled and clambered over several blocks, filled with broken buildings, cars, trees, furniture, bridges and dead bodies, till they reached the hill.

What a spectacle of human misery was there presented!

THE GORGE AT THE BRIDGE.

Fully three thousand people were gathered, weary, wet, cold, haggard, hungry, homeless, shoeless, hatless, coatless, ragged, muddy, many almost naked, gazing in mute despair, in awful anguish that could shed no tear (for no tears were shed) upon miles of wreck, containing by the thousand the dead bodies of husbands, wives, parents, children, lovers, and precious friends. Could humanity be called to suffer more?

Mr. Horace W. Rose, Esq., a prominent attorney about fifty years of age, had spent his life in Johnstown, and remembered distinctly all the great floods it had experienced. The highest he had seen was in 1887, and he had little fear that ever he would see another higher. He was not alarmed when the water entered the lower story of his dwelling, but as he saw it advance above the wash board, and with its foul freight stain the beautiful paper recently put upon the wall, he was not without a feeling of sadness. He conversed pleasantly with his neighbors, and twitted their children with invitations to come across the way and make a friendly visit. Fifteen minutes before the catastrophe he was engaged in shooting rats, and continued the occupation until hearing a loud crash, he ran to the back part of his house, and saw that the water had broken down his carriage-house and was driving the carriage into the yard. At the same moment he heard cries, the alarm of a bell, and the loud screams of a steam whistle. Feeling that something awful must have happened, he ran to the third floor, followed by all his family, and looking out through a window, which permitted a view of nearly a mile up the Conemaugh, the awful fact was at once apparent. "I saw stretching from hill to hill, a great mass of timber, trees, roofs and debris of every sort, rapidly advancing, wrecking and carrying everything before it. It was then about the midst of what was known as the Gautier Works, a department of the Cambria Iron Works, which covered perhaps ten or eleven acres of ground. A dense cloud hung over the line of the rolling debris, which I then supposed was the steam and soot which had arisen from hundreds of fires in the Gautier Works as the waves rolled over them. I stood and looked as the resistless tide moved on, and saw brick buildings crushed in an instant pass out of sight, while frame tenements were quickly crushed to atoms.

"Members of my family asked me if there was no escape. I answered, 'No; this means death to us all.' My wife with blanched face said, 'Won't our big strong house stand?' I replied deliberately: 'No, Maggie; no building can stand this awful jam, and we are all lost.'

"The press of the heaving, surging mass rolled steadily on, and in less than three minutes, as nearly as I can estimate time, from the moment I saw the front of the angry torrent it was upon us. The great Municipal building above me fell with a crash. The stately dwelling of my neighbor, John Dibert, was broken to atoms. I walked rapidly to the southeast window, and saw the front of the brick dwelling above and adjoining mine, crushed to rubbish. Several persons were floating directly down Main street, in front of me; a large frame building directly opposite me careened, at the attic windows of which I saw a number of ladies, one of whom held an infant in her arms; there was a crash, a sensation of falling, a consciousness that I was in the water, and all was dark. A moment later, I felt the press of a heavy shock, a sense of excruciating pain, involving my right breast, shoulder and arm. The thought came upon me that I was being crushed to death, that I could not long endure the agony I then suffered, and that death would come soon. I watched for the change, expecting in a moment to know the reality of eternity. I heard the moan of my eldest son, who was at my side when the crash came.

"I felt myself struggling, with my left hand clutching at something, I know not what. I heard the voice of my youngest son, as I thought, imploring me to aid him. I told him I was powerless to succor him. A moment later I realized that he was endeavoring to have me reach a higher elevation, when I told him my whole right side was crushed; he came to my relief and aided me in getting upon a fragment of the slate roof. A moment after, a little boy whom I had sheltered, appeared and informed me that my wife was drowned; he had barely made this announcement when I saw my only daughter, June, rise up out of the water among the debris to perhaps her waist, and immediately sink out of sight. As she sank, I saw my wife rise out of the water to about her waist, and almost immediately sink out of sight; a moment after, they rose together, and I saw my son Winter, a lad of twenty years, a strong, robust person, and heard him say, 'Ma, hold on to me, and I can save you.' I was lying on my side, perhaps twenty or twenty-five feet distant from where my wife, daughter and son were struggling, the skin torn from the right side of my face, the blood flowing profusely from the wound, the skin torn from the back of my left hand, my right collar-bone broken, my shoulder-blade fractured, the ribs crushed in upon my lung, my right arm from shoulder to wrist lying limp on my side, powerless to give aid or assistance to my loved ones. At this moment a young man seemed to shoot up and out of the debris at my side; I realized that he was an acquaintance, but could not name him. I at once, however, addressed him, saying, 'Young man, won't you go and help Winter save my wife and daughter? I am helpless; my whole right side and arm are crushed.' He made no reply, but

THE BATTLE WITH THE WATERS.

at once hastened across the debris, and aided in relieving my wife from the timbers in which she was pinioned. Then he immediately disappeared from my sight; but I afterward learned he was Harry Philips, who was reared in Johnstown, was then practicing his profession of dentistry in Pittsburg; was home on a visit, and in the house of Dr. L. T. Beam, and was the only person who escaped with his life, while his mother, niece, nephew and brother-in-law were lost in the flood. My eldest son had disappeared. I believed I had heard his dying moan. All the other inmates of my house at the time it was struck, were now floating on different fragments of houses, and being rushed with fearful velocity in a westerly course to and across the Stony Creek River.

"They saw a stout roof on the edge of the debris and succeeded in reaching it; an old lady on bended knees and holding with her hands, floated by on a shutter, and Winter assisted her to gain the roof; the current suddenly turned and swept them rapidly up Stony Creek, a distance of half a mile; they came to rest above Morris street in the Fifth Ward, and lay for a considerable time; some inexplicable force then carried them across the river, and they lay for a while in the mouth of Franklin street; the Catholic church was on fire, and the town clock struck five; a cold and pitiless rain poured down upon them; the current now changed and buildings and wreckage were borne rapidly down the stream; as houses were broken to pieces, clinging wretches with wild shrieks sank to watery graves; the two sons were separated from the remainder of the family on the roof; it drifted once more down the stream, was struck by a heavier building and pushed upon the bank; over various drift they climbed till they reached a three-story brick which stood intact; they entered it just as the town clock struck six—two awful hours, and yet no member of the family lost. Happier far their fate than that of many others. The two boys returned to their parents at four o'clock the next day."

These incidents will suffice. Thousands of the same sort might be given. No wonder that many were crazed with grief. One woman, wife and mother, sole survivor of a happy family, was found sitting in the wreck, holding in her arms her family clock which she had found. She told her story without a tear. Her mind was unbalanced. A man who had never been known to touch liquor was found the day after the flood, reeling to the bridge, drunk and raving, determined to drown himself. In agony at the loss of all he held dear, he had taken to drink, that he might remember his misery no more; but in vain: whisky could not destroy his terrible memories. Talmage in a letter to the New York *World*, said: "Such an avalanche of horrors never slipped upon any American city. Horrors piled on horrors, woe augmenting woe; bankruptcy, orphanage, widowhood, childlessness, obliterated homesteads, gorged cemeteries and scenes so excruciating it is a marvel that any one could look upon them and escape insanity * * * *

"Was the work of devastation as great as I supposed? Far worse. Types can not tell it. Only the eye can make revelation. But the worst part of it can not be seen. The heart-wreck caused by the sudden departure of so many can be open only to one eye, and that the All-Seeing. Think of one family of fourteen all dead except one, and that the wife and mother, and she the witness of their drowning. I saw the grave trench in which two hundred and sixty were buried, and the whole graveyard like a national cemetery, in which the unrecognized dead have a particular number placed above them and are recorded in the undertaker's rooms with a description of the body and clothes."

On many a life a shadow has been cast that will never be lifted. Many a heart will ache until it breaks. One who had lost wife and children and was alone, whose verses and whose name the world has never heard, more than thirty years ago wrote the following most touchingly beautiful lines, which will find an echo in the hearts of thousands of survivors of the Johnstown flood, as well as among countless millions of others in every age of the world:

> Down by the cedar sitting,
>   Lonely and sad and still,
> Watching the shadows flitting
>   Over the distant hill.
> Yearning for by-gone hours,
>   Never again to come;
> Longing for beauteous flowers,
>   Never again to bloom.
>
> Ever there flits before me
>   A shadowy form and face;
> Ever it hovers o'er me,
>   Wearing a nameless grace.
> Above my brow there lingers
>   A breath like summer air;
> Unseen and loving fingers
>   Stray through my tangled hair.
>
> Silence, slow creeping nigh me,
>   Out from the leafy shade,
> Bringeth the dead hours by me,
>   And rests on the darkening glade.
>
> O ye beloved of spring time,
>   Can ye come back no more?
> Bending I trace your footsteps
>   Over the distant shore;
> Down to the misty river,
>   Into the depths of death,

Seeking your presence ever,
  Praying with sobbing breath,
"Can ye come back no more?"
    Echoing clear from the unseen shore,
      Answer sweet voices "No more, no more!"

O for the pearly gates
  Of the golden nightless plain,
Where your gentle spirit waits
  For the hour we meet again.

Out from the darkness, soft and plain,
Comes the glad echo, " *We meet again.*"

CHAPTER XVIII.

RELIEF MEASURES.

> "Abou Ben Adhem (may his tribe increase)
> Awoke one night from a deep dream of peace,
> And saw within the moonlight of his room,
> Making it rich and like a lily in bloom,
> An angel writing in a book of gold:
> Exceeding peace had made Ben Adhem bold,
> And to the presence in the room he said,
> "What writest thou?" The vision raised its head.
> And with a look made all of sweet accord,
> Answered: "The names of those who love the Lord."
>
> "And is mine one?" said Abou. "Nay, not so,"
> Replied the angel. Abou spoke more low,
> But cheerily still, and said, "I pray thee then
> Write me as one who loves his fellow men."
>
> The angel wrote and vanished. The next night
> It came again with a great wakening light
> And showed the names of whom love of God had blessed,
> And lo, Ben Adhem's name led all the rest!"

IT goes without saying that the destitution and suffering occasioned by the flood were fearful. Everywhere might be seen hundreds of sad-eyed, disconsolate, almost famished creatures, groping about the wreck, almost unconscious of present necessities by reason of present woe. Scores were compelled to drag their precious dead from the wreck and bury them with their own hands—a trying task. Other scores found never a trace of many whom they sought. Hundreds of telegrams of anxious inquiries will never be answered.

The pressing necessities of the hungry people soon drove many to seek escape from the place. Yet all railroads were damaged, and in Johnstown itself one could hardly get about the streets. A stranger describes it as it appeared on June 1:

"Johnstown proper was partly a lake, partly several small streams, partly a vast sandy plain, and partly clusters of more or less ruined houses. Around, among, between, inside and on top of these houses, wherever the rushing torrent had been checked, were piled masses of wreckage; trunks of mighty trees, household furniture, houses whole and in fragments, bridges, locomotives and railroad cars, hundreds of tons of mud and gravel. Thickly strewn through it all were hundreds of corpses and carcasses. The only communication between this section and the Pennsylvania Railroad and the village of Peelerville on the north, and Kernville on the south, was across swollen torrents in skiffs, which required constant bailing to keep them above water. From the Stone Bridge of the Pennsylvania Road, for a distance of half a mile, no river could be seen, simply a dense mass of drift from twenty to fifty feet deep, apparently inextricable, bound together with miles of wire, here blazing and there smoldering, and enveloping the bridge in a cloud of nauseating vapor and smoke, giving unmistakable evidence of the presence of burning flesh. Not a thoroughfare was passable for a team, and very few for a horse. Locomotion was difficult, the mud was deep, the streets obstructed often to the roofs of houses, the rain was incessant.

> "How poor, how rich, how abject, how august,
> How complicate, how wonderful is man;
> How passing wonder He who made him such,
> Who centered in our make such strange extremes
> From different natures marvelously mixed."

The flood quickly called forth the best and the worst exhibitions of human nature. We shall mention first the evil, as a back-ground against which the good may stand more conspicuous. We believe that to most men it will be simply incomprehensible that anybody should think of adding so much as the weight of a hair to the calamities of Johnstown, as they were seen on the morning of that first day of June. Ghouls were quick to enter, snatching from the living, robbing the bodies of the dead. Johnstown doubtless had her complement of thieves, and these were speedily reinforced by many more—crooks and jailbirds, pickpockets and burglars, from cities like Baltimore, Philadelphia and Pittsburg; for "where the carcass is, there will the eagles be gathered together." Residents guarding silverware and other valuables were, in some instances, overpowered in broad daylight and their goods taken away from before their eyes. These crimes were diligently laid at the door of the Hungarians, but better knowledge acquitted them of the charge and proved that they were not more guilty than others.

The American, accustomed by republican training to regard himself as the chief source of law, is never slow to take things into his own hands in cases of extremity. We are told that a few of these ghouls were summarily dealt with; and under the circumstances the most conservative find it hard to condemn the grief-crazed men. One correspondent asked Deputy Sheriff "Chall" Dick if the reports of summary execution were true. Chall replied slowly:

"There are some men whom their friends will never again see alive."

"Well, now, how many did you shoot?" was the next question.

"Say," said Chall. "On Saturday morning I was the first to make my way to Sang Hollow, to see if I could not get some food for people made homeless by the flood. There was a car-load of provisions there, but the vandals were on hand. They broke into the car, and in spite of my protestations carried off box after box of supplies. I only got half a wagon load. They were too many for me. I know when I have no show. There was no show there, and I got out.

"As I was leaving Sang Hollow and got up the mountain road a piece, I saw two Hungarians and one woman engaged in cutting the fingers off of corpses to get some rings. Well, I got off that team and—well, there are three people who were not drowned and who are not alive."

"Where are the bodies?"

"Ain't the river handy there?"

Another form of robber appeared in the relic-hunter. He is a phenomenon inexplicable—at least to the writer of these pages. Why men should think to chip off pieces of the Washington Monument, or from Lincoln's coffin, or from the granite sarcophagus in the great pyramid, and carry them home and put them in a cabinet, and call people to admire them, without thereby simply advertising themselves as vandals, passes comprehension. Why a chip from Johnstown should be better than the same kind of a chip from any other place, no man can tell. But the world has always had a good stock and store of this kind of fools, well described by our neglected and forgotten poet, Robert Pollok, as men who roamed about the world searching for pieces of old pottery and the like, and

> "Wondered why shells were found upon the mountain-tops,
> And wondered not at that more wondrous still,
> Why shells were found at all."

These relic-hunters, commonly of genteel appearance, were in force at Johnstown, picking up knives, forks, silver spoons, communion vessels—anything they could call fools like themselves to gape at because it came from Johnstown, and sometimes judiciously preferring as mementoes the things that were of greater value.

JOHNSTOWN AFTER THE FLOOD.

There were professional thieves who entered the morgues and identified, with expressions of sorrow, their dear departed dead, strangers never seen before, in order that they might secure the valuables found on their persons. There were others who offered their services for the recovery of the dead, and who were placed upon the details sent out for that purpose, and plundered many corpses before the arrival of Mann's detectives pointed them out as the worst of thieves and robbers.

Besides these there were sleek scoundrels, too base and black for respectability even in the pit, who approached weeping, orphaned, beautiful young girls with alluring offers of jewelry and fine clothes and delightful homes in great cities. Their object has no need to be stated.

It is pleasant to turn from these few ghoulish and degraded human reptiles to the mighty army of noble men and women who succored Johnstown.

The story of the help rendered, how much, by whom, and in what ways can not be detailed in this place. It will be enough to give a brief and general statement, while for full particulars, even to the long list of the dead, known and unknown, the reader must be referred to Dr. Beale's most interesting book.

The faults and evils of government have been conspicuous since man was upon the earth. The contemplation of these has turned some shallow-brained people into anarchists, who think the ideal state of the race must be one in which there is no government at all.

There was no government in Johnstown while the flood was sweeping it away. All human laws were then suspended, for there was no human power that could enforce them. It is curious and instructive, in a condition of complete anarchy, to note the spontaneous movements towards organized government—movements simply evoked by the popular need. Government was introduced into Alma Hall almost before the sun had set on that dreadful day. Two hundred and sixty-four men, women and children, from various directions clambering out of the debris, had been gathered there. They were wretched enough already, but disorder would only add to their woes, and for the sake of order, and to feel that the strongest and wisest were at the helm, they were ready to submit themselves to command. Accordingly, a meeting was at once called on the stairway to elect a director to control the whole building and one of the stories, and two subordinates to take charge of the other two stories. Orders were at once issued that there should be no lights, lest the escaping natural gas should explode, and that all persons having spirituous liquors should surrender them to the directors. These orders were cheerfully obeyed.

As this company was wending its mournful way the next morning to Adam street, Dr. Beale saw a man taking some valuables, and ordered him to put them down. With this hint as to the capabilities of bad men, he sent a boy a little later to the nearest telegraph station with a message to Governor Beaver to send the military. The response came soon in the presence of the National Guard, the services of whose officers and men were, in almost every way, of inestimable value.

But the necessity for government was instant, and could not await the coming of a National Guard. The community called Johnstown consisted of seven straggling boroughs, each with its own officers. Some of these were dead, all were scattered and paralyzed, while furthermore, the common calamity demanded common action, and this called for a single government instead of seven. Accordingly, before the sun was high in the heavens on that first day of June, government had been organized. According to our Declaration of Independence, it must have been a lawful government, for it had for its basis the consent of the governed.

But it was not a republican government; it was an absolute monarchy—Charles L. Dick, Esq., was elected generalissimo to direct all matters according to his wil',—the best government in the world if always there were a wise and good man at the head; for the wisdom of one man is better than the folly of a multitude.

It makes one proud of his race as he watches this stricken community in the midst of overwhelmning sorrow and loss taking action immediately for preservation and recovery. Barbarians would not have done it; Asiatics would not have done it; nor would anybody else have done it so quickly and so well as Anglo-Saxon English-speaking republicans, full of energy, resource, and indomitable courage, and habituated to the idea of a "government *of* the people, *for* the people, and *by* the people."

Avoiding details let us see in brief what was done.

Within eighteen hours after the flood, there was a force of three hundred qualified policemen guarding the vaults of the First National and Dibert's banks, and patrolling the town. A few were armed with shot-guns, the most with base ball clubs extracted from a wrecked store. The size of their batons was an indication that they were not on dress parade, but were equipped for war. Committees were quickly appointed on finances, on supplies, on morgues, on the removal of dead animals and debris, on police, on hospitals; and these committees entered on their respective duties without an hour's delay. Farmers and others were now crowding to behold the ruin, and there were many with hearts to sympathize and hands to aid. Dr. Wm. Caldwell, one of the oldest and best known merchants in the place, met the wondering comers and engaged many of them for service in the removal of the wreckage and the recovery of the dead. Details were at once constituted and sent forth under proper leaders for these purposes. Within a brief while, Charles Zimmerman had removed more than two hundred dead animals, and Thos. L. Johnson, his assistant committeeman, one of the owners of the great plant at Moxham, had made visible progress in clearing the streets of debris.

A crying and instant need was a hospital. Before the flood there was only one hospital in Johnstown. This was built by the Cambria Iron Company for the use of their own men. This hospital was now almost instantly filled and running over; but before sunset on this memorable Saturday, June 1st, the committee had opened another. Telephonic communication was broken, but a boy was sent on horseback to Shoyestown with a message to Pittsburg for hospital equipments—cots, mattrasses, pillows, medicines and other necessities; and such was the energy of all concerned that by two o'clock on Sunday, less than twenty-four hours from the sending of the message, the equipment was in Johnstown. At that time every bench and counter and even the floor was crowded with the sick and wounded from all parts of the city.

It is impossible to describe the varied movements of that dreadful day. There was little shelter and less food, death everywhere, and some doubtless imprisoned in heaps of wreck, and not yet dead, but dying of wounds, or of cold and exhaustion. The first patient in the Bedford street hospital had been taken up, presumably dead, and carried to the morgue; there he was found to be yet alive, was removed to the hospital and died of congestion the next day. The claims of the dead and of the living seemed to be equally urgent. Many of the living, for food and shelter, pushed to the country; the farmers received them with

AT THE MORGUE.

open doors. They sent wagon loads of provisions to the valley of death; the dairymen came with milk and distributed it freely; but what was this among so many? It is needless to say that the flood, even where buildings had escaped wreck, had overflowed cellars and lower stories and destroyed or badly damaged almost everything eatable in the city.

Not a few of those who survived the flood are notable for their untiring and abundant labors. It was no time for perpetuating sectarian differences. Dr. Beale pays a warm tribute to Father Davin, a Catholic priest, who stood at his post, laboring with superhuman energy, though constantly urged to take even a short rest. But he could not rest in view of so much misery. He and Dr. Beale turned their respective churches into morgues, and labored like heroes, incessantly. Father Davin's health gave way under the terrible strain, and he finally went to the mountains; but it was too late. He died of overwork and exhaustion.

Nor must the work of that much abused fraternity, the newspaper reporters be forgotten. None but reporters can appreciate the difficulties under which those men worked; and one, a pale, earnest, sympathetic little Philadelphian, toiled on till his health failed. He died at the sea shore, whither he had gone to recuperate. These men we must thank for the prompt and full reports sent throughout the country, stirring it to prompt and energetic measures of relief.

The advantages of Christian over Asiatic civilization are never more apparent than when the calamity of some calls for sympathy and help of all the rest. Then, in an hour, the news is borne to every city and hamlet in a broad continent, in another hour the press has thrown it off in millions of sheets, and every street is vocal with the cry of the newsboy proclaiming the disaster, millions of hearts are throbbing with sympathy, voices from opposite sides of great cities are talking to each other over the telephone, a meeting is called and quickly assembled, counsel is taken, performance is prompt, and before the day is done, the railroad train, bearing the necessary forms of aid, is flying with the speed of the wind to the relief of the sufferers.

Not often, even in a Christian land, has relief been so prompt or so bountiful as it was to Johnstown. Pittsburg read the news in the papers of Saturday morning. The Mayor called a meeting for one o'clock. It was crowded to overflowing, for the interest was intense. A committee was appointed, and work began instantly. By four o'clock nearly twenty cars were ready. Seventy volunteer aids were on board—all that could be taken—and the train was flying towards Johnstown. At 10:30 p. m. Sang Hollow, four miles from the scene of death, was reached. Here three-quarters of a mile of track had been washed entirely away, and the train stopped. But the men from Pittsburg stopped not. They sprang out, and trip after trip through the mud and dark, in the use of hands and shoulders, they bore onward their precious burdens of food for the starving brothers and sisters. Long before daylight, the installment of provisions—a car load and a half—was deposited at the Stone Bridge. Further than this it was impossible to go. The flood had broken the embankment beyond the bridge and a furious river a hundred feet wide was sweeping through.

But while these valiant relievers were struggling forward under boxes and parcels, the railroad management was working a veritable miracle. Men and material were placed on the ground, the grade was restored, the track was laid, and at seven o'clock the next morning the train was quietly standing at the Stone Bridge!

Was ever human energy more conspicuous, or in a better cause? Some corporations must have souls—at least, the Pennsylvania Railroad—for this triumph was stimulated not by self-interest, but by the interests of thousands dead or ready to perish. And it was General Superintendent Pitcairn of the Pennsylvania Road who moved the mayor to call the Pittsburg meeting.

The Baltimore & Ohio Road also signalized its achievements and generosity. By Monday morning it had entered the south side of Johnstown, bringing relief, or exit to the suffering people. Superintendent Patton called on the villages and towns along the road to load as many cars as they pleased, and they would be transported to Johnstown without charge. The services of both the Baltimore & Ohio and the Pennsylvania Roads were of inestimable value, and from first to last, in a spirit of true philanthrophy, they co-operated with the efforts for the relief of a stricken people.

The labors of the Pittsburg committee knew no pause nor rest for ten days, until the State, whose duty it was in so great a calamity, stepped in, and through the Flood Commission, took hold and continued the work. Even then their labors did not cease, but were continued in hearty co-operation with the officials appointed by the State. During those ten days from the first of June to the eleventh, they had placed in the field under the most efficient management between 6,000 and 7,000 laborers, they had supplied a population of about 30,000 people with food; they had looked after sanitation and hospitals and morgues; they had accomplished much in the way of opening the streets and clearing the properties of filth and debris deposited by the flood. They had been the ministers not only of the charities of the twin cities, Alleghany and Pittsburg, but of other and more distant cities.

These, recognizing the integrity and efficiency of the Pittsburg committee, directed their benefactions to them, with the request that they would control their administration. A total of $831,295 passed into their hands; of this $560,000 was turned over to the Flood Commission, the balance having been expended by themselves. Of this total, $250,770 was contributed by the cities of Pittsburgh and Alleghany.

In the ladies' committee, Pittsburg developed another agency that was vastly beneficial. Established in rooms of the Second Presbyterian church, they began work on the 4th of June, and their doors thereafter were open day and night. A special committee was always on duty and waiting to receive every train, both of the Baltimore & Ohio and the Pennsylvania Roads. These brought scores and hundreds of refugees who had lost everything, and who did not doubt that in Pittsburg, at the hands of people they had never seen, they would receive sympathy and aid. They were met at the depots, conducted to the rooms of the committee, fed and clothed, and sent to comfortable quarters till they could see a way to provide for themselves. Many were seeking homes in the country or cities beyond, and the railways generously furnished free transportation to all who were certified by the ladies' committee. Situations were procured for many, and many fragments of families, seeking permanent homes in Pittsburg, were aided even to the anticipation of their winter supplies.

Philadelphia has long been an example to other cities, in that it has had a permanent committee of relief, ever ready with men and means to answer the call of some unusual distress. At the announcement of the great calamity, this committee was at once summoned by the mayor. R. M. McWade, city editor of the *Public Ledger*, a gentleman who had raised $25,000 and sped with it to Charleston, South Carolina, at the time of the earthquake, was present, and at once moved the appropriation of

CONEMAUGH VIADUCT.

$5,000, saying that when the facts should become known, ten times the sum would be required. Others did not wait for organized effort, but hastened with medicines, surgical instruments, shoes and carloads of prepared food

—bread, butter, bacon, cheese, coffee—to the field of disaster. Personal contributions were many and liberal. On the 11th of June the committee placed $500,000 subject to the order of Governor Beaver. As late as the 4th of August the committee was induced through Dr. Pancoast to appropriate $10,000 to the Red Cross Hospital in Johnstown. Philadelphia is truly a city of "brotherly love." Newsboys and bootblacks anxiously offered their mites; and in the penitentiary hundreds of convicts gave eagerly of the hard-earned pennies gained by working extra time, till the warden placed a limit upon the amount each might give. The total contributions of Philadelphia amounted to nearly $800,000.

New York went promptly to work on the 2nd of June. The churches beginning. Monday, the 3d, liberal contritions were placed in the hands of a committee, by individuals and corporations. The poor or bad boys in the charity and reform schools were an example to many, for they of their penury cast in all that they had. The boys in the House of Refuge on Randall's Island, gave $258.22. Perhaps such lads may be yet worth saving.

The total amount contributed by the City of New York was very close to $1,000,000.

Boston gave upwards of $500,000, Chicago about $200,000, Baltimore gave liberally, and received and cared for a multitude of refugees. Fifteen hundred rendered homeless by floods at Johnstown and elsewhere arrived in Baltimore in one day.

We may not detail further. The reader who desires the fullest account of what was done, and how, and by whom, must be referred to Dr. Beale's most interesting book. It may suffice in this place to say, that contributions were forwarded, not only from the principal cities and from every State in the Union, but from foreign countries. Ireland sent $18,252.21; England, $33,158.36; Canada, $4,454.64; Mexico, $130.40; Turkey, $876.57; Italy $9.46; Austria, $481.70; Germany, 34,199.36; Prussia, $100; Wales, $68.60; Saxony, $2,637.20; Persia, $50; France, $24,511.13; Australia, $1,251.12. Total, $120,187.79. These figures prove that there are men everywhere who love their fellow men, and that the whole world is of kin.

The total loss in the Conemaugh valley was between $8,000,000 and $9,000,000; the total bestowment about $3,000,000. The loss of life is estimated variously; from 4,000 to 10,000. It will never be definitely known.

The aid of the sympathetic public—was it charity? No, it was duty. I *owe* to help my fellow man in distress just as much as I *owe* to pay my debts, and sometimes more. Mercy is *due* to men no less than justice. "If any man seeth his brother have need and shutteth up the bowels of his compassion against him, how dwelleth the love of God in him?" We might add: How dwelleth the love of *man* in him? He that does not love his fellow men is not entitled to a place among them, any more than fleas or serpents are entitled a place in human beds.

> "That man may last, but never lives,
> Who all receives, but nothing gives;
> Whom none can love, whom none can thank,
> Creation's blot, creation's blank."

CHAPTER XIX.

FAMINE AND PESTILENCE.

"Then—see those million worlds which burn and roll,
Around us—their inhabitants beheld
My spher'ed light wave in wide Heaven; the sea
Was lifted by strange tempests, and new fire
From earthquake rifted mountains of bright snow
Shook its portentous hair beneath heaven's frowns,
Lightning and inundation vexed the plains,
Blue thistles bloomed in cities; foodless toads
Within voluptuous chambers panting crawled;
When plague had fallen on man and beast and worm,
And famine: and black blight on herb and tree.
* * * * * *
* * and the thin air, my breath, was stained,
With the contagion of a mother's hate,
Breathed on her child's destroyer."

SIGNS and wonders, grave omens, strange portents, have by the ignorant and superstitious been believed to precede and presage the approach of famine and pestilence. Comets have terrified the multitudes; the rabble has quailed at the aurora, and blanched with fear at the sight of colored rain and snow. And yet nothing is clearer than that famine is the result of the simplest meteorological causes. A deficiency in rainfall is sufficient cause—is almost the only cause. Elsewhere we have noted how dependent we are upon the winds and clouds, and we need spend no further explanation of their causes and variations.

Owing to the decidedly local character of our own rains, the probability of a general famine in this country is very slight, though local droughts are of continual occurrence. Europe has been affected with serious famines at various periods; but the greatest "harvest of death" has been in Oriental lands. During the present century there have been two or three severe famines in Asia Minor, the last but two or three years since. But it is in India and China, with their overcrowded populations and lack of facilities for inter-communication, that famine becomes most terrible in its ravages. The story of one is that of another; a deficient rainfall, a failure of the rice crop, a multitude eating grass, dead leaves, straw, offal—millions starving. As these lines are written come reports of great dearth in some provinces in Japan.

One of the best known famines of recent date is the great Bengal famine of 1866. When the rice crop failed the British government at once used every possible means to facilitate the importation of rice and established large systems of public works that the people might earn money wherewith to buy. Yet it was but the chief of many great employes. Great companies pushed great projects. The customary wages remained steady; but rice had trebled in price. Hence, even by doing double work the people could not procure their usual food. And no allowance had been made for the scores of isolated villages where the news of relief measures penetrated not. So the employed grew weaker continually and less able to labor and earn; those unemployed perished by hundreds. Private charity supported thousands; for the Hindoo dreads the beggars' curse as much as the loss of caste. The women added their labors to those of the laboring husbands, but this did not suffice to support the weakening families.

Then government charity was broached; but it was at once seen that efforts in this direction would cause the cessation of individual charity. Every village looks after its own poor; every noble family continues to dispense alms, even when every vestige of wealth and greatness is gone. It would not do to take steps that might instantly suspend this work. Yet the famished crowds grew daily greater, and the residents of the European quarter of Calcutta were horrified by the influx of thousands of squalid creatures in the last extremity of hunger.

At this crisis another factor came into play. Every pious Hindoo merchant writes at the top of his day-book each day the name of the divinity whose favor he courts, and immense sums—even millions of dollars—are spent in the annual celebration in honor of Kali, the especial favorite of Bengal. A wealthy and humane Hindoo merchant suggested that Kali would be better pleased if her celebration fund were used to relieve her starving worshippers. The idea became popular at once; and the fund, promptly swelled by the exigencies of the case, aided greatly in the relief of the destitute. When we remember that Kali is a fiend incarnate, who delights in human blood, and wears a necklace of skulls, we can but consider the suggestion of the pious merchant as savoring of the ludicrous.

Another objection to government charity was in the fact that the government could only hope to establish a few great central depots. Again, the Hindoo does not discriminate between the professional beggars, fakirs, hermits, yogis, and those whom we consider more deserving: and such discrimination as it was certain the government would make would only render it odious, and probably cause grave disturbances. So the government lost three weeks when it should have been actively at work. Meanwhile English residents were spending liberally their means in private relief depots.

The government found its way out by making quietly large grants to the private relief committees established.

But it was two or three months ere the best scheme was adopted. Rice could be imported in abundance. How to place it within the purchasing power of the people was the problem. The government turned merchant, and established depots where the laborer could buy at a price within his means. But while placing the market rate within reach of the needy one-third, the rate for the remainder must not be disturbed, or the merchants would be antagonized. It was easily accomplished. The market was opened but a short time each day; and the "respectable" Hindoo would never expose himself or his family to be jostled by the hungry labor-stained multitude that at once thronged the places. And public opinion, all-powerful in little Bengali towns, strongly condemned any one who without good reason, bought at the relief depots.

By June, every one was anxious to know if the rains would come and insure the September crops—there are two rice harvests each year. Thousands of sacrifices were offered, and sometimes human beings were offered. But the rains came, and the fall brought abundant crops.

The total loss of life was about 1,250,000, of whom one-fourth starved outright, while the remainder perished from disease and pestilence resulting from the scarcity of food. A famine in the same region in 1769 carried off 6,000,000; but then the government did nothing, and after the scourge immense tracts of cultivated land returned to their original wilderness. The reverse was the result in 1866. The methodical work of the government and the great corporations left the land far more improved than ever before; with the increasing facilities for communication and transportation, a repetition of the disaster even of 1866 is almost impossible—certainly beyond probability.

We may not go into details of scores of famines, ancient and modern; we have selected this one, showing how, even in adverse circumstances, prompt work lessens the ravages of the destroyer. Judging from the percentage of 1769, the loss of life in 1866 would, but for the relief work, have been about 9,000,000—one-third the population of Bengal. The only other calamity in recent years at all comparable, is the terrible famine of 1876 in China. How many perished then may not be definitely known; but it has been variously estimated at from 15,000,000 to 50,000,000. We may not dwell upon the horrors of such things—the hideous cannibalism that has at times resulted; as when we are told that during one famine in Egypt, in the dark ages, human flesh was openly sold in the markets!

A terrible scourge that frequently visited the old world in the middle and dark ages is that known as the "Black Death." As to its real character and source, the world is yet in ignorance. Whether it was readily conveyed in the atmosphere or not seems a mooted point. Modern medical science has robbed many contagious diseases of their terrors. Small-pox is easily guarded against. Diptheria has no terrors for clean streets. Yellow Jack has little chance against sound sanitation and hygiene. The germ theory of disease has greatly aided disinfective measures.

In contagious diseases, infection proceeds chiefly from personal contact with a diseased person or objects that have been touched by him. In malarial diseases there is no danger from personal contact; the disease resulting clearly from a poisoned atmosphere. But in the case of what are known as epidemics, the source of infection is not clear. The disease may attack thousands in a short time, and yet not appear readily communicable by personal contact. Doubtless in these cases the atmosphere is the medium of infection. Hence, disinfective measures are of little or no use against them. So while such can not properly be classed among atmospheric phenomena, yet it would seem that in the atmosphere we find the chief vehicle of the disease.

We may not here undertake any discussion of the several deadly contagious diseases that are known to modern medicine. Suffice it to say nearly all of them may be classed as filth diseases, arising from impure food or water, or filthy streets. Most notable of these is perhaps the terrible Asiatic cholera, that has swept Europe frequently, and which is now known to originate in the overcrowding and filth attendant upon the great twelve-yearly festival in honor of a Hindoo idol. Had the people of the middle ages, who regarded its ravages as a visitation of God upon them for their sins, been aware of its origin, they might have been disposed to wonder why they should be punished for the idolatry of a people thousands of miles away Possibly such reflections might have originated either a new species of crusade, or have opened the missionary movement several centuries earlier than it really began.

Comparatively speaking, there is little mystery left in connection with the greater contagious plagues known to modern medicine. But the famous Black Death, or Plague, or the Pestilence, as it is variously called, remains a secret so far as its origin and its proper treatment are concerned. Its symptoms are somewhat variously described by various ancient writers. In one point all agree: that when near death the body of the victim was covered with dark, gangrenous or carbuncular spots and swellings, or boils made their appearance in the glands of the neck, armpit and groin. It may be that the plague of boils and blains sent upon the Egyptians was none other than this Black Death. And doubtless it is identical with the terrible plague that visited Athens, B. C., 430, continuing its ravages through three years. People died in swarms, and the dead lay about the streets.

During the middle ages it appeared in Europe on an average, every fifty years, its last visitation being upon London, in 1665, when 100,000 people perished. Here its danger was increased by the fact that its character was more insidious than usual. The plague described by Thucydides was characterized by high fever and unquenchable thirst, and a reddish inflammation or eruption of the skin lasting seven or eight days before the appearance of the fatal spots; while from Defoe's account of the plague in London, these symptoms, though common, were anything but universal; and frequently persons felt no special disorder till the appearance of the spots told that death was at hand. Both in Athens and London, contact with the dead bodies seems to have been fatal to any animal. The suddenness of death in many cases calls to mind the last plague of Egypt, or the fate of Sennacherib's host:

> "Like the leaves of the forest, when summer is green,
> That host with their banners at sunset were seen;
> Like the leaves of the forest, when autumn hath blown,
> That host in the morning lay withered and strown.
>
> For the Angel of Death spread his wings on the blast,
> And breathed in the face of the foe as he passed;
> And the eyes of the sleepers waxed deadly and chill,
> And their hearts but once heaved, and forever grew still.
>
> And there lay the steed, with his nostrils all wide,
> But through them there rolled not the breath of his pride;
> And the foam of his gasping lay white on the turf,
> And cold as the spray of the rock-beating surf."

The horrors of the plague are beyond description. The panic consequent upon the appearance of Yellow Jack in the South gives but a faint idea of it. And this very panic was a most—we had almost said the most—powerful factor in the augmentation of the plague's fatality. It is also the case with cholera that a disturbed condition of the mind is fatal in the mildest form of the disease. Some one has thus embodied the case, though of course with exaggeration: A traveler leaving Bagdad met Cholera entering. "For what are you come?" "To slay 10,000 people." Each went his way. On returning, the traveler met Cholera once more. "But you killed 30,000!" "Nay, friend, I killed but 10,000; *scare* killed the rest!"

Occasionally this panic took a terrible form; as when during a season of plague in Germany, the idea seized the people that the Jews had occasioned the plague by poisoning the wells; and Jews were murdered, tortured, and burned by the hundreds; which reminds one of a modern writer's sarcastic definition of hydrophobia. "A peculiar periodical madness, impelling men to destroy dogs."

Of the thousand tales of interest that have come down to us, we may give place to one, a story of Florence. This city had twenty-three visitations of the plague; the first in 1325, the last in 1630. The plague of 1338 is the noted one described by Boccaccio. The story which we condense here is an incident of the plague of 1400.

Among the noble families who were sworn foes, were those of Rondinelli and Almieri; and one might as soon have expected the lion to mate with the serpent, as to hope for an alliance between the two families. But Cupid has never bothered his meddlesome pate with politics or theology; and so it came about that, as with Montague and Capulet, Antonio Rondinelli fell in love with Ginevra Almieri, one of the most beautiful women of the time—certainly unsurpassed in Florence. Of course, Signor Almieri could not for a moment think of such a hateful match, and so Ginevra was given to Francesco Agolanti. The young wife remained faithful; but she gradually faded; and in four short years sunk into a sort of lethargic stupor, resulting in death. The plague was then at its highest, and the panic was great. Every death from uncertain cause was a source of alarm, and burials were informal and hasty. The poor young wife was promptly bundled off to the family vault beneath one of the great cathedrals.

It seems that it was merely a case of coma, or suspended animation. The lady revived, only to find herself entombed with the skeletons of her husband's ancestors. Horrible as this would be for any one, it is a wonder that the weak nerves of Ginevra did not give way entirely under the strain. She screamed and called—only the dead heard. She groped about her tomb, and found a ladder; clambering up, she found a ray of moonlight streaming through a crevice, and learned her location She looked abroad

> " Upon the moonlight loveliness, all sunk
> In one unbroken silence, save the moan
> From the lone room of death, or the dull sound
> Of the slow-moving hearse The homes of men
> Were now all desolate, and darkness there
> And solitude and silence took their seat,
> In the deserted streets: for the dark wing
> Of a destroying angel had gone by
> And blasted all existence, and had changed
> The gay, the busy, and the crowded mart
> To one cold speechless city of the dead."

After desperate effort, and with strength astounding in a frame so weak, she forced up one of the paving stones that formed the roof of the vault, and dragged herself out. Sitting wearily down for a brief rest, a sudden shower came up and chilled her to the bone. She rose and went to her husband's house. He, at a second story window, astounded at the ghostly figure in grave clothes that roused him in the dead hour of night, "when ghosts do mostly walk abroad," and doubtless remembering that his treatment of the living wife had not been such as to recommend him to the favorable notice of her ghost, shut the window with alternate imprecations and invocations, and covered his head with the bedclothes—well-known in all ages to be thoroughly ghost-proof. Ginevra was similarly repulsed from the houses of her father and of various relatives. As a last resort, though exceedingly repugnant to a woman of her delicate feeling, she betook herself, almost chilled to death, to the house of Rondinelli. To his inquiry as to who was there, a weak voice responded, "Do you not know me, Signor Antonio? It is I—Ginevra. Neither my father nor my husband will receive me. Will you, too, turn me away?"

Great as was Antonio's fear of ghosts, the bare possibility that Ginevra was actually there in the flesh was a far stronger consideration; and he hastened to test the reality of his fair visitant. Having her properly cared for, he hastened to the vault, where the displaced stone confirmed her story.

A few days later, Antonio boldly applied to the civil authorities to marry the "late Ginevra degli Agolanti," and backed his application with certificates of the death and burial of the lady! The authorities hearing the facts—and mayhap being romantically disposed—decided that the lady was legally dead, that her relatives, by their own unwilling confession, had persisted in so regarding her; hence, she was no longer bound by any legal tie to the living, father or husband! She was absolutely free!

So Antonio and Ginevra were married, and of course, "lived happily ever after."

CHAPTER XX.

THE VOLCANO.

"And it bubbles, and seethes, and hisses, and roars,
As when fire is with water commixed and comblending,
And a hell-molten surf thunders wild on its shores,
While a red-tumbling flood from its caverns outpours,
Hurling hills from their place, and the mountains downrending,
So the chaos eternal
Born of fury infernal,
Rolls and belches and rumbles, unreined and unending."

IT is an axiom that there are three misstatements in the popular description of a crab: "A fish, of a red color, that runs backward."

Ques. What is a volcano?

Ans. A volcano is a burning mountain, from the summit of which issue smoke and flames. (*Old Geography.*)

The writer remembers the surprise he felt when a lad of nine, full of childish confidence in the infallibility of text-book misinformation, on reading in Prescott's "Conquest in Mexico" that Cortez obtained sulphur to replenish his stock of powder by lowering one of his soldiers into the crater of Popocatepetl. He wondered how so reputable a historian as Prescott had been induced to credit such an extravagant "yarn" on the part of the Spanish chronicler. To his youthful fancy, fired by the teachings of primary geographies, a volcano was a sort of chimney to a titanic iron furnace in full blast; indeed, he would have supposed it safer to descend into an iron furnace than into the crater. He speculated long on the matter, and wondered if fire-proof dresses were known in those days.

No small part of the non-traveling public has similar misconceptions of the character of volcanoes; and to obtain the truth it is not so necessary to learn as to unlearn. The description quoted from the old text-book is false in every particular. The mountain can not be said to be burning any more than melted lead. Nor does anything that answers to either smoke or flame issue from it. Be it known to all, that the greatest portion of the surface of an active crater is usually covered with a solid crust, in which there may be a small fiery lake, or inner secondary cone or crater. Into many craters it is possible therefore to descend: and into one volcano of the Mediterranean Sea an enterprising Scotch firm have long had quite remunerative chemical works.

The name is taken from one of the Lipari Islands—a small group near Sicily—which was known to the ancients as Vulcano. When the Romans imported the Grecian god, Hephaistos, to be their chief blacksmith, they assigned him Vulcano as his forge, and rechristened the lame old fellow with the adjective appellation of Vulcanus.

Men much prefer the marvellous or mysterious to the true. And, while their reverence is of a merely superstitious sort, the reverence of the ignorant often surpasses that of the learned. A superstitious people readily manufactured a myth to explain the awe-inspiring demonstrations of volcanoes; and the myth itself, because of its religious character, would discourage any attempt to closely investigate volcanic phenomena as sacrilege and impiety. There are similar volcano myths in the island and Asiatic world. So firm was the belief of the Sandwich Islanders in the certainty of dire vengeance upon all who trespassed on the domain of Pele, the goddess of Kilauea, that when a princess of the blood royal safely defied the goddess, ate her sacred berries, and threw rocks into her boiling lake, the people at once abandoned their whole race of gods. If there was no Pele, they knew of no god. Such reasons prevented the ancients and the barbarian world from obtaining any light on volcanic action.

Similar causes operated with equal force to hinder investigation during the middle and dark ages. Christian teachers seized upon them as convenient openings to the abode of eternal torment. The Arian heretic, the Emperor Theodosius, was assigned to Vulcano; while poor Anne Boleyn, for whose sake the "Defender of the Faith" defied the Pope, was sent by the latter to Mt. Ætna, as the shortest route to her destination.

Similar ideas are noticed among semi-barbarous races. The Aztecs deemed Popocatepetl, the greatest of their volcanoes, to be the place of punishment for wicked rulers. These gentry were supposed to cherish no good will toward their subjects, whose complaints had brought them to that place of torment, and to be always seeking opportunity for vengeance. The people held them in great awe, and were wont to invoke the aid of the gods when it became necessary to travel near the volcanoes. It is related that the highpriest, Tezozomoc, was wont to give aloe-leaves inscribed with sacred characters, to such persons. These leaves were amulets to preserve the wearer from harm. Southey uses this story in *Madoc:*

> "So ye may safely pass
> Between the mountains, which in endless war,
> Hurtle with horrible uproar, and frush
> Of rocks, that meet in battle."

This mountain was in eruption when Cortes reached Tlascala on his march to Mexico. It was believed to bode evil to the people of Anahuac. Learning the native superstition, Diego de Ordaz, captain of artillery, determined to beard the demons in their den, and with some companions ascended the mountain. Their safe return convinced the natives that the Spaniards were in league with the spirits, and did much to dishearten them. In memory of this feat, the Ordaz family has a volcano pictured on its coat of arms.

The Javanese call their greatest volcano Maha-Meru.

AT THE SUMMIT OF POPOCATEPETL.

Meru, in the Sanscrit mythology, was the home of Brahma, and the Malays, having adopted the legend, consider their greatest volcano the fittest symbol of his throne and power.

Virgil's Æneid affords a passage containing the Roman myth concerning Mt. Ætna, and showing that the people of Virgil's day were acquainted with the phenomena of that mountain. Thus Dryden has translated:

> "The flagging wind forsook us with the sun,
> And wearied, on Cyclopean shores we run.
> The port, capacious and secure from wind,
> Is to the fort of thundering Ætna joined,
> By turns a pitchy cloud she rolls on high,
> And flakes of mountain flames that arch the sky;
> Oft from her bowels massy rocks are thrown,
> And shivered by the force, come piece-meal down;
> Oft liquid cakes of burning sulphur flow,
> Fed from the fiery springs that burn below.
> Enceladus, they say, transfixed by Jove,
> With blasted limbs came trembling from above,
> And where he fell, th' avenging father drew
> This flaming hell, and on his body threw.
> As often as he turns his weary sides,
> He shakes the solid hill, and smoke the heaven hides."

This conception was borrowed from the Greeks, one of whose poets has told us

> "How shaggy-breasted Typhon lay,
> From sea-girt Cuma to Trinacria's bay."

Yet, even among the ancients an occasional great mind disregarded popular superstition, and enunciated just and rational views upon the matter. The elder Pliny lost his life in an effort to observe closely an eruption of Vesuvius. But the ideas advanced by these men were speedily forgotten; and the exact scientific examination of volcanoes is of the past hundred years, the great Italian, Spallanzani, being the first to publish a series of valuable observations on the volcanoes of his own land.

The ancients were acquainted only with the few active volcanoes distributed about the Mediterranean Sea, and the casual thinker might hence suppose their opportunities for observation were quite limited. But volcanic principles are the same everywhere, differing only in violence. In the Lipari Islands is situated the volcanic cone of Stromboli, which has been in a state of constant activity, though very mild, for at least two thousand years. This affords excellent opportunities for study, and much of our most valuable information on the topic is derived from careful observation of it. When the wind is steady in any quarter, a person may sit to windward for hours within a few yards of the boiling mass, while the noxious vapors and gases are borne away in the other direction.

The expulsive agent is in all cases steam, mingled to a greater or less degree with other vapors or gases. Its operation may be simply illustrated. Pure water does not readily boil over in any open vessel of ordinary dimensions. But if the vessel be very deep in proportion to its width, and the heat is applied at the base only, it boils over more readily. Now, if instead of water, we substitute porridge, thick molasses, or any similar thick or viscid material, the bubbles of steam rise slowly; and if rapidly generated, they force the matter out at the top ere they escape. Such bubbles as reach the top, burst, throwing tiny particles of the mass into the air.

How great a portion of the material expelled from volcanoes consists of steam and other gases is not easy to determine. But that the quantity of vapor is enormous is indisputable. Vesuvius is noted for the "pine tree" of vapor that overhangs it. The ascending steam and gases, on reaching an upper atmosphere as light as themselves, spread out horizontally in every direction, thus much resembling in outline the stone-pines that are a prominent feature in the Neapolitan landscape.

Some effort has been made to connect volcanic eruptions with atmospheric pressure; for, say the theorists, a fall of two inches in the barometer removes a pressure of over 2,000,000 tons from each square mile. A sufficient answer to this is, that this, after all, is only one pound to the square inch; while the force that can cast up volumes of melted matter from a great depth must needs be many tons to the square inch. Clearly these gentlemen would perch us on a sort of universal fire-box, and poise the lid on a hair trigger.

But heavy rainfalls and terrific thunder storms are almost invariable accompaniments of explosive eruptions. That these are the result and not the cause of volcanic action is clear. An electrical machine was invented by Sir William Armstrong, in which electricity was generated by forcing steam at great speed through a narrow orifice. This same principle would produce volcanic thunder storms. The immense volumes of vapor, reaching the open air, must rapidly cool and be precipitated as rain. The Italians dread these torrents, sweeping down immense quantities of mud, more than they do the streams of lava.

If an eruption causes an immediate fall of two inches of rain over an area seven miles square, it will be found that such a rainfall amounts to more than seven millions of tons of water. Yet the rainfall often is greater, and the area affected is larger; while it is not to be supposed that the entire volume of vapor cast forth is at once precipitated on the earth. This computation can not be assumed as anything more than a mere illustration of the tremendous forces brought into operation.

The solid substances emitted by volcanoes are popularly styled ashes, cinders, or scoria and lava. But what is called ashes would be more appropriately named dust; for it is merely finely divided lava, and in no way resembles genuine ashes.

Lavas present a general resemblance to the slag and clinkers of smelters and brick-kilns, but vary considerably in appearance and chemical composition. We need not touch this question further than to state that oxygen forms nearly one-half the weight of all lavas, silicon one-fourth of most, and aluminum one-tenth. From fifteen to twenty per cent. is made of various others, magnesium, calcium, iron, sodium and potassium being most common. Hence, the compounds present are always of the class known to chemists as silicates, substances requiring great heat to

VIEW IN ACTIVE CRATER.

melt. These, from being long melted, abound more or less in crystals; but if any one re-melts them and cools them suddenly, the result is a simple glassy mass, with no trace of crystals.

26

Scoria or cinders differ from ordinary lava only in the peculiarity of having partially crystallized in some portions and then stiffened or solidified while large bubbles were yet imprisoned or in the act of bursting; thus leaving the mass very ragged and cellular. But if the lava contains no readily formed crystals, the imprisoned bubbles of steam slowly rise to the surface, and being greatly elongated by the flowing of the lava, produce the beautiful material known as "pumice." It is to lava exactly what froth or foam is to water. Usually it is much lighter colored than the lava on which it floats, for the same reason that well-worked molasses candy is nearly white: they both contain a vast number of minute air bubbles. Pumice floats on water, and its decomposition being generally very slow, it drifts about the sea currents, and is often found thousands of miles from any volcanic region. In the immediate neighborhood of volcanoes it often accumulates on the sea to such an extent that vessels can hardly force their way through it. In the Sunda Islands it has been seen on the sea three feet in depth. During the year 1878 the accumulation of pumice near the Solomon Isles was so great that it took ships three days to force their way through. Sometimes such masses accumulate along the coast line to such an extent that a person can not readily tell where the shore line is. One may land and walk about on the great floating raft of pumice, unable to guess within even a mile of the actual shore. Deep sea soundings show that the entire ocean bottom is covered more or less with the pulverized pumice and volcanic dust. From the wide distribution it is not probable that the layer attains any great thickness.

The Mangaians of the South Pacific told the earlier missionaries of a feat of one of their heroes which at first was unaccountable. This demigod, Maui, a sort of Pacific

Hercules, raised the sky to its present position. Not getting it high enough to suit him, he put his head between the legs of his old father Ru, and heaved him and the half-raised sky up together. Ru stuck fast among the stars, and Maui left him there till his body dropped to pieces and his bones fell over the ground below. To prove the truth of their story they brought the missionaries bits of pumice, which they said were the bones of Ru. Singularly enough the white porous stone looked much like bone. The myth had been invented by the simple folk to explain the origin of pumice.

The ashes, or volcanic dust, is excessively minute, and in consequence readily penetrate crevices that are hardly visible. Professor Bonney, examining dust thrown out by Cotopaxi, has calculated that it would require from four thousand to twenty-five thousand particles to make up a grain in weight. The substance known as tufa is merely volcanic dust or ash upon which rain has fallen while the former was still hot. The resultant paste solidifies into a porous and loosely compacted rock.

Why some volcanoes nearly always throw out dust and fragments, while others throw out mere molten streams, was for a time not clearly understood. Some suggested the dust was the result of the continual collision of fragments as they rose and fell, and hence would increase in quantity as the eruption continued. This clearly would not meet the case of volcanoes which, without showing any previous signs of activity, burst into action with tremendous volumes of dust.

It was at length noticed that dust and fragments always were accompanied by tremendous explosions; while eruptions of melted lava were far more quiet, shocks being few and the explosions insignificant as compared with the former. This gave a clue to the mystery.

Many liquids and solids have the power of absorbing vast quanties of gas. Under pressure their absorbing powers may be vastly increased. Sometimes the property appears only at high temperatures. Silver when melted absorbs twenty-two times its volume of oxygen. If suddenly cooled the oxygen is given off with a rapidity verging on explosion. This is called the "spitting" of silver. Tiny cones and melted streams appear on the cooled surface—volcanoes in miniature. The same property belongs to the oxide of lead, and some other metals.

Now water can be made to absorb more than a thousand times its bulk of ammonia; more than five hundred times its bulk of hydrochloric acid. Alcohol may absorb three hundred times its volume of sulphurous acid. Charcoal may absorb one hundred times its volume of ammonia, eighty-five times its volume of hydrochloric acid, sixty-five times its volume of sulphuretted hydrogen, fifty-five times its volume of sulphurous and thirty-five times its volume of carbonic acid. Iron, steel and melted sulphur absorb many gases.

We have already seen that immense volumes of gases are thrown off in volcanic action. Now if a column of lava rises comparatively slowly in its "chimney," the imprisoned gases rapidly escape, producing violent boiling, but not a positive explosion. But if it rises very rapidly, the sudden removal of the pressure causes so sudden an expansion of the compressed gases in its upper portion as to amount to a tremendous explosion, which reduces the lava to microscopic dust.

This very principle was made practical use of in a mechanical contrivance invented to make paper pulp out of common cane, such as the farmer's boy delights in for a fishing pole. The hard, woody fibre was placed in a powerful iron cylinder full of water. A strong lid being adjusted, the whole was heated far above the boiling point of water. Naturally, every cell would be forced full of moisture by the immense pressure. After some hours heating, the lid was suddenly removed, and by the sudden expansion of the water into steam the cane was blown to atoms.

CRATER OF ORIZABA.

A beautiful product of the volcano of Kilauea is the substance known as "Pele's Hair." Small particles of glass shot violently into the air leave behind them long, glittering filaments, like gossamers. Birds often build their nests of these beautiful threads. Man, taking a hint from nature, has learned to manufacture the **glass hair** for himself by passing jets of steam through the **molten slag of iron furnaces.** It much resembles cotton wool, and is used for packing boilers and piston-heads, and similar purposes.

The appearance of fire at the summit of a volcano is rarely ever real flame. Any who has seen the peculiar appearance occasioned by brilliant illumination on a moist or foggy evening may readily perceive the cause. The phenomenon popularly known as the " sun drawing water " is of the same character. The immense cloud of vapor ascending from the volcano glows with the light sent up from the molten mass below. So it may be seen brilliant by night, and only a dark cloud by day. Stromboli has been called the light-house of the Mediterranean. In constant action, the brilliant light at night slowly fades: then suddenly breaks out as bright as before. This alternating results from the bursting of bubbles in the crater, which expose a new, hot surface. This rapidly cools; then another bubble bursts; and so the process continues. This may have suggested the alternating light now in common use in great light-houses.

In the Galapagos, and other volcanic islands of the Pacific, occurs another curious feature of volcanic action. Some places abound in seeming mounds or domes, which may be sometimes readily broken in with a heavy stone. These are produced by bubbles which partially cooled, when the lava below found some rent or outlet in another quarter and flowed away, leaving the solidified bubble.

Sometimes the cavern left by the retreating lava abounds in strange beauties. A sailor, who with a comrade, explored one of these volcanic caverns, gives the following account of it:

"In a sharp, deep valley of Albemarle we had broken in the roof of a bubble; and as we looked in we saw we had opened the way into a tunnel about fifteen feet in width, and extending either way as far as we could see from our position. By the lights which entered from above, we made out the floor as about twenty feet beneath us, and that the walls were curiously marked with columnar forms. My companion, who had dabbled in the sciences, proposed that we should take an underground view of volcanic action and appearances.

"So, on the following day, provided with a couple of lamps, a coil of knotted line, and a couple of waist-lines and iron poles for staves, we proceeded on our exploration. We descended with the knotted rope around our bodies, and stuck our feet into the rough side, lighted in our way by a single lamp. We carefully watched for any side openings which might confuse us or lead us astray in returning, but we saw none and felt safe. It soon became evident that the tunnel had not been formed by a rent of the mass after cooling, but rather by the molten lava's having drained away after a crust had formed upon it. This may account for the singular and beautiful formations by which we found ourselves surrounded. After proceeding some distance through a passage with a pretty uniform width of fifteen to twenty feet, and of about equal height, we paused to examine the formation of the cavern. The dim light of our lamps illuminated the pilastered walls, and a roof raftered and groined with straight and curved beams of crystalline structure many feet in length. Some of these were of a reddish appearance, and others had a vitreous lustre, resembling immense crystals, in places broken into the semblance of foliage, which reflected an olive green light. The gloomy splendor of this solemn architecture was relieved by the gold or amber reflections of crystals of sulphur, which, like marigold or sunflower, gleamed in the passage.

"The broad bases of the pilasters were enriched with counterfeits of fern, palms, and growths intricate and delicate as the penciling of the frost spirit's pictures. But these metallic pictures, under the limning of the fire-fiend had been inlaid with the brilliant facets of igneous minerals, green and brown in tint. Tempted onward by the increasing beauty of the scene, our lamp revealed new objects of interest in the increasing lustre of the arched ceiling, and the carved and painted walls. Our lamp was multiplied by the sparkle from the faces of unknown minerals. In places the passage was divided by central columns of basalt crystals, which terminated in curves, and were in form and tracery varied beyond man's power. The rude Goth for his cathedral, the Moslem for his mosque, the Celestial for his pagoda, might have drawn inspiration from this solemn portal to Nature's vast workshop.

"As we advanced further into the recesses of the mountain, the character of the the cave changed. The angular crystaliine forms which indicated the sudden withdrawal of the molten matter, or the deposit of elements sublimed by intense heat, yielded to smooth and rounded structures, like the worn rocks of the river side, giving the impression that the walls had served as a sluice to fiery torrents pouring from the volcano. A few steps farther showed us the singular curtain-like foldings of a substance resembling lampblack. Absolutely without lustre, and absorbent of every ray of light, it was present, as it were, only to the touch. With certain misgivings under this curtain of gloom, we entered a cavern the form or extent of which could only be known by touch of hands, for no possible brilliancy of light would command an answering reflection from the absorbent surface. Broken as was the surface to the touch, to the eye it was without form. The floor was invisible, and we were guided in our steps by our staves alone. It was like stepping into primal chaos, before light and form had birth. A profound chasm seemed to yawn at our feet; yet the rocky floor rang to the blow of the staff, and with cautious tread we proceeded. The flame of the lamp met no responsive glow; save from the two intruders who stood awe stricken in this strange emptiness; it stood in the still blackness unflickering, like a solid. Feeling the broken walls, the hand was met by an oily softness; the eye was useless, and even the touch now failed to guide us. Solid walls were not to the eye; rocky barriers seemed simply impenetrable darkness to the hand.

"From repeated contact with sooty walls, we also became covered with this strange, light-absorbing powder, until we were enveloped in an invisible mantle, and also passed from each other's sight. Eye alone answered to eye in their reflections of light. Too deeply impressed for conversation, we stood still with outstretched hands. My comrade asked at length, 'May it not be even so in the valley of the Shadow of Death?' And we looked for strength into each other's eyes and linked our arms that we might have the companionship of touch. We were now thoroughly frightened, and turned to retrace our steps; but which way? We stood in a sea of nothingness—locked in the foundations of the mountain. The walls were lost to the sight, and were nothing to the touch. We stooped to the deep dust of the floor and held the flame to read our foot-prints; but the soil absorbed the light, as the sand of the desert does the raindrop. We reached forward, and the hand failed to meet the wall; we reached downward; there, too, was empty space. The light showed no defining edge between the solid rock and the void. We swung the lamp from the brink on which we lay; it revealed nothing. We dropped a heavy stone into the chasm and listened for the rebound. No sound was returned as it sank into the profound. We cast another stone across to test the width, but this, too, was lost to the senses. Silently they passed away, as the mist wreath on the hill side. And then we knew we had been preserved from death. A careless step and we had found a grave in the depths of the world's foundations. We realized that we were lying in trembling safety on the threshold of the extinct volcano, and lifting our useless eyes from the impenetrable blackness, the awful whisper 'Lost!' passed between us. We were afraid to move; but the wasting oil of our lamp warned us that time must not be lost. Presently our ears caught the beat of surf on the rock as the tide came in, and following this direction, we finally reached the entrance, almost fainting from joy when we stood beyond this chamber of gloom. Once more we stood under the wondrous tracery and reflections of the outer gates of the inter-world of mysterious."

A most thrilling experience, and one giving a fine picture of what may be found in the mysterious depths of a lava bubble. In some cases the bubbles are very thin; and an unwary passer might be suddenly plunged into unfathomable depths should he tread on one. Usually, however, they are formed over horizontal currents or passages.

We have endeavored to give the well-established facts concerning the principles of volcanic action. It only remains, ere we leave this phase of the subject, that we notice the one point on which as yet our knowledge is not clear. That point is, the source of the heat which produces the remarkable effects.

Several theories are advanced. One class of scientists believes that the earth is a mass of molten matter, with only a thin outer shell of cooled material. That a very high temperature exists at no very great distance from the surface is beyond a doubt. The observations made in mines and artesian wells show that the average increase

ERUPTION OF MOUNT VESUVIUS.

in the temperature is one degree for every fifty-five feet in depth. One noted variation exists in the deep wells at Buda-Pesth, in Austria, where the temperature. increased up to 3,000 feet; but beyond that depth it became cooler again. The Comstock lode in Nevada, the richest mineral vein in the world, is nearly at the limit of practicable working, the normal temperature being as high as one hundred and fifty degrees.

Even if it be conceded that the material of the earth is a molten mass, there would be two theories to explain it: one, that the earth was originally in a state of fusion, and was slowly cooling; the other, that the great pressure from without keeps an otherwise solid center greatly compressed and heated, and consequently liquid. Either supposition is based on well established facts; but it does not appear clear that the molten globe with a cool shell can settle the entire question.

The objections to this are several. One, the complete absence of uniformity in the increase of heat as we descend. While the total average is as given above, the variations are so many and vast, that there does not seem to be any general law, as there should be if the molten interior possessed the least uniformity. In some shafts the increase is one degree for twenty feet; in others, one for every one hundred; in some, the temperature increases much more rapidly at great depths, in others, much less rapidly.

A second objection is, the vast difference in the character of lavas, even in districts very near each other. Thirdly, there seems no definite connection between volcanoes in the same region. Two adjacent ones may exhibit very different conditions. Mauna Loa is about 10,000 feet above Kilauea, a great crater of the same mountain. Yet the upper is often in a violent state of eruption when the latter is perfectly quiet. It would be difficult to conceive how these are supplied from the same source. If the interior were a molten mass in a state of equilibrium, as would be necessary if the uniformity of its motions in the solar system were to be preserved, any undue pressure would compel the molten matter to escape from the lowest opening. This would be in accordance with the simplest laws of liquids. Then we should find volcanic action most vigorous at the lowest active volcano; but such is not the case. The idea of a uniformly liquid interior seems hardly tenable.

There is still other objection to this theory. Experiments have been made with various materials to ascertain the change affected in them by heat. It is found that a block of granite five feet long, by a change of ninety-six degrees in temperature, is expanded .27792 of an inch; crystalline marble, .03264; sandstone, .0549. If, then, a portion of the earth's crust ten miles in thickness be heated six hundred degrees, its crust would be raised two hundred feet; or a change of one degree, the rate of expansion being fairly uniform to five hundred or six hundred degrees, would raise the surface four inches. How important this matter is may be better understood when we consider that if the interior of the earth be a uniformly molten mass, with a crust ten miles thick, a contraction of one-twelve thousandth of an inch should force out of the crust a cubic mile of lava. We should find then a change in temperature one forty-eight thousandth of a degree should effect this, if the crust were ten miles thick.

We are then forced to conclude that the earth is not cooling to any appreciable extent; or that the liquid interior is still capable of indefinite compression without necessarily being forced out through orifices in the crust; or that the interior is not a uniformly molten mass.

Such are the arguments against a melted interior.

The reader should avoid the assumption of a uniform rate of contraction or expansion of heat. Within very narrow limits, such a hypothesis may be allowed; but to assume that it is universal, would be to affirm that if you could only make the earth cold enough it would shrink to nothing at all! The earth and the temperature would swallow each other, like the two snakes, till neither was left. To illustrate more seriously, suppose a race of men existed whose only experience of temperature ranged between forty and two hundred degrees. They could consistently calculate, from the change of water between these limits, that it would require a temperature of many thousands of degrees to expand it to seventeen hundred times its bulk. Yet we know they would have to raise it only to two hundred and twelve degrees to produce the required effect. And if they could go below forty degrees, they would be astonished to find that water then expanded instead of contracting.

That the earth, if it cools, does so very slowly is clear, from the character of the materials thrown out. Lava from Mt. Ætna has been observed slowly moving nine months after the eruption. Lower portions of the beds have been found to be abnormally heated ten years after pouring out. Compare the thickness of a lava bed with the depth from which it is thrown, and it will be seen that little heat is lost in the subterranean depths. One instance, showing how slowly the lava is to part with its heat, may be given:

In the year 1828 a great mass of ice was discovered on Mt. Ætna. In consequence of the protracted heat of the season, supplies of ice at Catania and the adjacent regions failed entirely, and the people suffered considerably for the want of an article considered necessary to health as well as comfort in that hot climate. The Catanian authorities caused search to be made for some crevasse or natural grotto on Mt. Ætna, where drift-snow might exist. Near the base of the highest cone was found a vast mass of ice, covered by a lava bed. How old it was there is no means of knowing; nor can we tell how much of the ice might have originally been melted by the overflowing current. But there it was, so hard and firm that the workmen quarried it with great difficulty.

Lastly, it appears that the causes of earthquakes and volcanic action must be the same. A violent volcanic outbreak causes earthquake shocks at once, as though relieved by a safety valve. The experiments of Mr. Robert Mallet, the best known authority on earthquake phenomena, tend to prove that the shocks necessarily originate at a comparatively short distance below the surface. So, from two independent lines of investigation, the same conclusion is reached.

These objections have caused inquiry to be made as to what causes might locally develop heat. Here there are so many possible methods that scientists may not be expected to unite. One is the chemical theory: water coming in contact with quick-lime, or metallic sodium or potassium, would evolve intense heat. One or two locomotives have been invented which need no fuel, obtaining their heat supply thus.

But it is objected to this that the products of volcanic action are not such as would result from such a cause; that all experience indicates that water has already penetrated every portion of the earth, the deepest borings always crossing veins, and all great mines requiring to be artificially drained.

One other theory is, that the slow contraction of the globe from the radiation of heat into space necessarily affects the outer portion most directly, and in consequence, the shrinking of the crust at the weakest points produces unusual pressure there, which can evolve intense heat, as is shown by the fact that nearly all rocks so twisted or strained are more or less changed in their internal structure by heat. It is also evident that a region once thus weakened and seriously broken would necessarily form a fairly permanent volcanic tract. As the work of nature all goes to preserve equilibrium or balance of forces, an unusual upheaval would necessitate unusual subsidence near at hand; and in fact the highest mountain is always near the deepest ocean.

This explanation, combined with that of chemical action seems to us the more tenable. None of these theories conflict with the nebular hypothesis of Kant and Laplace.

In looking over the areas of volcanic action, we will find they have changed considerably from the areas of the past.

In the continent of Europe there is but one active volcano—Vesuvius; but there are six others on islands in the Mediterranean. Africa has four active volcanoes on the west coast, and six on the east; while ten others are to be found on adjacent islands. Austria has no volcanoes, so far as is known. In Asia are twenty-four active volcanos; but twelve of these are on the peninsula of Kamtschatka. On the American continent we find a larger proportion. North America has forty-five, most of which are in Mexico and Central America; and South America has thirty-seven. Of these continental volcanoes all are near the sea, except four which are reported to lie in the great unexplored tableland between Siberia and Thibet; and some are said to exist in the Chinese province of Mantchooria. No white man has visited them.

But it is in the island world that we must look for the most numerous volcanoes.

A great ridge runs through the Atlantic; and along this lie a number of islands with active centres. Jan Mayen, in the Arctic circle, has an active volcano; Iceland, thirteen; the Azores, six; the Canaries, three; east African islands, eight; the West Indies, six; three submarine volcanoes have been observed at different times in the Atlantic. But through the same region the number of extinct volcanoes is far greater. Of those which exist several seem approaching extinction.

But in the isles of the Pacific and between the Pacific and Indian oceans we have a vast series of volcanic vents of wonderful activity. In the Aleutian Islands are thirty-one; in the Kurile Isles, ten or more; Japan and the adjacent groups have twenty-five. Southeast of the Asiatic continent is the most active region on the globe. Fifty volcanoes are here known. Farther south are four in New Guinea, one or two submarine vents, a number in New Britain, the Solomon group, the New Hebrides, three in New Zealand, and Erebus and Terror in the Antarctic circle. Add to these the islands of the Central Pacific, and we have more than one-half the volcanoes of the globe. Besides there are a large number of nearly perfect volcanic cones which must recently have become extinct.

In conclusion, we find all the oceanic islands are either of volcanic or coral formation; and as we find that the coral polyp can not live at a greater depth than one hundred and twenty feet; as we know the ocean in the immediate neighborhood of these islands to be many thousand of feet in depth; as we know coral islands to be circular, often enclosing a lagoon of water, it is fair to suppose that the polyps have not built through long ages of subsidence, as is usually supposed; but that they have built upon the rims of extinct craters lying near the surface. The fact that these circular reefs always have one or more breaks in their circuit is additional reason for the belief. The fact of a coral island lying within a barrier reef, then,

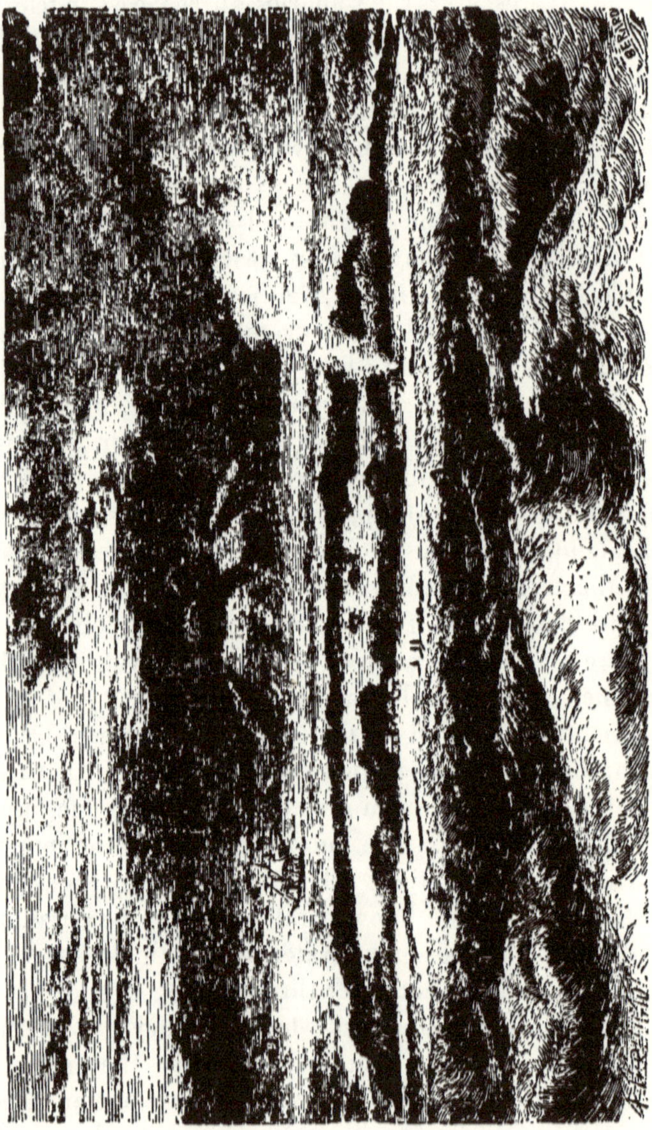

CORAL REEFS.

resolves itself into a volcanic crater with an inner cone, as every active volcano has. It is rather ludicrous to suppose that polyps, among the lowest of created beings, leading an ephemeral existence, should yet have such unanimity of purpose, such perfect mutual understanding, as to undertake to build their reefs in a more or less circular form; it is preposterous to suppose the unvarying form of the structure is the result of mere chance. Clearly we must find some other influences; and the most reasonable is to suppose the foundations of these islands were laid by the same agency that raised all other Oceanic islands from the bed of the sea.

The volcano thus plays an important part in the earth's economy. Not only does it add to land areas by upheaval from the deep. The amount of material thrown out by the Javanese volcanoes alone during the past hundred years is greater far than all the silt borne to the sea by American rivers during the same period. Krakatoa, in its recent eruption, threw out more than the Mississippi bears to the sea in sixty years.

There is some doubt as to how much volcanoes effect by direct upheaval. The formation of many observed cones shows that the majority are mainly built up by the materials thrown out, and not by any great elevation of the adjacent surface. In the case of a volcano already existing, it is of course not easy to know what proportion of its mass is merely accumulation of lava, cinders, or tufa.

As to the form of volcanic cones, those of ashes, cinders, and scoria are of course steepest; those of lava thrown out when liquid having a very gradual slope. The difference may be readily illustrated by comparing a heap of sand and pebbles with a heap of stiffening molasses candy. One is steeply conical; the other, rounded or dome-like. But either form of volcano may abound in crevices and apertures from which issue sulphurous vapors and gases. These fumaroles, as they are called, are usually surrounded with mineral deposits, often resembling the most delicate filigree work.

Having considered the general phases and principles of volcanic action, we may now notice some of the more famous eruptions of the past.

CHAPTER XXI.

GREAT ERUPTIONS OF VESUVIUS.

> "E'en while they cheered the gladiator's thrust,
> And shouted as the lion crunched his bones,
> Up sprang the Fire King from his ages' sleep
> Shook wide his robe of ever-deepening night,
> And flung his fiery banner on the wind.
> The groaning earth then trembled at his tread,
> And thousand thunders rent the raging mount,
> While prince and pauper, 'mid the scorching gloom,
> Groped through the gaping streets; the ocean hissed,
> And palaces and marble temples reeled,
> And crushed or prisoned; still the ashes fell,
> Till mansions, statues, homes and colonnades,
> And Strength, and Beauty, Love, and Life, and Death,
> Lay heaps on heaps, in one black ruin blent."

FOR nearly seventeen hundred years there lay beneath a sea of ashes near the Naples Bay, a city whose destruction had not been described by the younger Pliny; and in the lapse of years its site had been forgotten. During the construction of an aqueduct in 1592, workmen frequently came upon foundations of buildings. No curiosity seems to have been aroused. Nearly a hundred years later other buildings were discovered, with the inscription "POMPEII." Still there was no practical interest. Then the attention of the learned was drawn to the discoveries at Herculaneum; and Alcubierre, a Spanish colonel of engineers, in examining the subterranean canal, was led by the discovery of a house and statues to conjecture that some great treasures might lie buried there. Obtaining permission of the King of Naples, he began excavations in the year 1748. In a few days he unearthed "a picture eleven palms long by four and one-half high, containing festoons of eggs, fruits and flowers, the head of a man, large and in good style, a helmet, an owl, various small birds and other objects." Then was found the skeleton of a man, covered with the lava mud. By his side were eighteen brass coins and one of silver. Then was found an amphitheatre, with a seating capacity of ten thousand. But the work was poorly conducted: valuable pictures were detached from the walls, and the buildings again covered with rubbish. No strangers were allowed to copy anything.

When the French occupied Naples, the work was for a time better conducted; then it again declined. When Victor Emmanuel became King of Italy, a distinguished antiquarian scholar, Guiseppe Fiorelli, was appointed director-general of the works. Since then, the work has been well done, Signor Fiorelli noting "every appearance or fragment which might afford or suggest a restoration of any part of a buried edifice; replacing with fresh timbers every charred beam, propping every tottering wall or portion of brick work," till the tourist sees to-day a town in the integrity of its outlines and order of its arrangement. "Temples, baths, markets, tombs, stand out just as they stood eighteen hundred years ago. The villa of the port, the forum, the counting-house, the baker's shop, the school-room, the kitchen, carry us into the very heart of Roman life in the brightest days of the empire. The jewelry of beauty, the spade of the laborer, the fetter of the prisoner and the weapon of the soldier are all there, reproducing and realizing the past with a vividness which can scarcely be conceived."

Relics and historic records give us an ideal of the past. How correct is the ideal may be inferred from the fact that no two antiquarians have the same conception of a

Druid temple With all the details of Scripture and Josephus, we have not an exact model of the temple. Inhabited ruins change with their possessors: those uninhabited decay in the war of elements. But Pompeii was, so to speak, hermetically sealed, in the height of its prosperity, preserved from Goths and Vandals, and is laid before us to-day as it stood over eighteen centuries ago, allowing us to see how sudden was the storm that burst upon it long years ago. The paintings are "undimmed by the leaden touch of time; household furniture left in the confusion of use; articles, even of intrinsic value, abandoned in the hurry of escape, yet safe from the robber, or scattered about from the trembling hand which could not pause or stoop for its most valuable possessions; and in some instances the bones of the inhabitants, bearing sad testimony to the suddenness and completeness of the calamity that overwhelmed them."

"There are the very ruts which were made by the wheels of chariots, flying, perhaps, from the impending ruin; there are water-pipes, in the cavities of which, sealed by the hand of time, the splashing fluid can still be heard; there are rude and grotesque inscriptions, scratched by some loiterer on the stucco, and as fresh as when they excited the mirth of the passer-by; there are egg-shells, bones of fish and chickens, and other fragments of a repast of which skeletons lying near were partaking when the catastrophe overwhelmed them; there is fuel ready to be supplied to furnaces for heating the baths; there are the stains left upon the counters of drinking shops by wet glasses; there are the vials of the apothecary, still containing the fluids he was wont to dispense; there are ovens in which loaves of bread, carbonized, but otherwise perfect, may yet be seen; there are vases with olives still swimming in oil, the fruit retaining its flavor, and the oil

DESTRUCTION OF POMPEII.

burning readily when submitted to the flame; there are shelves, on which are piled stores of raisins, figs and chestnuts; there are amphorae containing the rare wine for which Campania was so famous."

Here you saw a new altar of white marble, wondrously beautiful, just from the hands of the sculptor; "an enclosure was building all round; the mortar just dashed against the side of the wall was but half spread out; you saw the long, sliding stroke of the trowel about to return and obliterate its own track; but it never returned; the hand of the workman was suddenly arrested, and the whole looks so fresh and new that you would almost swear that the mason had only gone to his dinner, and about to come back immediately to smooth the roughness."

The younger Pliny tells us of his uncle's death, and of the suddenness of the calamity. The people were in the amphitheater when the volcano burst forth. The elder Pliny, in command of the fleet at Misenum, was called by his sister to notice a strange cloud that had just appeared. He had just returned from a walk, bathed, and gone to his study. This was August 24, A. D. 79, about 1 P. M. The dense cloud occasionally glowed with light; again, it was of inky blackness. It was the "pine tree banner," since become so familiar to the Neapolitans. Pliny at once started for his galleys, determined to have a closer view of the strange scene. As he went to the shore he received a note from a lady who lived at the base of the mountain, urging him to come to her assistance. He set out at once to render what aid he could; "for the villas stood extremely thick upon that lovely coast." They neared the mount; cinders, pumice, ashes, and glowing stones fell on and among the vessels. Sternly ordering the frightened crew to press on, Pliny stood in the bow of his vessel, calmly dictating notes and observations on the awful scene. Reaching Stabiae, he found a friend in great fear, preparing for flight, and waiting for a change of wind. Pliny ordered baths, and sat calmly down to supper, assuring his friend that the lurid flames on the mountain sides were but villages fired by the heated stones. Retiring to rest, his anxious friends heard him snoring. Finding they were about to be entombed in the falling cinders, they roused him, and all, tying pillows on their heads as protection from the showers of stones, sought the seashore; but the waves ran too high for them to embark. It was still dark as Erebus in the limit of the cloud, though already broad day. Drinking some water, Pliny stretched himself on a mat; but an unusual rush of sulphurous vapor compelled the company to disperse, and two servants assisted him to rise, but he at once fell back dead. Perhaps the noxious vapors were in greater quantity near the ground. His nephew tells us he always had weak lungs. The company fled. Three days later, Pliny's body was found "looking more like a man asleep than dead." At Misenum, fourteen miles away, the earth was constantly and violently shaken. Houses were toppling down. Chariots could not be steadied, even by supporting them with large stones. The sea rushed back, leaving many marine animals stranded high and dry. The dark cloud on Vesuvius flamed and roared. The cloud enveloped Misenum and spread to Capreæ. "Nothing was to be heard but the shrieks of women and children, and the cries of men; some were calling for their children, others for their parents, others for their husbands, and only distinguishing each other by their voices; one was lamenting his own fate, another that of his family; some wished to die that they might escape the dreadful fear of death; but the greater part imagined that the last and eternal night was come, which was to destroy the gods and the world together." Then came the flash of flames; then darkness and ashes, blinding, crushing, burying. Stabiae also was buried. But the destruction of the two great cities is given no word; it was sudden and complete. The ruins show they were shattered by an earthquake. Then showers of broken lava rushed upon Herculaneum; while Pompeii, farther away, was reached only by the cinder-showers. Dion Cassius tells us the people were seated in the theatres when the shock came.

In their terror, every object was distorted and magnified. "A multitude of men, of superhuman stature, resembling giants, appeared sometimes on the mountains, sometimes in the environs; stones and smoke were thrown out; then the giants seemed to rise again, while the sounds of trumpets were heard."

Cassius, however, wrote a century and a half after the disaster; and the chief value of his testimony is to show how terrible and lasting an impression had been made upon the Campanians, from whom he derived his narrative.

After the desolation, the site of Pompeii was searched for such relics as might be of practical use elsewhere. The search was rough and destructive. The Emperor Alexander Severus made the place a "sort of quarry from which he drew a great quantity of marbles, columns and beautiful statues which he employed in adorning the edifices which he constructed at Rome. Modern research has discovered but few gold and silver articles, coins, and statues. It has developed however, a far more fearful and faithful picture of the eruption than has been given by any historian. The clouds of falling ashes so enveloped each object as to preserve an exact impression, from which casts have been made, showing every curve and line, even to the texture of the clothes. So we look upon the death-agony, and conceive the terrors of the scene.

Here is the arena. Here were skeletons; perhaps of gladiators already slain; perhaps of wounded men, unable to rise, who rolled and gasped, and struggled in the choking gloom. There is the prison; you may see the fetters still round the leg bones of the inmates.

Here stood the temple of Isis. On that pedestal was a beautiful image of her, draped in purple and gold. In the next room lay a priest beside the battered wall, with axe in hand. In the next room sat a priest overtaken at his dinner. In other cloisters lay other priests, who had remained at the temple, perhaps deeming Isis would protect them in that awful hour. Close by the prison door lay a skeleton with a handful of silver coins. Mayhap some one had perished there while endeavoring to bribe the jailor to release a prisoned friend. Close by that column, in his narrow niche, a Roman sentry stood, full armed; observing to the last, stern, unflinching obedience to superior powers, who neglected to relieve him in the terror of the time.

In the vault of a beautiful suburban villa of Diomed, lay eighteen adults, a boy, and an infant, huddled together in attitudes terribly expressive of the agony of a lingering death. To the skulls of the children still clung their long, blonde hair. There was the impress left by the bust of a young girl of striking beauty. Near the garden gate without the house were two skeletons; one with a bunch of keys and a quantity of money; the other with a number of silver vases. Doubtless the family had thought to escape by retiring to the well-provisioned cellar; while two slaves endeavored to profit by the confusion to escape with their booty. The stifling sulphureous vapor found them out.

In the house of the Faun stood the skeleton of a woman; her hands raised over her head. Her scattered jewels lay about the floor. Endeavoring at length to leave the house, she found the doorway blocked with ashes. The flooring of the upper rooms began to fall, and she lifted her arms in vain attempt to stay the crumbling roof. Thus was she found.

In a garden near by a woman was found seven feet from the earth. She had surmounted many obstacles, but perished as she scaled a wall.

Beneath a staircase lay a man who had with him a vast treasure of gold and silver. He had preserved it at a terrible cost. Near by were five others who had met a similar fate. They lay fifteen feet above the earth. Plunderers were these, overpowered by a rush of mephitic gas while delving for buried treasures.

Here lay two bodies, feet to feet—mother and daughter, perhaps. The former lay outstretched and tranquil; the young girl of fifteen, in an attitude expressive of frightful agony. Her legs are drawn up and her hands clinched. With one hand she had drawn her veil about her head, to screen herself from the ashes and smoke. The form and texture of her dress are clearly seen; and through its rents the fair young skin appears like polished marble.

Close by lay a young woman of high rank; young, richly dressed and beautiful. One upraised arm and her clenched hands tell plainer than words her agony and despair. A man—tall, stalwart, in coarse dress and nail-studded sandals, lay at hand. Upon his back, with straightened limbs and extended arms, he had resolved, since unable to escape, to die like a man. His powerful features are clearly shown, and a portion of his moustache adheres to the plaster cast.

Such are sights from which the veil of time has at last been lifted. How many perished in that fearful outbreak we shall never know. Seven hundred skeletons have been found in one-third of the city of Pompeii. Perhaps two thousand perished there. But of the scores who fled from the city, from suburban villas, from villages along the mountain, and who were overtaken by the fiery storm ere they reached a place of safety, who shall tell? Who may declare the fate of the lady who appealed to the Roman admiral Pliny for relief? Such questions each may determine for himself. History will preserve an eternal silence.

Such are the facts concerning the first great historic eruption of Vesuvius. That volcanic phenomena were known to the ancients we have already seen; but the character of Vesuvius seems to have been unsuspected. The Greeks knew of the mountain top as a depressed plain, covered with groves and wild vines. Spartacus and his gladiators, with their thousands of followers, had their fortified camp there. Strabo called it a volcanic mountain, but Pliny the elder did not include it in his list of volcanoes. The fertile, rounded slopes were covered with well-tilled fields.

But the neighboring regions were active, though Vesuvius was not. Pithecusa, the modern Ischia, was often and terribly shaken, and various attempts to settle upon it were in consequence abandoned. Poisonous gases poured forth, even when there was no active eruption.

Still nearer Vesuvius lay the noted lake Avernus, which in Roman mythology was the gateway of hell. It was said to exhale noxious vapors so powerful that birds could not cross it. At the present day it is only a pretty lake, without any unusual properties. It appears to cover an extinct crater.

In the year 63 a great earthquake was felt in the Vesuvian region. Hundreds of lives were lost, and great damage was done in many cities; and numerous lighter shocks occurred during the next sixteen years. No one seems to have apprehended any danger from the mountain. How long it had remained dormant is unknown. But Pompeii and Herculaneum are both built upon lava beds. That Pompeii itself was a very old city is clearly established. In general outline it is elliptical, nearly two miles in circuit, the entire area being one hundred and sixty acres. Characters upon many of the foundation stones would seem to indicate a period earlier than the Etruscan occupation; while other portions, especially the towers, are certainly of later date. It is quite fair to suppose that Vesuvius, from these facts, had lain quiet for a thousand years or more.

One effect of this first eruption of Vesuvius was to break down the western wall of the crater and destroy the entire side of the mountain next the sea, leaving as the only remains of the ancient crater a little ridge on the south flank, and that portion, which under the name of Somma, still encircles the present cone.

From the time of its first eruption, the restlessness of Vesuvius has been well observed. The next action occurred in the year 203. In the meantime the sides of the crater had become overgrown with brushwood and forest trees, and the basin itself was a favorite haunt of wild boars. In the year 472 the mountain broke forth with more violence than at either of the former periods. The roaring was simply indescribable. The clouds of ashes spread over the entire adjacent region. Houses toppled down miles away. Scores of people were suffocated. The ashes fell in showers at Constantinople and Tripoli.

Other eruptions followed in 512, 685, and 993. No stream of molten lava issued at any of these. But in 1036, a great eruption took place, during which, we are told, the lava poured forth from fissures in the sides, as well as from the top, and ran in a broad and deep stream into the sea. Thirteen years later another similar outbreak occurred; then ninety years passed without any disturbance.

Of these eruptions, little beyond the bare fact is known. But from the time of the last one referred to, 1139, scientific men have carefully watched each outbreak. In 1198, the neighboring crater of Solfatara Lake was in eruption; in 1302, Ischia, dormant over fourteen hundred years, exhibited wonderful activity. For more than a year earthquakes shook the island, and at length there burst forth a lava stream from the southeast side of the mountain, flowing two miles, to the sea. Many houses were destroyed during the two months' eruption; and not a few of the inhabitants abandoned the island. But Vesuvius was quiet till 1306. Again it broke forth in 1500. During this time Ætna was in a state of unwonted activity.

The eruption of 1538 broke forth at the foot of the mountain, and was marked by some peculiar features. The plain between Avernus, Monte Barbaro, and the sea, was first raised a little, and many cracks made in it, from some of which water issued. The sea retreated about two hundred paces, leaving many fish on the sands at the disposal of the people of Pozzuoli, a little watering place on the Bay of Baiæ. On the evening of September 29, numerous shocks of earthquake occurred, and about two o'clock in the night an immense fissure opened near the lake and extended toward the town. Smoke, fire, stones, and mud made of ashes, were vomited furiously, the whole process being attended by a terrible roaring, as of continual loudest thunder. Stones and masses of pumice larger than an ox were thrown out. The gulf in the town widened, and not a few houses were broken to pieces, or swallowed up in the chasm.

The large stones were thrown about as high as a crossbow would carry, and then fell, sometimes into the lake, sometimes into the chasm again; but mostly upon either side of it. The mud was ash-colored, very liquid at first but rapidly thickening; and within thirty-six hours the site of Pozzuoli was covered by a volcanic cone. A contemporary chronicler, present at the time, says this cone was one thousand paces in height; by which he probably meant slant height. The cone at present is four hundred and forty feet above the Bay of Naples. Two days later it again began to cast forth stones and ashes; and again on the seventh day. Several persons who had ascended the hill were killed in this sudden outbreak by falling stones, or smothered by the sulphurous vapors. This "Monte Nuovo" or New Mountain, is a mile and a half in circumference at the base, and four hundred and twenty-one feet deep. It is apparent, then, that its bottom is nineteen feet above the sea level. The Lucrine Lake was almost filled up. Only a shallow pool remains.

Falconi writes that from Naples the flames were seen, bursting forth in the night, between the hot-baths and Tripergola. The next morning might be seen the poor people flying in terror, begrimed with the black and muddy shower, which continued throughout the day. Flying from death, death was painted in their countenances. Some bore their children in their arms; some carried sacks full of goods; some led donkeys loaded with valuables, or such as were unable to walk.

The few eruptions after 1039 had been feeble. We find the mountain coming to be regarded as extinct as a volcanic crater. Nearly five centuries passed. Bracini, who visited it in 1631, writes that "the crater was about five miles in circumference, and above a thousand feet deep; its sides were covered with brushwood, and at the bottom was a plain on which cattle grazed. In the woody parts wild boars frequently harbored. In one part of the plain, covered with ashes, were three small pools; one filled with hot and bitter water, another salter than the sea, and a third hot but tasteless." Such was the general character of the crater in A. D., 78, save that it was not so deep.

In December, 1631, with a sudden, tremendous roar, the mountain flamed into action. This outbreak has never been surpassed in fury and destructiveness by any eruption of Vesuvius, unless we except the one which destroyed Pompeii. The fatalities between the two eruptions had been few, the most of the mischief being damage to property. One of the eruptions failed to throw out any marked amount of matter of any sort.

. But in 1631 the woods and pastures, vines, and fields within the crater, were annihilated. Explosion followed explosion in swift succession. The great crater was filled with molten rock. Stream after stream poured swiftly forth, till seven rivers of fire were desolating the land. Crops were fired by the cinder showers. Millions of tons of ashes were scattered over the land. The mountain slope was dotted with ruined villages. Resina, a populous little town on the site of Herculaneum was completely destroyed. Storms of wind and rain swept the mountain, and the huge rivers of mud buried whatever had escaped the lava and ashes. The crater itself was shattered and nearly destroyed. Hundreds of cattle were destroyed by the fiery storm. Not less than eighteen hundred people perished in this great convulsion. Thirty-five years later another outbreak occurred; and since then the mountain has been in constant activity.

The next unusual activity of especial note occurred in 1737. Breislak has estimated the outflow of lava at

VESUVIUS IN 1737.

10,237,096 cubic meters; enough to cover a square mile twelve and a half feet in depth. Immense quantities of white ashes were thrown out, and the entire mountain was filled with rents and fissures, from which poured volumes of noxious vapors that suffocated man and beast. The quantity of ashes thrown out doubtless exceeded the volume of lava. In 1766 occurred another unusual convulsion, the mountain continuing vigorously active from March till December, vomiting lava streams and huge volcanic "bombs." These last are masses of lava enclosing a bubble of gas, which is set free by the breaking of the bombs as it falls. In 1779 the lava streams for a time threatened Naples itself.

Sir William Hamilton, long time English ambassador in Italy, has left a careful record of the eruption of 1793-94. Passing by such features as, common to all its eruptions, we have noted elsewhere, we may note the more striking particulars: Millions of heated stones were thrown high in the air, and fell in beautiful curves about the cone. It might be likened to the bursting stars of our pyrotechnic displays. Nearly half Vesuvius was covered with fire. "Huge masses of white smoke were vomited forth by the disturbed mountain, and formed themselves at a height of many thousands of feet above the crater into a huge, ever-moving canopy, through which, from time to time, were hurled pitch-black jets of volcanic dust, and dense vapors, mixed with cascades of red-hot rocks and scoriæ. The rain from the cloud canopy was scalding hot."

"As the lava rushed forth from its imprisonment it streamed a liquid, white and brilliantly pure river, which burned for itself a smooth channel through a great arched chasm in the side of the mountain. It flowed with the clearness of honey in regular channels, cut finer than art can imitate and glowing with all the splendor of the sun." Various were the effects of stones thrown in. "Light bodies of five, ten or fifteen pounds weight, made no impression; but bodies of sixty, seventy and eighty pounds were seen to form a kind of bed on the surface of the lava and float away with it. A stone of three hundred weight that had been thrown out by the crater, lay near the source of the current of lava. I raised it up on one end and then let it fall in upon the liquid lava, when it gradually sank beneath the surface and disappeared. If I wished to describe the manner in which it acted upon the lava, I should say that it was like a loaf of bread thrown into a bowl of very thick honey, which gradually involves itself in the heavy liquid and then slowly sinks to the bottom."

As it flowed down the mountain the brilliant whiteness disappeared. Then it began to wrinkle, where flowing slowly, like the cream on a pan of milk when poured off. Crusts formed, which were speedily cracked to pieces, as the current underneath pressed on. On such crusts a person may cross the stream, if not particular as to singeing his boots. Being cooled when near the bottom, yet forced on by the pressure behind, the whole mass "resembled nothing so much as a heap of unconnected cinders from an iron foundry, rolling slowly along and falling with a rattling noise over one another."

This eruption continued from February, 1793, to July, 1794. Rocks were hurled two thousand feet into the air. The lava flowed from fifteen different sources, and pouring in one stream from twelve to forty feet thick, flowed three hundred and eighty feet into the sea, requiring but six hours from the time of the outbreak to reach the shore. The sea boiled for one hundred yards around. The town of Torre del Greco was destroyed, and a number of persons were killed. The natives insisted, when the paroxysm was over, on rebuilding on the old site. The Neapolitans have a jest concerning their own exemption from the calamities which Torre has endured: "Naples sins and Torre is punished." The lava of this discharge is estimated at about twenty-one million cubic metres.

Several eruptions of Vesuvius have occurred during the present century. Of these, the most notable are those of 1822 and 1872. They have given us exact information upon a point where formerly there was only conjecture, viz: the height which the material thrown out may reach.

In 1822, the ashes for twelve days fell in a continuous shower. The lava which had boiled up and hardened till the appearance of a depressed crater was lost was blown away. An immense abyss was formed, three-fourths of a mile in length and two thousand feet deep. The entire top of the cone was then blown away. Masses of lava weighing many tons were hurled two or three miles. Darkness prevailed in broad day, as far away as Amalfi, where the ashes fell to the depth of several inches. The dense column of ashes and vapor was thrown ten thousand feet above the level of the sea. In no known eruption has the electrical display been so brilliant and continuous. The roll of thunder could be clearly distinguished from the rumble of the volcano.

In recent years an observatory has been erected on the mountain, and all its phenomena carefully noted. During the eruption of 1872 instantaneous photography was pressed into service. A comparison of the whole view with the height of the mountain, showed that the vapors and fragments were thrown twenty thousand feet into the air—nearly four miles. This outburst began on April 24, and reached its climax in two days. The entire mountain filled with fissures and cracks—in the words of Prof. Palmicri, "sweated fire." Enormous volumes of steam poured from the crater, with such a prodigious roar, that the terrified Neapolitans rushed from their houses, and spent the night in the open air. The lava floods rushed down the mountain side; and one of them destroyed two villages, besides many country houses adjacent. The whole region for several days quivered with shocks of earthquake.

Such have been the more important eruptions of Vesuvius. Its position, by an ancient and populous city, has made it the most celebrated of volcanoes. There seems no doubt that it is supplied from the same source which feeds the others in the neighborhood, as well as Mt. Ætna. When Vesuvius is quiet, Ætna is active, and vice versa. Close observation has established a well-defined daily periodicity; so that the most favorable period for visiting the crater may always be known beforehand.

In fine, about sixty eruptions of Vesuvius are on record. Of these, twenty-three were during the last century, and twenty-five during this. The activity of the entire region seems on the increase.

CHAPTER XXII.

OTHER GREAT ERUPTIONS.

> "Hast thou observed the ancient tract,
> That was trodden by wicked mortals,
> Who were arrested on a sudden,
> Whose foundation is a molten flood?
> Who said to God, Depart from us,
> What can Shaddai do to us?
> Though he had filled their houses with wealth.
> (Far from me be the counsel of the wicked!)
> The righteous beheld and rejoiced,
> The innocent laughed them to scorn,
> Surely their substance was carried away,
> And their riches devoured by fire."

SUCH is Dr. Henderson's translation of Job XXII, 15-20. By many the passage has been supposed to refer to the destruction of the cities of the plain, and used to support the theory that a volcanic eruption was the means of their overthrow. If the theory were true, the catastrophe is the earliest historic eruption. A brief statement of the reasons for the belief may interest the reader.

The entire Dead Sea valley is depressed far below the level of the sea. From the Dead Sea to the head of the Red Sea is a well-marked trough, supposed to indicate that the Jordan once emptied into the Red Sea. The adjacent Sinaitic peninsula is a volcanic region, which may have been in eruption when the Israelites passed it. Dr. Robinson reports water marks left high on the cliffs, far to the south of the Dead Sea. Fragments of lava have been picked up among the salt-crusts and bituminous deposits on the shores.

In short, the region is one in which, at some time, volcanic action occurred. It lies between two great volcanic

DESTRUCTION OF SODOM.

centers; Sinai, and the volcanic region of Arabia and Syria. The question really is, whether any disturbance occurred there at so late a period as the destruction of Sodom.

The idea advanced by several thoughtful men is, that in the bituminous plain occupied by the cities, fissures opened and flames and cinders issuing, rained upon the inflammable surface, speedily destroying the cities, which sunk with the earth till the sea covered them. Such cases, minus the bitumen, have several times occurred. And, again, the sea might have existed before, and merely have been extended by the convulsion. Such is the substance of the theory.

Cases in support of it are not wanting. The city of Euphemia, in Calabria, was so swallowed up in 1638. Kircher, who was near at the time, tells how he and his companions, unable to keep their feet, during the violent earthquake, lay upon the ground till the paroxysms were somewhat abated. Rising and looking for Euphemia, only a frightful black cloud was seen. It slowly cleared away revealing a loathsome and putrid lake. No trace of the city or its inhabitants was ever found.

In the island of Trinidad is a vast lake of pitch, of which the Indian legend tells the origin. The words are Kingsley's:

> "Once that dark and loathly pitch-lake
>   Was a garden, bright and fair,
> And the Chaymas, from the mainland,
>   Built their palm ajoupas there.
>
> There they throve, and there they fattened.
>   Hale and happy, safe and strong,
> Passed the livelong days in feasting,
>   Passed the nights in dance and song.
>
> Till they cruel grew, and wanton,
>   Till they killed the colibris,
> Then outspoke the Great good Spirit,
>   Who can see through all the trees."

The spirit proceeded to remind the Chaymas of all the good things he had provided for them; how he had allowed them unlimited use of all things which could be of any possible good to them; how he had even been patient with their thanklessness. Only the colibris or humming-birds, useless to the Chaymas, he had reserved for himself, that he might have pleasure in their beauty and happiness. The story continues:

> "But the Chaymas' ears were deafened.
>   Blind their eyes, and could not see,
> How a blissful Indian's spirit
>   Lived in every colibri.
>
> Lived, forgetting pain and sorrow,
>   Ever fair and ever new,
> Whirring round the dear old woodland,
>   Feeding on the honeydew.
>
> Then one evening roared the earthquake,
>   Monkeys howled, and parrots screamed,
> And the Guaraons, at morning
>   Gathered here, as men who dreamed.
>
> Sunk were gardens, sunk ajoupas,
>   Hut and hammock, man and hound,
> And above the Chayma village,
>   Boiled with pitch the cursed ground."

The salient points of the evidence being presented, the reader may draw his own conclusions. Perhaps the cities were fired in the manner suggested—perhaps lightning ignited the bitumen. But it is generally supposed that their site lies beneath the sea.

After the account given of Vesuvius, the reader will no doubt be surprised to learn that this noted mountain can not rank as more than a respectable fourth-rate volcano. It will require but a brief comparison with others to show that such is the case.

By far the largest volcano in Europe, and next to Vesuvius, the most noted, is Mt. Etna, in the island of Sicily. It was well known to the ancients, and appears to have been in eruption from the most remote historic times. Diodorus Siculus records that a violent eruption caused an adjacent district to be deserted by its inhabitants before the Trojan war. Thucydides tells of three eruptions between the colonization of Sicily by the Greeks and the Peloponnesian war—431 B. C.

Notwithstanding the great antiquity of the records of this mountain, but little detail is known of its earlier eruptions. The first of which any extended account exists is the great outbreak of 1669. The convulsion began with a tremendous earthquake. Many villages and towns in the adjacent districts were leveled to the earth. In the plain of St. Lio, a fissure six feet wide and twelve miles long and of unknown depth opened from north to south with a terrific, crashing noise, and extended nearly to the top of the mountain. Flashes of intense light poured from it. Five other parallel fissures afterwards opened, one after the other, emitting smoke, and the most horrid bellowings, which were heard to the distance of forty miles.

This explains the manner in which dykes or banks of lava are thrown up amid other rocks. The light emitted by these fissures would indicate that they were, to a certain height, filled with glowing lava.

The lava, during this eruption, having overwhelmed and destroyed fourteen towns, some of them containing three or four thousand inhabitants, at length arrived at the walls of Catania, a populous city, situated ten miles from the volcano. These walls had been raised sixty feet high, towards the mountain, in order to protect the city, in case of an eruption. But the burning flood accumulated against the wall, so as to fill all the space around and below that part, and finally poured over it in a fiery cataract, destroying every thing in that vicinity.

From Catania the lava continued its course until it reached the sea, a distance of fifteen miles from its source, in a current about eighteen hundred feet broad, and forty feet deep. While moving on, its surface was, in general, a mass of solid rock, or cooled lava, and it advanced by the protrusion of the melted matter, through this hardened crust.

As an illustration of the intense heat of volcanic matter, the Canon Recupero relates that in 1766 he ascended a small hill composed of ancient volcanic matter, in order to observe the slow and gradual manner in which a current of liquid fire advanced from Ætna. This current was two and a half miles broad; and, while he stood observing it, two small threads of lava, issuing from a crevice, detached themselves from the main stream, and approached rapidly towards the eminence where he and his guide were standing. They had only just time to escape, when they saw the hill on which they stood a few minutes before, and which was fifty feet high, entirely surrounded, and, in about fifteen minutes, entirely melted down into the burning mass, so as to be incorporated with, and move on along with it.

According to Hitchcock, 77,000 persons perished during the eruption of 1769, and eighty-four square miles were covered with lava.

The slowness with which lava cools may be inferred that ten years later, workmen endeavoring to sink a shaft through the bed were forced to abandon the work when near the bottom, by reason of the heat.

While this was Ætna's greatest outbreak, several of terrible destructiveness have occurred since. In 1693 an eruption was accompanied by earthquake shocks, which in three days did more damage than the lava. Catania was almost destroyed; great sea-waves rolled in upon the

446 GREAT DISASTERS.

DESTRUCTION OF CATANIA.

wreck; the vessels in the harbor were dashed against each other or upon the beach: the ringing of the bells and the roar of the mountain and sea was mingled with the cries of thousands of unfortunates struggling in the ruins. Not less than 16,000 people perished in Catania alone.

In 1755 occurred an eruption which is memorable for the great flood which attended it. Immense quantities of snow and ice, accumulated about the summit, were melted by the intense heat, and the waters rushed down in a column thirty feet deep and one and three-quarters miles wide, into the plain below. The lower portion of the valley was filled with the debris. Those who were not buried in the rubbish were swept out to sea. The total loss of life is not exactly known, but amounted to many thousands.

Second in volume to the eruption of 1669, but very slightly destructive, is the eruption of 1852-53. It began August 20, 1852, and continued nine months. "The united width of the lava streams was two miles, with a depth of from eight to sixteen feet, piled up in some places to one hundred feet. It reached to near Zarafana, —almost six miles, descending thirty-five hundred feet in sixteen days. The Val del Bove, from the upper part of which it proceeded, looked like a sea of fire. Explosions as of artillery were frequently heard, and the scoriæ were sent up to great heights." The intense heat set fire to the trees in the vicinity.

In January, 1865, a considerable eruption took place from an immense fissure on the northeastern slope of the mountain. Seven active craters developed along the fissure, sending out a lava stream one and one-half miles wide.

Three other eruptions have taken place from Ætna since 1853; but, save some damage to property, these have been comparatively unimportant, save from a geological standpoint. One began in 1874 from a fissure on the north side, but suddenly ceased. Prof. Silvestri, after examining the locality, asserted that the next eruption would take place from this same fissure. Five years later his assertion was verified, large streams of lava being sent out, with heavy showers of ashes and sand. Large areas of forest were destroyed, and the stream drew alarmingly near some populous villages, but stopped not far from a small river. The area of the lava bed was about seven hundred and fifty acres, the volume being about twenty-three and a half million tons.

Ætna's last eruption was in May, 1886; a few houses were destroyed, but no lives were lost. Ætna and the adjacent Lipari Islands exhibited unusual activity during the entire seventeenth century, having a total of fourteen eruptions; as many as are recorded in all their previous history. The next century witnessed fifteen outbursts from Ætna, and during the present one there have been eleven.

It will be noticed that both Vesuvius and Ætna seem to have reached their maximum activity at the close of the last century. The same is true of the volcanoes of Iceland. This island, which is as large as Ireland, is built up entirely of volcanic matter. It doubtless began with a single, great submarine volcano; but to-day it has at least thirteen active vents. It presents us with the most tremendous outpour of matter in the history of the world. For seven hundred years there has not been an interval of forty, and seldom of more than twenty, without eruptions and earthquakes in some portion of the island. Single eruptions of Mt. Hecla have lasted six years. Often during violent earthquakes, old mountains have disappeared; new ones have been raised up; rivers turned from their courses, or dried up altogether. The old Norseman who discovered the island might much more appropriately have named it Fireland. Doubtless had his ancestors known the island they would have chosen it as the home of the terrible fire giants.

But Iceland is the realm of both frost and fire; and there is no more romantic or painful chapter in history than the story of this hardy and spirited race to maintain their foothold in the face of such terrible odds. Those who hold that a nation's progress and stamina are in proportion to its material advantages, would have to make an exception in favor of blood. The plucky Norsemen have held their own in this region for nine centuries; nor is there any deterioration. No nation can to-day show a better intellectual or moral condition than these poor but hardy islanders. Yet there is not a region of the world that has been more frequently or terribly scourged than this semi-barren island.

The best known volcano in Iceland is Mt. Hecla, which ranks with Ætna and Vesuvius in fame. It is not the highest nor most remarkable of Icelandic volcanoes; but the frequency of its eruptions, together with the fact that it may be easily reached, have brought it to the front. It is five thousand feet high, and lies but thirty-five miles from the sea. The larger portion of the material thrown out by it consists of slag, cinders, pumice, and ashes, the slope of its cone being about 35 degrees. It has nothing answering to the customary crater; the eruptions break from fissures in its sides; and, in consequence, it may emit several streams or showers at once.

Hecla has been in eruption about thirty times since its character was first known, and has at times made fearful havoc. Its last great outbreak was in 1878.

Hecla has adjutants in this volcanic field that are more savage and relentless than the generalissimo. One of the most destructive outbursts of recent times occurred in the Vatna district in 1875. In this region, about sixty

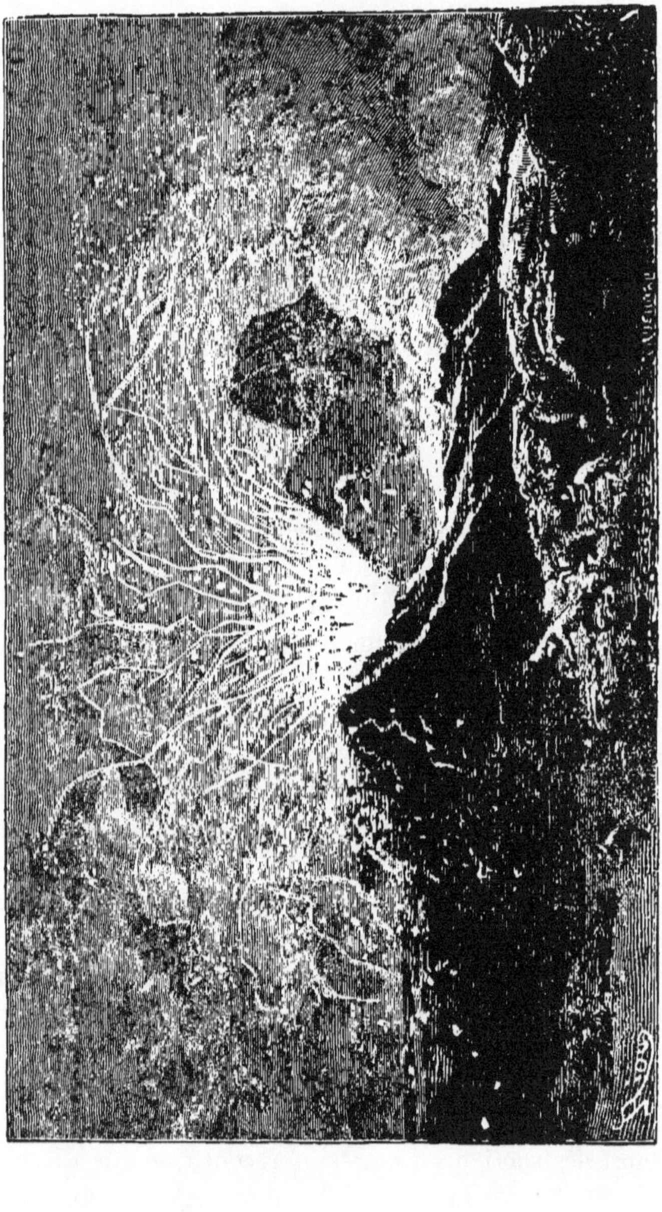

MT. HECLA.

miles by one hundred and fifteen, is a very nest of volcanoes. The convulsion lasted several months, the entire region being active; and great numbers of people perished. So great was the destruction of property, crops, and flocks that the people, reduced to starvation, were compelled to appeal to Britain and Denmark for assistance. This has happened more than once in Iceland's history.

But far up in the impenetrable deserts of the interior is a mountain which has seldom shown any activity; but when in full blast, its power is unsurpassed by any volcano on the globe. This is the fearful Skaptar Jokul, or Skaptar mountain. A single instance of its power will suffice.

One of the most stupendous outbreaks recorded in history is that of Skaptar Jokul in 1783. In the quantity of lava ejected, it is hardly surpassed by any single eruption; and few disturbances of the sort have surpassed it in fatality. Immense volumes of ashes were hurled into the air, spreading over the whole island in dense clouds. Streams were poisoned by the minerals and alkalies thrown out. Immense numbers of sheep and cattle perished. Thousands of acres of pasture lands were ruined. Where the grass was not killed, it often was rendered poisonous, like the water, by the mineral dust falling upon it. The hills were dotted with the decaying carcasses. The air was filled with horrible stench. The ashes fell in such volumes into the ocean that the fish deserted the coast. The flying clouds of dust spread to Europe. The appalling horror of the scene can hardly be imagined. Death stalked abroad in his most repulsive form.

"The river Skapta, a considerable stream, was for a time completely dried by a torrent of liquid fire. This river was about two hundred feet broad, and its banks from four to six hundred above the level of the water.

This defile was entirely filled for a considerable distance by the lava, which crossed the river by the dam thus formed, and overflowed the country beyond, where it filled a lake of considerable extent, and great depth.

"This eruption commenced on the 11th of June. On the 18th of the same month, a still greater quantity of lava rushed from the mouth of the volcano, and flowed with amazing rapidity, sometimes over the first stream, but generally in a new course. The melted matter having crossed some of the tributary streams of the Skapta, completely dammed up their waters and caused great destruction of property and lives by their overflow. The lava, after flowing for several days, was precipitated down a tremendous cataract, called Stapafoss, where it filled a profound abyss, which that great water-fall had been excavating for ages, and thence the fiery flood continued its course.

"On the 3rd of August, a new eruption poured forth fresh floods of lava, which, taking a different direction from the others, filled the bed of another river, by which a large lake was formed, and much property and many lives destroyed.

"The effect of this dreadful calamity may in some measure be imagined when it is known that, although Iceland did not at that time contain more than fifty thousand inhabitants, there perished nine thousand human beings by this single eruption, making nearly one in five of the whole population. Part of them were destroyed by the burning lava itself; some by drowning, other by noxious vapors which the lava emitted, and others in consequence of the famine, caused by the showers of ashes, which covered a great proportion of the island and destroyed most of the vegetation. The fish, also, on which the inhabitants depended, in a great measure, for food, entirely deserted the coast."

OTHER GREAT ERUPTIONS. 453

The quantity of lava which Skaptar Jokul emitted during this eruption was almost beyond belief. The two principal branches were respectively forty and fifty miles long. The branch which crossed the Skapta was from twelve to fifteen miles wide; the width of the other was seven miles. The usual depth was one hundred feet; but two and three hundred were frequent; and where the streams dashed across gorges or narrow valleys the depth was six or seven hundred. It would be quite safe to estimate the average depth at one hundred and fifty feet. These two principal streams were, then, sufficient to cover one thousand square miles to a depth of one hundred and fifty feet. Contrast with this the twenty million cubic meters estimated to have been poured forth in one of the great Vesuvian eruptions. This last would cover one square mile to a depth of twenty-five feet. Vesuvius sinks to an insignificance that is pitiable; its great outbreak produced but one-six thousandths as much as the single eruption of Skaptar Jokul! Such calculations may give us a comparative estimate of the two; but no figures can give us any conception of the force required to elevate such a stream of melted rock through the crust of the earth. And if we compare the resultant fatality, it is clear that this great convulsion, in a very sparsely settled island, destroyed more lives than all the outbursts of Vesuvius in its densely populated neighborhood.

This eruption of Skaptar was preceded by several outbreaks in the sea; some of them close to the shore; some many miles from land. Such phenomena have become tolerably familiar. Livy informs us that a disturbance of this kind near Sicily, occurring with similar phenomena at the time of Hannibal's death, so terrified the Romans as to induce them to proclaim a day of supplication to the gods to avert their displeasure. Santorin in the

Grecian Archipelago is a similar production. And in 1831 an island was thrown up to the southwest of Sicily, where previous soundings had shown a depth of six hundred feet. It was preceded by a violent spouting of steam and water. The sea around was filled with floating pumice and dead fish. The crater reached a height of two hundred feet, being three miles in circumference. Its circular basin was full of boiling, dingy, red water. It continued active three weeks, and then slowly sank, leaving a dangerous reef eleven feet below the surface; while a single black volcanic rock projected from the sea near the center of the reef. It is known as Graham's Island. Thus we see that volcanic action is not confined to the land, and that the areas affected are continually shifting.

Jorullo, in Mexico, affords an example of the way in which new volcanoes are constantly being formed. In the parallel of the City of Mexico exist five volcanoes, extending in a line across the country as if thrown up along some immense fissure or subterranean fault, extending from sea to sea. Of these Popocatepetl is perhaps the largest, and Jorullo the most recent.

There formerly existed in Mexico an extensive plain of remarkable fertility, covered with fields of cane, cotton and indigo, and watered by irrigation from the reservoirs in the basaltic mountains that bounded it. This region, the *Malpays*, had no volcano within eighty miles, and lay twenty-six hundred feet above the sea. In June, 1759, alarming rumblings were heard in the earth, which were succeeded by severe earthquakes. These phenomena lasted several weeks, to the great consternation of the inhabitants. In September it seemed that quiet was restored, when suddenly, on the night of the 28th, a fearful subterranean noise was again heard; fissures opened, and hot stones were thrown out. Part of the plain rose up like

OTHER GREAT ERUPTIONS. 455

an immense bubble to the height of sixteen hundred feet. Imagine the astonishment of the natives when morning showed them a mountain where the night before was a

JORULLO.

level plain! It almost seemed as though some magic had transported them to another land. Smoke and ashes spouted forth; five smaller cones were thrown up, the least of which was three hundred feet in height. The plain was dotted with thousands of small conical mounds, called by the natives *hornitos*, or ovens. Each emitted vapor for a time; but at length all the upheavals, save Jorullo, ceased action, though the plain remained so hot as to be uninhabitable for many years. Jorullo continued to throw out lava several months, and has been in more moderate action ever since.

In some respects the terrible outbreak of Skaptar Jokul has been several times exceeded. While almost alone in the immense quantity of lava thrown out, we have seen that great streams of lava are not accompanied by the most violent explosions. In the number of lives destroyed, Skaptar has also been exceeded; but if Iceland had been as densely populated as Ireland, which it equals in area, the convulsion might have destroyed half a million or more.

One of the best examples of the force of steam on a smaller scale is seen in the eruptions of volcanoes, is to be found in the geysers of Iceland. These lie in a strip of ground one hundred yards wide and about a quarter of a mile in length. The ground is dotted with numerous dark apertures and conical mounds, from which clouds of steam ascend continually. Of these the Little Geyser is no longer active, being merely a pool of still, hot water. The Great Geyser is periodically active, and the Strokr, or Churn, may be excited at any time by throwing a quantity of earth into it. As a matter of course, these boiling springs never do any damage, the quantity of water thrown out being of no consequence. The water holds in solution a vast quantity of silicious matter, which is deposited around the mouth of the geyser, forming sometimes a saucer-shaped basin, sometimes a nipple-shaped mound. From the rate at which the deposits are

OTHER GREAT ERUPTIONS.   457

made, it is estimated that the Great Geyser is about ten hundred and sixty years old.

One of the most tremendous outbursts of which we have any authentic account occurred in the island of Sumbawa. It is one of the Molucca islands; and the mountain from

GEYSER.

which the outbreak occurred is called Tomboro.

"This eruption commenced on the 5th of April, 1815, but was most terrific on the 11th and 12th of that month; nor did it cease entirely until some time in the following July. The explosion so much resembled the firing of heavy cannon at a distance that the people of many vessels at sea supposed there was a great naval engagement within hearing, but could not imagine what nations were engaged.

"The commanders of some ships, and several English forts, gave orders to prepare for battle, though they were several hundred miles distant from the mountain. At Sumatra these tremendous explosions were distinctly heard, though not nearer than nine hundred and seventy miles from Tomboro. They were also heard at Ternate, in the opposite direction from Sumatra, at the distance of seven hundred and twenty miles from the mountain.

"So immense in quantity was the fall of ashes, that at Bima, forty miles from the mountain, the roof of the English resident's house was crushed by the weight, and many other houses in the same town were rendered uninhabitable from the same cause. At Java, three hundred miles distant, the air was so full of ashes that from this cause, at mid-day, it is said, the darkness was so profound that nothing like it had ever before been experienced during the most stormy night.

"Along the coast of Sumbawa the sea was covered with floating lava, intermixed with trees and timber, so that it was difficult for vessels to sail through the mass. Some captains, though at a long distance at sea, mistook this mass for land, and sent out their boats in order to ascertain the safety of their situations. The sea, on this and the neighboring coast, rose suddenly to the height of twelve feet, in the form of immense waves, and, as they retired, swept away trees, timber, and houses with their inhabitants. All the vessels lying near the shore were torn from their anchoring and cast upon the land. Violent whirlwinds carried into the air, men, horses, cattle, trees, and whatever else was in the vicinity of the mountain. Large trees were torn up by the roots and carried into the sea. But the most calamitous part of the account still remains; for such were the tremendous effects of the burning lava—the overflowing of the sea, the fall of houses, and the violence of the whirlwind, that, out of twelve thousand inhabitants on this island, only twenty-six individuals escaped with their lives, all the rest being destroyed in one way or another.

"The whole island was completely covered with ashes, or other volcanic matter. In some places the bottom of the sea was so elevated as to make shoals where there was deep water before; and in others, the land sunk down and was overflown by the sea. Adding those who were killed on other islands, the total death roll was over twenty thousand."

This entire region is one of wonderful activity. Mount Api, in the island of Banda, in the same group, has had twelve violent eruptions in two hundred and thirty-four years; and, indeed, it is hardly ever really quiet. The volcano of Abo, in the island of Sanguir, broke out in 1711, burying a large number of villages in cinders, covering extensive areas of forest and plain, and destroying many thousands of people. This same volcano burst forth suddenly in March, 1856, vomiting torrents of mud, streams of lava, and clouds of ashes and scoria, doing almost as much mischief as on the former occasion. In the island of Timor, a gigantic volcano, long known as the Peak, began a violent eruption in 1638. When the convulsion was over the mountain had disappeared; partly blown away, partly sunken, and the site is to this day covered by a great lake.

But the center of this great volcanic region lies in the island of Java, which possesses about fifty craters, half of them still active. The heat and vapors poured out, combined with the power of the sun, combine to make this one of the most noted tempest regions in the world. Nowhere else are such terrific thunder-storms so common; and more than twenty water spouts are sometimes seen at one time.

One of the most remarkable eruptions of modern times is that of Papandayang, in this island, which occurred in 1772. The mountain burst forth suddenly, with a tremendous roaring. Cinders and ashes were almost insignificant. Immense boulders were hurled about the neighboring regions. The mountain was veiled in a cloud of glowing vapor. A tract of land seventeen miles long and seven miles wide, with over forty villages, was swallowed up. Several thousand people perished. When the cloud finally vanished it was found that four thousand feet of the upper portion of the mountain had been blown away. The broad, ragged mass remaining was of little more than one-half the original height. Two other mountains in the island were in action at the same time; while several intervening active cones remained quiet. Mt. Guntur, in the same island, has had a number of violent eruptions. The last, occurring in 1800, sent forth in addition to lava streams, a torrent of white, acid, sulphurous mud, which swept a populous and fertile valley, engulfing hundreds of men and animals in its course. We shall notice by and by a still more remarkable Javanese convulsion.

Time would fail were details to be given of the numerous volcanoes of Sumatra and Celebes and the adjacent islands, or of the eruptions and boiling springs of New Zealand, or the towering cones of New Guinea, or of the peaks of the Canary, Cape Verde and Azores. Let us notice briefly a few of the more noted volcanoes of America.

Our own land is free, for the most part, from such disturbances; the only recorded outbreaks being those of

Rainier and St. Helens, in 1842. But in prehistoric times it had numerous volcanic areas. The Raton peaks in New Mexico once sent out lava streams that spread over the country between the Upper Arkansas and Canadian rivers; and St. Helens, Hood, Edgecombe, Baker, Rainier, Fair Weather and Shasta, are cones well known to the western tourist. These, except Hood and Shasta, are still active.

But better known examples of great internal heat are found in the hot springs of different portions of the country; though these merely show the existence of subterranean heat, and afford no conception of its power or violence. Quite as famous is the famous geyser basin of the Yellowstone. Here is a region surpassing greatly the geyser district of Iceland, both in area, and in the number and power of the geysers. The whole region is pierced with fumaroles, around which sulphur and other minerals crystalize in beautiful forms; and steam jets break through the soil in countless places. Certain of the geysers are exceedingly periodic; and others, like the Strokr of Iceland, may be incited to action at almost any time by casting in earth or stones. The more powerful of these "toy volcanoes" send water to a height of four hundred feet.

In the southern portion of the continent and in South America we find a region of remarkable activity. Central America has had several violent convulsions at a comparatively recent period. The volcano of Las Virgines, in Lower California, had a great eruption in 1746; but the country being sparsely peopled, little harm was done, and the fact of the eruption was made known by the light and clouds seen from vessels at sea, and the ashes and cinders that fell in the adjacent regions of Mexico.

If eruptions be measured by the violence of explosions,

THE YELLOWSTONE PARK.

then the famous outburst of Cosequina must rank among the greatest, if not itself the greatest, that is known to history. The narrative of its eruption, as related by an eye-witness, seems almost beyond belief; but the facts are too well authenticated. The extent of the destruction of life, though certainly reaching many hundreds, was never definitely known. The personal narration serves to show the fearful impressions made upon those who experience such awful convulsions:

"The wonder to me is how any man could live through such a burst as Cosequina's in San Salvador. 'Twas the 21st of January, 1835—as fine a morning as ever was seen on earth. The Bay of Fonseca was smooth as silk; never a cloud in the sky. The lazy folks of Playa Grande and Nagascolo were lying in the hammocks beside the doors, smoking and dozing, and not a soul had a notion of ill from any side on that sunny morning, which was to be the last for half of them. They lay in hammocks and smoked and dozed like worthless cusses, as they are; and most of 'em, no doubt, had full in sight the big mountain on t'other side the gulf. They'd nigh forgot to call it a volcano. Not for a thousand years, as the Indians told, had smoke or mischief come from that hill; they'd ha' laughed silly any one as had talked danger from Cosequina.

"At ten o'clock that morning that mountain burst out again, and in a fury such as never yet was known in the upper world—no, nor ever will be again, as I believe, till the last day. Suddenly it burst out—not muttering beforehand, nor smoking—but crash! all on the moment, as if to remind men what evil power was yet left in nature to destroy them. At ten o'clock that day the voice of the mountain was heard after one thousand years' silence—in such a thunderous roar was it heard that beast and bird fell dead with the sound alone, and great cliffs pitched headlong into the sea! There's thousands still alive to witness. For a while the streets of Playa Grande and Nagascolo must have seemed like streets of the dead; for every soul was stunned. Folks were lying in their hammocks or on the floor, motionless and senseless as corpses. The sky was still bright and blue, but on the mountain side was a cloud like ink, which rolled down like a cap to the foot. Naught afterwards seemed so horrible as the sudden heaping of that jet black mound in the place of the sunny, green hill.

"But it didn't long offend any man's sight—over heaven and sea the cloud opened and spread. Lightning and thunders burst from the heart of the ocean, and sheets of flame glared luridly the sides of Cosequina. The darkness spread so quick, that at Leon, two hundred miles away, they were lighting the church candles within an hour after the outbreak. But candles, nor torches, nor houses aflame couldn't disperse that darkness. For three days no soul in Leon saw another's face, nor ventured out but to the howling churches, to grovel there. Night dragged after night, but no day shone over the land. A lighted torch could not be seen at arm's length! The ashes fell softly and silently, till buildings crushed down headlong with the weight. Tigers were in the churches, and panthers entered house doors in search of companionship and protection. Hundreds committed suicide in their madness, and hundreds more became simple for life. Men's faces were blistered by the hot winds; the paint fell from the statues; the crash of falling, and the faint light of burning houses doubled the horror of darkness. Such a time as that was never seen on earth since the plague of Egypt, I guess!

"But of course the most awful work was around the Gulf of Fonseca. The water rose in waves twenty feet high, dashed over the Estero, and swept off the towns of Playa Grande and Nagascolo, slick as a prairie fire. Scarce a soul escaped for twenty miles about. The cattle crushed over the barrancas in search of water, and were destroyed in herds of thousands at a time; for none could see, nor hear, nor breathe. Rivers were dried by the heat, and choked with ashes; forests burned up; the very grass withered throughout the whole length and breadth of Nicaragua, and hasn't sprung since. *Sacate* ('a broad flag-like blade') alone escaped, and the country which was once the grazing land of Central America was ruined till eternity, for that business.

"During this time of death, as they still call it, at Balize, one thousand miles away, the commandant called out the garrison, and kept them under arms twenty-four hours, thinking all the navies in the universe were at action in the offing. There 'twas too dark to see fifty yards oceanwards. The roar of Cosequina was heard miles around, spreading fear and perplexity. Four thousand miles in radius the ashes fell; they lay on the roofs at San Francisco, California.

"Well, the mountain's behaved like a decent sort of powder-cask ever since. The fuse has always been burning and spitting; but you see there's a big consumption of power in such a burst, and I guess the old machine wants to recuperate awhile."

Those familiar with the terrific effects produced on the gunners by the discharge of heavy artillery, can understand that the atmospheric concussion produced by tremendous volcanic explosions might kill large numbers of birds and small animals in the vicinity.

As to the distance to which ashes may be carried, a late eruption in Iceland was announced by a Professor in Germany long before any vessel brought the news. The atmosphere was unusually full of dust which, on examining with a microscope, he pronounced to be pulverized Iceland lava. The detonations of Cosequina were heard over the peninsula of Yucatan, along the shores of Jamaica, eight hundred miles distant, and as far as Bogota in South America—nearly ten thousand feet above the sea. Ashes fell on vessels twelve hundred miles westward at sea. Fortunately the eruption was soon over.

Another unusual outbreak occurred in Central America from the volcano of Leon in 1867, beginning November 27. First there were a number of violent explosions, which shook the earth for a great distance. Immense quantities of black sand were then thrown out, and a column of vapor and fire, filled with meteor-like specks, was hurled to a height of three thousand feet. Closer observation showed the "specks" to be rocks four or five feet in diameter, and weighing thousands of pounds. The showers of sand lasted three days, covering the earth for fifty miles around. The forest for leagues was scarred by the swift-falling showers of sand and stones; and for half a mile around the cone the trees were leveled to the ground.

Central America contains twenty-nine volcanoes, eighteen of which are active. Twenty cones are in sight from the town of Leon. One cone, Izalco, suddenly manifested signs of activity, but no eruption took place. But the sudden heating rapidly melted the snow on the mountain, and the torrents of water inundated the town of Guatemala, destroying thousands of dollars worth of property, besides many lives. The mountain has since been known as "Agua," or water.

South America is noted for the frequency and extreme violence of its earthquakes; of which more hereafter. Though possessing a greater number of very lofty volcanic cones than any other region, the direct effect of its eruptions have not been so disastrous as the results of many eruptions elsewhere. There is but one very notable exception; the earthquake that destroyed Riobamba in 1794 was followed at once by an outpour of mud from Tunguragua, which overwhelmed forty thousand people, still dazed by the shock, or struggling in the ruins of their villages.

One notable incident is the continual subterranean roaring heard for a considerable period over twenty-three hundred square miles of Northern Venezuela, a number of years ago, during a violent outpour of lava from the volcano of St. Vincent, an island six hundred and twenty-three miles to the northeast. No motion of the earth was perceptible. It has been supposed that the noise was merely the roar of St. Vincent conveyed through the crust of the earth; but this would raise the question as to why the same noise was not audible at points nearer to St. Vincent? Another suggestion is that the source from which the lava of St. Vincent was derived lay beneath Northern Venezuela; and a fact brought in support of this is, that the great earthquake of Caracas was immediately followed by action at St. Vincent. Similarly, the great eruption of Cotopaxi, in 1744, was attended by subterranean rumbling at Honda, four hundred and thirty-six miles away, and eighteen thousand and one hundred feet lower. Between are the colossal mountains of Pasto, Pichincha and Popayan, with countless valleys and ravines.

The cone of Cotopaxi is the smoothest and most symmetrical in the world; perhaps because its eruptions are almost entirely of ashes or fragmentary lava. As no villages lie in its immediate neighborhood, the clouds of ashes have not done so much damage as might be expected.

The first sign of an eruption is the melting of the snow upon the cone. Torrents of water sweep down the mountain. Such an outbreak occurring in 1741, after two centuries repose, the amount of snow accumulated may be imagined. The rush of the water tore away blocks of lava, ice and scoria; the plain below was covered with dashing waves. Twelve miles from the mountain the waters still had a velocity of fifty-six feet per second, or about two-thirds of a mile a minute. Escape from such a current would be impossible. Six hundred houses were swept away and one thousand people destroyed. The sides of the cone glowed in the night with a reddish light. Cotopaxi also had a great eruption in 1533, which hurled lava blocks containing one hundred and thirty cubic yards to a distance of nine miles. Such masses would weigh more than two hundred and eighty tons. Such feats will serve to give clearer ideas of the immense power of volcanic action.

Perhaps a statement of the force required to raise a column of lava would interest the reader. Lava being about twenty-eight times as heavy as water, a column of it eleven and three-sevenths feet high, and one inch square, would weigh fifteen pounds. Then to raise lava to the tops of various volcanic cones would require pressure or initial velocity as follows:

	Height.	Pressure per square inch.	Initial velocity per second.
Stromboli	2,168 feet.	2,640 pounds.	371 feet.
Vesuvius	3,874 "	4,710 "	496 "
Hecla	5,106 "	6,195 "	570 "
Ætna	10,892 "	13,230 "	832 "
Teneriffe	12,464 "	15,135 "	896 "
Mauna Kea	14,700 "	17,865 "	966 "
Popocatepetl	17,712 "	21,525 "	1,062 "
St. Elias	18,079 "	21,975 "	1,072 "
Cotopaxi	18,869 "	22,380 "	1,104 "
Sahama	22,965 "	27,756 "	1,212 "

OTHER GREAT ERUPTIONS. 469

When we remember that our powerful steam engines are operated by pressures varying from one hundred and twenty to two hundred pounds per square inch, it is evident we can have no adequate conception of the magnitude of a force of twenty-seven thousand pounds to the square inch. And yet such a power must be but a tithe of the force exerted; for it represents only the force necessary to throw the lava from the surface to the tops of the mountains; whereas the lava reservoirs are far beneath the surface. Also, the above calculation considers only the mere weight of the lava; it allows nothing for the resistance of cohesion, friction, or a heavy crust to be often burst through. When we consider all these, each of which must far surpass the weight of the single column of lava, it is evident that the pressure that can hurl lava blocks of two hundred and eighty tons nine miles from a mountain must reach a million pounds per square inch. These are meaningless figures. Human thought cannot grasp so stupendous a power.

Perhaps the best known of the great volcanoes are those of the Sandwich Islands. We find there the largest extinct crater in the world. The great dead crater of Haleakala, in East Maui, is thirty miles in circumference. The crater of Kilauea, on the flank of Mauna Loa, is about seven miles in circumference. Several great eruptions have occurred in these islands during the past fifty years; and in one of these convulsions the volume of lava poured out was at least equal to the great outburst of Skaptar Jokul in Iceland. And when we consider the frequent recurrence of the Hawaiian eruptions, it at once appears that in this region lies the greatest lava producer on the globe.

But in regard to destruction of life or property, there has so far been no more harmless region in the world.

There are two reasons: The lava poured out is very liquid, and cools slowly; hence a cone formed from it has a very gradual slope. The actual grade of Mauna Loa is but five or six degrees. So a lava stream descends it very slowly; and the light on the mountain warns the people of the outbreak. The shore region is the only one inhabited, the interior being covered with dense forests. So the lava may burn a path directly through to the sea, and yet do no great damage to the interests of the people. The greatest damage done to the island has not been from an outpour of lava, but from earthquakes and sea-waves. The great eruption of 1868 was accompanied by continual shocks—two thousand being felt in a fortnight, and numerous tidal waves being produced; yet the total fatality was but one hundred, and nearly all of these were old or weak persons who were unable to swim well enough to escape from waves that overtook them. A few were overwhelmed by a torrent of soft, red clay that broke from a fissure in the mountain. Cliffs and crags were thrown down by the earthquakes, and the top of one hill was thrown one thousand feet. The lava stream reached the sea at Nanawale, fifty miles from its source, and pushed three-fourths of a mile into the sea.

Again, in an eruption in 1880, two lava streams poured out toward the town of Hilo; and though the great crater continued in full blast, it was nine months before the people could be sure whether the streams would destroy the town or not. At length the lava was within five minutes walk of the town. Many collected their chattels and left. Then the action on the mountain suddenly subsided; and in a few days the "great red dragon" lay stiff and cold, almost at the people's doors.

Since the natives build their houses almost invariably of one story and of the lightest materials, earthquakes can do comparatively little damage to most property. Hence, with all the activity of the great volcanoes, the inhabitants are far more secure than those of many other regions apparently not so dangerous. Persons may readily visit the great crater in eruption, though at full blast; and excursion parties are organized to visit this "Niagara of fire" on every occasion of unwonted activity. Nowhere else in the world can volcanic action on the grandest scale be so carefully observed.

The details given hitherto will serve to illustrate the terrible havoc wrought by subterranean forces. So far only outpouring of volcanic matter has been especially noticed. But ere examining the terribly destructive force of earthquakes alone, it is meet that the story of the tremendous eruptions of the century be closed with the story of the greatest of the age; and indeed, when all details are considered, it may rank as the most tremendous convulsion of all history. In certain details, Skaptar may have exceeded it: in destruction of life. Ætna surpassed it in 1669; but as a whole, it is simply without a parallel.

The reader will rightly judge that such a convulsion could hardly occur elsewhere than in the Malayan archipelago. Already the terrible outburst in Sumbawa has been noted; also several others in Java.

Java and Sumatra formerly formed a single island, but were separated by a terrific earthquake in 1115. Shocks are felt in one of the two islands nearly every month. The list of calamities occurring there during the past hundred years is appalling. Besides the convulsions before noted, an eruption of Galung-gung, in 1822, overwhelmed one hundred and fourteen villages and destroyed four thousand people. In 1843 Mt. Guntur cast forth 30,000,000 tons of ashes, doing immense injury to life and property. In 1867 there was a tremendous earthquake which killed many thousands in the interior of the island, and dried up or greatly obstructed the water courses. Immediately afterward the volcano of Gunung-Salak ejected such a quantity of cinders and lava that the work of obliterating or obstructing the streams was complete. The cess-pools and marshes bred pestilence and epidemics, which have carried off from Batavia alone nearly a million of inhabitants in the past twenty-two years. In 1872 the volcano of Mirapi burst out and destroyed several thousand people in the province of Kadu. Sixteen severe earthquakes were felt in 1878, and another one in 1879.

At length, in 1883, Krakatoa, a volcano on a small island in the Straits of Sunda, in the very center of the greatest subterranean furnace on the globe, began to manifest some uneasiness. As in the case of Cosequima, people had almost forgotten to call it a volcano. And when the mountain muttered and fired a little in February, they regarded it with some curiosity, and then, when it quieted down, thought no more about it.

On the 25th of August the people of Batavia heard peculiar subterranean mutterings, as they thought, but the roar increased till it might have been compared to a battery of fortress artillery. An avalanche of stones and ashes began to fall, and continued all night. Krakatoa had begun.

By morning it was impossible for Batavians to reach the Straits of Sunda. The bridges were down and the roads impassable. The waters of the straits were in fearful turmoil. Explosions beneath the sea followed each other in rapid succession. The waters were sixty degrees hotter than usually. The rebounding waves were dashing upon Madura, five hundred miles away, mountains high.

CATTLE IN VOLCANIC MUD.

The dance of death had hardly begun. Louder and louder roared Krakatoa; ere noon, Maha-Meru, the greatest of Javanese volcanoes, had joined in. Then Gunung-guntur opened; others rapidly followed, till fifteen volcanoes of Java were in eruption; most of them in full blast. The awful scene was beyond description. Krakatoa could still be heard thundering above all the rest.

Before nightfall Gunung-guntur, the greatest active crater in the world, four miles in diameter, was spouting enormous streams of lava and sulphurous mud. Tremendous explosions followed with showers of cinders and stones, as though the old giant were endeavoring to out-do the leader of the dance. Terrible was the slaughter by the flying fragments.

The sea was more violently agitated. Dense clouds of hot, sulphurous vapors, charged with electricity, hung over the waters, and added whirlwinds and thunderstorms to the scene. Fifteen large waterspouts could be seen at one time.

On the shore, men, women and children ran wildly about. There was no safety upon sea or land Houses were crumbling, the atmosphere darkening, the storm increasing. Hundreds of people were buried beneath ruined houses. Hundreds more were struck down in their flight. Immense crevices opened and swallowed; huge waves rushed inland and devoured. It seemed as though Java were to buried, with a rain of fire, in the unfathomable depths of the sea.

Towards midnight, it seemed as though the Prince of Darkness might be present in person to direct the work of destruction. " A luminous cloud far more colossal than that which had appeared above Gunung-guntur, gathered above the chain of the Kandangs, which run along the southeast coast of Java. This cloud increased in size each minute, until at last it came to form a sort of a gray and blood-red color, which hung over the earth for a considerable distance.

"In proportion as this cloud grew the eruption gained fresh force, and the floods of lava poured down the mountain sides without ceasing, and spread into the valleys, where they swept all before them. On Monday morning about two o'clock, the heavy cloud suddenly broke up, and finally disappeared. When the sun rose, it was found that a tract of country extending from Point Capucine to the south as far as Negery Passoerang, to the north and west, and covering an area of about fifty square miles, had entirely disappeared.

"There stood the previous day the villages of Negery, and Negery Babawang. Not one of the inhabitants had escaped. They and their villages had been swallowed up by the sea. The population was not so dense in this part of the island as in others, but for all this the total number of victims fell little short of fifteen thousand.

"The chain of the Kandangs, which runs along the coast of Java in a semi-circle for sixty-five miles, had also disappeared.

"The waters of Welcome Bay, in the Strait of Sunda, those of Pepper Bay to the east, and those of the Indian Ocean to the south, had burst in upon the country, where they formed a raging torrent."

All the furies of the deeps of earth and sea seemed freed to work their will and wreak their wrath. The great Papandayang now joined in the chaos. The cannon-like reports could be heard fifty miles away.

Then Sumatra was infected with the wild fury. From one of her volcanoes three columns of lava shot up from three different places, and three leaping red streams of lava dashed forth for the plains below. The mountain hurled after them showers of stones. Volumes of black dust flew after, making thick, stifling darkness which could be felt. Banks of ashes lay upon the roofs of houses, or muffled the city streets. A tornado hurried by, bearing stones, dust, roofs, trees, houses, and men.

In Java the fierce Papandayang burst open. From the seven great fissures the lava in its basin plunged out and reached for miles from the mountain's base. On the site of the island of Merak, which was swallowed up by the sea, the next day fourteen volcanic mountains sprang up, forming a chain from St. Nicholas Point, Java, to Hoga Point, in Sumatra.

In Batavia and Anjer were three thousand five hundred European residents; eight hundred of these never saw the light again. An overwhelming avalanche of rock, mud, and lava, poured upon their quarter in Anjer; then the sea leaped upon those struggling in the ruins and swept away all. Not so much as a trace of them was left. Two thousand inhabitants perished, besides a large number of fugitives from other quarters. Bantam was submerged, and one thousand five hundred people drowned. Waves dashed completely over the island of Serang, and not a single inhabitant escaped. The storms of rock and lava numbered their victims at Cheribon, and at several noted pleasure resorts.

The great temple of Boro-Buddor was ruined, its dome being beaten in by the showers of rock. This is a most deplorable architectural loss. It was the largest Buddhist Temple in the east, and had no equal in the world. Erected eleven hundred years ago, it stood on an eminence in a circular valley. It had a great central dome one hundred and forty-five feet high, surrounded by seventy smaller domes. On the platforms beneath were four hundred and fifty chapels, cut in openwork out of granite, and each having a statue of Buddha. The walls of the temple contained a complete picture-history of Buddha, there being four thousand beautifully chased bas-reliefs. Not a stone was left uncarved. The great chapel under the central dome was reached by a series of four grand staircases of five hundred feet each. No other structure is comparable to it. A few may be even more splendid; but it was decidedly *sui generis*.

The list of calamities grew rapidly. The town of Tamarang was devoured by the lava. Red-hot stones fired many houses. Eighteen hundred people perished. The island of Onius was terribly shaken and then plunged into the sea. The island of Midah was swallowed up. No one escaped. The lighthouses on Sunda Strait were wrecked. The town of Tjeringen was destroyed with ten thousand people. Nine hundred people perished at Waronge. Three hundred corpses were dug from the ruins of Talatoa. The river Jacatana was blocked with lava and ashes, and leaving its bed poured through Batavia.

The island of Merak, a fortified place three miles from Krakatoa, was a valuable Government stone quarry, six or seven years in use. Thousands of native workmen were assembled there, with engineers and overseers. Their huts were on hills one hundred and fifty feet above the sea. The end of the season was at hand. The 1st of September would see them returning to their Java homes. The island trembled, paused—sank slowly—the sea plunged over it. Two natives and an European bookkeeper escaped.

A steamer put out from the port of Telok Betong. Two inches of lava lay upon her deck. Pumice stone lay ten feet deep on the sea around her. When but a short distance out "we saw a gigantic wave of prodigious height suddenly advancing upon us at great speed from the di-

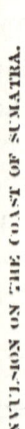

CONVULSION ON THE COAST OF SUMATRA.

rection of the open sea. Immediately the captain brought his vessel round so as to meet the wave stern foremost. After a moment of most piquant anxiety, we found ourselves lifted up with terrific speed; our vessel bounded upward, and then we felt ourselves plunged into the abyss. But the wave had passed us and we were out of all danger. Like a high mountain the gigantic wave sped furiously towards the shore, while immediately after three other great waves followed it. The waters rushed in and destroyed the town, sweeping away first the light house, which fell in like a pack of cards, then all the buildings beyond. In a few moments all was over, and where once Telok Betong stood there was nothing but water."

Livid with terror, the captain steamed rapidly to warn the town of Anjer. There was no longer an Anjer, a Dutch fort, a garrison. A single sailor, who had caught a floating tree, stalked about among the corpses.

Krakatoa, which had opened this fearful carnival of death, sank slowly into the sea. Of the island, twenty-five miles long and seventeen wide, a small portion of the terribly shattered cone remained in sight. New islets were made; vast shoals created. Sailors discovered new islands and landed, only to find themselves on vast floating pumice rafts, miles from land. New charts had to be made. For a time the seas were hardly navigable.

Such is the story. The damage to property was millions of dollars. The loss of life will never be definitely known. First estimates placed it at 80,000. Conservative judges pronounced it in all probability between 50,000 and 60,000.

The explosions were heard as far away southward as Australia; to the westward as far as Southern India; to the eastward, they are said to have been heard in the Caribbean Sea. Even if we reject the latter, we may take the others, and obtain some idea by imagining volcanoes at St. Louis to be heard at New York and San Francisco, at Mexico and in Hudson's Bay.

The great sea wave rushed from Krakatoa to the Mauritius in eight hours. It rolled around the coasts of the Australian continent, dashing into the southern harbors, sweeping through the narrow Bass Straits. It rose and fell upon Hawaiian coasts in a perplexing manner. It surged against South America; against East Africa; it rounded Cape Horn and made itself known on the coasts of France, upon our Atlantic shore. It encircled the world—the greatest sea wave ever known.

The volcanic, microscopic dust remained long in the air, and occasioned the singular redness of the sky at morn and eve that prevailed throughout the world for the next two years. Apart from this suspended dust, the volcano threw out as much matter as the Mississippi bears to the gulf in two hundred and fifty years.

The atmospheric wave of low barometer was even more marked than the oceanic wave. On the day when Krakatoa sank into the sea, the barometric oscillation was noticed all over the world. From the time at which it reached Berlin, it is found to have travelled eight hundred and seventy-five miles an hour. Thirty-six hours later the barometic oscillations were repeated, but less pronounced. Thirty-seven hours afterward there came a third, and still fainter series. It appears, then, that the atmospheric wave, set in motion by this stupendous outbreak, was powerful enough to thrice encircle the world.

It has been but a short time since geologists believed the magnitude of the subterranean forces to be greatly decreased; but in view of a century of great eruptions closed by such an appalling convulsion, it must be said that the fiery forces are at least as active and powerful as ever.

CHAPTER XXIII.

EARTHQUAKES.

"Diseased Nature oftentimes breaks forth
In strange eruptions: and the teeming earth
Is with a kind of colic pinched and vexed
By the imprisoning of unruly wind
Within her womb; which for enlargement striving,
Shakes the old beldam earth, and topples down
Steeples and moss-grown towers."

SUCH is the theory of earthquakes as laid down by "Wild Will Shakespeare." Whether it be an expression of the popular belief of the day, or a personal opinion, is not easy to determine. If the latter, he had, as we shall see by and by, many predecessors in the same belief. His metaphor, though more elegantly expressed, cannot compare with the Indian's for terseness and force: "Ground heap sick—heap belly ache—no good!"

We have already seen that the forces producing earthquakes and volcanic action are conceded to be practically identical. The latter seldom occurs without the former; but the former are frequent in districts far removed from any known vent of subterranean heat. So the expression of Shakespeare is not so far wrong as might be, so far as our present knowledge goes.

In the Hindoo cosmogony successive ages of the world are separated by periods of chaos; and no wilder image of unreined destruction has fancy ever dreamed. The earth is to be eternal. There is one eternal, invisible spirit, Brahm, from whom springs Brahma, who creates a race of gods. These frame the earth into orderly condition, and rule it for four hundred thousand years. At the end of that time, the land and sea and sky meet in gigantic ruin; the gods are no more, save only Vishnu, the preserver. The sea covers all things and eternal night is accompanied by eternal tempest.

Eternal is not strictly correct, however. This reign of destruction lasts four hundred thousand years, during which time Vishnu sleeps on the coils of the great seven-headed serpent of eternity, which floats upon the gloomy sea. The long night over, Vishnu wakes and remodels the earth, and peace and light resume their sway. Seven such cycles pass; all things are annihilated, and Brahm sets about a new creation which goes the same round.

The eastern wise men, fond of allegory and parable, doubtless intended by this to express the persistence and order in the universe, even in periods of the most inexplicable disaster; and to picture for the ignorant the absolute eternity of God.

The thing was too good to let drop; and others added to it by asserting the earth was upborne by an elephant who stood on the back of a tortoise. The tortoise rested on a fish; the fish on water; the water on air; the air on light; the light on darkness; the darkness on the Lord only knows what. When these animals were somewhat wearied, they changed their position, and the earth trembled.

Greece had a somewhat better myth of the giant Atlas, who bore the world on his shoulders; but the old fellow's gait was not of the steadiest. Rome, not much given to manufacturing her myths *de novo*, imported the Grecian fable. We have to-day appropriated the old fellow's title for a geography supposed to contain the whole earth. The figure is lost on most.

But the alleged drunkenness of Atlas did not consort precisely with the popular ideas of the proper conduct of a steady old porter in a responsible position; and the myth-makers dragged in a new scapegoat in the person of the Titan Typhon, or Enceladus, supposed to be entombed in Mt. Ætna, as we have elsewhere noticed.

Inhabitants of parts of Farther India and of some Malayan islands believe that far down in the bowels of the earth an immense tiger, Pelu, lies asleep. The sole object of his existence is to destroy the earth; but he may not do this till the human race is extinct. Then he will rise to his feet, the earth will burst into fragments and fly into the distant realms of space. It must of necessity follow that our feline friend's existence is a somewhat monotonous one, and to avoid ennui in his cramped quarters, he passes much time in sleep. Waking occasionally, and wishing like the German Barbarossa, to know if his time is come, he cautiously raises a few hairs on his back. The earth trembles, and the natives, rushing from their tottering houses throw themselves upon the ground, shouting loudly "Pelu! Pelu!" to assure his tigership that they are certainly alive. Satisfied on this point, the worshipful beast composes himself for another nap.

Thor, the war god of the Norsemen, wielded a mighty hammer, Miolnir. In the "Saga of King Olaf" we find Thor shouting:

> "The blows of my hammer,
> Ring in the earthquake."

Another myth attributes the earthquake to the restlessness of the serpent Midgard, who encircles the universe, his tail in his mouth. Also, the wolf Fenrir, who is to take part in the final contest that produces Ragnarok, is supposed to have occasional differences of opinion before the time with certain of the fire giants. The earth is then liable to be shaken.

Natives of the Tonga group, in the South Pacific, be-

484 GREAT DISASTERS.

lieved that their hero-god, Maui, upheld the world on his breast. When he became restless and shook the earth, they would rush out and beat the ground with sticks to make him lie still.

From traditions concerning Mohammed we learn that

EFFECT OF A POWERFUL EARTHQUAKE ON MASSIVE MASONRY, ITALY.

the circular earth lies in the midst of a vast sea, and is encircled by an immense whale, upon whose back 700,000 gigantic bulls walk up and down. Said whale swims about the earth very cautiously, but occasionally jostles it slightly. On the night when Mohammed was born this noble animal was so agitated with joy, that had not the Lord restrained him, he would assuredly have overturned the earth.

The Sandwich Islanders believed that the goddess Pele, who dwelt in the great volcano of Kilauea, was displeased with the conduct of man; she proceeded to admonish him of her power, by shaking him out of bed in the night, or tumbling his house about his ears. If especially angry, she set her volcanic home to fuming and firing.

So-called scientific theories on various topics have in time past been little more respectable, and need not be given any detailed attention. The pious gentry who deemed Roger Bacon a wizard and Columbus and Galileo heretics, would have listened with horror to any effort to explain the phenomena of earthquakes as anything else than a direct manifestation of the wrath of God. Researches in any branch of natural science met with decided discouragement in Christendom during the dark and middle ages; and the goddess of wisdom found a decidedly more congenial atmosphere at Moorish and Saracen courts.

Hence the modern science of seismology, as the investigations of earthquakes are called, is comparatively in its infancy. Yet the subject of seismic phenomena has been of interest to the thoughtful from a very early period, earthquakes being of far greater frequency than most persons suppose. Some of the earliest philosophers ventured opinions on the topic; for the records of earthquakes, more distinctly than those of volcanoes, go back to the earliest times.

We find Aristotle, in his treatise on natural events, rejecting the explanations of three other philosophers as untenable, and propounding a theory of his own. Anaximenes, of Miletus, suggested the drying and moistening of the earth occasioned irregular contraction and expansion, and from the cracking and readjusting shocks resulted. Democritus, of Abdera, shook his earth by means of vast subterranean bodies of water which some force compelled to move from one cavity to another. Doubtless the peculiar wave-like motion of the earth in many earthquakes suggested his theory. Anaxagoras, of Clazomenae, believed that ether—by which the old Greeks seem to mean air—was confined in underground cavities, and in its efforts to escape upward produced the vibration of the earth. Aristotle substitutes for the disturbing agent wind, which has flowed into fissures and caverns and is endeavoring to flow out again. Virgil and Pliny stand by the old Greek; and it is quite probable that Shakespeare acquired his idea from one of the three. And these, with Anaxagoras, are but little out of the way; for as seen in the discussion of volcanic action, the explosive or disturbing agent is generally steam, though other gases are present in large quantities.

We have already noticed that earthquakes and volcanoes are produced by the same causes; but as the myths of many nations do not connect the two, it is evident that such people did not recognize their essential identity.

But after knowing they are but variations in results, we cannot so readily explain the reason of the variations. Certain facts are well established; and from these common premises widely different conclusions have been deduced.

We know to-day that in active volcanic regions, an earthquake almost invariably precedes an eruption; and a violent one has never, within the historic period, followed an eruption. So the most reasonable inference is, that the earthquake merely betokens the presence of a vast quantity of imprisoned vapor which has not found an outlet; and that so soon as a volcanic vent is found, the pressure is relieved, and the earthquake subsides.

But this leaves us just where the theorists of volcanic agency have stopped. The question of the sudden formation of volumes of gases in sufficient quantities to produce such terrible effects is to be solved.

Mr. Mallet, who is one of the best authorities on the subject, considers that submarine eruptions must account for them. A volcanic upheaval of the sea bottom would produce crevices, by which the sea is brought directly in contact with subterranean fires. An explosion is the result, like those that have occasionally occurred at foundries from dumping masses of fiery slag into a snowbank. So what began with a gradual upheaval ends with a sudden concussion, the vibration of which passes along the sea bottom to the mainland. Every one who has lived in the city is familiar with the fact that the vibration produced by a carriage may be felt at the top of a very tall building.

But the idea that the explosion always occurs at the sea bottom leaves no way to account for the fact that a volcanic eruption acts as a safety-valve. Mr. Mallet's conclusions are largely based on personal observations of earthquakes in England, where no active volcano exists.

That earthquakes are more violent and volcanoes more numerous on islands or near the sea coast is well-known. It is also well established that shocks frequently occur at sea, which are not perceptible on the land. The shock is similar to that produced by striking on a reef. Often have sailors been mystified, on receiving such shocks and hastily heaving the lead, to find the ocean unfathomable. Again, shocks which are most violent on land are not perceptible at sea, unless a great sea wave be produced; but such a wave in the open sea, as often experienced, produces no shock but passes under a vessel like a heavy swell. And a shock at sea is sometimes severe enough to snap a spar, or wrench loose bolts like the blow of a reef, yet no trace is perceptible on shore. Lastly, earthquakes often happen in inland regions, and affect but a small area. Clearly it will not do to attribute effects so different to explosions at the sea-bottom.

Those who attribute all earthquakes to subterranean heat and gases, whether local or general, find it easy to account for the occurrence of violent earthquakes in regions remote from active volcanoes. In case of the gradual decline of volcanic action, such as we know from the great numbers of extinct volcanoes, old trap-dykes, and ancient lava beds, to be continually taking place in one region or another, the old vents or safety-valves would cool and close. The pent up power would in consequence gradually accumulate, till finding no outlet, it would burst the crust over a wide area, and so relieve the pressure.

This finds further confirmation in the fact that the noted non-volcanic regions which are seriously shaken are all coincident with or adjacent to regions of extinct fires; while in such regions as are very seldom shaken, such as Germany, portions of North America, Brazil, the eastern slope of the Andes, the traces of such agency are less common, or of older date. Noted regions of volcanic action of comparatively recent extinction are Asia Minor, Turkey, Spain, Southern France and Greece. These, belted together by the active regions of Western Asia, the peninsula of Arabia, the Mediterranean, and Azores and Canaries, form a region which has suffered from earthquakes as much as, if not more than, any other tract upon the globe.

Those who have been puzzled by the appearance of earthquakes some distance from any actively volcanic region, have endeavored to divide earthquakes into two classes, which they have called volcanic and plutonic. This second class they have considered as originating, like the other, in the depths of the earth; but have endeavored to account for them by supposing them to be occasioned by the falling in of great caverns at a considerable depth. This theory has found a fair objection in the fact that in such cases an earthquake should always be a sinking of the ground: while the wrecking power and peculiarities of some earthquakes indicate a decided upward concussion as the first of shocks; and at the seashore, where any change in level is at once detected, upheaval is quite as common as subsidence.

Much speculation has been spent upon the fact of an earthquake being very severe in two or three different localities, but being imperceptible or very mild in intervening places. In South America it has become so common a peculiarity that the natives speak of such localities as "bridging" the earthquakes. Not improbably the reason is the same that produces calm when two waves interfere, crest to trough; the motions destroy each other. It may be also that the character of the underlying rocks has much to do with such cases. Experiments with explosions in mines show that vibrations of the soil travel over three hundred yards per second through sand beds, or about as rapidly as in the air; over five hundred yards in granite; while through iron they travel over three thousand eight hundred and fifty yards per second. So a vibration extremely destructive to a region underlaid by massive rocks might be comparatively harmless to a town on a sand-bed or mud-bank. Observations on earthquakes themselves have shown great variation in the rate of speed. The earthquake of Germany of 1846 moved four hundred and ninety-two yards per second; while the earthquake of Viege in 1855 traveled nine hundred and sixty yards a second toward Strasburg, but only half that speed towards Turin. So, also, the Lisbon earthquake traveled three times as rapidly around the coast as down the Rhine valley. So it must be that certain regions owe their comparative immunity from earthquakes to the nature of the ground beneath.

One or two ingenious savants have suggested that the earth is a vast thermo-electric pile, and that disturbances in the electrical equilibrium of the earth are the cause of earthquakes and volcanic eruptions. But as already seen, the electrical phenomena of volcanic eruptions are fairly considered an effect, and not a cause, of the eruptions, as the hydro-electric machine illustrates. In the theory of these men, the molten veins of the interior represent conductors which are too small or imperfect to allow the electricity to pass freely, and are fused in consequence. One of these men, Steffens, alleges that such phenomena can only occur where large veins of coal exist, because large masses of carbon would be necessary to keep up a strong electric tension in the interior. Herr Steffens must account for the fact that the great coal regions of the world have been peculiarly favored in their comparative immunity from shocks.

Still others have advocated the idea that atmospheric whirlwinds and cyclones produce earthquakes. While not a few shocks have been accompanied by violent storms, the exception seems to be the rule. And in the case of storms, we have seen that the outpour of heat and vapor in a volcanic eruption would necessarily produce one. As concerns the winds that have accompanied earthquakes, they have as often come after the shock as before.

But these bring up certain phenomena that must be noticed. It is not easy to say how great is the connection between electrical and atmospheric disturbances, and the shiverings of the earth; but that there is some peculiar bond between them has been thought indisputable. It is only in the present century that scientists have carefully conned this matter, and generally rejected the belief. But the opinion is very ancient, and has a strong hold upon the people. It is generally adhered to by South Americans, Italians, West Indians, Japanese, and the inhabitants of Central Asia. Kamtschatkans, Kurile Islanders and Japanese, assert shocks are most frequent at the equinoxes. In equatorial America, the natives say an earthquake is preceded by drought, and is the precursor of rain. In the Dauphiny Alps, the people regard earthquakes as the result of avalanches; and the latter are readily started by the slightest atmospheric disturbances. In Central America the equinoctial idea prevails.

These things set the wise men to investigating. Much to their surprise, they began to discover that the idea of connection between the seasons and shocks seemed well-grounded. In 1834 Professor Merian announced that of one hundred and eighteen earthquakes at Basle, the majority had occurred in the winter. Volger made a list of twelve hundred and thirty shocks in the Alps; seven hundred and seventy-four occurred in autumn and winter. December showed one hundred and sixty-eight; July forty. Of ninety-eight quite severe shocks, but one had occurred in the summer. Of five hundred and thirty-nine earthquakes in the Rhine basin, one hundred and three occurred in the spring, one hundred and one in the summer, one hundrd and sixty-five in the autumn, one hundred and seventy in winter. Observations in the Antilles show a slight predominance of autumn and winter.

Another peculiar fact is that most shocks seem to occur at night. Out of four hundred and seventy-two earthquakes in 1855-56, whose time was exactly noted, but one hundred and seventy-two happened in the day. Of those at night, three-fifths were during the latter half, forty-four being between one and two o'clock. Squier has told us that during several years residence in Central America, nearly all shocks occurred at night; also, that he experienced none save at the change of seasons. Hence, one is almost compelled to conclude that, while the primal cause of earthquakes must exist in the depths of the earth, yet external and climatic influences are strong modifiers.

Some other peculiarities are adduced to show the connection between atmospheric disturbances and earthquakes. In Central and Tropical America the temperature is said to fall after any shock. After the earthquake at Lechsand, Sweden, in 1856, the temperature fell eighty-six degrees. The same shock was violent as far as Smyrna in Asia Minor, where the thermometer fell at once twenty-nine degrees, the night being the coldest of the winter. Many similar cases are mentioned. But in view of the fact that one hundred times as many sudden and marked changes of temperature occur every year in various localities without the intervention of an earthquake, it seems difficult to regard the above instances as more than mere coincidences. The greatest fall in temperature the writer ever experienced occurred within three hours of a transit of Venus; but one swallow—nor a flock of them—cannot make a summer.

Barometric observations have been dragged into the combat. The great Lisbon earthquake, and the convulsion in Calabria, were preceded by low barometer. Similar observations have been made in this century. The constantly recurring shocks of 1855-56 were in each case preceded by fall of barometers. But Humboldt, in South America, and Ehrmann, in Central America, were unable to find such order; though the shocks were so invariably followed by such changes that unusual earthquakes were believed by the natives (as is also believed in India) to advance the rainy season. The resultant electric phenomena might produce this expedition.

But in this field all at present is mere guess work. The exceptions to any association of earthquake and storm are so far the rule; except in case of a volcanic eruption also occurring. In the latter case a storm invariably follows, so far as present observations go; but then the storm is not co-extensive with the earthquake, but is usually confined to the neighborhood of the volcano.

It should be noticed that certain scientists have endeavored to prove these convulsions are due to planetary influence. It does not appear that they have been able to find the least trace of any connection between the earth's convulsions and the planets; but some affirm the existence of an earthquake cycle coincident with the Saros of the moon. Effort is also made to connect earthquakes and volcanoes with the gigantic convulsions of the sun, known as "sun spots." It is argued by certain advocates of the molten interior that the attraction of the sun and moon produces an interior tidal wave, like that of the sea; and any irregularities in this produce the phenomena of earthquakes and volcanic eruptions. Objections to the molten interior have been already noted; and in regard to the other suggestions, so long as the great convulsions are peculiarly prevalent in certain regions, so long it will be necessary to seek their chief cause or most powerful modifiers in entirely local influences.

In conclusion, it does not yet seem clear that we can rely absolutely upon a single cause as productive of all the convulsions of the earth's crust. Internal local heat, pent up gases, suffice for volcanic phenomena; but earthquakes present so many peculiar variations that it seems almost imperative to many men to admit, at least, the modifying influence of other agencies. But so long as these agencies appear to be quite as frequently the modified as the modifier, no laws concerning them can be announced. Hence, internal conditions are the only clearly identified factors so far.

There is quite as much difference of opinion as to how far beneath the surface the shocks originate. Robert Mallet's investigations have led him to believe the depth cannot be over thirty miles, and that seven or eight miles is the limit for most, and his views are those of most scientists. But a few others conclude that we cannot find molten matter and gases to produce the concussion at a less depth than seventy-eight miles. But, as their conclusions are based largely upon the idea that the melting point of minerals is raised uniformly with increasing pressure, their conclusions must be rejected as unreliable.

The character of the motion is well known. Each point of the surface begins to move with the vibration first upwards, then away from the center of shock, then downward and backwards. Thus, each point describes a small ellipse, which is repeated with each wave of vibration. If the longer axis of the ellipse be vertical, the main force of the concussion is directed upwards; if the shorter one be upright, the shock is an undulatory one. An alternation of the two forms the most destructive combination. The difference is readily perceived in the effects produced. A sudden upward shock may wreck the roofs or floors of buildings, while an undulatory one brings down the walls.

Houses erected on sand, immediately overlaying compact rock, usually suffer most during earthquakes. The effect is that of the vibration of a sheet of glass covered with sand. But, if a second sheet of glass be placed on that, the vibration is hardly communicated to it at all. So, while sand is a bad foundation, a sand-bed beneath the surface seems to deaden the shock.

It is not difficult to understand that lofty buildings, and those of stone or brick, must be vastly more dangerous than those of wood, and low and broad. Throughout many portions of Central and South America, the people endeavor to compromise, by building houses of stone, but low and massive, with very light roofs. These are far less safe than light structures of wood; also, it is clear that cupolas and towers must be peculiarly liable to injury. For this reason, churches have often suffered more from shocks than other buildings, and the throngs of penitents who flock to them in the hope of propitiating an offended providence are often the first victims of an earthquake.

"It is to earthquakes, rather than to barbarians, from the fifth to the ninth century, that Rome owed the loss of so many superb palaces and temples. One might imagine that in these great disasters, the architect is the ally of the subterranean scourge. The Indian's hut and the Arab's tent, may be overturned without any great loss or injury to their owners; but the marble of the patrician crushes him as it falls, and the inhabitants of a great city meet their death under the ruins of their sumptuous buildings. The Peruvians of old were not far wrong in making merry at the folly of their Spanish conquerors, who, in erecting great buildings upon a soil so constantly agitated, were preparing, at great expense, their own tombs."

It will be shown, by and by, how the motions of earthquakes are becoming so carefully noted that their path can be pointed out beforehand. Ere many years are past, the prediction of earthquakes may become as important a feature of the Signal Service Department, as the foretelling of storms.

CHAPTER XXIV.

EUROPEAN EARTHQUAKES.

"The thunder roared his signal to the sea,
While shook the frightened earth through all her coasts,
And mountains bowed their trembling heads in awe,
And yawning gulfs leaped up amid the plains.
The fountains of the mighty deep were rent,
The waves, long prisoned in their rocky bounds,
Roared, in a strange new freedom rushing forth,
And sprang on forest, plain, and mount, and hill, and vale,
Exulting in destruction; while the frightened hordes
Of men, with birds and beasts of every sort,
Fought each with each for refuge from the flood,
    Yet none escaped."

RECORDS and myths of great earthquakes go back almost to prehistoric times. The Greeks tell of an immense flood—perhaps a sea wave—which overwhelmed Attica immediately after an earthquake in the nineteenth century before Christ. It is known as the deluge of Ogyges, from the name of the reigning king. Some three centuries later is the story of a great earthquake and flood in Thessaly, from which Deucalion and Pyrrha escaped. There is a still vaguer legend of an immense earthquake about 2400 B. C., that shook all Southern Europe, and Asia Minor, opening an outlet for the Black Sea, which had before been entirely inland. In the convulsion of the seas, we are told almost all the people of Greece and Asia Minor perished. Chinese traditions and monuments tell of an immense earthquake at the same period, which suddenly raised the bottom of the great Northern Sea, pouring its waters out upon all North China and drowning the people. Where the great sea once was is now the great Mongolian Desert.

THE DELUGE.

Likewise the Egyptian priests told Plato of a great island, Atlantis, lying off the coast of North Africa, stretching an unknown distance to the west; the home of a mighty nation that ruled all the western world, to the shores of the Mediterranean, and threatened the liberty of the European world. It is said that they made war on the combined forces of Greece and Egypt; and in the crisis of the struggle a fearful earthquake swallowed up the Grecian soldiery in a single night, and sunk Atlantis in the ocean since called from its name, Atlantic.

Doubtless all these traditions relate to the same terrible catastrophe described in Genesis. The Chinese even tell us in what way the "fountains of the great deep were broken up." It would seem that a great sea once extended northeastward from the present basin of the Caspian over the deserts of Central Asia; and that an awful upheaval of this basin was the chief factor in the flood. Isthmuses were torn asunder: vast oceans hurled their gigantic waves over the continents, and over islands engulfed forever. The extraordinary evaporation from the unusual expanse of water, the sudden chilling of the atmosphere, produced torrents of rain. "The same day were all the fountains of the great deep broken up, and the windows of heaven were opened." Whatever be the truth of the traditions, it is certain they preserve the memory of a catastrophe unparalleled in recent days.

Of a later date, there is the story that the Ciminian and Alban lakes near Rome were created by a terrible earthquake; but the date of this event is not very definite. The Japanese tell us that the great volcano, Fujiyama, was thrown up in a single night, and at the same time the lake in Oomi was created, near by, on the site of a number of flourishing villages.

Occasionally an earthquake has brought about a historic

crisis. In the year 464 B. C., "in the fourth year of the reign of Archidamus, there happened the most dreadful earthquake in Sparta that had ever been known. In several places the country was entirely swallowed up: Taygetus and other mountains were shaken to their foundations; many of their summits, being torn away, came tumbling down; and the whole city was laid in ruins, five houses only excepted. To heighten the calamity, the Helots, who were slaves to the Lacedemonians, looking upon this as a favorable opportunity to recover their liberty, pervaded every part of the city, to murder such as had escaped the earthquake; but finding them under arms, and drawn up in order of battle, by the prudent foresight of Archidamus, who had assembled them around him, they retired into the neighboring cities, and commenced that day open war, having entered into an alliance with several of the neighboring nations, and being strengthened by the Messenians, who at that time were engaged in war with the Spartans." But for the timely aid of others, Sparta might have been overthrown. The most striking feature is the astonishing coolness and presence of mind of the Spartans in the face of such a dire calamity.

This is, perhaps, the earliest earthquake of which careful historic mention is made. But from that time, the record thickens rapidly. In the year 373 B. C., a great shock did fearful damage throughout all Greece, destroying thousands of lives and damaging millions of dollars worth of property in a single night. The inhabitants of the Peloponnesus, roused by the convulsion, waited in fear for the morning. Dawn showed that the two beautiful cities of Bura and Helice were no more. The sea rolled above. Long after, on calm, clear days, Helice, once an inland town, could be seen at the bottom of the Corinthian Gulf: silent and beautiful in its ruin, marble temples and shattered homes presenting a literal "city of the dead."

The year B. C. 217 found Rome and Carthage locked in

RUINED ROMAN COLONNADE.

deadly combat. While Hannibal and Flaminius fought by Thrasymene, earth felt the throes of war, and shook Italian cities down, while lakes and streams were tumbled from their beds. North Africa suffered, perhaps, the greatest shaking recorded in her history; one hundred towns were lost, and tens of thousands of people perished.

In A. D. 17 thirteen cities of Asia Minor were thrown to the ground. The Emperor Tiberius rebuilt them at his own expense. The grateful people presented him with a magnificent pedestal, which he had placed in the forum at Pozzuoli.

A. D. 27 Egypt was shaken, and the great statue of Memnon overthrown. In A. D. 63 came a great earthquake in Central Italy.

The earthquake in A. D. 33, at the time of the crucifixion, was felt throughout Asia Minor, Greece, Sicily and Southern Italy. In the Syria corpses were tumbled from their rock-hewn tombs. The town of Nicaea, in Bithynia, was totally destroyed. How many perished in this widespread shock is not known. Tradition has it that a fissure in a great rock, which overhangs the shore at Gaeta, was made by this earthquake. Till quite recently passing vessels were wont to salute the rock in commemoration of the great event.

No city has suffered from these terrible throes of Mother Earth as much as Antioch. In the year 115, the Emperor Trajan, extending his territories to the wilder regions of the Caucasus, was in the city with his army. There came heavy thunders, great winds, fearful subterranean rumblings; the earth shook; down tottered temples, towns, palaces, colonnades, statues, homes and huts, in irretrievable ruin. The Emperor sprang from a window and ran for his life, like a peasant, through the streets resounding with the groans and cries of the unfortunates buried in the ruins. Mountains were rent asunder, rivers turned from their courses, new streams were created, old valleys disappeared. Eighty thousand people are believed to have perished at Antioch alone.

GREAT DISASTERS.

In A. D. 365 a fearful earthquake was felt throughout the entire Mediterranean region. The sea rolled back, leaving fishes and vessels high and dry; then, suddenly return-

ANTIOCH.

ing, it carried large boats two miles inland. Fifty thousand people were lost at Alexandria. Shortly before, a number of towns in Palestine had been destroyed. This second great disaster shook all Asia Minor. In every town men began to talk, with bated breath, of the fearful wrath the Lord manifested because of those who had lent a willing ear to heretical doctrines. "This was why only the priests and holy men of the church could appease the Divine wrath; and if the town of Epidaurus had escaped the ruin which befell all the other towns along the coast, it was because the inhabitants had taken the statue of St. Hilary to the sea-shore. The Saint made the sign of the cross, and the mountain of water, bending low before him, forthwith receded." Whence, it seems the Lord was supposed to have greater regard for crooked saintly fingers than for heretical doctrines. Numerous were the direful prodigies said to have accompanied this fearful shock.

The next century brought calamities once more upon Asia Minor. A series of tremendous shocks were felt in 458, wrecking many of the finest cities. The renowned Antioch, rebuilt in its pristine splendor, was once more humbled in the dust. Eighty thousand people perished within its walls; many thousands more in the adjacent regions. Probably one hundred and twenty-five thousand in all were slain in this earthquake.

Years passed by, bringing, from time to time, minor shocks which destroyed hundreds in different locations, but which passed with but little notice amid so many greater disasters, and wars and rumors of wars. Antioch had been gradually rebuilt, and was more splendid than ever before. The first quarter of the sixth century was past. The time of the great festival of the Ascension was at hand, A. D. 526. From all the country round came people flocking to the celebration, to witness the pageantry and procession. Without a moment's warning, a great earthquake came, as fearful as the shock four hundred and eleven years before. The destruction was vastly greater. The tottering walls crushed thousands in the crowded streets. Every avenue and alley became a death-trap. There is not, in all the pages of history, record of an

MASSIVE ARCHITECTURE WRECKED, ASIA MINOR.

earthquake of greater destructiveness. Gibbon estimates the number of victims at two hundred and fifty thousand.

Nor was Antioch the only sufferer. The number of victims at other points in Asia Minor might be fifty thousand more. The whole sixth century is noted for the unusual number of appalling disasters of this sort which occurred at different places in the then known world. Probably a million people perished during this period in earthquakes alone. Such unwonted havoc may well cause us to wonder what manner of convulsions were occurring in the great volcanic regions of the Pacific and the then unknown western world. If the same general rule prevailed then that has been noticeable in more recent periods; if great convulsions were then, as now, comparatively synchronous, it would be difficult to form any adequate idea of the magnitude of the disturbances.

In 742 there was a tremendous earthquake in Egypt and Arabia, which overturned scores of cities and villages, rent mountains asunder, buried people in the wrecks of their dwellings, tossed the sea to and fro, swallowed up towns, wiped out thriving seaports, and numbered its dead by many tens of thousands. Four years later Jerusalem and all Syria experienced a dreadful shock, which made terrible havoc. In 823, Central Europe was shaken and Aix-la-chapelle nearly destroyed. In 860 Persia and Syria were again shaken; and in 867, Antioch, after its three centuries of comparative rest, was again ravaged by the destroyer. This shock extended to Mecca, which was fearfully rent. Part of a mountain in Syria was hurled into the sea. The century closed with a fearful convulsion in far distant India, wherein no less than one hundred and eighty thousand people were killed. Western Syria suffered again in 1169 and 1202. All the cities of the Mediterranean coast were shaken to pieces, with the usual terrible loss of life. The valleys of the Lebanon district were upheaved and altered throughout their whole extent.

Shock after shock came in the succeeding decades. One of these destroyed forty thousand persons at Bagdad alone. In 1759, the long list of catastrophes in Asia

RUINS NEAR CAIRO.

Minor was increased by one of the most terrible on record. At the first shock the proud Antioch was once more totally destroyed. Within the next forty-five days Baalbec, Sidon, Acre, Foussa, Nazareth, Safit, Tripoli, and scores of lesser towns and villages were almost blotted out. The horrors of that period are too awful for description. Even more fearful, if possible, was the earthquake of 1822, which once more made Antioch a shapeless mass of ruins. Aleppo, Djollib, Riha, Gisser, Chugra, Dieskrich, and Armenas shared a like fate. In the whole pashalic of Aleppo not a house or hut was left standing. Several severe earthquakes have followed during the century. In one, we are told the force of the shocks was so peculiar

RUINS NEAR NINEVEH.

and powerful that in some places stone walls were converted to heaps of dust or lime.

This record, which is but a partial one, is enough to explain the utterly ruined condition of Baalbec, Palmyra, and many other relics of ancient grandeur. They have contended with a force more terrible than ever was shot or shell of the cannonier. Thousands are familiar with the views of such massive columns and walls of the Temple of Jupiter as are still standing, eighty-four feet high from base to capital. The marvel is, that after such a succession of fearful quakings there is the slightest semblance of their former condition remaining.

Terrible as these calamities are, not a great deal beyond the bare fact is known of many of them. To learn more exactly the dreadful capabilities of this stupendous agent, it is necessary to examine European and South American earthquakes that have come directly under the observation of scientific men. From these we may learn more particularly of the details of various fearful shocks.

In all Italy, so famed for its warmth and beauty, there is not a more lovely district than Calabria, which lies in the Southern portion of the peninsula. Yet no part of Italy has suffered such great calamities. An earthquake in 1693 shook the whole of Calabria and Sicily, totally destroying sixty towns and villages, and not fewer than one hundred thousand people. Eighteen thousand perished at Catania alone. Forty-eight years later a violent earthquake shattered one hundred and ninety towns in Calabria and completely swallowed up Eufemia, leaving only a stinking lake. But these were before the day of minute scientific observation.

In 1783, a series of shocks, unequalled in recent years in violence, began in Calabria and continued through four years. The scene was visited and carefully examined by several able men, and from their accounts a fine conception of the whole may be obtained.

The subterranean concussions were felt beyond the confines of Sicily; but if the city of Oppido, in Calabria, be taken as the center, a circle around it, whose radius is twenty-two miles, would include the space which suffered the greatest calamities. Within this circle all the towns and villages were almost entirely destroyed. A radius of seventy-two miles would include the whole region affected.

It was a calm, hazy day in February, 1783. At a

quarter to one o'clock was felt the first shock, which "threw down, in the space of two minutes, a greater part

REMAINS OF ANCIENT HEBREW MASONRY.

of the houses within the whole space above described. The convulsive motion of the earth is said to have resembled the rolling of the sea, and that in many instances it produced swimming of the head, like sea-sickness. This rolling of the surface, like the billows of the sea, was like that which would have been produced by the agitation of a vast mass of liquid matter under the ground.

In some walls which were shattered, the separate stones were parted from the mortar, so as to leave an exact mold where they had rested, as though the stone had been carefully raised from its bed in a perpendicular direction; but in other instances the mortar was ground to powder between the stones, as though they had been made to revolve on each other.

It was found that the swelling, or wave-like motions, and those which were called *vorticose*, or whirling, often produced the most singular and unaccountable effects. Thus, in some streets in the town of Monteleone, every house was thrown down, except one, and in some other streets all but two or three;" and these were left uninjured, though differing in no respect from others. In some houses which were wrecked, deep foundations were thrown clear out of the ground, as though upheaved by a direct lifting. Sometimes very massive buildings escaped; sometimes they suffered most. Obelisks and pillars made in sections showed the effects of the vorticose motion. The separate portions were partly turned upon each other, without being thrown down.

The number and size of the fissures in the soil is astonishing. "In many instances, these fissures were so wide, as in an instant to swallow up men, trees, and even houses; and when the earth sunk down again, it closed upon them so entirely, as not to leave the least vestige of what had happened, nor were any signs of them ever discovered afterwards. In the vicinity of Oppido, the center of these convulsions, many houses were precipitated into the same great fissure, which immediately closed over them; and,

EUROPEAN EARTHQUAKES. 511

GREAT EARTHQUAKE IN CALABRIA.

in the same neighborhood, four farm-houses, several oil-stores and dwelling-houses were so entirely ingulfed that not a vestige of them was seen afterwards.

In some instances these chasms did not close. In one district a ravine, formed in this manner, a mile long, one hundred feet broad and thirty feet deep, remained open; and in another a similar one remained, three-quarters of a mile long, one hundred and fifty feet wide, and one hundred feet deep; in another instance there remained such a chasm, thirty feet wide and two hundred and twenty-five feet deep." In another place a gulf three hundred feet square was left open; again, we are told of one seven hundred and fifty feet square. A calcareous mountain, Zefirio, was rent in twain for half a mile. Similar effects were observed in Sicily, where Messina was almost totally destroyed, and the ruins devoured by the flames. "In various places the ground sunk down, and lakes were formed, which, being fed by springs, have remained ever since. The convulsions also removed immense masses of earth from the sides of steep hills into the valleys below; so that, in many instances, oaks, olive-orchards, vineyards and cultivated fields, were seen growing at the bottoms of deep hollows, having been removed from the side hills of the vicinity. In one instance, a mass of earth two hundred feet thick and four hundred feet in diameter, being set in motion by one of the first shocks, traveled four miles into the valley below.

The violence of the upward motion of the ground was singularly illustrated by the inversion of heavy bodies lying on the surface, and which can hardly be accounted for, except on the supposition that they were actually thrown to a considerable distance into the air. Thus, in some towns, a considerable portion of the flat paving-stones were found with their lower sides uppermost. Mr.

EUROPEAN EARTHQUAKES. 513

DESTRUCTION OF MESSINA.

Lyell accounts for this effect by supposing that the stones were propelled upwards by the momentum which they had acquired, and the adhesion of one end of the mass being greater than the other, a rotary motion had been communicated to them. It is difficult to conceive how a whirling motion, so rapid as to produce such an effect, could have been communicated to a whole town without producing some consequences still more extraordinary."

In many places in the plain of Rosarno, funnel-shaped pits were formed, with crevices radiating in every direction like fractures in a pane of glass. These were partially filled with sand and water.

Polistena was so absolutely wrecked that not the least semblance of the plan of the town could be detected. Terranova was precipitated, with its fourteen hundred inhabitants, three hundred and twenty-five feet into a deep gorge, and turned upside down. Moluquello, on an opposite hill between two streams, was rent in twain—one-half fell into the stream on the right, the other on the left. There was left a ridge so narrow at the top one could not keep his balance on it. Santa Cristena was hurled from the top of a sandy hill into the valley beneath. Out of three hundred and seventy-five towns and villages, three hundred and twenty were destroyed. Two hundred and fifteen lakes and morasses were created by displacements of the ground and blocking of water-courses. The pestilence bred by these vied with the direct power of the earthquake.

Some slight disturbance was manifested on the day before the great shock. Prince Scylla, an old man, warned his people to take to their boats, and himself set the example. When the first shock came, many of these people were sleeping in their boats near the shore, while the others were on the shore at a little place elevated above

THE DISASTER OF SCYLLA.

the sea. With this convulsion the earth rocked, and suddenly there was precipitated a great mass of rock from Mount Jaci on the plain where the people had taken refuge; and immediately after the water arose to a great height above its ordinary level and swept away the sleeping multitude. The wave then instantly retreated, but soon after returned again with increased violence, bringing back many of the people and animals which it had carried away. At the same time every boat in the vicinity was overwhelmed, or dashed against the beach, and thus destroyed. The Prince, who was an aged man, with thirteen hundred of his people was swept away and perished in the sea. The total loss of life resulting from this earthquake is estimated at eighty thousand. A shock which came on the 4th of March was as violent as the first one. Eleven hundred shocks were felt in two years.

Doubtless not a few of those who perished died merely from hunger or confinement. Quite a number of those rescued after several days were uninjured.

If it be true that prosperity shows men in their true colors, the reverse is equally marked. It is hard to believe the tales of barbarous inhumanity of the occasion. Says Dolomieu: "As egotism and the instinct of self-preservation crushed all other feeling, no help was brought to the unhappy victims buried beneath the ruins; yet many of them might have been rescued. When calm was restored, the lower orders, succumbing to the vilest passions of nature, thought of nothing but pillage."

Like a certain class of ghouls who follow in the wake of armies to enrich themselves by plundering the slain, "men might have been seen scouring the fallen ruins, braving imminent danger, and treading under foot dying persons who appealed piteously for help, in order to go and plunder the houses of the wealthy. They robbed the very injured, who would have paid them handsomely for rescuing them. At Polistena a person of quality had been buried head downwards beneath the ruins of his

LISBON BEFORE THE EARTHQUAKE.

house, and when his servant saw what had happened he actually stole the silver buckles off his shoes, while his legs were in the air, and made off with them. The unfortunate gentleman managed, however, to rescue himself from his perilous position. For several days cries of anguish were heard coming from underground." For days afterward the fearful stench of putrefying corpses filled the atmosphere. Such were the horrors of this memorable occasion.. So sudden was the calamity that many of those buried supposed only their own houses were overthrown and wondered why their neighbors were so slow to aid them. Many suffered greatly from thirst, and in consequence hardly felt the pinch of hunger, though entombed several days.

One of the most notable of the earthquakes of the last century is the one which overturned Lisbon, November 1, 1755. In extent of territory affected, it is the greatest of any known; but because it bears the name of the place where it was most violent, it is supposed by many to have been confined to a single district.

The morning was magnificent. At 9:35 A. M. there was a loud underground roar, like distant thunder, followed at once by a tremendous shock, which overthrew churches, convents, and many others of the finest buildings of the city. This shock lasted five seconds. There was two minutes pause, during which thousands of shrieking people rushed about the streets to escape the falling ruins. Then came a second shock, and two minutes later a third. In five minutes the Portuguese capital had become a ruin, filled with fifty thousand corpses.

The churches were filled with people, it being All Saints' Day, and the hour of high mass. The great cathedrals were but death-traps. All apparatus that could be of use in the work of rescue was buried in the wreck. The streets were crowded with sobbing multitudes, calling in vain for friends and kin.

At the sea-shore was the magnificent quay, Cays de

Prada. It was built entirely of marble, and just finished at an immense expense; and on it, after the first shock, a vast concourse of people had collected as a place of safety, having left the city to escape the fall of the houses. But it proved the most fatal spot in the vicinity; for at the next shock the earth opened and instantly swallowed up the whole quay, with the multitude which had there assembled; and so completely were the whole retained by the closing of the earth, that not a single dead body ever rose again to the surface. A great number of small boats and other vessels near the quay, and filled with people as a place of safety, were also precipitated into the yawning vortex; and it is stated that not a single fragment of any of these boats was ever seen afterwards. When the disaster was over, soundings were taken. Six hundred feet of water rolled above the marble quay and its countless victims. St. Ubes was swallowed up by sea-waves, while rocks fell from its promontory into the sea.

Then the sea suddenly retired, leaving the bed of the harbor exposed. A moment later a gigantic wave, fifty feet in height, rolled in upon the doomed city.

Two hours later fire broke out in the wreck, and driven by a high wind, swept the ruins, and also the houses left standing. The furious flames raged three days, burning hundreds imprisoned in the wreck. Every element seemed in conspiracy against the city.

In addition to threatened famine and pestilence among the survivors, the rabble, as in Calabria, showed a disposition to indiscriminate plunder. Upon this " the King gave orders immediately for gallows to be placed all round the city, and after about one hundred executions, amongst which were some English sailors, the evils stopped." The King was very prompt and energetic, initiating every practicable system of relief, and having the really needy cared

EARTHQUAKE AT LISBON.

for at the expense of the State. Several lighter shocks were felt in the succeeding two months. At the end of three months the Government began to rebuild the town. In fifteen years it was well restored, and to-day is one of the handsomest in Europe.

The immense area over which this earthquake was felt is very remarkable; for not only was every part of Spain and Portugal convulsed, but the shocks were perceived, with greater or less intensity, in England, Holland, Italy, Norway, Sweden, Germany, Switzerland, Corsica, the West Indies, at Morocco and Algiers in Africa, and in a part of South America. At Algiers the shock was so violent as to throw down many buildings; and an oasis, with all its population, not far from Morocco, was swallowed up. Fez and Mesquinez were destroyed, with fifteen thousand people. The town of Setubal, seventeen miles from the Tagus and twenty-two miles southeast of Lisbon, was almost entirely swallowed up. The shock was almost as severe at Oporto as at Lisbon. The premonitory roar was compared to the rattling of many carriages over a rough road. The loftiest mountains were shaken, and many cleft or shattered. Masses of rock tumbled from the crags into the valleys. At Colares, seventeen miles from Lisbon, flames and smoke were seen to burst from the Alviras, and also out of the sea. These phenomena continued for some days. A chasm fifteen miles long opened in the Pyrenees. Towns were seriously damaged in Switzerland, France and Italy. Vesuvius, in a state of eruption for a period, suddenly ceased. The shock was also felt by ships far at sea, and, in several instances, the concussion was such as to make the people suppose their vessels had struck on a rock. In one instance, it is said that the people on board a vessel off the West Indies were thrown up a foot and a half from the deck. This circumstance may be ac-

RUINED CATHEDRAL, LISBON.

counted for by the inelasticity of water; so that a violent and sudden movement of the bottom of the ocean would be communicated to the surface and to the ship, through the medium of the fluid, with nearly the same force as though the vessel had been on the ground itself.

Quite as remarkable was the immense wave produced. At Cadiz its height was sixty feet, and the damage in proportion. Rolling to the northward it inflicted vast injury upon Cornwall, England. At the Canaries and Azores the waves rose repeatedly to an immense height; and at Madeira the injury was still greater. In less than an hour the wave had traveled to Leyden. Norway and Sweden felt its presence, even to the recesses of the Gulf of Finland. On the western border of the Atlantic, among the lesser Antilles, where the tide scarcely exceeds twenty-nine inches, a black wall of water twenty-two feet high rushed upon the coasts. The steep and rocky islet of Stabia was dashed over by the waves. In Martinique the water rose to the roofs of the houses, and then receded from the shore for more than a mile. The unusual commotion stirred up the bituminous sediment of the sea bottom, and at Barbadoes the waves were in consequence black as ink.

There have been numerous earthquakes since in Europe which must pass without mention. One in 1817 completely destroyed Vostitza, a town in Greece not far from the site of ancient Helice. Another well-remembered one in 1855 desolated the Canton of Valais in Switzerland. This country has had numerous shocks—sixteen hundred or more, in the past few centuries, and once or twice Basle has been almost totally destroyed. Valais itself is a beautiful vale accessible only by a cleft in a mountain range eighty-five hundred feet deep. Numerous small towns and hamlets are scattered about the vale, and the precipitous slopes around are dotted with shepherds' and hunters' huts.

On July 25, 1855, after an extremely hot morning, the people were astounded by a great earthquake—an abrupt and vertical shock. Then came wave-like motions throwing every one prostrate. Houses tumbled in all directions. People were rolled about like logs of wood. Nearly every village in the canton was destroyed. Great landslips and avalanches rushed down from the hills. So tremendous was the shock that the mountain tops could be seen to sway to and fro. Crags and blocks of ice fell into the vales, crushing and grinding. The terrible uproar sounded as though the whole range of the Alps was about to collapse. The terrible shocks were felt at Lyons, at Paris, at Heidelberg, at Milan, at Genoa. Lisbon had no severer shock. And this great convulsion, that dandled mountains as though mere puppets, and destroyed towns and villages by the score—killed one person. It is one of the most remarkable occurrences in European history.

Among the more destructive recent shocks in Europe are those of 1881-84. Chio, one of the most beautiful islands of the Grecian archipelago, and the home of a thrifty and enterprising people, was visited by an earthquake on April 3, 1881. The whole city, with its hospitals, schools, libraries and works of art, was laid in ruins in a few seconds. This convulsion forms a strange contrast to the more violent one just described. Numerous adjacent villages were overthrown; and after the shock was past it was found that more than five thousand persons were killed and ten thousand others more or less injured. After making all possible efforts at restoration, the authorities were compelled to pull down many still tottering walls and scatter disinfectants over the wreck to

SCENE AT CHIO.

avoid an epidemic from the thousand corpses left beneath the ruin.

The entire adjacent coast of Asia Minor was more or less shaken, and several scores of people were killed in some seaport towns. The shocks continued several days, each being accompanied by a peculiar subterranean roaring. Two years later, ere the town was fairly rebuilt, there was another earthquake, which, however, did more damage in Asia Minor than in Chio.

But the most striking example of great damage done by an earthquake in a very small tract is the case of the island of Ischia. This tiny islet, the Imarina of Horace and Virgil, was well known to the Greeks, who at one time endeavored to establish themselves upon it, but were finally driven away by repeated volcanic outbursts. Since the activity of Vesuvius, Ischia has remained quiet, though a dozen extinct craters bear witness to its former fury. Its highest point is two thousand, seven hundred and seventy-two feet above the sea, while the entire island is but six miles in diameter. It is evidently cast up by an ancient, submarine volcano.

Situated a few miles from Naples, Ischia has for years been a favorite summer resort for the Italians of the neighboring coast. A score of little towns and villages dot its shores and hills, and the view of the Gulf of Naples, Baiae, and adjacent islands and coasts forms one of the most beautiful landscapes in the world.

After its abandonment by the Greek colonists the islet was quiet for sixteen centuries. In 1302 an eruption and earthquake occasioned considerable loss of life and property. After that, though the main peak, Epomeo, has been occasionally muttering and fuming, no serious disturbance occurred for nearly six centuries. The subterranean heat occasions numerous hot springs, the water reaching a temperature of 178 degrees. These baths, and the abundance of choice fruits afforded by the island, afford additional attractions to visitors, and the twenty-five thousand inhabitants would seem to have an earthly paradise.

March 4, 1881, the people were suddenly roused from their slumbering security by two sharp shocks half an hour apart, which overthrew seven hundred houses in the little town of Casamicciola, killing one hundred and twenty-six people and wounding one hundred and seventy-seven more. The only premonition was that a few minutes before the hot springs suddenly reached the boiling point.

Yet this disaster was comparatively insignificant when we consider the one of July 28, 1883.

It was the height of the summer season. The little island was thronged with pleasure-seeking visitors. The night was dark and cloudy; the sea was unusually agitated. The small theatre at Casamicciola was filled with an animated throng, who cared not for the boding storm. The play opened with an earthquake scene. As the clock pointed to 9:32, the *Punchinello* rushed on the stage, shouting, "Un terremoto! un terremoto! alla mare! alla mare!" (An earthquake! an earthquake! to the sea! to the sea!) The audience thought it was part of the play; but ere they could applaud the vigorous acting, the lights were out, a thundering sound was heard, and the crashing roof was upon them. The appalling roar was followed by profound silence, as clouds of stifling dust were whirled up by the wind. Then in the darkness were heard the cries of terrified people, seeking one another in the gloom, and groping for the shore as in the days of Pompeii.

A visitor who was in the theater said, that at the first noise, which resembled the discharge of a heavy battery of artillery, "not a cry was uttered, though terror was depicted in every countenance; but when the first shock was followed by several others, a shriek of despair went up from every lip. The lights went out, pieces of timber were falling all about us, and cries of terror were succeeded by shrieks of pain from those who had been injured. It was a trying moment. When the shocks ceased, I crawled, like many others, out of the ruined building in order to reach the shore. The dust was literally blinding. Several times I stumbled over heaps of masonry and rubbish from which heart-rendering groans and shrieks were proceeding. Upon the shore I encountered many others as frightened as I was, and endeavoring to escape in fear of there being more shocks. Seeing that all remained quiet, we retraced our steps in order to relieve the injured. But it was not until the morning, upon the arrival of the authorities and the troops sent from Naples, that it was possible to take any effective steps for surmounting the difficulties by which we were surrounded. The firemen, assisted by volunteers, then set to work energetically to clear away the rubbish, laying the dead bodies in a row, and handing the injured over to the doctors. It was necessary to go to work very carefully, so as not to injure those still unhurt; and so the work continued very slowly, during which time we felt our heart-strings torn by the piteous appeals for relief. Some people were covered by so much debris that it took hours to reach them, and when we did so, some of them had succumbed to their injuries, while others had gone out of their minds. The dense clouds of dust had choked many of those who were not killed on the spot."

Some strange scenes occurred; and there were instances of remarkable coolness. An Italian professor of surgery who had taken his child to the theatre, coolly took out his watch at the first crash, and noting the exact time, sat

THE PANIC AT CASAMICCIOLA.

perfectly still while the surging crowd endeavored to escape. There he sat with his child till morning, when the light enabled him to find his way out of the wreck.

The sea shore was a weird spectacle. Lighted up by a pile of blazing drift might be seen scores of naked children, and grown persons in their night clothes, scurrying wildly about. An eye-witness tells of many crazy with fear and grief. All night long the wreck resounded with groans and cries. One woman, whom he heard continually moaning, and crying "My children! my children!" was found at daybreak on the edge of a shattered terrace, and clad only in a chemise. Wondering what he could say by way of consolation, he chanced to observe two little ones playing not far away amid a tottering wreck that threatened at every moment to crush them. They were hers.

Further down a woman's jewelled arm and shoulder protruded from the wreck, while her husband, buried nearly, kept crying "save her, never mind about me." As a helping hand was reached to her a sudden landslip crushed out the remaining life.

A young English lady sat playing a funeral march. An Italian count sprang up, saying, "I cannot stand such music!" Just as he cleared the door the hotel fell in ruins behind him. The young lady was found dead at the piano.

For days the work went on, pressed by the energy of the Italian government. All the native police had been killed in the wreck. King Humbert in person visited the scene and had the work pressed as rapidly as possible.

There was no more complete wreck of any town than of Lacco Ameno. Of fifteen hundred and ninety-three people but five escaped. At Casamicciola but one house was left intact. Not a few houses in the former place were swallowed up in fissures. Floria was totally destroyed. Yet the largest town on the island, Ischia, with the adjacent villages, was scarcely hurt; and at Naples, on the mainland, the news of the catastrophe was a complete surprise. Yet on the half of the islet that was most severely shaken the earthquake numbered four thousand victims. A greater contrast to the great Valais earthquake could hardly be imagined.

Still more recent is the catastrophe of Southern Spain, one of the loveliest regions in the world. This district has several times been shaken; but notably at the time of the Lisbon earthquake, when so much damage was done by shocks and sea-waves at Cadiz; again in 1833, when in the single province of Murcia more than four thousand houses were destroyed, with hundreds of the inhabitants. Again the ground was in a state of constant tremor from November, 1855, to March, 1856.

But more severe than these was the shock of 1884. About the end of November slight vibrations were perceptible in Spain, Portugal, Italy, and Southern France. The shocks did not manifest especial intensity at any especial locality, and no attention was paid to them, as such occurrences are so frequent that they cannot be regarded as indicative of greater shocks to come. For example, there were forty-six hundred and twenty shocks recorded in different portions of the earth during the years 1850-57; yet none of these were followed by earthquakes of great severity. So in the case of the November shocks of 1884, no one seemed concerned to know where they originated, or if they boded evil.

But on Christmas day, 1884, there came, a little past nine at night, an intense subdued roar like that of a hurricane; and at once the plateaux of Andalusia, the mountains of Murcia, and the sunny plains of Granada, Jaen

GREAT EARTHQUAKE IN ANDALUSIA.

and Cordova shook from one end to the other. At Seville the terrified people rushed into the streets and camped there all night; but this city did not suffer so much as in the shock of 1755. In Granada the motions followed in rapid succession for several weeks; but though many other buildings were overthrown, the far-famed Alhambra was not injured. Twenty thousand people camped without the city gates.

The shocks were much severest in the mountainous districts. Villages and hamlets in ravines and along mountain slopes were speedily destroyed. The town of Alhama lost thirteen hundred and twenty houses at the first shock. Five hundred and seventy-six bodies were taken out of the ruins. Two hundred and eighty houses were overthrown by subsequent shocks. Abumelas lost five hundred and seventeen people, and four hundred and sixty-three houses out of four hundred and seventy-seven. More than three thousand houses were wrecked throughout Andalusia and Granada. Fifty-six towns and hamlets were greatly damaged, twenty of them entirely destroyed. Parts of mountain slopes slid slowly into the valleys. Deep crevices, like those of the Calabrian earthquakes, were opened in some localities. One of these is two miles long and of unknown depth. Boiling water burst from fissures in the mountains. The course of the river Gogollas was changed. Portions of the country was upheaved; others depressed. Shocks were felt at sea near the Azores.

Several thousands were killed and wounded, and the survivors suffered much from cold and hunger. The young King Alfonso took active part in the work of relief; but so numerous were the dead that many of them had to be buried in heaps or covered with quick-lime. There was not time to bury all properly.

Such are details of the more prominent European earthquakes. There have been others of almost equal importance; but three years ago a severe earthquake killed two thousand or more in the Italian Riviera; but the cases given well illustrate the destruction wrought in Europe, and other regions claim attention.

CHAPTER XXV.

EARTHQUAKES IN THE UNITED STATES AND ENGLAND.

> The fowls of every hue,
> "Crowding together, sailed on weary wing,
> And hovering, oft they seemed about to light,
> Then soared as if they deemed the earth unsafe.
> The cattle looked with meaning face on man,
> Dogs howled, and seemed to see more than their masters,
> And there were sights that none had seen before.
> And hollow, strange, unprecedented sounds,
> And earnest whisperings ran along the hills,
> At dead of night: and long, deep endless sighs
> Came from the dreary vale; and from the waste
> Came horrid shrieks, and fierce unearthly groans,
> The wail of evil spirits that now felt
> The hour of utter vengeance near at hand.
> The winds from every quarter blew at once,
> And shapes, strange shapes, in winding sheets were seen,
> And voices talked amid the clouds: and then
> Earth shook, and swam, and reeled, and oped her jaws,
> By earthquake tossed and tumbled to and fro."

IT is a common assertion that when persons are drowning, all the events of past life rush suddenly before them with startling distinctness: sometimes in amusing combinations: generally the reverse.

Something of the same effect is produced by the earthquake; but in a far more terrifying way. Each one is witness to the panic of his neighbor; and no fright is so terrible as that which is infectious. In moments of great peril a single calm master-spirit may quiet a mob. But when the eternal hills are shaken, when the groaning earth reels beneath the feet, and the mountains are removed and cast into the midst of the sea, who is there that retains his presence of mind? Man's social arrangements are calculated upon a supposition of the earth's stability : **and when he finds himself the victim of misplaced confidence, there is neither courage nor spirit nor reason left in him.** Numerous are the cases where men have been rendered insane by such convulsions.

To the ravage of the hurricane, the roar of the storm, the surge of the sea, the rush of the flood, one becomes in a measure accustomed, and in the moment of danger may take precautions for personal safety. But in the case of earthquakes the reverse is the rule; none dread them more than those who know them best. The stranger in tropical America may sit at his ease on a summer evening, enjoying the beauties of the landscape; or he may stand in a crowded hall, amongst a galaxy of wits and beauties, observing the kaleidoscopic movements of the gorgeous costumes before him. There comes a faint peculiar quiver of the earth, so insignificant that the unitiated foreigner may hardly observe it: but there goes up a wild shout of "Tembla! Tembla!" and in an instant a terror-stricken, breathless throng surges wildly into the streets, the fields, the parks—anywhere: anywhere away from the heavy roofs and massive walls that would defy a hurricane; all blindly seeking to be under the open sky, only too often to be engulfed in gaping crevices.

It is preternaturally terrible; this emblem of solidity quivering beneath our feet, reminding us that the days of unbridled chaos, the wild war of all the elements, the tremendous geological convulsions that have exterminated so many races of animals in the days of the past, may be as ready and powerful for destruction in the present! The sensation of utter powerlessness is so overwhelming, that amid the crash of falling houses, the cries of entombed victims, the shrieks of flying multitudes, the rumblings in the earth beneath, and the trembling of the soil like that of a steed in the presence of a lion, the boldest and bravest can but sit with bowed head, in silent, motionless despair, awaiting whatever fate a grim capricious chance may determine. In the strange mysterious phenomena, which strike and do their work in a few seconds, one is disposed to see the disturbing dreams of fever, or the touch of a horrible nightmare, rather than any possible reality.

It is no wonder that insanity, hallucinations, or graver nervous disorders, in such moments fasten themselves on people for life. When a power, which despite its constant recurrence, remains almost unknown, holds the lives of untold thousands in its grasp, the mind is affected beyond the power of pen to describe. Long stress of poignant grief finds its effects equalled in a few seconds. People dash convulsively on the ground, as though seized with epilepsy. Some may become paralyzed : paralytics may recover the use of their limbs : others lose the power of speech : yet others are hopelessly idiotic. Not less marked are the effects on the brute creation. The owl, with nervous twitching head, and feathers all awry, flits to the trees near the house, as though imploring the protection of man. The panther forgets his ancient enmity, and creeps within the city gate. The screaming swallow leaves the eaves, and wings her way to other lands. The long-silent crocodile scrambles from his native lair and rushes moaning about the sand. The frightened nightingale forgets her song. The doleful dog howls loudly in the street. The trembling ox and horse together huddle, and groan as they tremble. The air itself is chill, as though it were turned cold at the manifestation of some awful being. All things are awed by the terrible " Wrath of God."

The " Wrath of God ! " Yes, such is the actual name of the earthquake among the modern Greeks—Theomenia. No other title will they give it. They have braved the

WRECK OF THE CHARLESTON EARTHQUAKE.

storm and the flood, the famine and the pestilence for three thousand years, and recognize in each the operation of law, and against each may take precautions; but the earthquake, absolutely beyond control, is to them inexplicable by natural causes, and any attempt to explain it is resented. They know the quicksand in which the victim, erect, vigorous, in full possession of his faculties, stares his fate in the face; stands for hours with death grinning from the sand at his feet, as it slowly drags him down; but this fearful opening of the soil, that in an instant swallows young and old, rich and poor, the loved and hated, the city and the castle—it can only be the "wrath of God!" So to the Jew was the fall of Sodom.

Not a single agent of nature can equal it in sudden destruction. It comes and it goes in a few seconds; almost ere you are aware of its presence it has claimed its thousands. There is no escape; no ruin so absolute; no desolation so pitiful; no death so remorseless. You stand chatting with a friend, the earth shakes, gapes,—and the friend at your side finds a grave in the foundations of the earth. "Two women shall be grinding at the mill, the one shall be taken and the other left."

"Think ye that those twelve on whom the tower of Siloam fell were sinners above all that are in Jerusalem? I tell you nay."

So, as we have already seen, the phenomena of earthquakes are as clearly under the domination of law as any other forces of nature. We know the forces that produce them, and though we can not tell with certainty what combination of them existed at the location of any particular shock. We can not hope to control the causes, but we can to a large extent avert the seriousness of the results. With this in view, we can consider seriously the extent of the ravages of this strange destroyer, without considering them as direct visitations upon the sins of a people.

Such views as those of the Greeks, however, have been common among all Christian nations of non-Saxon origin, and still prevail to no small extent. But the peculiar sense of personal responsibility and power that belongs to the Teuton, Scandinavian and Saxon stock has given a different impress to British and American ideas. Perhaps, too, the fact that Britons and Americans have suffered less from earthquakes than many others, has gone far to modify the trend of their thought. Be that as it may, the dominant element of the race—reverence, awe, and with common sense and a dash of contempt for those of more superstitious disposition, may be found in the old hunter's comment on the outburst of Cosequina: "What was the meaning of those shakes in New Granada a month agone? Natur' don't mostly toss about this big earth just for sport and idleness; there's a meaning and a reason and a secret in every movement she makes. But eighty earthquakes in twenty-four hours aren't sent just to scare a pile of Nicaraguan Greasers. Guess earthquakes don't take no more regard of Greasers than of other big folks!"

So long as superstitious ideas prevail among a multitude of people, it is not surprising that they find portentous signs in earth and sky betokening the near approach of the dread visitation. This is naturally increased by the desire to have due warning. The ancient Greeks were especially anxious in this regard. So we find one of their grave geographers, Pausanias, declaring that earthquakes are preceded by unusual rain or drought, eclipses, sudden disappearing of springs, great hurricanes, fiery apparitions in the sky with long trains of light, and the appearance of new stars in the sky. The people of Mendoza, South

America, when overtaken by a great earthquake, suddenly remembered that but a short time before, a flaming meteor of a brilliant blue color and awful appearance had hissed past their town. So before the Riobamba earthquake, a brilliant shower of meteors took place; so, also, at the Cumana earthquake. At other times the weather has been unusually rainy; again, long drought has prevailed. Sometimes springs have become suddenly muddy, and cleared as suddenly after the shock. Again, muddy streams have become clear till the shock passed. Again, we are told that all animals manifest great fear before the earthquake comes; that lizards, snakes, mice and rats rush from their holes in terror. Doubtless many smaller animals perceive tremors of the earth that pass unnoticed by men; but as to the efficacy of such signs in general, it is suggestive of Hotspur's reply to Glendower. The fiery Welshman, endeavoring to prove that he, too, is some great one, asserts that at his nativity

> "The front of heaven was full of fiery shapes,
> Of burning cressets: and at my birth,
> The frame and huge foundations of the earth
> Shaked like a coward."

To which Hotspur answers:

> "Why, so it would have done,
> At the same season if your mother's cat
> Had kittened, and yourself had ne'er been born!"

So much for popular beliefs. Quite generally there are subterranean rumblings, or slight tremors preceding the more violent shock; but even these are not sure signs, as they may occur alone, or the earthquake may come unannounced. A notable case of the former sort is the remarkable subterranean roaring heard at Guanaxuato, in Mexico, in 1784. It lies in a rich mining district, with no volcano in the vicinity. On January 9 there broke out, after some preliminary muttering, a great uproar which seemed as if a thunder storm were going on beneath the surface of the earth. A short distance from the town it could not be heard; and not the slightest tremor of the soil was perceptible, even in mines sixteen hundred feet deep. But so great was the panic it created, that thousands fled from the town, leaving it entirely to the mercy of thieves and bandits. The alcaldes, with true Spanish grandiloquence, asserted that the government would " be able in its wisdom to say when danger is imminent, and to take measures for enabling the people to fly for refuge;" and it determined to impose a penalty of one thousand

HOUSES THROWN INTO A RAVINE BY AN EARTHQUAKE.

piasters on the rich, or of two months imprisonment on the poor who fled ere the word was given. But though it was easy to make laws, it was not so easy to feed the people; for the affrighted peasantry would not set foot in the city; so the month of uproar became one of famine as well.

A similar rumbling occurred in Melada, an island off the coast of Dalmatia, in 1822, and the frightened inhabitants besought the Austrian government to transport them to a place of safety; but though the explosions continued during two years, sometimes more than one hundred in a single night, nothing ever resulted therefrom.

So with regard to all popular beliefs on this topic—no dependence can be placed on any of them. There is nothing to warn us of the approach of the earthquakes, neither in the heavens above, nor the earth beneath, nor the waters under the earth.

Has the reader ever experienced one of these strange earthstorms? Perhaps not. Is it believed they are rare? They are as common as storms in the atmosphere. Within a period of seven years, four thousand six hundred and twenty have been recorded. Many more, doubtless, occurred completely beyond the pale of civilization. Hundreds have passed unnoticed save by delicate instruments. Not a day passes without several being recorded. They are as widely various in power as the storm and the breeze. Not a region on earth is unvisited by them.

Yet the reader will be disposed to think that the United States is almost free from these visitants. To a certain extent it is; we have not in all our history, had a shock of extreme violence, or one that can compare in destructiveness with the strange convulsions of tropical regions: but in the rarity of shocks we are not so favored as might be supposed. A few moments consideration of the records will be sufficiently convincing.

In the memoirs of the "Academy of the Arts and Sciences" in Boston, is a paper read in 1783 by Prof. Williams, recounting the story of some of the earlier earthquakes in our history.

The first one noticed after the landing of the Pilgrims occurred June 1, 1638. We are told it was preceded by a rumbling noise like remote thunder, which gradually grew louder and nearer. Then the earth began to quake till pewter and crockery tumbled from the shelves, stone walls

WRECK ON KING STREET, CHARLESTON, S. C.

toppled over, and chimneys crumbled and fell. The shock passed from northwest to southeast, and was followed by a second in half an hour. People found it difficult to keep their feet. It occurred in the afternoon but there is no means of knowing what area was affected. As the country was then unsettled, the damage done was of course nil. Nearly four years later occurred a light shock, barely noticeable, in the same region. In 1653 an earthquake on the 29th of October stirred up the Puritan divines to admonish their flocks of the wrath of God. Still another occasion of the same sort was given in 1658. But of this latter, though we are told it was a very great earthquake, we have neither day nor month, nor any record of its violence, extent or duration.

The first convulsion of which there is any detailed account, occurred in 1663, January 26–28, Old Style. An old narrative thus records it:

"About half an hour after five in the evening a most terrible earthquake began. The heavens being serene, there was suddenly heard a roar like the noise of a great fire. Immediately the buildings were shaken with amazing violence. Doors opened and shut of themselves with a fearful clattering. The bells rang without their ropes being touched. Cracks appeared in the walls of buildings, and floors separated and in some cases fell down. Chasms appeared in the fields, and the hills seemed to be in motion. The fright of the inhabitants was shared by the beasts and birds, who sent forth fearful cries, howlings and bellowings. The duration of this earthquake was very uncommon. The first shock continued half an hour before it was over, but it began to abate about a quarter of an hour after it began." (Probably there were a considerable number of shocks, gradually lessening in violence.)

"The same day about eight o'clock in the evening, there came a second shock, equally violent as the first, and within the space of half an hour, there were two others. The next day about three hours from the morning, there was a violent shock, which lasted a long time, and the next night counted some thirty-two shocks, of which many were violent. Nor did the trembling of the earth cease until the July following. Many trees were torn up, and the outlines of the mountains appeared to be much changed. Many springs and small streams were dried up; in others the waters became sulphurous, and the channels in which some had run were so altered as to be unrecognizable. Half way between Tadousac and Quebec two hills were thrown down and formed a point of land which extended half a quarter of a league into the St. Lawrence River. The island Aux Coudres became larger than it was before, and the channel of the St. Lawrence was greatly changed."

This is, perhaps, as severe a shock as has been felt in this country; but though the shock extended southward to Pennsylvania, its chief energy was centered in a narrow strip on the St. Lawrence, giving our Canadian neighbors the lion's share of the fright. Other light shocks were noticed in New England in 1665, 1668, 1669, 1670, 1705, and 1720.

October 29, 1727, another severe earthquake was experienced about 10:40 P. M. It seems to have had Southern New Hampshire as its focus, extending thence to the Delaware and Kennebec rivers. Its approach was heralded by a subdued roar from the northwest, which, as it drew nearer, "was thought to be the roar of a blazing chimney near at hand, and at last was likened to the rattling of carriages driven fiercely over pavements. In about half a minute from the time the noise was first heard, the earthquake was felt. It was observed by those who were abroad that, as the shake passed under them, the surface of the earth rose and sank." Houses trembled and rocked, as though about to fall to pieces. Movables were dashed about with a fearful clatter. Crockery was smashed; stone walls and chimneys thrown down.

At Newbury, ashes and sulphur were cast forth from the earth, and also volumes of sand. Sulphuretted hydrogen seems to have been present in large quantities: also chemicals readily decomposed by warmth and moisture.

A correspondent of the Royal Society wrote that a clergyman near Boston assured him "that immediately after the earthquake there was such a stink that the family could scarce bear to be in the house for a considerable time that night." Another clergyman writes that in the following April the fine sand thrown up by the earthquake "had a very offensive stench—nay, it was more nauseous than a putrefying corpse: yet, in a very little while after, it had no smell at all. How long it was before it began to have this stench, I am not certain; but I believe it was covered with snow until a little while before." Another minister records that "about three days before the earthquake there was perceived an ill-stinking smell in the water of several wells. Some searched their wells, but found nothing that might thus affect them. The scent was so strong and offensive that for eight or ten days they entirely omitted using it. In the deepest of these wells, which was about thirty-six feet, the water was turned to a brimstone color, but had nothing of the smell, and was thick like puddle water." Some wells, dry just before the shock, immediately filled up. Occasional shocks were felt for some months after.

From the phenomena present here, and in many similar cases, it will appear that large volumes of pent-up

SCENE AT CHARLESTON.

gases may be discharged in districts remote from any volcanic region. In some instances, we are informed that immediately after severe shocks, the streams and vegetation have proved poisonous to cattle. There were light shocks felt in 1732, 1737 and 1744; but none of these are said to have done any damage beyond throwing down a few stone walls. Thus we find within a century fourteen earthquake periods in New England alone; and in several cases the shocks were numerous, extending over a period of several months. Comparing the small area with the whole region, and remembering that shocks are more frequent in the central, southern and western portions of the country, it is fair to conclude that the merest tithe of those actually occurring could have come under the notice of our ancestors.

The most violent shock ever known in New England came eighteen days after the great Lisbon earthquake of 1755, preceded by a peculiar, rumbling roar. Then came a "rapid, jarring, vibrating motion," with an upward shock: then a "violent, prodigious shock, as suddenly, to all appearances as a thunderclap breaking upon a house and attended by a great noise." Then followed a series of "quick and violent concussions, jerks and wrenches, attended by an undulating, waving motion of the whole surface of the ground, not unlike the shaking and quaking of a large bog."

Several writers give a graphic account of the behavior of the good people of Boston at this juncture. The shock came at a little past four in the morning. Some sprang from their beds and ran into the street; some lay shivering with fear, not daring to rise; others rushed to the windows, and, seeing in the gloom their unclad neighbors rushing about the streets, shrieked aloud that the judgment day was at hand. Others thought that they heard

Gabriel's horn, and fell on their knees, crying for mercy, or fainted away. The boldest feared the crash of tottering houses; children ran about crying for their parents; dogs howled dismally; birds flew aloft with frightened cries; cattle bellowed with fear as they dashed about their pens. Screaming horses struggled in their stalls. Numbers of fish were killed by the shock. Changes were wrought in springs and streams, after the manner of 1727.

The damage done was not so great as might have been expected from the unusual alarm shown. A large number of chimneys in Boston were thrown down; clocks were stopped; a new vane was broken from the market house, the spindle being snapped at a place where it was five inches thick; but we are not told of any serious loss of life or property. The shock extended southward, and was plainly felt along the east side of the Chesapeake, but not on the western shore. The sea wave set in motion travelled southward, and it is supposed to have occasioned the unusual commotion of the water in the West Indies. At St. Martin's the sea suddenly fell five feet below its level, and then rose six above.

The time of the shock was determined exactly by an accident. Prof. Winthrop, of Cambridge, had placed a long glass tube in his tall clock, as a safe place. This tube, thrown against the pendulum, stopped the clock, which the day before had been adjusted to meridianal noon; and as Prof. Winthrop had compared his watch and clock the night before, he was able to show that the shocks began at eleven minutes and thirty-five seconds after four A. M., November 18, and continued about four and a half minutes.

Eighteen periods of earthquakes are noted in the next fifty-five years; and at one of these, in 1791, nearly one hundred and fifty shocks were felt.

OLD STATE HOUSE, CHARLESTON.

In 1810–11–12, a series of remarkable shocks were felt throughout a large portion of the United States, but with especial force in the central Mississippi valley. The first were noticed near St. Genevieve, but the center of violence seemed to lie around New Madrid, Mo. The shocks became so sharp and frequent that Dr. Robertson was sent out to observe and record them carefully. He kept count up to five hundred, and then abandoned that portion of the work.

The phenomena were much like those of the milder type of earthquakes everywhere. Around New Madrid huge fissures opening in the earth emitted volumes of sand and gas, occasionally spouting water, or sending out bursts of flame. Some of the fissures were six hundred feet long and twenty feet wide. The sand and water was sometimes thrown as high as forty or fifty feet. During the whole period there were unusual disturbances in other regions. On the night of the most violent shocks occurred the great earthquake at Caracas, Venezuela, which destroyed so many thousands. Had the Mississippi region been a very thickly settled one, the loss of life would have been fearful. Upon the upheaval of a new island, Sabrina, in the Azores, to a height of three hundred and twenty feet, and an eruption of the St. Vincent volcano, in the Antilles, the disturbance ceased. It is not safe to assert positively that there was no connection between these phenomena; but there is little probability that there was. They serve rather to show how universal are the subterranean forces with which man must deal. The year 1811 was also marked by a storm of unusual violence, and by the appearance of a brilliant comet. But, as noticed before, efforts to establish any especial connection between such phenomena have not met with any marked success.

These earthquakes were so violent in the river itself as to almost shatter boats in mid-stream. Trees at some distance from the bank were hurled into the water with tremendous force. Flashes of fire and molten matter were thrown to great heights. The explosions seemed like a battery of artillery. Sunken logs and snags were thrown from the deep bottom of the river to a height of thirty feet above the surface. Sulphurous streams dashed from a thousand rents, leaving unfathomable fissures. Great forest trees lashed their heads together, or were snapped off by the shocks. Small islands sank to the bottom of the river. Quantities of coal and charred wood were thrown up; some lying a considerable distance from the fissures that discharged them. Many boats were lost; quite a number of people were buried under falling banks. It was undoubtedly the most violent convulsion in the history of our country. Reelfoot lake, now a noted fishing resort, we are told was formed by this earthquake.

Time would fail us to give an especial notice of the many shocks received since the country has been more widely settled. With a notice of the recent Charleston earthquake this list must be closed.

This convulsion owes its importance rather to its location than to its violence. It was felt over about one-fourth of the entire country, its greatest force being felt along the Atlantic coast from New Haven to Savannah. The area affected was elliptical, and the shock was but little less severe at Atlanta, Georgia, in East Tennessee, and many North and South Carolina regions, than in Charleston itself. At was felt at Charleston at 9:51, August 31, 1886, and reached Toronto, Canada, in four minutes. It did not travel so readily westward as northward.

It is of course impossible to estimate exactly the damage done. A considerable number of important cities suffered more or less; but the majority were forgotten in the unusual severity at Charleston. The city appeared as though it had been through a siege, or as if a gigantic charge of dynamite had been exploded beneath it. In

CHARLESTON, S. C.

all directions might be seen heaps of ruins, houses tottering, cracked, twisted—in all stages of destruction. Ever and anon a fresh shock brought down some crumbling edifice with a sullen roar, and a cloud of stifling dust veiled it from view. The night resounded with the screams of terrified fugitives, the tread of hurrying feet, and the groans and cries of the wounded. The parks swarmed with those in search of a place of safety. Hundreds were bruised or maimed by falling stones and timbers; not a few were killed outright; others, crushed in the wrecks, died a lingering death.

Appeals for aid were promptly responded to by all portions of the country. Even those localities which had themselves suffered severely, came to the aid of the city that had been more sorely stricken.

The greatest injury to life was indirect. Only forty-seven people, it is said, were killed outright. But few houses were left safe; and for a considerable time young and old, rich and poor, the feeble and the strong, were out of doors in tents, booths, or such rude shelters as they could hastily erect. The alarm was perpetuated by occasional recurrence of the shocks during several days. The continued exposure and lack of necessaries created a vast deal of sickness; and the deaths thus indirectly occasioned far exceeded those killed outright.

The damage to buildings in Charleston is estimated at $5,000,000. But in comparison with the whole number injured, comparatively few of the houses were shaken completely down. Hundreds were shaken and shattered to the point of falling, and had to be pulled down as unsafe. The shock was just short of a point where it would have made terrible havoc. If violent enough to overthrow the many houses it merely shattered, its victims would have been numbered by thousands, instead of tens. We may be thankful, with Lord North, that things were no worse.

The nature of the shocks varied. In some parts of South Carolina chimneys and brick walls remained upright, but crushed to atoms at the base, as if shattered by a powerful upward concussion; in other locations, evidences of a twisting motion were present; houses were turned partially around, and left almost unharmed. Again, as in most cases in Charleston, the chief movement appeared to be a horizontal one—the upper portions of walls and buildings being thrown down, while the lower suffered little harm. More of these singular effects will be noticed in connection with other shocks. Crevices and fissures were opened; railroad rails bent in a snake-like form; mud, sand, and small stones were thrown out. There was no tidal wave, and artesian wells four hundred feet deep were not disturbed. There was no barometric variation, though the air is said to have suddenly become oppressively hot at the moment of the shock. Some Pennsylvania gas wells diminished, and a geyser in the Yellowstone Park, four years quiet, burst suddenly into action. These we must deem mere coincidences.

As a whole, this has been the most destructive single earthquake in our history, while far inferior in real violence to the convulsions last noticed. For frequency of shocks, and total damage in consequence, the Pacific States far exceed all the rest of the country. Their position with active volcanic regions in Oregon and Washington and Lower California, renders them peculiarly liable to such disturbances. Within the years 1872–1885, inclusive, there were registered seventy-five earthquakes in New England, sixty-six in the Atlantic States, seventy-five in the Mississippi Valley, and two hundred and thirty-seven in the Pacific States.

These facts ought to be conclusive evidence against the belief that, because storms and earthquakes are sometimes simultaneous, the one is in any way responsible for the other. These figures show the fewest shocks in the region

EARTHQUAKES IN THE UNITED STATES. 557

WRECK OF FACTORY, CHARLESTON.

most frequented by tornadoes; while the section never visited by the latter shows more shocks than all the rest combined. Add to these the previous shocks recorded in our history—231—and it is evident that we have our full share of such convulsions.

In respect to earthquakes, our British cousins have been even more fortunate than ourselves. A cursory glance at British geology shows that at a remote age in the past, volcanic action was frequent and violent; but the whole region has long buried or healed the wounds inflicted upon the face of nature by the petulant giants of fire. Now and then there is a premonitory tremor; but the warning seems not to be for the grandchildren of the Druids; and the latter have been lulled to a sense of almost absolute security.

Yet at some periods of the past they have been seriously disturbed, if we may credit the old chroniclers; but their records are so brief, and at times so conflicting, that it is not always easy to determine the extent of the disaster. And it must be remembered that in the dark and middle ages the mass of the people knew absolutely nothing of affairs not in their own immediate neighborhood.

Perhaps the most striking feature of British earthquakes is the fact that, like the shocks in the Vesuvian neighborhood, the area they disturb is very small; it may be, however, that incompleteness of reports is responsible for this apparent peculiarity. Up to the last century but one general shock is recorded; this being the first of which there is definite mention, occurring in 974 A. D. Five others are recorded in the next century, all local.

Perhaps the most violent of the earlier earthquakes was the one which in 1110 shook the region between Shrewsbury and Nottingham, tumbling down many houses and injuring many people. At Nottingham the bed of the river Trent was laid dry and remained so some hours. Probably a large fissure opened temporarily in the channel, allowing the water to escape into subterranean cavities. Three other earthquakes occurred in the Lincolnshire fens in the next thirty-two years, doing considerable damage.

In 1158 mention is made of a most extraordinary earthquake which shook London and vicinity, destroying much property, injuring several people, and causing the Thames to become so low as to be passed on foot. Seven years later there was a general tremor observed throughout all England.

John of Brompton relates a remarkable circumstance in connection with an earthquake in 1179. The ground belonging to the bishop of Durham, at Oxenhall near Darlington, was raised suddenly to a level with the adjacent hills, remaining so from 9 A. M. till sunset, when it fell again, leaving a deep cavity in place of a hill. Three other earthquakes occurred ere the close of the century; the last one, in Somersetshire in 1199, being violent enough to throw men off their feet.

Forty-seven years passed without any further experience of the sort, when a series of severe shocks, especially violent in Kent, overthrew a number of churches and other buildings of the more pretentious sort; and the same thing happened next year, affecting especially London and the Thames Valley. Again, in the year after, Bath and Wells suffered considerably; and two years later St. Albans was shaken.

Of other earthquakes in the next century no especial mention need be made, save of one of unusual violence in 1385. A revolution in Scotland followed, and the superstitious populace, looking backward, concluded that the earthquake had been meant as a warning which they had not been able to interpret. A second shock which fol-

RUINED DWELLING, CHARLESTON.

lowed the revolution was supposed to express the Divine displeasure at their short-sightedness.

But one shock, though a very general one, is recorded during the next one hundred and sixty-six years. Then in 1551 a slight tremor upset the people's furniture and dinner pots in a portion of Surrey. Twenty years afterward a severe shock in Herefordshire was accompanied by a landslide. A large portion of a hill slowly descended during two days, turning a half circle as it came, as though on a pivot.

In 1574 a sharp vibration shook northern and western England at the hour for vespers. Suppliants in Norton Chapel were thrown prostrate and fled in terror, believing the dead were rising through the floor. Part of Ruthin Castle was thrown down.

In 1580, April 6, nearly all England was alarmed by a violent shock. The great bell at Westminster rang the alarm; others joined in. Students of the Temple rushed into the streets; stones fell from St. Paul's; showers of chimneys in the streets maimed several persons; a panic ensued at Christ Church, where two people were killed by falling stones, and several were maimed in the wild rush to escape from the building. Parts of the fortifications at Dover were overthrown; also several churches and castles were damaged. May 1 of the same year the shocks were again felt in Kent, during the night. This is one of the most notable of British earthquakes; it passed eastward through Belgium to Cologne.

But it is needless to pursue the record further. Only two unusual features are presented among the many earthquakes following: one in 1731 was confined to an area six miles by five; and one in 1734 exhibited a peculiar rotary motion, shaking persons in bed around at right angles to their former positions.

Summing up the record, we find that in the 10th century one earthquake is recorded in England; during the 11th, ten; during the 12th, twelve; during the 13th, thirteen; during the 14th, four; during the 15th, one; six in the 16th; twenty in the 17th, and eighty-four in the eighteenth. The present has also had a fair quota. But if we consider the damage to property, or the fatality, we must conclude that no country in the world is so favored in this matter of earthquakes as Great Britain, unless it may be Germany.

Finally, all the disasters of this sort, in both England and the United States, so far as all historic records go, do not equal a single one of the many terrible convulsions recorded in the history of other nations. From the earliest times to the present, we find a constant succession of appalling disasters, many of which are almost beyond the power of comprehension. The most cursory glance at these horrors of the past should render every Anglo-Saxon peculiarly grateful that his lot is not cast in a land so cursed with terrors, and more ready to sympathize with the stranger in his woe.

CHAPTER XXVI.

EARTHQUAKES IN TROPICAL AMERICA.

" Hark! louder on the blast come hollow shrieks
Of dissolution; in the fitful scowl
Of night, near and more near, angels of death
Incessant flap their deadly wings, and roar
Through all the fevered air: the mountains rock
And thousand meteors flame about their heads;
The thunder long and loud gives out his voice,
Responsive to the ocean's troubled growl,
While bellowing chasms rend th' eternal hills.
Earth trembles at the mighty march of death."

THE reader will be assured, from the facts given concerning volcanic eruptions, and the earthquakes of Asia Minor mentioned in the former chapter, that great earthquakes are as numerous in Asiatic districts as elsewhere; but beyond the bare fact, little is known of most of these. India has preserved no written history; and China and Japan have been till recently almost inaccessible to Europeans. So while the disturbances there are equal in importance to those of other lands, it is but lately that any definite information has been accessible; and our chief knowledge has come from personal narratives of white settlers and visitors to the islands of the western Pacific. In Japan, there is, to say nothing of numerous volcanoes, strong circumstantial evidence of the frequency of earthquakes in days past. Almost all dwellings are constructed of bamboo and lightest woods, one story high, with screens of paper as partitions: houses of stone are feared, the people preferring to take their chances on a great fire than on an earthquake. The same fact is notice-

EARTHQUAKE IN CHINA.

able in the Philippines, Moluccas, and adjacent groups. Almost the only stone buildings are those of Spanish and Dutch settlers. China has apparently suffered less; but we learn that in 1556 two entire provinces were laid waste. The extent of the loss of life can not be estimated. The earth vomited ashes and flames, and ten great sea waves occurred in twenty-four hours.

Since European occupation of the East Indies, the convulsions have been frequent and alarming. The city of Manila was completely destroyed, with thousands of people, in 1645. Not one stone remained on another. Severe shocks occurred there again in 1699, 1796, 1825, 1852, and 1863. The last named wrecked the cathedral while filled with worshipers. The loss of property was from $8,000,000 to $10,000,000, or twice that of our Charleston earthquake. Four hundred people were killed. The shock lasted about half a minute, but opened many fissures, emitted volumes of gas and spoilt the river water. Again, in 1880, after some vague or irregular tremblings, there were several violent shocks. There was first experienced a peculiar sense of nausea and faintness, with a feeling of powerlessness or inability to flee. Horses stopped trembling in the streets, "standing with ears erect, with staring eyes, and stiffly extended legs, as though conscious of extraordinary peril." The natives, heedless of appeals for help, wildly sought their own safety, or knelt devoutly invoking the saints. Clouds of dust filled the air, and heaps of ruin blocked the streets. The terrible hush that prevailed was broken only by an occasional cry for aid, or the crash of a ruined home. Portions of ground between great crevices were raised five or six feet; other parts fell as much. But the confusion rapidly subsided, and occupations of all sorts were resumed. One newspaper, true to the traditional enterprise of the fraternity, dragged its paraphernalia from its ruined building, and went to work in the middle of the street. An American publisher could hardly beat that.

But a region whose earthquakes have attracted greater attention, and have been more carefully noticed by scientific men than those of the eastern archipelago, is to be found along the western slope of the Andes, extending thence into Central America and Northern Venezuela and the West Indies.

Ever since the Spanish conquest, earthquakes have been numerous and violent in this whole region; and judging from the character of the native dwellings, the aborigines were for centuries accustomed to such movements. But it remained for Humboldt, in the last century, to give us a more careful description of some of the greater of these disasters.

Of the preceding disturbances, one of the most notable occurred in 1698, when the crater of the volcano Carguirazo fell in with a great crash during a shock of earthquake, and an area of twenty square miles was covered with mud containing numerous dead fish. A few years later, a similar occurrence north of Quito produced an epidemic of pernicious fevers.

But of the many great convulsions, that of Riobamba, in 1794, must rank as exceeding all within the range of authentic history, unless we except the one which destroyed Antioch in the year 526. The area disturbed was the great volcanic plain on which Quito stands.

No subterranean noise announced or accompanied the shock. Adjacent volcanoes were quiet; but the volcano of Pasto, sixty miles to the northward, had for three months been violently smoking; and at the moment the shock sixty miles away began, it suddenly stopped, nor did it again begin. The volcano of Cayambe, near Quito, seemed surrounded by meteorites. The pious people, alarmed at this manifestation of the divine wrath, formed a religious procession which walked through the principal streets. The result justified their belief in the potency of their prayers; for Quito remained unharmed. A great roar, since known as *el gran ruido,* was heard under the town some twenty minutes after the disaster; but at the scene of the latter it was not heard at all.

In the immediate vicinity of Riobamba, the destruction was fearful. The entire plain seemed rent into small independent fragments, which rose or sank at will. Humboldt tells that an eye-witness might have seen "fissures which alternately opened and closed, so that persons partially engulfed were saved by extending their arms, that they might not be swallowed up; portions of long trains of muleteers and laden mules disappearing in suddenly opening cross fissures, whilst other portions, by a hasty retreat, escaped the danger; vertical oscillations, by the non-simultaneous rising and sinking of adjoining portions of ground, so that persons standing in the choir of a church, sixteen feet above the pavement of the street, found themselves lowered to the level of the pavement without being thrown down; the sinking down of massive houses, with such an absence of disruption or dislocation that the inhabitants could open the doors of the interior, pass uninjured from room to room, light candles and debate with each other their chance of escape, during two days which elapsed before they were dug out; lastly, the entire disappearance of great masses of stones and building materials. The old town had possessed churches, convents, and houses of several stories; but in the places where they stood, we found, on tracing out among the ruins the former plan of the city, only stone heaps of from eight to twelve feet in height."

Of some of the villages in the adjacent plain not a trace was left. They sunk bodily, and the earth closed over them. Of the others, only heaps of ruins were left.

Nor was this all. The great volcano of Tunguragua, at the southern extremity of the plateau, was rent asunder by the shock, or, according to others, had an eruption from the side. Immense torrents of thick, dark, sandy mud, mingled with pebbles, poured out and flooded adjacent portions of the plain, smothered scores still entan-

AFTER THE SHOCK.

gled in the ruins of their dwellings, filling numerous ravines and valleys, one of which was one thousand feet wide and seven hundred feet deep.

The total loss of life was terrible. One authority places the destruction at two hundred thousand. Forty thousand Indians were suffocated by the torrent of mud alone. It is the most destructive earthquake in modern history.

The town of Cumana has been visited almost as frequently as the far-famed Antioch. In 1530, we are told, the sea rose four fathoms, the earth was rent, a fort laid in ruins, the town wrecked, and dark, noisome liquids ejected from fissures. In 1766, a long drought, fifteen months in duration, had turned the thoughts of the people once more upon their manifold transgressions, and they were prepared for further chastisement. This came upon them. October 21 an earthquake blotted the town out of existence in less than a minute. The earth vomited sulphurous waters. The shocks were continued during fourteen months. The good people instituted an annual fast and procession in commemoration of the event.

Again, in 1794, Cumana was nearly prostrated. December 14, 1797, there was a tremendous upward shock, with a noise like a mine explosion. Four-fifths of the town was laid in ruins. The atmosphere seemed converted to water, so great were the torrents of rain. The Indians held a religious festival and dance, believing the destruction and regeneration of the world was at hand.

The first days of November, 1799, were noted for the peculiar redness of the sky and the oppressiveness of the atmosphere, though the weather was not especially warm. At nightfall the sea breeze failed to begin, and the dusty earth began to crack in all directions. The people were sure some evil boded. November 4, as a heavy storm came up, there was a sharp gust of wind, which the natives say always precedes an earthquake; and a few minutes later came the shock; two others followed during the evening; but though all the tokens of a great shock, according to native ideas, were present in such force that the people abandoned their homes and slept in the parks and fields, the great quake never came. The redness of the sky continued, and a few nights later occurred a brilliant shower of meteors. Despite these signs and wonders,

Mother Earth refused to tremble. Humboldt concluded native prognostications were unreliable.

During the past eighty years destructive earthquakes have been more frequent in South America than in any other region of the earth. First on the list is the great disaster at Caracas.

This town lies six miles from the seaport of La Guayra, in a valley "where reigns eternal spring." Shut in by lofty mountains, its aspect is somewhat gloomy. The cold mountain air keeps the evening veiled with clouds. But as a whole, the situation is so fine that the people would hardly exchange it for a site less liable to earthquakes.

In December, 1811, when the disturbances were so great in the valleys of the Mississippi, Ohio and Arkansas, there was a sharp shock, which did no especial damage. At this time there was a severe drought, which continued during the succeeding months; but no word of the disturbances to the North, or in St. Vincent, reaching the people, they were not especially alarmed. So the days passed till Holy Week came, and hundreds were in the great churches.

At a few minutes past four there was a sudden shock which set church-bells to ringing. Then came a second, which made the ground seem as though it were boiling. This ceased, and the people supposed the danger was past, when there came the fearful subterranean roar but too well known in tropical countries, followed by series of alternating shocks at right angles to each other, and at once the beautiful city, with its palaces and homes and works of art was a shapeless ruin, with twelve thousand corpses lying amid the wreck. Four thousand people were slain in the churches alone. The great church of Alta Gracia, one hundred and fifty feet in height, whose nave was supported by pillars fifteen feet in diameter, was turned into a heap of rubbish but five or six feet high. Nearly all had sunk in the earth. Scarce a vestige of pillar or column could be found. A regiment of infantry, mustered in San Carlos barracks, was engulfed, but few escaping. Nine-tenths of the town was annihilated.

Night came. The cloud of dust, that like a mist had risen from the wreck, had settled to the ground. The full moon shone as calmly on the scene as in the past; and by the spectral light were seen strange figures hurrying to and fro. Here passed a mother with an infant's corpse;

SCENE AT CARACAS.

while there a father groped amid the wreck, and called by turns the names of wife and child. No tools were left in reach in all the town; bare-handed creatures grappled with the stony heaps, and groaned in answer to the moans beneath. The aqueducts were shattered and the springs were stopped; the Guayra River was the sole supply. Scarce vessels could be found to fetch it in. Here hurrying feet bore wounded creatures to the stream; but lint and bandages were all beneath the wreck. Two thousand injured people lay upon the turf, with little of the needed help; but all their friends could do was done. Not even food enough could be procured at first.

Then anguish-stricken souls repented of their sins, and marched in procession that the wrath of God might be changed to mercy. Some driven to the verge of madness loudly confessed their sins in the open streets. Some promised to restore ill-gotten gains; often the peculation was known only to themselves. Marriages were solemnized between many who had hitherto not considered a ceremony necessary. Children were formally recognized by parents who had before repudiated them; long standing fueds and enmities were dropped.

Caracas was not the only place injured. La Guayra, Mayquetia, Antimano, Baruta, La Vega, San Felipe, and Merida were totally destroyed. Five thousand deaths occurred at San Felipe and La Guayra alone. It was impossible to give burial. Vast funeral pyres were made and corpse after corpse consigned to the flames. The total number of deaths from the earthquake, including those who perished from want and sickness induced by the exposure, was probably forty thousand; some have estimated fifty thousand. The shocks were felt as far westward as Bogota.

It does not appear that any especial commotion was felt in Central America, though shocks in the latter regions are nearly always felt in Venezuela or Columbia. Every portion of Central America has been repeatedly shaken. The town of Guatemala has been four times destroyed, the people each time selecting a new site and adhering to the old name. The people of San Salvador, on the other hand, have obstinately clung to their site, though visited by violent earthquakes in 1575, 1593, 1625, 1656, 1798, and 1839; and minor shocks are of such constant recur-

RUINS OF SAN SALVADOR.

rence that the locality is nicknamed "the hammock." But the shock of 1839 was so severe that they seriously meditated leaving; but they finally settled in the old place, when four-fifths of their town had just been destroyed.

But in Holy Week, in 1854, as Mr. Squier tells us, unusual rumblings were heard on the morning of Holy Thursday. The inhabitants, somewhat alarmed, still went about their customary avocations. The remainder of the week passed without further cause for fear. At half past nine o'clock on Sunday night a severe shock so alarmed many people that they prepared to camp out for the night. At ten minutes to eleven there came without any warning a fearful quaking, which levelled the city to the earth in ten seconds; clouds of dust filled the streets; wells and fountains were choked; not a drop of water could be obtained. Not a house was left inhabitable; scarce one preserved the semblance of being erect; yet the town was composed chiefly of low, one-story structures. The air was filled with fumes of sulphur; the neighboring volcano threatened an eruption; and in addition to the usual horrors of an earthquake, other features were added.

The ex-president of the republic was so badly hurt as to be almost incapacitated for duty. Indians roamed pillaging the wreck, dropping on their knees and praying as fresh shocks terrified them; then returning to the plunder; for they were good Christians. Justice, police, clergy—all were gone. The venerable bishop, Soldana, when dragged from the ruin, bade the people flee in all haste, for "God had given the city over to the Evil One as a punishment for its sins; and in spite of the name it bore '(Holy Savior)' it would be cast into the bottomless pit." The good bishop promptly headed the retreat of the clergy from the forces of Satan, evidently under the impression that if the people could only leave the accursed locality, the devil would not be so scrupulously exact in tormenting them before the time. The people flocked after the clergy in large numbers, believing they would be safest in the neighborhood of the holy men. It is well known that even the devil respects the cloth.

The republic had been rent by civil war for years; and in this critical juncture, it seemed that it was about to be

PEOPLE OF SAN SALVADOR FRIGHTENED.

renewed. But a man of strong will and energy and coolness stepped forward—Duenas, ex-monk, lawyer, deputy, and president—from his farm, like Cincinnatus. Collecting a few friends and digging some arms from the wreck of the barracks, he inspirited the new president, and martial law was proclaimed. The shooting of a few Indian robbers imparted to the remainder a respect for law equalled only by their practical Christianity, and the work of rescue began. Large numbers of the populace permanently forsook the site.

Two years later there was a great earthquake in Honduras; but the area of disturbance was not so densely peopled, and the damage done was proportionately less. Disasters of this sort cause most Central Americans to emigrate. "Then women and children form themselves into groups and travel through the country. They set the drama in which they have taken part to music, and they go through the country singing the rude verses which they have run together in the different villages, and then send the hat around. After they have visited the whole of their own country, they cross the frontier into the neighboring State, where they are also assured of doing pretty well."

During three centuries of Spanish occupation of South America, while scores of convulsions had visited the Pacific seaboard, none had shaken the eastern slope of the Cordilleras, or the great plains beyond; and there had resulted a settled belief that the entire region was, so to speak, earthquake-proof. But the illusion was rudely dispelled.

In the extreme west of the Argentine Republic, on the high road from Valparaiso to Buenos Ayres, lies the town of Mendoza, in full view of Tupungato and the mighty Aconcagua. Never having, in all their history, experienced any harm from these mountains, the people anticipated none.

"Mendoza had about 20,000 inhabitants and five hundred houses, nearly all of them very handsome. It also contained two very large hospitals, several schools, a splendid cathedral, and several churches. Its trade was prosperous, and more than a hundred large shops testified to the extent of its commerce. There was no such library in the whole of the Argentine Republic. Its theatre was most sumptuous, and the Alameda, its public promenade, was regarded as the finest in South America.

"One evening, an immense red and blue meteor slowly traversed the sky from East to West, and the volcano of Aconcagua broke into an eruption upon the night following—20th March, 1861—without any premonitory sound or sign: the earth quaked violently, and in less than a minute the town of Mendoza had disappeared. It was

SHOCK AT LAKE IN HONDURAS.

transformed into a vast field of ruins, the highest of which were not more than three feet from the ground. Never within the memory of man has a town been so taken by surprise; for in this case the earthquake was not preceded by the underground mutterings which, even if only a few seconds in advance of the shock, give some sort of warning. Upon that night, and in less than four seconds, fifteen thousand people were buried in the ruins. Horrible noises, cries of terror, the heartrending howls of men and animals filled the air, and a thick cloud of dust darkened the sky."

Mendoza was not the only place injured. At San Juan, one hundred miles northward, three thousand people were killed. Three hundred and fifty miles further away, Cordova lost a number of houses, and a slight shock was felt at Buenos Ayres. The wreck presented the scenes common in such cases; and, as in several similar disasters, bands of brigands pounced upon the town to pillage the ruins.

Of the many touching incidents, we must give place to two:

That the town was absolutely unwarned is hardly correct. A French geologist, M. Bravard, sent on a scientific mission by the Russian government, had found the volcanoes near by violently roaring, yet emitting no smoke or fire; and, nearing the valley of Mendoza, he found the soil in a constant tremor. Alarmed at these manifestations, he expressed his belief that if the pressure were not speedily relieved by eruption, a severe earthquake might follow. His assertion caused serious apprehension, for his high attainments gave his opinions great weight with the people. For nearly a week the possibility of a catastrophe was seriously discussed. One evening he stood at the door of M. Matussiere, wishing his friends good-night. Again he alluded to the earthquake—the shock came, and he was caught by the fall of the house.

Matussiere himself was on his way home from Valparaiso. When fifteen miles from Mendoza, in the mountains, a tremendous roaring was heard, but he felt no shock. The moon shone as calmly and clearly as ever, and no disturbance followed. Oppressed, however, by terrible fear, he hastened to Mendoza. He could not even guess where was the wreck of his own home. After a

WRECK AT MENDOZA.

long, despairing search, he saw his great house dog come bounding toward him. The dog led him to the wreck; and, after wearisome toil, the merchant found his wife and one child alive. The rest of the family, and the French geologist, were dead.

Another episode is related by M. Charton: There was at Mendoza a rich, French hotel keeper, M. Tesser. After the shock, "one of his intimate friends wandered among the ruins. His eyes were dry: he could shed tears no longer. He stopped on the site of the hotel, trying in vain to recall the old arrangements. He was retiring—his heart filled with sighs, thinking of the honest man and the family he had loved so well—when he perceived, through the shapeless mass of girders and calcined stones, M. Tesser's dog, which moaned; he approached it. The poor animal, the two hind legs and part of the body of which were crushed, forced itself, in spite of his sufferings and weakness, to scratch with his front paws, and uttered, from time to time, a plaintive howl. As it saw its master's friend come near, it exerted itself and howled louder. The friend understood that Tesser must be beneath this rubbish, and hoped he was not dead. He ran to fetch some persons, and, with their help, after much labor, he indeed discovered the body of poor Tesser; his left arm and leg, lying under the beams, were broken, his mouth and eyes full of earth, but he still breathed. Before trying to disengage his limbs, they washed his face, which seemed to relieve him; without saying a word, he instinctively stretched his right arm toward his dog, who drew himself to him, and died a few moments afterwards.

"Tesser scarcely was in a state to pronounce any words, before he asked where his family was. All had perished in the great disaster. Hearing this answer, he closed his eyes with despair; then, making a fresh effort, he pronounced the name of his little girl, and showed with his finger a separate place where he had put her to bed. Some of the people, in compassion for his grief, although without hope, made further search; others occupied themselves in dressing his broken limbs. A few minutes later, those rendering him this service saw him suddenly raise himself up—he gave a cry—they brought him his daughter, still living. A beam had fallen across the bed of the child and had protected it; but she was seriously wounded in the head; she had also her mouth and eyes filled with dirt, and was exhausted with hunger." For two months the pair lay under a tent against a tree, more dead than alive. They only remained to each other of the once rich and happy family. But in this respect, they were no worse off than hundreds of others.

The people abandoned the site, unable to remain in view of so many monuments of former happiness. Strangers came in and a new Mendoza rose, but not so lovely as the former one. This town was also severely shaken in 1885.

With a notice of one other earthquake, which demands attention because of unusual results, this chapter must close.

This shock occurred August 13, 1868, in Peru. The center of the convulsion was at Arequipa, at the foot of the lofty volcanic mountain of Misti, which has not shown signs of activity since the great outburst of 1542. So far as their volcanic neighbor was concerned, the forty-four thousand people of Arequipa had apparently no reason for apprehension.

At five minutes past five, there came a light shock like the jar of a distant explosion. Half a minute later began the subterranean rumbling, with a rapidly increasing vibration, which made the people run for their lives into the streets. Then "the swaying motion changed into fierce, vertical upheaval. The subterranean roaring increased in a terrifying manner; then were heard the heart-piercing shrieks of the wretched people, the bursting of walls, the crashing fall of houses and churches, while over all rolled thick clouds of a yellowish-black dust, which, had they been poured forth many minutes longer, would have suffocated thousands."

Tacna and Arica suffered little less. But the greatest damage in the coast region was from the sea wave. A few minutes after the shock, the sea rolled back, falling twenty-five feet; then a huge, black wall of water leaped up, fifty feet in height, and rushed for the shore. The American vice-consul at Arica, well versed in the phenomena of earthquakes, left his house at the first shock, and ran with his family to the hills to avoid any probable sea wave. The monster billow struck the mole to pieces, and swept clean the lower part of the town. Six vessels were lost in the bay, or tossed over rocks and houses; two, a Peruvian corvette and a United States war-ship, were carried inland and left high and dry, half a mile north of Arica, without a broken spar or tarnished flag. Similar feats were recorded at Iquique. Twelve hundred miles of sea-coast were more or less affected. Sixty million dollars worth of property were destroyed, and twenty thousand people killed.

The great sea wave was especially remarkable. Recoiling from the Peruvian coast, in three hours its southern expansion was observed at Coquimbo, eight hundred miles south. An hour later it was at Constitucion, four hundred and fifty miles further. Northward, the wave rushed, sixty feet high, into the harbor of San Pedro, California, five thousand miles from the shock.

To the westward, the Sandwich Islands were reached

that night, and irregular waves broke upon the coast for three days. Before midnight it broke upon the Marquesas and the Paumotu archipelago. At half-past three in the morning it was at New Zealand. By daylight it was

THE GREAT SEA WAVE REACHES CHILI

surging along the coasts of Australia, and by mid-day it was tossing even on the southwest coast of Australia. The same day, it was heaving on the shores of Japan.

This wave is doubtless surpassed only by the great wave

set in motion by the convulsion of Krakatoa, mentioned
in the chapter on volcanoes. It travelled to a distance of
10,500 miles from its starting point, at a speed of from
400 to 500 miles an hour, according to the direction. Yet
it has had several strong rivals. Had the great wave of
1867, at the time of the earthquake at St. Thomas, been
raised in the open sea, instead of in the comparatively
shut in Caribbean, it might have travelled to an equal
distance. The sea wave which followed the earthquake at
Simoda, Japan, in 1854, completely wiped out that town,
leaving only fragments of a temple-wall, and some
wrecked vessels, two miles inland. Most of the people
perished. Recoiling from the coast, the wave rolled in
upon the shores of California, travelling 5,000 miles in
twelve hours.

The terrible earthquake that ravaged Jamaica in 1692,
produced a wave that swept thirty-three feet of water over
the highest house in Port Royal, destroying 3,000 persons
An English frigate, the *Swan*, was deposited on the top
of a large building, breaking in the roof. The waves of
the Lisbon and Calabrian earthquakes have been noticed
elsewhere.

This same district in Peru has suffered similarly several times. Callao, with the ground on which it was
built, was swept away in 1746. Only fifteen of its people
ever reached Lima, six miles inland. When the town was
rebuilt, a second disaster of this sort nearly destroyed it.
Iquique and Arequipa, in Peru, were again destroyed May
9, 1877; and a wave seventy feet high swept the coast,
and recoiling reached Japan next day, travelling two hundred and eighteen yards per second.

The cases given illustrate well the stupendous power
and destructiveness of vibrations in the earth's surface.
But few have been given, nor have all the greatest been

detailed. Mention only must suffice for the one which shook Naples and vicinity, December 5, 1456, destroying forty thousand people. Another in Persia, June 7, 1755, destroyed Kaschan, with forty thousand people; one at Cairo, Egypt, the preceding year, killed twenty thousand. Another in the Abruzzi, Italy, November 3, 1706, killed killed fifteen thousand persons; one at Palermo, Sicily, September 13, 1726, killed six thousand; one hundred thousand perished in the Pekin earthquake of November 30, 1731; two thousand were destroyed by an earthquake in the Kutch district, India, in 1819. Constantinople was overturned in the year 1800; six thousand people perished in an earthquake in Murcia, Spain, in 1829; fifteen hundred were killed by Italian earthquakes in 1835–36; Southern Syria suffered greatly in 1836; Hayti was shaken, and four thousand people perished, in 1842; one hundred thousand houses and thirty thousand people destroyed by an earthquake in Japan, 1854; Montenerro, Calabria, and ten thousand people in 1857; five thousand people in Ecuador, 1859; Northwestern Khorassan, Persia, with thirty thousand people, in 1871; Antioch again nearly destroyed in 1872; three thousand people killed in Cashmere, 1885.

Terrible as this list seems, the total but little exceeds the havoc wrought by the single Bengal famine of 1866. There would be little difficulty in proving that drought, with the consequent famine, has proved the most terrible agent of destruction known to man; and yet it is one that facilities for rapid transit should render least destructive.

Scientific men have within forty years made efforts to keep a sort of catalogue of shocks; but the frequency of earthquakes has rendered this a profitless task. Great ones are long remembered; but as for numbering the minor shocks, one might as well count rainfalls; several

EARTHQUAKE IN SPAIN.

occur every day; and it is only when unusually destructive, like extraordinary tempests, that they attract any attention; so that their being recorded depends even more upon location than upon actual force.

All the phenomena of volcanoes and earthquakes point us to one conclusion: that the earth may in time become as dead and deserted as the moon. The telescope shows the latter to be thickly dotted with volcanic craters, whose immensity, in comparison with those of our own globe, is astounding; yet all are extinct. It is not probable that the interior of our earth is molten; and we have seen that fractures and subsidence, caused by gradual cooling, seem to be the main cause of the local phenomena of volcanoes and earthquakes. As the ages roll on, these weak places may become still higher; and the belt of warm climate will grow narrower and narrower. Cooling at the present rate, 2,500,000,000 years will be necessary to render it as lifeless as the moon.

"As the cooling progresses, a sheet of snow and ice, from north and south, will descend from the mountains upon the table-lands and valleys, driving before it life and civilization, and covering forever the cities and nations that it meets on its passage. All life and human activity will press insensibly toward the inter-tropical zone. The great cities of the world will fall asleep in succession under their eternal shroud. During very many ages, equatorial humanity will undertake arctic expeditions to find again under the ice the place of Paris, Lyons, Bordeaux, and Marseilles. The sea-coasts will have changed, and the geographical map of the earth will have been transformed. No one will live and breathe, except in the equatorial zone, up to the day when the last family, nearly dead with cold and hunger, will sit on the shore of the last sea, in the rays of the sun, which will thereafter shine here on a dead, cold earth, revolving, like a satellite moon, about a sun unseen by mortal eyes, and distributing to an extinguished planet a useless heat." So will end the history of our planet and its great disasters.

> "All worldly shapes shall melt in gloom,
> The sun himself must die,
> Before this mortal shall assume
> Its immortality!
> I saw a vision in my sleep,
> That gave my spirit strength to sweep
> Adown the gulf of time!
> I saw the last of human mold
> That shall creation's death behold,
> As Adam saw her prime!
>
> The sun's eye had a sickly glare,
> The earth with age was wan;
> The skeletons of nations were
> Around that lonely man!
> Some had expired in fight—the brands
> Still rusted in their bony hands.
> In plague and famine some!
> Earth's cities had no sound or tread,
> And ships were drifting with the dead,
> To shores where all was dumb!
>
> Yet prophet-like that lone one stood
> With dauntless words and high,
> That shook the sere leaves from the wood
> As if a storm passed by!
> Saying, We are twins in death, proud Sun,
> Thy face is cold, thy race is run,
> 'Tis Mercy bids thee go:
> For thou ten thousand years
> Hast seen the tide of human tears
> That shall no longer flow."

CHAPTER XXVII.

PREDICTION AND PREVENTION.

> " Fain would th' ephemeral pigmies then aspire
> To drive, like Phäethon, the sun's coach of fire,
> To grapple with the lightning in the sky,
> Or with the restless winds abroad to fly.
> Not all the bolts of Jove, nor Phœbus' wrath,
> May fright them from their wild, self-chosen path.
> Though poplars wave above ten thousand graves,
> And myriad Icari lie beneath the waves,
> The rest, as once the Titans, still press on,
> And strive to thrust the great gods from their throne."

EVER since man has dwelt upon the earth, there has been a constant effort, not merely to foretell the future, but to control it. So strong is man's faith in his own capacity, that wizards, jugglers, fakirs and tricksters, and necromancers have always found their vocation a lucrative one. It is easy to make one's living by imposing upon the credulity of the public. Not merely the American people, but every other people, like to be humbugged. So strong is the tendency to gullibility, that the most extraordinary pretensions are the most readily credited. The capability of the public to judge in such cases is well illustrated by the Grecian story of the famous mimic, whose imitation of the grunt of a pig was so perfect, that thousands came to witness his performance. A countryman remarked that he could do still better, and, concealing a pig under his coat, he stole upon the stage. Pinching the animal's ear, the pig squealed violently, but the audience hissed the squeak as a miserable fiasco. Whereat the countryman produced the pig, and left the audience pondering the situation.

The same tendency causes men to desire to attribute unusual appearances to causes beyond the domain of natural law. The savage finds thunder and lightning in the discharge of a gun; mysterious magic in a telescope; downright sorcery in quinine; witchcraft and incantation in a written prescription. If one, a little shrewder than his fellows, after long study of an ant's nest, conceive the idea that they have a regularly constituted community, with a queen at the head, he needs only to suggest such a thing to his neighbors, to be set down as having communications with the Ant Queen; and he may readily aspire to the chieftainship, thence to be known as the Ant Chief. Imagination is so much easier than observation. Doubtless old Numa's thoughtful air in his daily retreat, gave rise to the tale that he was in consultation with the nymph of a fountain. Any one who had devoted an hour each day to gazing pensively into a stream, might have achieved a like reputation, as the Hindoo fakir is held in high repute for sanctity, because he preserves strict silence and gazes for years at the end of his nose.

So when men achieve new results by natural means, it is preferred to assume otherwise. Good Roger Bacon invented gunpowder by witchcraft. The early chemists were in league with the Evil One. Faust and Gutenberg sold their souls to the devil, in order to get Bibles printed. The Magdeburg physicist, who made a water barometer in which a wooden figure rose or fell as the atmosphere varied, was the devil's own child. Cows sickened and died at the will of shrivelled dames who rode through the air on broomsticks.

Foreknowledge is always confounded with foreordination. The weather prophet is transformed into a weather-maker. The myth of Aeolus is thus explained. Once a king of the Lipari Isles, by careful observation of the vapor cloud over Stromboli he was enabled to announce changes of weather a day or two in advance, as every observant man in that region can do to-day. The simple subjects attributed his knowledge to supernatural powers, and after his death perpetuated the story of Aeolus, the king of the winds, who dwelt in a cave in one of the islands.

In the time of Elijah, the prophets of Baal were confident of procuring rain by howling, cutting and slashing; while Ahab believed Elijah was responsible for the drought. The negro and the red man to-day show the same characteristics in this respect. The negro rain-maker makes fetich; the red chief, "big medicine," to bring rains. The reputed success of each is proportioned to his shrewdness in recognizing tokens of change in the weather.

The great white man is often little better. While no longer trusting in the power of any one to control the weather, he has set up a god of false science, whom all must bow down to and worship. True knowledge is often flouted and scouted; but every one who would attract attention must assume at least the appearance of learning. College degrees are bought and sold at reasonable prices. No questions asked. The dancing-master is professor. The pugilist has become professor. The man who fiddles for beer in the corner saloon is professor. Weep, O Minerva!

So any one who wishes especial importance to be attached to his utterances, needs but assume a title, or a few mystic letters. Every great catastrophe produces a plentiful brood of them. As soon as the Charleston earthquake alarmed the country, it was announced that a grave "Prof." had predicted it. He was the hero of the hour. Interviewers flocked from many quarters. For weeks the words of

"Prof." —— , were as ointment poured out. The papers gave him great space—published sketches of his career. So much adulation was too much for human nature; besides, he owed a duty to the public. A man so gifted should continue to give warning of impending dangers. He did so. They didn't materialize. The "Prof." has had little attention for three years.

The Louisville tornado afforded other cases. A woman in the west predicted a combined deluge and earthquake, with other minor horrors on the side, as prepared for the Pacific coast. Some of the gullible people sold out at great sacrifice, that they might lose as little as possible by the greatest cyclone and earthquake of the century. Others drew up a formal petition to the Governor, calling upon him to proclaim a day of supplication and fasting for the doomed cities of Oakland, San Francisco and Alameda. The end of the world drew nigh, and these three cities, as eminently wicked, would be first punished; after which Chicago and Milwaukee would suffer.

Bands of believers met and wrestled mightily in prayer that the unparalled horrors might be averted. They were eminently successful.

Another came forward and announced that the entire Mississippi valley was to be visited with a cataclysm, such as no man had ever conceived. The floods were to break all the levees, wash away everything that was within a hundred miles of the stream, tear up the delta built by the deposits of ages, and leave the site of New Orleans at the bottom of the sea. At this writing the Crescent City is in hourly expectation of its doom.

Yet another seer, warned of the Lord in a vision, perhaps, has just declared the fate of the Atlantic coast. Before the end of the century there will be an earthquake such as no man ever before has known. The fountains of the great deep are to be broken up. All the cities of the New England coast will be desolated by immense sea waves. Manhattan Island, with the city of New York, and Long Island, are to be sunk to the bottom of the sea. Our hearts fail us for fear for the things that are coming upon the earth. Let us hope that peradventure there be yet five righteous men in Sodom.

Some years ago great sensation was occasioned by the discovery of Mother Shipton's prophecy among some old English manuscripts. It began:

> "Carriages shall without horses go,
> And accidents fill the world with woe;
> Around the world men's thoughts shall fly,
> In the twinkling of an eye."

After a few statements of this sort, it closed by saying:

> "The world to an end shall come
> In eighteen hundred and eighty-one."

Great was the fright of not a few timid believers. Many arranged their affairs for the end of the world. Some, as the Millerites have several times done, prepared their ascension robes. Finally, the whole thing proved to be a hoax. A wag had endeavored to amuse himself at the expense of the public.

Such are fair specimens of predictions that continually appear in the newspapers. Certain men will always endeavor to astonish the ignorant by their words and works. Seldom do sober-minded people pay the least attention to them. As for minor changes in weather, they are so constant, and so limited in area, that, as stated elsewhere, any one is safe for announcing the character of the weather for any day in the year. From a score of places, he could obtain testimonials of the correctness of his prognostications; while nine score more, if they spoke, might declare him altogether mistaken.

But many will ask in all seriousness, if there is no

means of prediction upon which all may depend. Is any more reliance to be placed upon the prognostications of the Signal Service than upon those of the self-constituted prophets?

A brief statement of the principles relied upon will be satisfactory on this point.

Our weather bureau was established in 1870. Such organizations are maintained, at the public expense, in Great Britain, France, Germany, Italy, Australia, Russia, India, Algeria, and Japan. Several smaller countries share in the expense and benefits. Men long trained in the work grow more reliable. Each must first master the topography and the prevailing movements of the atmosphere of any region, ere he can presume to know anything of the probable changes.

How extremely important a knowledge of the country is, will be understood when it is remembered that mountain ranges may turn aside great storms, and hills of any considerable size may modify small ones. And in general, storm paths are so narrow, in comparison with the whole country, that the slightest variation at the start may be very important at the end of six hundred or seven hundred miles—or a day's travel. So, announcing twenty-four hours beforehand the exact locality a storm may reach, is really a very delicate piece of work. If a tyro should announce rain for North Georgia, he might be astonished to find a difference of twenty-one per cent. between Atlanta and Augusta. He would find in Tennessee sixteen per cent. difference between Knoxville and Nashville; or twelve and a half per cent. in Iowa between Dubuque and Davenport.

The Signal Service does not endeavor to forecast entirely new conditions so much as to give warning of storms already on the way. It can not safely say where a storm will arise; but it can declare with tolerable certainty the path a storm will pursue after having once started.

Yet, there are certain signs of rain that can be of use to the public. Americans, as a rule, pay less attention to the actions of the animal kingdom at change of weather than other nations; and the lower animals detect changes of weather more quickly than man. Slugs and snails often leave their crannies, and endeavor to find some drier retreat at the approach of rain. Swallows fly lower; chiefly because the insects they pursue abandon the upper air. Crickets and grasshoppers become less noisy, and seek snug retreats. Fish leap more frequently from the water. The oft-praised tree-frog seems not to have deserved the confidence placed in him as a barometer.

Quatremere Disjonval, when made a prisoner of war by the Dutch, made a careful study of the habits of the house spider, while in confinement. His observations played an important part in the war. "General Pichegru, being prevented by the mild weather from carrying out his intention of invading that country, was about to retire with his army from the Dutch frontier, when Disjonval found means to inform him that, from the signs he had observed in his spiders, a severe frost was sure to take place in the next ten days. Pichegru trusted to the prognostic: the frost came in time. Holland was conquered, and Disjonval released from his prison."

Voigt asserts that the spider is so reliable a barometer because of its anatomy: the long, slender, unmailed legs being peculiarly sensitive to atmospheric changes. That is, when Madam Spider finds herself with a touch of rheumatism, she wraps herself in a thicker blanket and takes to her den. In fine weather the garden spiders are much more plentiful; and the tiny gossamer spiders also are numerous, and fly at greater heights.

These serve to illustrate the class of phenomena most relied upon by those in every land who must spend much time in the open air. The scientist may understand the laws of winds and rains: but the farmer, the shepherd, the fisherman, and sailor, to whom every phase of weather means much, can, relying upon the actions of the lower animals, detect approaching changes as readily, in many cases, as the Signal Service; and far more readily or correctly than the quasi learned theorist whose stock in trade is a hobby and an unlimited quantity of assumption.

It is one thing to understand law; it is quite another to be able to make practical application of it. Franklin identified lightning with electricity; a century passed before practical use of the electric light resulted. We know now the general laws of air currents, but little application of them has been made.

As to the possibility of controlling the winds, no one has thus far had the temerity to propose it. But that rainfall can be partially controlled is well known. The heaviest rains occur in forest areas; and in turn, the matted roots of the forest and jungle retard the descent of the rain into the water courses, and hinder the washing away of the soil. Floods have become more sudden and destructive in the lumber regions since the timber has been cut away, while the actual rainfall is not so great. So a number of our Western States require a "homesteader" to plant a tree claim.

A bold genius has recently asserted that we may produce rain at will, by sending up balloons loaded with dynamite or other powerful explosives, and then firing them. It has been observed that almost every great modern battle has been followed by a heavy rainfall; and the idea is, that the continued explosions have had much to do with them. Frequenters of Fourth of July picnics will readily vouch for the correctness of the theory. Doubtless a more effective plan would be simply to apply the well known first principle of air-currents and storms—heated air; but this would be immensely expensive. Every year sees exemplifications of it, however, in the heavy rains that follow the great forest fires or prairie fires of our own land. Natives of tropical regions frequently burn the jungle at the close of the dry season; and the unusual heating of large areas in this way doubtless has much to do with hastening the advent of rain.

The expedient of firing the sawgrass ponds is frequently resorted to in Florida, and has been brought to the notice of the public in official meteorological reports. It is directly in accordance with the principle of restoration of the balance of forces, whereby a long heated term is followed by unusually heavy rains.

But, in contending with subterranean forces, man is hitherto balked. Numbers of instruments exist for measuring the force and direction of earthquake shocks, but these can be made of little practical use; for we have seen that the vibrations travel from forty to one hundred and fifty miles a minute, according to the nature of the soil. Hence, could we know a certain shock would travel around the world, it would not be possible, after it was first felt, to send warning ahead in time to be of any especial value. But we have seen that unusual disturbances of this sort are confined to certain regions, and are of constant recurrence; while in other lands, they are almost unknown. So any one understands pretty well what risks he runs in any particular district.

The Chinese were the first to invent a seismometer, or instrument for ascertaining the force and direction of any shock. Their apparatus consists of an upright pillar bearing a number of dragons' heads—each one holding a ball in its mouth. So any slight tilting or vibration of the pillar would cause a ball to drop on the side toward which the shock travelled. The distance to which the ball was thrown served as a rude measure of the force.

Equally simple is Mallet's contrivance—a number of cylinders of equal heights and different bases, placed upon a sanded surface. The more violent the shock, the larger the cylinder thrown down.

But observations of these vibrations, to be of use, must take note of the myriad tremors that will escape ordinary perceptions, or the powers of such rude instruments as the above. There are several sorts now used. Prof. Palmieri, of the Vesuvius Observatory, uses a delicate instrument, which records the slightest tremor on a dial-plate. The Italians have also applied the microphone to this work. The delicacy of this instrument may be imagined, when it is known that by its means a fly can be heard walking on the floor. So the slightest subterranean noise may be heard.

These instruments have taught us that the minor tremors increase in number and intensity as any unusual disturbance of Vesuvius approaches; just as the Signal Service can detect the gathering of a storm ere it actually bursts. Remembering also Bravard's warning of Mendoza, in the last chapter, it is clear that in certain regions such observations can be made of practical value to the people at large.

One of the most ingenious apparatus for observing the vibrations of the soil is that constructed by M. d'Abbadie, at his observatory near the Pyrenees. A conical cavity forty-six feet deep is excavated in the solid rock. At the bottom is a basin of mercury. A long-focus lens over this reflects upon the surface of the ground the image of the metal below. The slightest tremor is carefully examined by a microscope. In short, this ingenious Frenchman has applied the reflecting telescope to the observation of the interior of the earth.

After all, the chief precautions must be of a different type. As already noticed, long observation has taught the Japanese and others that their safety depends mainly upon the construction of houses of the lightest type; when the sea wave is more to be dreaded than the shock. This is the general principle of building now adopted in countries where earthquakes are frequent; and doubtless the earthquake is partially responsible for the fact that many intelligent savage races have made no progress in architecture.

It should be noted, however, that the ancients believed that deep wells were a safeguard against earthquakes; such is the expression of several ancient writers. And in this connection we may mention the remarkable case of Quito, in Ecuador. Here we have a city of magnificent cathedrals, public edifices, and other lofty buildings, which have not in three centuries been overthrown by an earthquake. Yet it lies on the plateau on which stood Riobamba, where such terrible destruction was wrought in 1794, and at the base of the great volcano of Pichincha. It has been shaken time and again more severely than towns in the vicinity that have been totally destroyed. Yet it remains intact, and the people have an indifference to earthquakes that is astonishing. They attribute their safety to the fact of having deep cellars under every house. When we remember that tropical races are not, as a rule, a cellar building people, it may be that the idea is worthy of serious consideration. But many idle races of the tropics might, in lower grounds, merely exchange the results of an occasional earthquake for malaria-breeding pools.

CHAPTER XXVIII.

THE REIGN OF LAW.

> " Man is born on a battle-field. Round him to rend
> Or resist, the dread Powers he displaces, attend
> By the cradle which Nature, amid the stern shocks
> That have shattered creation, and shapened it, rocks.
> He leaps with a wail into being; and lo!
> His own mother, fierce Nature herself, is his foe:
> Her whirlwinds are roused into wrath o'er his head;
> 'Neath his feet roll her earthquakes; her solitudes spread
> To daunt him; her forces dispute his command;
> Her snows fall to freeze him; her suns burn to brand;
> Her seas yawn to engulf him; her rocks rise to crush;
> And the lion and leopard, allied, lurk to rush
>   On their startled invader. * * * * * * *
> Not a truth has to art or to science been given,
> But brows have ached for it, and souls toiled and striven;
> And many have striven, and many have failed,
> And many died, slain by the truth they assailed."

THE original condition of the human race was not one of knowledge. When the first man and the first monkey were created and finished, the monkey knew as much as the man. Both found themselves in a world of forces, of the nature of which, beyond what was revealed to their native instincts, they knew nothing at all. The man's superiority lay not in knowledge, but in capacity to know.

Man learned the forces and facts of Nature by experience. He learned them at the cost to himself of fear and pain and toil and death. He plucked one fruit and found it wholesome; another, and found it bitter; another, and found it deadly. The surviving son learned to avoid the mistakes of his father.

Man was not long in gaining a knowledge of his environment, enough at least, if he would not be too venturesome, to conserve in some degree his happiness and life. He learned that fire will burn, that water will drown, that storms will blow, that floods will overwhelm, that winter will come, and that his life is dependent on continual quest and avoidance. But Nature held innumerable secrets which he did not know; many, which, even to-day, he has not learned. In proportion as he should become acquainted with these, he would be master of a situation, which, at the first, so nearly mastered him. He might acquire a magnificent fortune, if he would only work for it; accordingly, we are told that his Maker admonished him to "subdue and have dominion."

Whether man has been six thousand years, or sixty thousand, in learning the little that he now knows, no one can tell; but during these years of his primary tuition he could not through knowledge have the mastery of Nature, for knowledge was too meager. It was well, therefore, that he should, in the meanwhile, have a partial mastery through faith. Ignorant of natural forces, or without means of avoidance, is it any wonder that he should fly for refuge to the Supernatural? Accordingly, God was his "refuge and strength, a very present help in trouble." Believing himself watched and defended by infinite power and love, he could "run through a troop or leap over a wall;" he could fancy himself "immortal till his work was done," safe on the battle-field as in his chamber; he was not afraid of the "pestilence that walketh in darkness, nor of the destruction that wasteth at noonday;" of earthquake and storm and fire he was not afraid, for these were the ministers of Heaven's will—if not to be avoided, then to be accepted with submission and trust.

Such faith in the presence and interposition of the Supernatural was instructive to the young world, and as necessary as its mother's milk is to a babe. It gave comfort and repose and strength, for its subject felt that "underneath and round about him were the everlasting arms." It made heroes of cowardly men on battle-fields; heroines of weak women in humble homes. It produced the sublimest characters of history; it vanquished death. Sustained by it, it is literally true that men "subdued kingdoms, wrought righteousness, stopped the mouths of lions, quenched the violence of fire, escaped the edge of the sword; out of weakness were made strong, waxed valiant in fight, turned to flight the armies of the aliens."

The sudden loss of this faith from earth would be a calamity. It would be as though the sun and moon had been darkened, and the stars had gone out in the sky. Till men know more of Nature, they must continue to lean on the Supernatural. They may never do this less than they do it now; but they will do it more intelligently.

As the child, with growing strength, is weaned from the the breast, so increasing knowledge tends to the destruction of faith. It may be stated as a law that, other things being equal, faith in the manifestation of the Supernatural—in the miraculous—is most facile to him who knows the least. Accordingly, the men of highest attainments have commonly the least of this kind of faith. They still believe in something back of Nature; some cause of Nature—in the Supernatural—but they expect nothing from it outside the lines of natural law. They know nothing of miracle or special providence. They see everywhere cause and effect; the one not present without the other; the perpetual grinding of machinery and the wretch mangled who is caught between the wheels; the wisest and best of men, pillars of state or prophets of the Lord, crushed as surely as the vilest and the meanest. All the prayers of God's people will not make rivers flow back to their fountains, nor turn the Sahara into a sea; nor thaw the ice at the poles, nor relieve the famine, nor stop the pestilence, nor level a single mole-hill, nor make one hair white or black. The whole universe is held in the chain of cause and effect, with link joined to link forever and ever. The Supernatural may be the electric energy that thrills along the endless chain, but it never quits the conductor to find out new paths. What it does today, it did a thousand years ago, and will do a thousand years hence. So speaks and so believes the student of Nature. We may be extremely reluctant to admit his teaching, and yet the facts seem to be altogether with him. The evidence is overwhelming that men everywhere, good and bad alike, are dealing directly, not with the Supernatural, but, with Nature—with law; *nothing but natural law*. If any hesitate to accept this saying, we do not press them, for the time has not yet come when they could accept it with safety. The babe will cling to the mother's breast as long as he needs it, and sometimes longer; but by and by he will abandon it of himself.

A world of iron law is not our ideal world, though the evidence grows that it is the real one. We like law well enough when it defends us; we are not pleased with it when it chastises us. At such a moment we would flee to some friendlier power. We would go to God and tell Him that Nature is not treating us well, and that we desire His interposition. It is because we are afraid of Nature that we take so much interest in the Supernatural. But what reason have we to think that the Supernatural is better than Nature?

The Supernatural has had more prophets than Nature, and will doubtless continue to have them. Far be it from us to forbid them. Let them prophecy in the name of the Lord. Let them "strengthen the weak hands and confirm the feeble knees;" inspire courage in adversity, calmness in the face of death.

But we should like to remind them that if they have done much good, they have also done some evil.

They have greatly obstructed a lesson, the most important for men to know; a lesson which they must learn at last, whether they like to learn it or not; a lesson which they need to learn as soon as they can, because certain knowledge is better to shape the life than is uncertain faith; a lesson that will bring them face to face with the real conditions of their present and eternal well-being,— we mean this lesson, that *the Supernatural, the Primal Fountain of Force, goes forth only in streams of natural law*. So far as can be shown, it manifests itself in no other way. Contrary to this, the prophets of the Supernatural have often encouraged man to believe that he shall not reap as he has sown; that he may sow to the flesh, and yet reap to the spirit; that outside and alongside the machinery of law is another and more masterful machinery of Providence and Grace; that the latter is ordained a sure corrective and deliverer from the evils of the former; that so almighty is this invisible, ever-active and presiding energy, that it can, by a momentary display, transform the most inveterate sinner into a saint, and crown him with everlasting happiness, although, meanwhile, it supinely leaves the innocent child the victim of Adam's fall, to sink into the flames of hell. Our sense of justice is shocked, virtue is dismayed, vice is emboldened, and the so-called scheme of grace, less pitiful and just than that of nature, is seen to differ from it chiefly in this, that it offers greater encouragement to sin.

Nature throughout all her regions proclaims the dominion of law. She has incessantly denounced woe to its violator. A million times has she shown us the delinquent writhing under the scourge. Never once has the transgressor escaped. His transgression,

> "Like a staunch murderer steady to his purpose,
> Follows him through every lane of life,
> Nor misses once the track,"

and soon or late he is overtaken. Privation or pain is the inexorable penalty. Nature with trumpet voices shouts incessantly, " Whatsoever a man soweth that shall he also reap."

The dominion of law is shown in the punishment of *intentional disobedience*—what men call *sin*. Its natural consequences are remorse, degradation, and spiritual death. A being of loftiest make is reduced to the likeness of a vile and venomous thing, crawling on its belly through the dust. Higher enjoyments are exchanged for such as are brutish and vile,—so to speak, the life of a humming-bird, flitting through all sunny climes and scenes and feeding on nectar, is exchanged for the life of a swine, feeding on offal, and wallowing in the mire. And never once is a wound made by the lash of law healed without a scar; in other words, transgression leaves its permanent impress on the soul, and the transgressor, despite the incantations of priest or prophet, finds himself poorer forever. He has forfeited the peace of them that do well. He has peopled the past with bitter memories; the future with gloomy forebodings. Reason untrammeled, loyal to the truth and pursuing it with success, has been substituted with reason fettered with chains of prejudice and vile affection, loving and making a lie.

Habit, with every successive stroke of action, has riveted these chains more firmly, till the victim is fast bound hand and foot, and delivered over to despair. The order of downward progress is, transgression, spiritual pain, stupor, insensibility, permanent degradation, which is spiritual death. In all this, there is no immediate or special judgment of God; no working of the Supernatural apart from natural law. If there were no God at all, while the constitution of man and the universe should remain as they are, the consequences to the transgressor would, in no wise, be altered. The sinner has nothing to fear but natural law, and sooner or later he finds this terrible enough.

But the punishment of sin is not the most impressive proof of the dominion of law. We feel that the willful transgressor is entitled to the punishment of his deed; hence, even when his punishment is severest, he fails to command our fullest sympathy. That the organization of Nature should be such as systematically to afflict the sinner, is not more than our sense of justice would prompt us to expect.

But the punishment of *ignorance* offers a more impressive spectacle—a more striking exhibition of the dominion of law. It seems that ignorance, especially when absolutely unavoidable, might be pleaded in bar of punishment; but nature obviously does not accept the plea. Nor does it avail us in this emergency to appeal from Nature to the Supernatural. The Supernatural refuses to entertain the appeal—positively declines to interfere—and natural law is left to take its course. The ignorant must suffer as surely as the guilty, and often his suffering is not less severe. For the slightest mistakes men forfeit happiness or life,—mistakes not of themselves alone, but mistakes of others. The sin or the error belongs to one man; the weight of the suffering often falls to another. Even our benevolence seems to be punished; for quite frequently the effort to help others brings disaster to ourselves—to our fortunes, to our families, our lives. Seeking to rescue another from fire or water, from the assassin or the robber; from the domestic tyrant or the foreign invader, we lose life, and, for lack of our help, our children are uneducated, exposed to moral evil, neglected, turned out of doors. The very tramp whom, for pity, we took in from the street, robs us, or murders us. Meanwhile the Supernatural beholds and makes no sign—gives no indication that it is at all concerned.

The suffering which comes through unavoidable ignorance, or which is visited upon the innocent through the deeds of the guilty, is, in its sum total, appalling and unspeakable. It is a dark and fathomless ocean, whose waves have been incessantly beating on the shores of this dreary world since time began. Every drop of this mighty ocean has been wrung out through the operation of natural law. An omniscient eye, every hour of the day and night, through countless ages, has gazed into these waters of anguish, and has declined to lessen their quantity by a single atom. No order from the Supernatural has gone forth to countermand any decree of Nature. Man has stood alone, grappling with his antagonist; and though he has cried incessantly, heaven has left him to his fate. Could there be a more awful demonstration of the supremacy of natural law?

Nature slays in babyhood one-third of all the children that are born into the world, just because they have not strength to resist her; meanwhile she carefully preserves such tyrants as Tiberius to finish their three score years and ten, though every added year means the murder of a thousand of the best men and women to be found in a wide empire. Why does not the Supernatural rise up from his place and smite the tyrant to the earth? Is it not plain that we are dealing with natural forces alone?

For six thousand years—God knows how long—Africa has been a hell, than which perhaps no man need ever fear a worse. If the pulpit may convince a sinner that as a result of his ways he shall be turned black, body and soul, and sent to Africa, there perpetually to renew his life as often as it is extinguished by the superstition and fiendishness of his fellows, and the said sinner do not then begin to live more wisely, it will be useless to talk to him of fire and brimstone. Upon this horrible theater of action perhaps 600,000,000 of human beings have been projected in every century, coming without their will to a heritage of nakedness and superstition and barbarity absolutely prohibitive of happiness here or hope for the hereafter; and yet there has been no interposition of the Supernatural in their behalf. The laws of birth and death preside, just as if there were no power above us that cares for either.

It is one of the ordinances of nature that life without nourishment shall not be prolonged. There is reason to believe that God would see the last man starved from off this planet, and the planet itself plunged onward into the void, tenantless forever, before he would command that stones should be made bread. Not twenty years ago, 18,000,000 in the northern provinces of China starved to death in a single year. What horrible anxiety of hollow-eyed mothers for gasping babes; what hideous deaths day by day; what acres of unburied corpses; what throngs about religious altars, wringing their hands, and screaming to the heavens, till it would seem that the agony of their prayers would have shaken the very stars from the sky; and yet there was none that heard, nor any that regarded. Not a single stone was turned into bread; not a single life was sustained without food; and if any survived, it was the heartless brother who wrested the last morsel from his weak and dying sister. A ghastly instance of the dominion of law, attested by 18,000,000 of dead witnesses. Can we look upon such a scene and ever again expect a petty interposition in behalf of an individual when it has been denied to a nation, and when the Continent of Africa has waited for it through countless ages?

Instances might be multiplied to infinity. Every horror recorded in this book is a proclamation of the supremacy of law—a warning to men that if they would shun the effect they must avoid the cause; that they must foresee the laws and attributes of nature, and provide; or they must perish. Strange that after ages of such awful teaching man is yet a fool—too lazy, too stupid to open his eyes; vigorously fighting against knowledge when every interest of his soul and body are at stake; saying supinely, "it makes no difference whether you know much or little, or what you believe, provided only you are sincere;" and in the same breath dishonestly hearkening to his prejudices or his passions; becoming a compound of ignorance, superstition and self-will, which first defies and rouses the powers of Nature, and then flies howling to the Supernatural for deliverance. When we think how little man has learned, notwithstanding the severity of his schooling, we are less disposed to accuse the harshness of Nature's administration.

Our reflections on the course of Nature have not proved that there is no God, but rather that there is. The order, regularity and certainty of natural forces indicates a changeless, exhaustless fountain from whence those forces flow. Amid the ceaseless mutations of the universe, this primal energy seems to be the one thing in which there is "no variableness, neither shadow of turning." It flows on resistless along the same channels from age to age. It overwhelms whatever lies in its path. It would sweep away all the millions of earth like a grain of sand. It would sweep the very stars from the sky. Nothing can arrest it; nothing change its course. It accommodates itself to nobody; all must be accommodated to it, or suffer disaster. It is inexorable, like "that rock, upon which if a man fall, he shall be broken, but if it fall upon him, it will grind him to powder." It is not man who is running this puny world; it is a changeless, eternal Power. No fear that any human combinations in capitols or temples will swerve this infinite energy, or control it in the least. That which is according to its nature it will do, and it will do nothing else. It is absolute monarch, and woe to him who resists its sway. We are amazed, awed and subdued in the contemplation. We begin to feel that there is but one thing for us to do, and that is, to learn its ways and by increasing knowledge and obedience, as rapidly as possible to put ourselves in accord with its goings-forth.

Should we enter some vast factory where there are acres of floor-space, and wheels and cogs and pulleys and hands and machines of patterns innumerable, all propelled by a giant engine hidden away in the cellar; should we see all this wilderness of wheels moving in concert, and every machine turning out the work for which it was intended, we should neither doubt the existence of the power, nor the benevolence of the whole design: nor if presently we saw a workman, reaching after some fancied good, drawn between wheels and mangled, or a hundred ignorant or careless persons caught up and whirled round and round and dashed to death; would we find any occasion to reverse our judgment—to doubt either the existence of a controlling force, or its essential goodness? Rather we should be impressed with its terrible supremacy, and with the importance of seeking out the lines of its manifestation and learning to avoid a conflict.

Law is not an entity, but only the mode of an entity; not a thing existing, but the attribute of a thing; not in itself a power, but the manner of the action of a power.

When a power through a given cause produces a given effect, and the same effect from the same cause, this regularity of manifestation fulfills our idea of law.

The great original energy must act with this perfect regularity—that is, it must govern by law, and that equally, whether this original energy be a thing only, or a person. In either case, we must accept it as uncreated, necessary, having a definite constitution or nature. In this power or person, natural laws are rooted, and from it they proceed, as rays of light from the sun. To arrest the rays, you must quench the luminary; to arrest the current forces of nature, you must stay their author. The goings-forth of power from this exhaustless fountain are necessary, ceaseless, changeless, resistless. If this fountain is an impersonal force, we can no more expect it, on any account, to relax its energy, than we can expect the engine in the cellar to stop because some wretch up stairs has been caught between the wheels.

If it is personal, having the attributes of wisdom and goodness—which is the popular idea of God—still, from the very attributes with which it is invested, we must expect it to have all the uniformity, precision, and inexorableness of a machine. Its mode of action must be the same in all cases that are alike, though the series be infinite, else there will be more or less than perfect wisdom or perfect goodness in some of the series. More would be impossible: less would impeach the power; hence, the action must be uniform and resistless. It must show the characteristics of law—*nothing else but law.* God can not consent to do something that is not perfectly wise and perfectly good because He has been importuned so to do by fools, or because a creature is going to be crushed. Therefore, neither with Him—an infinitely wise and good being—nor with Nature's laws, which are but the effluence of

His nature, can there be any "variableness or shadow of turning."

The general acceptance of this truth will mark a step forward in the progress of humanity. Such knowledge will largely displace the faith of the past and the present, but there will be a net gain. We have been looking for God outside of Nature; but while some profess to have seen him, the majority have been weak in faith, or wholly unbelieving. When we learn to see God in nature, we shall see him every day. We shall then truly realize that "in him we live and move and have our being." We shall have substituted certainty in the governing power for something very like caprice. We shall not expect the Supernatural to forbid the Natural, any more than we shall expect the sun to quarrel with his beams. Knowing definitely what not to expect of God, we shall understand precisely what to expect from ourselves. We shall comprehend more fully the Maker's meaning when He said, "Subdue and have dominion."

Judaism alone, of all religions, took no cognizance of a future state. If man thoroughly adjusted himself to this world's laws, he needed not fear for the hereafter. Therein is the strongest proof of its divine origin. And along this line a thousand victories have been won—but much yet remains. The results of human folly are lessening daily as man progresses. The means of rational enjoyment have been already vastly increased, and there will be further enlargement. But men, not angels, must do the work. Moses and his people stood, the sea before, and Pharaoh and his hosts behind them. In this extremity, he lifted his hands and cried to heaven. The answer that came was hardly such as he expected, but it may be very suggestive to us: "Wherefore criest thou unto me? *Speak unto the children of Israel*, THAT THEY GO FORWARD."

www.ingramcontent.com/pod-product-compliance
Lightning Source LLC
Chambersburg PA
CBHW021228300426
44111CB00007B/457